Licence to Thrill

Cinema and Society Series
General Editor: Jeffrey Richards

Best of British: Cinema and Society from 1930 *to the Present*   Anthony Aldgate
& Jeffrey Richards

*Brigadoon, Braveheart and the Scots: Distortions of Scotland in Hollywood
Cinema*   Colin McArthur

Britain Can Take It: British Cinema in the Second World War   Anthony Aldgate
& Jeffrey Richards

British Cinema and the Cold War   Tony Shaw

Children, Cinema and Censorship: From Dracula to the Dead End Kids
Sarah J. Smith

An Everyday Magic: Cinema Culture and Cultural Memory   Annette Kuhn

The British at War: Cinema, State and Propaganda, 1939–1945   James
Chapman

*The Crowded Prairie: American National Identity in the Hollywood
Western*   Michael Coyne

Film and Community in Britain and France: From La Règle du Jeu *to* Room at
the Top   Margaret Butler

Film Propaganda: Soviet Russia and Nazi Germany   Richard Taylor

The Finest Years: British Cinema of the 1940s   Charles Drazin

From Moscow to Madrid: Postmodern Cities, European Cinema   Ewa Mazierska
& Laura Rascaroli

*Hollywood Genres and Post-War America: Masculinity, Family and Nation in
Popular Movies and Film Noir*   Mike Chopra-Gant

Hollywood's History Films   David Eldridge

*Licence to Thrill: A Cultural History of the James Bond Films (Second Updated
Edition)*   James Chapman

Past and Present: National Identity and the British Historical Film   James
Chapman

Powell and Pressburger: A Cinema of Magic Spaces   Andrew Moor

Propaganda and the German Cinema, 1933–1945   David Welch

*Spaghetti Westerns: Cowboys and Europeans from Karl May to Sergio
Leone*   Christopher Frayling

Spectacular Narratives: Hollywood in the Age of the Blockbuster   Geoff King

Typical Men: The Representation of Masculinity in Popular British Cinema
Andrew Spicer

The Unknown 1930s: *An Alternative History of the British Cinema,*
1929–1939   Edited by Jeffrey Richards

LICENCE TO THRILL
A Cultural History of the James Bond Films

James Chapman

second edition

I.B. TAURIS

LONDON · NEW YORK

New revised edition published in 2007 by I.B.Tauris & Co. Ltd,
6 Salem Road, London W 2 4BU; 175 Fifth Avenue, New York NY 10010
www.ibtauris.com

In the United States of America and Canada distributed by Palgrave
Macmillan, a division of St. Martin's Press, 175 Fifth Avenue, New
York NY 10010

First published in 1999

ISBN 978 1 84511 515 9

A full CIP record for this book is available from the British Library
A full CIP record is available from the Library of Congress

Set in Monotype Garamond by Ewan Smith, London
Printed and bound in Great Britain by TJ International, Padstow, Cornwall

Contents

General Editor's Introduction   vi
Acknowledgements   viii
Preface to the Second Edition   xi
Author's Note   xiii

Introduction: Taking James Bond Seriously   1

1   The Contexts of Bond   22

2   Snobbery with Violence: *Dr No, From Russia with Love, Goldfinger*   49

3   Bondmania: *Thunderball, Casino Royale, You Only Live Twice, On Her Majesty's Secret Service*   89

4   Bond in Transition: *Diamonds are Forever, Live and Let Die, The Man with the Golden Gun*   123

5   Keeping the British End Up: *The Spy Who Loved Me, Moonraker*   149

6   Cold Warrior Reborn: *For Your Eyes Only, Octopussy, Never Say Never Again, A View to a Kill*   170

7   Continuity and Change: *The Living Daylights, Licence to Kill*   196

8   Millennial Bond: *GoldenEye, Tomorrow Never Dies, The World is not Enough, Die Another Day*   212

9   Revisionist Bond: *Casino Royale*   241

Notes   253
Filmography   271
Bibliography   289
Index   298

General Editor's Introduction

The James Bond films are a cinematic phenomenon. The series was launched in 1962 and is still running after nearly fifty years and – if we exclude the spoof *Casino Royale* – six different actors in the leading role. The critics have frequently been vitriolic about Bond and his world, branding it variously as sexist, racist, snobbish, violent and juvenile. But this has not been reflected in the films' continuous box-office success worldwide. This disparity between critical perceptions and audience appreciation is one of the many subjects tackled by James Chapman in this wide-ranging analysis of the cultural significance of the Bond phenomenon.

The Bond films were born at a precise moment in British history, a decisive period of social and cultural change – the 1960s, which simultaneously witnessed sexual liberation, Britain's global political decline and the transformation of the United Kingdom from sober and responsible superpower to swinging symbol of fashion, music, youth and consumerism. Chapman perceptively charts the ways in which the Bond films negotiated a path through these massive changes.

The films achieved an unbeatable blend of conspicuous consumption, brand-name snobbery, technological gadgetry, colour-supplement chic, exotic locations and comic-strip sex and violence. But they have continually and cannily repositioned themselves as times have changed, the balance of world power has shifted, cultural norms have been transformed, and new cinematic genres have emerged to challenge the former pre-eminence of the secret agent action adventure.

With skill, wit and erudition, James Chapman examines the literary and cinematic precursors of the Bond films, their production strategies, their visual style, their attitudes to sex, violence and heroism and their distinctive Britishness. The whole adds up to an exciting, insightful and original study which throws new light on a cinematic phenomenon too often taken for granted.

Jeffrey Richards

Acknowledgements

Film historians, just as much as our colleagues in other branches of the historical discipline, are frequently concerned with identifying origins (of films, genres, trends, movements, etc.). In the long term, the origins of this book can be traced back to a family holiday in the summer of 1977 when, at the age of eight, I was taken on my first ever visit to 'the pictures'. The cinema in question was the massive and sumptuous Odeon in St Peter Port, Guernsey (sadly no longer extant). The film, equally massive and sumptuous, was *The Spy Who Loved Me*. In hindsight that evening marked the beginning of my fascination with James Bond. And, over twenty years later, *The Spy Who Loved Me* remains one of my three favourite Bond films (along with *From Russia with Love* and *On Her Majesty's Secret Service*).

However, as all historians know, long-term origins are only part of the equation. In the short term, this book is indebted in large measure to two people. Jeffrey Richards first suggested that I should turn my knowledge of James Bond into a book, over lunch at Pierre Victoire in Lancaster in late September 1995, shortly after I had completed a doctoral thesis (on a different subject) under his supervision. Philippa Brewster, my editor at I.B.Tauris, gave more concrete form to the idea by suggesting that I write a cultural history of the James Bond films, over another lunch, at the Spaghetti House in Bloomsbury Square in May 1997. Both of them have supported this project wholeheartedly from the outset, and my grateful thanks are due, therefore, to each of them in turn – even more so because they bought me lunch on each occasion ('Hearts and stomachs good comrades make').

My colleagues in the History Department of the Open University have endured my obsession with all things 'Bondian' with tolerance and good humour ('Oh, grow up, 007!'). In particular, my thanks to Tony Aldgate, who has provided much valuable encouragement as well as lending various source materials. Other colleagues, both home and away, as it were, on whom I have tried out my ideas ('And this one I'm particularly proud of!') include Rowana Agajanian, Ian Conrich, Sue Harper, Matthew Hilton, Peter Krämer, Derek Matravers, Arthur Marwick and Vincent Porter. All faults and flights of fancy in the book, I hasten to add, are entirely mine.

A special note of thanks must be recorded for all those friends past and present with whom I have viewed and/or discussed Bond films over the years, including Philip Adcock, Paul Bennett, Philip Chaston, Sarah Cobby, Bogdan Costea, Michael Coyne, Ian Darbyshire, Neil Harrison, Cathy Laing, Salim Mohammed, Eric Peterson, Thomas Ribbits, Melanie and Reg Ruse, Line Sevaldsen, Jimmy Storey, Andy Walker and George White.

Research for this book was carried out primarily at the National Library of the British Film Institute and at the British Newspaper Library, Colindale. My thanks to the staff of these institutions for their assistance. Mention must also be made of the inter-library loans service provided by the Open University Library, without which the process of tracking down so many journal and magazine articles would have been a much more laborious task.

Most of the illustrations in this book were provided by the Stills, Posters and Designs Division of the British Film Institute; others are from the author's private collection. They are from films originally distributed in the United Kingdom by Columbia-EMI-Warner, Exclusive Pictures, Metro-Goldwyn-Mayer (MGM), Radio Pictures (RKO), United Artists (UA) and United International Pictures (UIP).

The 'official' James Bond films (excluding the 1967 *Casino Royale* and *Never Say Never Again*) are produced by Eon Productions Ltd. Copyright in these films is controlled by Danjaq SA. Copyright in the James Bond novels is controlled by Glidrose Productions Ltd. Grateful acknowledgement is extended to these organisations for the use of production stills from the James Bond films and for permission to quote from the James Bond novels. However, if, for any reason, x   Acknowledgements

I have inadvertently included any copyright material without proper acknowledgement to the owners, I offer my apologies to all concerned and will be happy to make the appropriate amendment to any future edition of the book.

Finally, my thanks to my parents, whose loyalty to the cause extends far beyond the call of duty.

Preface to the Second Edition

Alfred Hitchcock once remarked that films are never finished but only laid aside. So it is with books. The publication of a second edition of *Licence to Thrill* provides me with the opportunity to revise certain features of the original that were not entirely to my satisfaction. I have revised the Introduction and have entirely rewritten Chapter 1, which in hindsight I thought far too unwieldy. Chapters 2 to 7 remain largely as they were, except for the correction of some minor errors. Chapter 8 has been expanded to include *The World is not Enough* and *Die Another Day*, while Chapter 9 is entirely new. (At the time of writing, January/February 2007, *Casino Royale* has not yet been released on DVD, and so this chapter is based largely on notes scribbled from repeated viewings in the cinema.) I have removed the Postscript, incorporating most of the material elsewhere in the text, and have updated the Filmography and Bibliography. Since the publication of the first edition of this book in 1999, there has been a significant level of scholarly interest in Bond to the extent that the subject is no longer as neglected as it was a decade ago. In particular, Jeremy Black's *The Politics of James Bond* (2001), Christoph Lindner's *The James Bond Phenomenon* (2003) and Ed Commentale, Stephen Watt and Skip Willman's *Ian Fleming & James Bond: The Cultural Politics of* 007 (2005) have all significantly expanded the field of Bond scholarship. The latter volume came out of an international conference held at the charming Bloomington campus of the University of Indiana in May

2003: I should like to record my thanks to Steve Watt for inviting me to deliver the opening keynote address.

Finally I would like to add to the list of acknowledgements for the first edition the names of Alexis Albion, Jeremy Black, Nicholas Cull, Sally Dux, David Ekserdjian, Tobias Hochscherf, Christoph Laucht and Nathalie Morris. A special note of thanks to Gary J. Firuta who took me on a James Bond bar crawl in New York in June 2003 ('All you can eat for only three hundred dollars') and who has remained a constant source of Bondology and friendship since.

Author's Note

I argue in this book that the enormous popularity of the James Bond films is more than just the sum total of their box-office receipts, that it has to do with questions of film culture in a wider sense. However, in dealing with a series of such commercially successful films, some indication of how they performed at the box-office becomes inevitable. Box-office statistics can be a minefield for the unwary. They are almost invariably quoted in US dollars, even for the Bond films, which are British-made but financed and distributed by an American company. Moreover, there is a crucial distinction to be made between the *gross* (or *gross revenues*) of a film, which refers to the total amount of money paid by customers at the box-office, and its *rentals* (or *rental receipts*), which is the amount received by the distributor. For films made before the 1970s the rentals (compiled annually by *Variety* from information provided by distributors) provide the most reliable guide to box-office performance, while it is usually possible only to estimate their overall grosses. In more recent years, as more reliable mechanisms have become available for calculating gross revenues, it has become more common to speak in terms of grosses rather than rentals. I have used both rental and gross figures in this book, while ensuring that where comparisons are made like is compared with like. According to *Variety*, the 'domestic' (i.e. in the United States and Canada) rental receipts of the Bond films have amounted to 47.5 per cent of their gross revenues.

Another caveat regarding raw box-office statistics is that they do not take account of inflation. A more useful indication of popularity is the number of paid admissions to see a film, though unfortunately such statistics are available only for the United States throughout the entire period covered by the Bond films. As an example, there were some 74.8 million paid admissions to see 1965's *Thunderball* compared to 29 million to see 1995's *GoldenEye*. If judged by the number of people who went to see the films, therefore, *Thunderball* attracted a considerably larger audience than *GoldenEye*. However, this fact would be disguised by a straightforward comparison of their US grosses, which amount to an estimated $63 million for *Thunderball* and $107 million for *GoldenEye*. The more recent the films are, the more inflated their grosses have become, though in real terms the most successful Bond films were those released in the mid-1960s (*Goldfinger, Thunderball, You Only Live Twice*).

Finally, all quotations from the James Bond novels are referenced in the main text by the page numbers of the current Coronet paperback editions of the books. The original publication details of the books can be found in the Bibliography.

Introduction: Taking James Bond Seriously

W hy should we take James Bond seriously? The question is worth asking, for, to judge by the pronouncements of his creator, James Bond was never intended to be taken seriously at all. Ian Fleming liked to give the impression that the Bond novels were nothing more than entertainments which he had started writing for his own amusement. He was fond of saying that he took up writing fiction on the eve of his wedding as an 'antidote' to his alarm at facing up to marriage at the age of forty-three. He disavowed any deep meaning in his books of either a psychological or a political nature. In an article entitled 'How to Write a Thriller' in 1963, Fleming was at pains to distance himself from the so-called 'angry young men' who had emerged in post-war English literature:

> I am not an angry young, or even middle-aged man. I am not 'involved'. My books are not 'engaged'. I have no message for suffering humanity and, though I was bullied at school and lost my virginity like so many of us used to do in the old days, I have never been tempted to foist these and other harrowing personal experiences on the public. My opuscula do not aim at changing people or making them go out and do something. They are not designed to find favour with the Comintern. They are written for warm-blooded heterosexuals in railway trains, airplanes or beds.[1]

[handwritten margin note: No hidden meaning in Bond]

It was characteristic of Fleming that he should dismiss his own books in such terms, as minor or insignificant works. It was equally characteristic that when he submitted the manuscript of his first novel, *Casino Royale*, to his publisher Jonathan Cape in 1952, it was accompanied by a self-deprecatory note describing it as 'dreadfully banal ... [a] miserable piece of work'.[2]

The James Bond books, with their improbable plots and their descriptions of fast cars, high-stakes gambling and gunplay, were set in a very different world from the gritty 'northern realism' of contemporary novelists such as John Braine or Alan Sillitoe. Fleming had become a novelist only at the onset of middle age. He had previously tried his hand at various careers, including banking, stockbroking and journalism. During the Second World War he had been personal assistant to the Director of Naval Intelligence at the Admiralty and certainly had first-hand knowledge of espionage, if not necessarily any personal experience.[3] James Bond, secret agent 007 of the British Secret Service, was a product of Fleming's vivid imagination. He said that Bond was 'the author's pillow fantasy', the sort of character he wished he could have been: 'I admit that Bond is very much the Walter Mitty syndrome – the feverish dream of the author of what he might have been – bang, bang, kiss, kiss – that sort of stuff.'[4]

Fleming's interview comments, however, were part of the self-effacing public persona of a complex man whose Old Etonian charm disguised a host of personal insecurities and contradictions. For someone who, albeit jokingly, described his own work as 'miserable' and 'banal', Fleming went to often quite extraordinary lengths to secure good reviews for his books by placing them with friends in journalistic and literary circles; and, although he was reluctant to admit it, he was highly sensitive to the criticisms which Bond attracted, particularly from his wife Anne's circle of *literati* friends such as Evelyn Waugh and W. Somerset Maugham. When he struck up a friendship with American thriller writer Raymond Chandler, whose work he greatly admired, Fleming was more candid. 'Probably the fault about my books is that I don't take them seriously enough and meekly accept having my head ragged off about them in the family circle,' he admitted to the creator of Philip Marlowe. Characteristically, however, he added the qualification: 'If one has a grain of intelligence it is difficult to go on being serious about a character like James Bond.'[5]

Critics were – indeed, still are – divided on the merits of the Bond

novels. On the one hand they have been attacked as harmful and perni- *too*
cious, particularly by critics from the left who dislike them on ideological *sexual for*
grounds, while on the other hand they have been disparaged as mere *etc*
entertainments which, well-written though they may be, do not really
deserve to be taken seriously. The attacks on the novels have tended
to focus on their content, with some critics reviling them for exhibiting in excessive measure all the unpleasant 'snobbery with violence'
characteristics of English crime fiction. This view is exemplified by
Paul Johnson's vitriolic review of *Dr No* for the *New Statesman* in 1958,
wherein he described it as 'without doubt the nastiest book I have ever
read'. 'There are three basic ingredients in *Dr No*,' Johnson declared,
'all unhealthy, all thoroughly English: the sadism of a schoolboy bully, *sex, bully*
the mechanical, two-dimensional sex-longings of a frustrated adolescent,
and the crude snob-cravings of a suburban adult.' As if that was not
damning enough, he added that 'this novel is badly written to the point
of incoherence'.[6] Other commentators, however, have accepted the Bond
novels on the sort of level which Fleming would have appreciated,
as superior thrillers with a sophisticated veneer. 'These books are not
meant to instruct the reader or to plumb the indecipherable problem
of life,' wrote R. M. Stern in the *New York Herald Tribune*. 'Their special
quality consists in the fact that they answer completely to the needs of
the popular novel – that is to say they amuse. Fleming is a story-teller
in the classical meaning of the word.'[7]

Yet just because a writer is first and foremost a story-teller who
disavows any notion of social commentary is no reason why his work
should not be taken seriously, particularly when, as in Fleming's case,
it was popular with the reading public. Following Fleming's death in
1964, there were signs that his books were starting to be noticed in
academic circles. Kingsley Amis, novelist, critic and former university
teacher, was certainly of the opinion that Fleming deserved to be taken
seriously. In an affectionate but nevertheless perceptive analysis of
the Bond novels, entitled *The James Bond Dossier*, Amis suggested that
'they were more than simple cloak-and-dagger stories with a bit of
fashionable affluence and sex thrown in'.[8] *The James Bond Dossier* – still
by far the most accessible study of the novels – was, in part, a plea
for popular, generic fiction to be appreciated on its own terms. Amis
argued that Fleming deserved to be ranked 'with those demi-giants of
an earlier day, Jules Verne, Rider Haggard, Conan Doyle'. 'Ian Fleming', Amis continued, 'has set his stamp on the story of action and

intrigue, bringing to it a sense of our time, a power and a flair that will win him readers when all the protests about his supposed deficiencies have been forgotten.'[9]

If Amis was rather impressionistic in his discussion of the narrative conventions and character types of Fleming's stories, the same could not be said of the work of Umberto Eco, the scholar who, more than any other, has brought academic respectability to the study of James Bond. Eco set out to identify and rationalise precisely what the pleasures to be had from reading Fleming were, to which end he applied the methodology of structuralist analysis that was becoming voguish in the 1960s. Structuralism, as Terry Eagleton has observed, is 'quite indifferent to the cultural value of its object ... The method is analytical, not evaluative.'[10] According to his structuralist analysis of the Bond narratives, Eco concluded that it was the essential similarity of the novels that was their main appeal. He used the metaphor of a game of chess, whereby different characters (pieces) make certain pre-determined moves, to explain the narrative structure of the Bond novels. 'The reader's pleasure consists of finding himself immersed in a game of which he knows the pieces and the rules – and perhaps the outcome – drawing pleasure simply from the minimal variations by which the victor realises his objective,' Eco argued. 'The novels of Fleming', he went on, 'exploit in exemplary measure that element of foregone play which is typical of the escape machine geared for the entertainment of the masses.'[11]

By the time that academics had started taking Fleming seriously, James Bond had transcended his origins as the hero of a series of popular novels and had become nothing less than a cultural phenomenon. This was due in no small measure to the immensely successful series of James Bond films starring Sean Connery which had begun with *Dr No* in 1962. But while the novels have attracted their share of serious analysis, the James Bond films have not on the whole received such attention. One of the reasons for this is that admirers of Fleming – the people who have been prepared to take the literary Bond seriously – generally dislike the films, seeing the cinematic Bond as nothing more than a parody of the literary original. This attitude was perfectly exemplified by Anthony Burgess, who, in a short essay written as an introduction for a new paperback edition of the novels in the 1980s, was particularly disparaging. 'The films, which grew more and more gimmicky, and less and less psychologically interesting, are

[handwritten margin note: reader knows pieces, rules, outcome of bond: but still interested]

grotesquely parodic of the novels, and the cinema version of *Casino Royale* is a disgraceful distortion of a fine taut story which owes nothing at all to lurid fantasy,' he declared. The 1967 *Casino Royale* had in fact been a spoof, not of Fleming's Bond but of the series of Bond films produced by the team of Albert R. Broccoli and Harry Saltzman, who had bought the rights to all the novels except the first. Even in respect of the 'official' Bond films, however, Burgess contended that 'the James Bond whom Fleming created has only a nominal connection with the leering hero of the screen'.[12]

book Bond ≠ Movie Bond

Critical reaction to the James Bond films has always been mixed. Indeed, it mirrors the reaction to the novels in that in the early days of the series the Bond films were either attacked for their excesses of sex and violence, or they were dismissed as nothing more than entertaining movies of no real importance. This was evident from the very beginning of the series, when *Dr No* polarised critical opinion. For Nina Hibbin, film critic of the communist *Daily Worker*, it was 'vicious hokum skilfully designed to appeal to the filmgoer's basest feelings'.[13] No less a moral authority than the Vatican condemned the film as 'a dangerous mixture of violence, vulgarity, sadism and sex'.[14] But while some critics despised *Dr No*, others thought it was simply good fun which was not meant to be taken at all seriously. For Penelope Gilliat, writing in the *Observer*, 'the film is full of submerged self-parody, and I think it would be as wrong to take it solemnly as it would be to worry that Sherlock Holmes's beastliness to Dr Watson encourages intellectual arrogance or the taking of cocaine'.[15] One American critic described it as 'the best bad film of the year'.[16] The film industry trade press, for its part, recognised that the Bond movies were going to win popular rather than critical acclaim. 'As a screen hero James Bond is definitely here to stay,' declared *Variety*. 'He will win no Oscars but a heck of a lot of enthusiastic followers.'[17]

Opinions of the early Bond films were split, therefore, between those who disliked them on ideological or moral grounds and those who accepted them on their own terms as popular entertainments. As the series went on, however, this division gradually disappeared, and the critics came to speak more and more with one voice – weary, resigned and despairing of the increasingly predictable and formulaic nature of the films. As the *Monthly Film Bulletin* said of *You Only Live Twice* in 1967: 'Really no better and no worse than its predecessors, the fifth James Bond is rather less enjoyable mainly because the formula

not match times

has become so completely mechanical (and Bond himself so predictably indestructible) without any compensation in other directions.'[18]
The longer the series continued, the more the critics lamented that
the later films had lost the vitality which had made the earlier ones
so fresh and exciting. Ronald Bergan, for example, considered that by
the time of the fourteenth 'official' Bond film in 1985, *A View to a
Kill*, 'both the hero – as interpreted by the 57-year-old Roger Moore
– and the formula were beginning to look somewhat old and tired.
What was fresh in the 60s and had a certain faded charm in the 70s,
began to look dated and mechanical in the 80s, despite the usual
technical expertise.'[19]

[handwritten margin note: 80's formula got old]

Even for those film journalists who do like the Bond movies, there
is a tendency to assume that they should not be placed under the
microscope of critical scrutiny. 'To me,' writes John Brosnan, 'the James
Bond films are fun, and to take them seriously would spoil the whole
game.'[20] This view is indicative of a critical culture in which there is still
great resistance to the notion that popular entertainments are legitimate
objects for cultural analysis. The special qualities of the Bond films
as popular cinema are, unsurprisingly, emphasised by the discourse of
the film industry trade press, which exhibits a similar disinclination
to engage with them on anything other than the superficial level of
'entertainment' and 'escapism'. And in his posthumously published
memoir, Bond producer 'Cubby' Broccoli similarly attributed their
success to their expensive production values. 'The success of James
Bond has always depended upon the values we put up there on the
screen,' he averred. 'People may argue about the relative merits of the
Bond films, but few would deny that they reveal the highest production
values and technical skill.'[21]

Nor has academic film study been inclined towards serious analysis
of the Bond films. The tone was set by Robin Wood who, in his classic
book *Hitchcock's Films*, compared the early Bond movies unfavourably
with Hitchcock's celebrated spy thriller *North by Northwest*. The Bond
films, in Wood's view, were mere formula pictures which lacked the
thematic maturity and stylistic artistry that Hitchcock had displayed in
North by Northwest. 'If I fail to be entertained by *Goldfinger*, it is because
there is nothing there to engage or retain the attention; the result is
a nonentity, consequently tedious,' he declared. 'The essential triviality
of the James Bond films, in fact, sets off perfectly, by contrast, the
depth, the charm, the integrity of Hitchcock's film.' Unlike *North by*

Northwest, which could be seen as a work of art because it was 'thematically organic', *Goldfinger* was nothing more than 'a collection of bits, carefully calculated with both eyes on the box office, put end to end with no deeper necessity for what happens next than mere plot'.[22] In the case of *From Russia with Love*, moreover, there is a direct comparison to be made between the sequence of a helicopter attack on Bond and the famous set piece in *North by Northwest* where Cary Grant is attacked by a crop-dusting plane. Wood was in no doubt which was the better of the two.

> The difference in quality will seem to some readers too great and too obvious for the comparison to be worth making; but its purpose is not to score easily off a bad film but to help us define the quality of the suspense in Hitchcock. It is worth, perhaps, pointing out that *From Russia with Love* represents precisely that pandering to a debased popular taste that Hitchcock is widely supposed to be guilty of; the most hostile commentator would find difficulty in paralleling its abuses of sex and violence in any Hitchcock film.[23]

For Wood, therefore, whereas Hitchcock's films were legitimate works of art, the Bond films were pale imitations pandering to the box-office. It has to be borne in mind, of course, that Wood had a particular agenda of his own. His book, first published in 1965, and which began with the question 'Why should we take Hitchcock seriously?', was one of the first major English-language texts to explore the notion of the film director as *auteur*, an idea that had developed mainly through the influential French critical journal *Cahiers du Cinéma* during the 1950s. Authorship theory was adopted by Anglo-American scholars in the 1960s as part of their bid to establish film studies as a legitimate academic discipline. Popular film could be taken seriously, it was argued, when the presence of an *auteur* could be detected as the overall artistic intelligence behind the films. Hitchcock was held up as the example *par excellence* of an *auteur* working in mainstream commercial cinema: a master of visual narration and *mise-en-scène*, whose films were characterised by recurring stylistic and thematic motifs and which consistently set out the director's own view of the world based on a sense of the chaos lurking beneath the apparent normality of society. It is easy, in hindsight, to point out the contradiction in Wood's theoretical position: concerned with elevating Hitchcock to critical respectability, he dismissed the Bond films in precisely the same terms (commercial, insubstantial, pandering to popular taste) that had for so long been used to condemn Hitchcock himself. However, this contradiction might not have been so evident at the time Wood was writing, when the notion of authorship prevailed in film studies and when individual directors with an identifiable 'world view' were championed above mere genre films. The Bond movies, with their formula-based plots, standardised narratives and stereotyped characters, were regarded as a sort of film-making by numbers, the antithesis of the cinema of personal expression exemplified by *auteurs* like Hitchcock.

Whereas Robin Wood clearly disliked the Bond films, other scholars have tended either to ignore them or to pay them only passing mention. There has been little or no place for Bond in most standard histories of British, or indeed world cinema. A partial exception to this is Roy Armes's *A Critical History of British Cinema*, which at least pays some attention to Bond – described as the 'most potent myth of British cinema in the 1960s' – and discusses the early films in relation to others of the period such as the Hammer horror films and the cycle of 'Swinging London' films in the middle of the decade. Armes admires the early films and rates *Goldfinger* as 'perhaps the best of the series', but echoes other critics in considering that by the time of *Thunderball* and *You Only Live Twice*, 'the formula was already showing signs of becoming purely mechanical'. By the time of *The Spy Who Loved Me* in 1977, there was evidence of an 'almost inevitable decline into routine', though Armes does acknowledge that, the mediocrity of the later films notwithstanding, 'the James Bond series remains a remarkable production achievement, totally recasting the source material so that the upper-class Englishness of Ian Fleming's original gives way to the more classless virility of the Hollywood action film hero'.[24] More recently, in her book *British National Cinema*, Sarah Street mentions the Bond films in relation to other traditions of popular film-making: 'Like other successful British genres (Gainsborough melodramas, Ealing comedies, Hammer horror and the *Carry On*s), a secure production base provided a long-serving technical and creative team who worked towards perfecting the Bondian formula.'[25] There is still much reluctance, however, to engage with the films as anything other than formula entertainments.

It is symptomatic of the neglect of Bond by serious film historians that, while there are numerous books on the Bond films, they have all emanated from what might be termed the Bond fan culture rather than from academia. The titles of some of these books – *The Official James Bond 007 Movie Companion, The James Bond Bedside Companion, The Incredible World of 007, Kiss Kiss Bang! Bang!: The Unofficial James Bond Film Companion* and *The Essential Bond: The Authorized Guide to the World of 007* – are indicative of their celebratory, anecdotal and uncritical content. The usual format for these books is to recount the production histories of the films, based on interviews and behind-the-scenes information, but what they lack in scholarly apparatus they make up for in their lively style and their extensive knowledge of all things 'Bondian'. The proliferation of James Bond fan clubs and magazines, moreover – most of which focus on the films rather than the original novels – is ample testimony to the existence of an international fan culture for whom the figure of James Bond has a special significance.

It would be fair to say that those who do take James Bond seriously today are divided into two camps. On the one hand there are the Fleming purists who have little time for the films and who deplore the fact that most of the films' fans are unacquainted with the literary original. 'It is time for the aficionados of the films to get back to the books and admire their quality as literature,' Anthony Burgess declared.[26] On the other hand there is the fan culture which has grown up around the films and for whom the cinematic Bond exists in his own right and on his own terms. 'We seek to reclaim Bond from the humourless Fleming pedants who view Bond as fixed, immutable, an unalterable period antiquity,' declare the authors of a recent addition to the plethora of fan histories. Alan Barnes and Marcus Hearn (respectively, a comic-strip writer and the editor of a *Star Wars* fan magazine) suggest that the mythic status of Bond 'owes everything to his incarnation on the cinema screen, and little to the novels of Fleming', whom they regard as 'tangential' to the on-going film series.[27] A more detached and balanced perspective is provided by cultural theorist Tony Bennett:

> The novels are undoubtedly privileged in the sense that, historically, they came first. They function as textual sources for the film, and as legitimators – both culturally (an authentic Bond film must, however loosely, be based on a Fleming source) and legally … From this point of view, the films are secondary and derivative in relation to the novels. From the point of view of their role in the construction and circulation of the figure of Bond, however, the films are clearly privileged in relation to the novels. This is

 film novel

not merely to say that many more people have seen the films than have read the novels; rather more important is the fact that, for most readers, the films came first and the novels second.[28]

[margin note: film become → novel]

The longer the films have continued, furthermore, the more privileged they have become: the film-makers have now run out of Fleming novels and have started using non-Fleming titles, thus extending the career of James Bond beyond the original corpus of texts.

[margin note: goes against idea of realism / quality]

How can the neglect of the Bond series in film scholarship be explained? The most obvious explanation is the nature of orthodox film criticism, particularly in Britain, with its emphasis on 'realism' (exemplified by documentary, social-problem films and kitchen-sink dramas) and notions of 'quality' (exemplified by adaptations of classic literature, from the Dickensian films of David Lean in the 1940s to the so-called 'heritage' films of Merchant-Ivory and others in the 1980s and 1990s). The writing of British cinema history, until very recently, has been done predominantly from the perspective of a critical discourse which privileges sober, unsensational narratives, believable character-isations and a restrained visual style. In a critical tradition which favours realism and quality at the expense of fantasy and escapism, it is easy to understand why the Bond films, with their fantastic plots, their glossy visual style and their origins in a tradition of 'shocker' literature, should have been excluded from the canon of critically respectable cinema.

Since the 1980s, however, there has been a greater willingness on the part of film historians to engage with those films which had been marginalised by the dominant realist discourse. The most persistent metaphor of recent British film historiography has been that of the 'lost continent', a term coined by Julian Petley to describe the 'repressed side of British cinema, a dark, disdained thread weaving the length and breadth of that cinema, crossing authorial and generic boundaries, sometimes almost entirely invisible, sometimes erupting explosively, always received critically with fear and disapproval'.[29] Recent scholar-ship has been much concerned with exploring this 'lost continent', and, concomitant to that, reclaiming certain genres and cycles of films which hitherto have been neglected. The main beneficiaries of this 'new film history' have been critically despised but commercially successful forms such as the Gainsborough costume melodramas and the Hammer horror films. Whereas orthodox film history had marginalised these films, largely on account of their lack of serious themes or literary pedigree, the tendency now is to see them as using their ostensible fantasy ingredients as a means to explore various identities – national, class and, especially, sexual identity – which have particular resonances for audiences at historically specific moments. The Gainsborough and Hammer films are now championed for their flamboyant *mise-en-scène*, which represents an alternative to the sober realism and restrained visual style of more respectable cinema, and for their flagrant transgressions of conventionally acceptable norms of moral and sexual behaviour – precisely the qualities which orthodox criticism had either overlooked or despised. This revisionist project was exemplified by the short-lived *Journal of Popular British Cinema* which sought 'to make known what has been called the "unknown cinema"'. The first issue, focusing on 'Genre and British Cinema', included a range of articles on such diverse topics as crime films, war films, *Carry On* comedies, 'Swinging London' films and sexploitation cinema, all of which, in the words of the editors, 'contribute to the welcome trend to treat British film genres in relation to their cultural and historical conditions, as well as dealing with them as particular stylistic and thematic configurations'.[30] Admirable as its intentions are and impressive as its range of coverage is, the inaugural issue of the *Journal* nevertheless omits any consideration of the Bond films, surely one of the most popular but neglected series in cinema history.

The absence of the Bond films from the new film history is more difficult to explain than their exclusion from the orthodox realist historiography. One possible reason is that the Bond films do not really belong to the 'lost continent' of British cinema in the same way as other popular genre films which have recently come in for critical reappraisal. Certainly there are some similarities between the Bond series and the Gainsborough and Hammer films, both in terms of their roots in popular literature (the Gainsborough melodramas in the 'bodice-ripper' tradition of romantic fiction, the Hammer films in nineteenth-century Gothic literature) and in terms of their richly decorative set design and expressive *mise-en-scène*.[31] But there are also some important differences. The Bond movies are big-budget films with lavish production values which are filmed on locations around the world, in contrast to the modestly budgeted and predominantly studio-bound Gainsborough and Hammer films. And, on a textual level, whereas the pleasures offered by the Gainsborough and Hammer films have generally been explained in terms of their transgressive characteristics, there is nothing particularly

[margin annotations: demonstrate era through these avenues; key to long term success]

transgressive about Bond. Indeed, the films are at best ideologically conservative, and at worst downright reactionary in their representation of, for example, race and gender.

Perhaps the main reason for the continued neglect of the Bond films at a time when other aspects of popular cinema are enjoying a long overdue critical rehabilitation is that they are, simply, unfashionable in the present intellectual climate. The character of James Bond, with his old-fashioned sense of patriotism and duty, his often contemptuous attitude towards foreigners, and, above all, his undisguised male chauvinism, is the antithesis of what is deemed 'politically correct'. The Bond films are unlikely to appeal to proponents of, say, the *Screen* school of film theory, not merely because the films are sexist, heterosexist, jingoistic, xenophobic and racist – they are all of these things, to varying degrees – but also because they seem to endorse and even celebrate those attitudes. In an age when academia is hidebound by the notion of political correctness, the Bond films are certainly beyond the pale of what is considered ideologically acceptable. And yet, despite their political incorrectness – or perhaps even because of it – the Bond films have been enormously popular with cinema-goers around the world, suggesting either that audiences do not pay as much heed to the ideological content of the films as do academics, or that the films provide a particular sort of pleasure which mediates their sexist and racist overtones.

For the evidence of the international popularity of the Bond films is overwhelming. They are, without doubt, the most successful series of films in box-office history: if the individual films have not quite achieved the super-blockbuster status of *Star Wars*, *Jurassic Park* or *Titanic*, nevertheless the cumulative grosses of the series as a whole have surpassed all other similar cycles of films.[32] Moreover, the Bond films have not been one-off successes, but have been consistently successful over a long period of time, a remarkable achievement in a period when the film industry has undergone far-reaching changes and in which film culture has been transformed out of all recognition from that which pertained when the series began in the early 1960s. The index of their success, indeed, is indicated not merely by box-office receipts, but by the fact that the films have proved so enduringly popular with audiences. They are, to borrow one of Raymond Williams's definitions of the word 'popular', evidently 'well-liked by many people'.[33] The Bond films have now won the approval of several successive generations of cinema-goers, while it has variously been estimated that between a quarter and a half of the world's population has seen a Bond film, either in the cinema or on television, video or DVD.

international

The international success of the Bond films is in itself worthy of particular attention, simply because it is so unusual for British cinema. Many commentators have berated the failure of the British film industry to compete in the international market. Nick Roddick, for instance, observes that Britain 'is a small country with a sometimes disproportionate belief in her world significance' and that this 'has fairly inescapable implications when it comes to film'.[34] The occasional high-profile international successes for the British film industry – from Alexander Korda's *The Private Life of Henry VIII* in 1933 to more recent hit movies like *Four Weddings and a Funeral* and *The Full Monty* – merely highlight how infrequent such films are. In almost all such cases, there are unique and peculiar reasons for the success of these films, while attempts to repeat them are usually doomed to failure. Those producers who have set their sights on conquering the world film market – including Korda in the 1930s, the Rank Organisation in the 1940s and Goldcrest in the 1980s – have invariably failed to sustain their ambitious production programmes and have seen their empires crumble. But while most standard film histories paint a gloomy picture of an industry unable to compete on equal terms with Hollywood, they all too often overlook the fact that in the Bond series the British cinema has produced a cycle of films which have enjoyed conspicuous and consistent success in the international market over a long period of time.

It might be argued, of course, that the Bond films are not really 'British' at all, given that they are backed by American dollars. By this token, however, films such as *Tom Jones*, *A Hard Day's Night* and *Chariots of Fire* would not qualify as British either. Ever since the 1930s, in fact, American studios have provided the financial backing for productions which are, to all other intents and purposes, British. The production base of the Bond films is British (only three so far have been made in overseas studios), most of the technical personnel are British, the generic roots of the films are British, and the ideology of national identity which the films themselves embody is British. Indeed, the Britishness of the Bond films has been one of their main selling points, a factor which differentiates them from all the other action movies which have followed in their wake. This has not prevented one commentator from claiming the films for American popular culture. In his book *American*

Mix American studio v British spy / Worker

Dreamtime, Lee Drummond argues that the key to understanding Bond's popularity lies 'in the *universality* of Bond's appeal, and not in a parochial Britishness that … others have insisted on ascribing to him'. Instead Drummond suggests that Bond 'has become fully incorporated into the larger, ongoing *story of America*, the Dreamtime chronicle of that rich, gimmicky and bizarre land that is less a place than a state of mind'.[35] He sees Bond as the first in a succession of 'international media sensations' whose other members are all American: Captain Kirk, Luke Skywalker, Indiana Jones, J. R. Ewing, Rocky and Rambo. Yet this argument is methodologically flawed and extremely impressionistic: it marginalises the motifs of Britishness that are so prominent in the films, ignores the cultural roots of Bond, and does not take sufficient account of the fact that the Bond film series has historically been more successful outside North America. It has long been a film industry rule of thumb that the rental income of a major studio release will usually be divided roughly equally between the 'domestic' market (USA and Canada) and the 'international' market (all territories outside North America), though since the 1980s the balance has shifted slightly in favour of the international market. Throughout their history, however, the Bond films have consistently taken significantly more in the international market: it has not been unusual for their international rental income to be twice or even three times greater. Overall the Bond series has taken approximately two-thirds of its revenues from outside North America.

The best academic study of the Bond phenomenon, taking into account both the novels and the films, is Tony Bennett and Janet Woollacott's *Bond and Beyond*, a book which has much to recommend it despite its heavily theorised slant and its leanings towards Marxist-based approaches to cultural studies. Bennett and Woollacott are interested 'in the figure of Bond, in the diverse and changing forms in which it has been produced and circulated, and in the varying cultural business that has been conducted around, by means of and through this figure during the now considerable slice of post-war history in which it has been culturally active'. The aim of their study, they claim, is 'to go beyond the Bond novels and films to take account of the broader range of texts and coded objects through which the figure of Bond has been put into circulation as a popular hero'.[36] Accordingly they analyse not only the books and the films, but also the images of Bond in other media – advertisements, newspapers, magazines – to show how Bond has functioned as a point of reference in popular culture. The principal

[handwritten margin note: SPY idea is universal]

[handwritten note: reference to Britain in pop culture]

theoretical assumption underlying *Bond and Beyond*, typically for cultural studies during the 1980s, is the Gramscian notion of hegemony which supposes that the role of popular culture 'is not that of imposing a range of dominant ideologies but that of articulating the relations between a series of ideologies (subordinate as well as dominant), overlapping them on to one another so as to bring about certain movements and reformations of subjectivity – movements whose direction has varied with different moments in Bond's career as a popular hero in response to broader cultural and ideological pressures'.[37]

A more historical dimension to Bennett and Woollacott's work is evidenced by their analysis of the various 'moments of Bond' throughout his 'career' as a popular hero. They chart how 'the cultural and ideological currency of the figure of Bond has been changed and adapted to changing circumstances'.[38] They identify three particular moments which defined Bond's place in popular culture. Pointing out that Fleming's novels did not immediately achieve best-seller status, Bennett and Woollacott identify 1957 – the year in which the stories were first serialised in the *Daily Express* and when a 'James Bond' strip cartoon began in the same newspaper – as 'the first stage in the transformation of Bond from a character within a set of fictional texts into a household name'.[39] The second key 'moment' of Bond was the mid-1960s when the success of the early James Bond films 'both significantly broadened the social basis of Bond's popular appeal in Britain and extended the horizons of his popularity internationally'.[40] The films transformed the essentially conservative, establishment figure of Fleming's novels into a modern, classless hero more in tune with the social climate of the 1960s. It was during the mid-1960s that the phenomenon of 'Bondmania', attributable principally to the success of the films, which in turn boosted sales of the novels, was at its height. The third 'moment' of Bond is the period since the early 1970s when the nature of Bond's popularity changed by becoming less of a cultural phenomenon and more of an 'institutionalised ritual' with the production of a new film on a regular basis every two years. Moreover, from 1975 onwards, 'the transmission of a Bond film by ITV on Christmas Day established a regular place for Bond in the "way of life" of the British people'.[41] Bond has now become a familiar and recognisable institution, a 'dormant signifier' which is inactive most of the time but is 'capable of being periodically reactivated' with the release of each new film.

Bennett and Woollacott provide a thoroughgoing, stimulating, theoretically informed investigation of the Bond phenomenon which contains much useful and perceptive analysis of both the novels and the films. What *Bond and Beyond* emphatically is not, however, is a contextual history of the James Bond films. The authors do not consider the films in the context of British cinema history more generally. Nor do they discuss the place of the Bond movies in *film* culture specifically (as opposed to popular culture in general). There is much scope, therefore, for further critical and historical analysis of the Bond films. For instance, whereas the place of the novels within the spy thriller genre has been thoroughly investigated by literary theorists – Michael Denning's book *Cover Stories* is exemplary in this respect – there has been no comparable generic analysis forthcoming from a film studies perspective.

This book arises from a desire to subject the James Bond films to the same sort of critical scrutiny that has recently been applied to other areas of popular cinema. In particular it seeks to locate the Bond films in the generic profile of popular cinema and to chart how the Bond series has both responded to and survived changes in the film industry, in popular film culture and in society at large. It seems to me that the Bond films can be located in various different generic contexts; that relationships can be identified between the Bond movies and other types of popular cinema, both past and present. The following list is not intended to be too schematic, but rather to suggest a general framework for critical investigation.

1. *The British imperialist spy thriller.* On one level the Bond films represent the last, glorious, big-budget flowering of the old-fashioned British imperialist spy thriller. The link here is predominantly a literary one in that Ian Fleming is widely regarded as having inherited the mantle of sensational British thriller writers such as John Buchan and 'Sapper' (H. C. McNeile), whose fictional heroes – Richard Hannay and Bulldog Drummond – have been seen as the literary predecessors of James Bond. Fleming's Bond is undoubtedly one of 'the Breed', that group of instinctively competitive, patriotic, honest and square-jawed defenders of the realm so memorably evoked in Richard Usborne's nostalgic tribute *Clubland Heroes.* But the imperialist spy thriller also successfully made the transition to the cinema, enjoying its heyday with the films of Alfred Hitchcock, and others, during the 1930s: *The Man Who Knew Too Much, The 39 Steps, Secret Agent, The Lady Vanishes, The Return of Bulldog Drummond, Bulldog Drummond at Bay, Sexton Blake and the Hooded Terror, Q-Planes*

and *The Four Just Men* were among the films which made the decade the golden age for the genre in British cinema. Subsequently the spy genre was modified, first through the secret mission narratives of the Second World War, then through the espionage films of the Cold War. The Bond films, in this sense, can be placed in a generic lineage of British popular fiction. The film critic of *The Times*, in reviewing *From Russia with Love* in 1963, described the screen Bond as 'the Four Just Men, 1960s style, all rolled into one'.[42] But already, by the time that Bond made his cinema debut, the values and ideologies of the imperialist spy thriller had been overtaken by events. Bond himself was an anachronism, a defender of empire in a post-colonial age. Raymond Durgnat certainly saw him in these terms, employing a typically British metaphor in suggesting that 'Bond J. is the last man in of the British Empire Superman's XI. Holmes, Hannay, Drummond, Conquest, Templar *et al.* have all succumbed to the demon bowlers of the twentieth century, while The Winds of Change make every ball a googlie.'[43]

2. *The cliff-hanger adventure serial.* 'If any cinematic genre inherited the mantle of the Saturday matinée serials and Pearl White tied to the rails, it was James Bond,' remarks film critic Andrew Rissik.[44] The film serial, or 'chapter play', can be seen as an alternative mode of film practice to the dominant classical cinema of Hollywood between the mid-1910s and the early 1950s, representing the continued existence of a cinema based on 'attractions' (stunts, chases, fights, death-defying escapes) and on the non-closure of narrative (at least until the final chapter). While the serials ranged across various genres, including westerns, adventure melodramas, science-fiction and crime-fighter serials, in the collective consciousness of cinema-goers they have come to represent a cinema of thrills, spills, master criminals and imperilled heroines. The Bond films have frequently been compared to the old movie serials, the only major difference being that they are made on a much bigger and more expensive scale. 'Certainly, the James Bond films and all the imitations of them were only movie serials made acceptable to adults,' write serial historians Jim Harmon and Donald F. Glut. 'The mad scientists were better characterized to make then more believable; their inventions were made to look more convincing; sexy girls were added; the week-to-week continuation was subracted [*sic*] for a jaded, impatient audience.'[45] Furthermore, it is not only through the cinema that the influence of the serial on the Bond films can be detected. The British radio serial *Dick Barton* of the late 1940s, for example, might be seen as another

forerunner of James Bond: a 'special agent' who, complete with his own distinctive theme tune, defended Britain against the fiendish plots of diabolical criminal masterminds.

3. *The modern Hollywood action movie.* If the links to the imperialist spy thriller and the serial suggest that the Bond films are best located in relation to genres and modes of the past, their influence on the modern Hollywood action movie illustrates that they can also be placed in the context of one of the most popular and characteristic genres of contemporary American cinema. The Bond series can be seen as the progenitor of the high-tech action film – a genre which one commentator has dubbed the 'big loud action movie' (the acronym does not need spelling out) – that is now a staple of Hollywood film-making. In the view of screenwriter Larry Gross, the Bond films represented 'an entirely new super-kinetic cartoon-type action movie'.[46] The Bond films are chiefly memorable for their outstanding action set pieces: the fight on the Orient Express in *From Russia with Love*, the battle of Fort Knox in *Goldfinger*, the underwater climax of *Thunderball*, the moonlit ski chase in *On Her Majesty's Secret Service*, the heart-stopping ski-parachute jump in *The Spy Who Loved Me*, the fight on the cargo net in *The Living Daylights*, the breathtaking free-running chase from *Casino Royale*, and dozens of other examples. The characteristics of the modern Hollywood action thriller – the emphasis on (usually violent) action over plotting and characterisation, the reduction of narrative complexity to a series of set pieces, the foregrounding of technology and firepower, and, perhaps above all, the hero who never dispatches a villain without a 'witty' one-liner – can all be traced back to the Bond films. The starring vehicles of Hollywood action-men such as Mel Gibson, Arnold Schwarzenegger, Sylvester Stallone, Bruce Willis *et al.* are nothing if not Americanised reworkings of the James Bond formula. Even the Indiana Jones films, in which the hero is characterised in contrast to James Bond (scruffy and crumpled rather than suave and sophisticated, relying on a bullwhip rather than technological gadgetry), owe as much to Bond as they do to the serials which inspired them. Bond, the first of the cinema's cynical, saturnine superheroes might be seen as the 'father' of Indiana Jones – literally so when Sean Connery was cast as Harrison Ford's father in *Indiana Jones and the Last Crusade*.

4. *The 'Bondian'.* For all the similarities which the Bond films share with other genres, the Bond series itself is nevertheless unique in that there is nothing else quite like it in cinema history. In this sense it

might be argued that the Bond series is a genre (or at the very least a sub-genre) in its own right. The Bond series is differentiated from other action movies through the character of James Bond himself. 'There is no other romantic anti-hero in existence at the moment,' remarked *GoldenEye* director Martin Campbell in 1995. 'They are all blue collar – Arnold Schwarzenegger, Bruce Willis, Sylvester Stallone. There are no sophisticated or British comparisons to Bond.'[47] The Bond film-makers have developed their own production ideology based on the notion of what is and what is not 'Bondian'. This production ideology constitutes a set of expectations about what a Bond movie should be like, what it should contain, how it should be made, and so on. This was a recurring theme in a series of interviews with production personnel conducted for an Open University case study of the making of *The Spy Who Loved Me* in 1976–77 and which is the basis of an essay on the production of the Bond films by Janet Woollacott. '"Bondian" was the phrase used by Broccoli and other members of the production team to mean "in the spirit of James Bond",' she writes. 'To a certain extent the term "Bondian" was used to describe the Bond films, which were seen as a distinctive formula, a specific genre of film.'[48] Another aspect of the 'Bondian' ideology is the existence of a core production team that has built up over the years. The first sixteen Bond films, for example, were made by five directors (Terence Young, Guy Hamilton, Lewis Gilbert, Peter Hunt, John Glen) and others who have been integral members of the Bond production team include title designer Maurice Binder (fourteen), screenwriter Richard Maibaum (thirteen), composer John Barry (twelve), stunt co-ordinator Bob Simmons (ten), cinematographer Ted Moore (seven) and production designers Ken Adam (seven) and Peter Lamont (nine to date). The existence of a core production team ensures a level of continuity and a commitment to the 'Bondian' production ideology unprecedented in popular cinema.

This book is not, I should emphasise, yet another account of the production histories of the Bond films, an angle which has been thoroughly described in the behind-the-scenes accounts already referred to. It is, rather, as the subtitle states, a cultural history of the James Bond films. I shall seek to place the Bond films in the contexts of British cinema history and film culture. This will involve, in the first place, investigating the various contexts of Bond, in particular considering their origins in the British film industry of the late 1950s and early 1960s. This will be followed by close analysis of the films themselves, both as text and in context. My textual analysis focuses on the narrative ideologies of the films, their visual style, their representation of gender and their construction of national identity (a problematic concept, of course, but one which is central to the Bond mythology through the notions of 'Britishness' which are attached to the central character). My contextual analysis focuses on the critical and popular reception of the films, and discusses how they have responded over time to changes both in the film industry and in society at large. The longevity of the series is due, in large measure, to the strategies which the film-makers have adopted for renewing and updating the Bond formula. Thus, the films themselves have always kept slightly ahead of the times through their displays of futuristic technology, while periodically new actors have been brought in to play the central character, who is always a contemporary rather than a period figure. The approach I have followed is to group two or three films together per chapter, in order to illustrate the generic and stylistic development of the series. For example, the first three films can be grouped together in that they came closest to the 'snobbery with violence' style of Fleming's books, while *The Spy Who Loved Me* and *Moonraker* are clearly a pair, if only because the latter is more or less a straight remake of the former. In order to locate them within film culture, I have drawn extensively on contemporary reviews of the Bond movies from a wide range of sources, embracing not only middle-brow and 'quality' publications but also the popular and trade press. Newspaper and magazine reviews are too often neglected by film theorists, perhaps because their approach to criticism seems unsophisticated in comparison to the academic jargon of most scholarly journals, but for the film historian they provide useful evidence of the cultural and intellectual climate within which the films were received, as well as providing a barometer of critical taste over a period of five decades.

Readers will find that I do not concern myself with the question of who is the 'best' James Bond. This is a question which has been debated within the Bond fan culture for years, generally in terms of a simplistic and tedious comparison of the acting styles of Sean Connery and Roger Moore, with the former usually emerging as the fans' favourite. It is my contention, however, that there is and can be only one definitive James Bond (just as there is and can be only one definitive Sherlock Holmes), and that is the original literary character. Ian Fleming's James Bond is definitive, while all the other James Bonds – including not only the actors who have played him on screen, but also the novels by other authors who have followed Fleming in writing Bond stories – are interpretations.

Finally, I should point out that I write this book both from the perspective of a film historian and as a Bond fan. As a film historian, it is my belief that the Bond series has been too long neglected in film history and is long overdue critical rehabilitation. At the same time, as a Bond fan, I accept that the Bond films are fun and can also be appreciated on that level. Too many academic writers seem to be almost embarrassed to admit to enjoying the movies they write about, as if doing so would somehow compromise their scholarly objectivity. Part of the process of taking the Bond films seriously, however, is to recognise that they are made for purposes of entertainment, an entertainment in which we all share. Ever since *Dr No* burst on to cinema screens in 1962, James Bond has held a licence to thrill audiences all over the world. It is high time that the most successful and enduring series of films in cinema history were accorded their rightful place in the sun.

1

The Contexts of Bond

It all began with a man called Ian Fleming.'[1] So producer Albert R. 'Cubby' Broccoli, when asked to identify the origins of the James Bond films, remarked in an interview towards the end of his life. On one level, of course, this is perfectly correct, as it was the British author Fleming who created the character of James Bond in a series of snobbery-with-violence spy thrillers published during the 1950s and early 1960s. On another level, however, to attribute the origins so simply does not account for the highly complex set of cultural and industrial determinants that turned Fleming's character into the most successful and enduring series of films in cinema history. Rather like Sherlock Holmes, to whom he has often been compared, James Bond has outgrown his origins at a historically specific point of British culture and has become nothing less than a cultural phenomenon recognised around the world. The transformation of Bond from relatively modest literary origins into a global brand-name and multi-media 'franchise' is a complex process that involves both Britain and America. This chapter explores the various contexts of Bond: it considers the ideological and cultural underpinnings of Fleming's books in the 1950s and their place in the history of the thriller genre; it discusses the first, albeit unsuccessful, attempt to adapt Bond for a different medium in the long-forgotten American television production of *Casino Royale* in 1954; and it charts various historical developments in the film industries on both sides of the Atlantic that made possible the production of the first Bond films in the early 1960s.

The first James Bond novel, *Casino Royale*, was published by Jonathan Cape in April 1953. Thereafter Fleming published another eleven Bond novels, and two collections of short stories, writing a book each year until his death in 1964 (the last novel, *The Man with the Golden Gun*, and the short-story volume *Octopussy and the Living Daylights* were published posthumously). Although Fleming was eventually to fulfil his ambition of entering the best-seller stakes, it was only towards the end of his life that the Bond books enjoyed mass popular success. Sales of the early hardbacks were respectable if not spectacular, though the print run was at first not very large (the first edition of *Casino Royale*, now a highly prized item for book collectors, had a print run of only 4,750). Fleming had considered killing off his hero at the end of *From Russia, with Love*, citing 'my waning enthusiasm for this cardboard booby'.[2] He was persuaded to continue when *From Russia, with Love* was serialised by the *Daily Express* in 1957 and by the prospect of selling the film or television rights. 'You don't make a great deal of money from royalties and translation rights and so forth ... but if you sell the serial rights and film rights, you do very well,' he later remarked.[3] From 1955 the Bond books were also published in paperback by Pan and the availability of these cheaper editions would seem to have significantly widened Bond's popularity. Combined paperback sales rose from 41,000 in 1955 to 58,000 in 1956, 72,000 in 1957, 105,000 in 1958, 237,000 in 1959, 323,000 in 1960 and 670,000 in 1961.[4] It was in 1962 – the year in which the first Bond film was released – that combined sales passed the million mark for the first time. To some extent, of course, these statistics reflect the fact that a new title was added to the list each year, but the appearance of new titles did not appreciably affect the sales of previous books in the sequence. *Casino Royale*, for example, had gone through six imprints by the end of 1960 and twenty-three by the end of 1965. The Bond books represented an important landmark in publishing, according to literary historian John Sutherland, who describes them as 'a breakthrough comparable in some ways to [Allen] Lane's, thirty years earlier'. 'The importance of the Bond books', he suggests, 'was that they revealed a new reliable market for a certain kind of book that was not trash and could be marketed as a "brand name" (i.e. "the latest Bond").'[5]

The early Bond novels were reviewed by 'literary' critics in terms that ranged from wry amusement to mild condescension. The anonymous reviewer of *The Times Literary Supplement*, for example, found *Casino Royale* 'an extremely engaging affair, dealing with espionage in the "Sapper" manner, but with a hero who, although taking a great many cold showers and never letting sex interfere with work, is somewhat more sophisticated'.[6] Simon Raven labelled the same book 'a kind of supersonic John Buchan' and felt that Fleming's success lay in 'taking the best elements of the [Peter] Cheyney method (speed, controlled savagery, a pungent and sceptical idiom) and yet combining them with the more spacious and gracious atmosphere of old-style international intrigue – monocles, medals, and milordos'.[7] It is significant that reviewers placed Fleming in the same generic lineage as John Buchan and 'Sapper' (H. C. McNeile), whose adventure thrillers were characterised by their upstanding patriotic heroes, fast-moving action-oriented plots and international villainy. Indeed, Fleming can be seen as the last of the 'old school' thriller writers, his career bridging the gap between 'Sapper' (who died in 1937) and Buchan (died 1940) and the more realistic spy stories of the 1960s by authors such as John le Carré and Len Deighton. Bond was characterised from the outset with all the trappings of the traditional fictional British gentleman hero, including his vintage Bentley and personalised cigarettes made for him by Morlands of Grosvenor Street. Fleming was 'an exact contemporary' of Richard Usborne, a schoolboy fan of the Bulldog Drummond stories, who averred that Fleming 'remembered the Drummond books shrewdly in planning his James Bond'.[8] However, Fleming, for his part, denied that he based Bond on Drummond at all, suggesting instead that it was the hard-boiled detectives of American crime fiction who were his models. 'I didn't believe in the heroic Bulldog Drummond types. I felt these types could no longer exist in literature,' he told one interviewer. 'I wanted my character to more or less follow the pattern of Raymond Chandler and Dashiell Hammett's heroes, who are believable people, believable heroes.'[9]

As the Bond books became more popular, however, they began to attract a different sort of criticism that was far more savage than the good-natured joshing of other reviewers. This trend reached a climax in 1958 around the publication of the sixth novel, *Dr No*, which attracted a barrage of criticism from critics on the left for what they perceived as its excesses of sex and violence. The broadside was led by Bernard Bergonzi, who detected 'a strongly marked streak of voyeurism and sado-masochism in his books' and deplored 'the complete lack of any ethical frame of reference'. Bergonzi described the 'erotic fantasies' of the books as 'decidedly sinister', comparing Fleming to 'a dirty-minded schoolboy' and complaining that he 'describes scenes of violence with uncommon relish'. The Bond books, he went on, 'have an air of vulgarity and display which contrast strongly with those subdued images of the perfectly self-assured gentlemanly lifestyle that we find in Buchan or even Sapper'. The increasing popularity of the books, Bergonzi believed, was a sign of a society in moral decline. 'Mr Fleming, I imagine, knows just what he is doing,' he concluded, 'but the fact that his books are published by a very reputable firm, and are regularly reviewed – and highly praised – in our self-respecting intellectual weeklies, surely says more about the present state of our culture than a whole volume of abstract denunciations.'[10] A leader in the *Manchester Guardian* similarly deplored 'the cult of luxury for its own sake' and what it saw as the 'pernicious' brand-name snobbery of the books, and though it attested that 'the readers are to blame' rather than the author alone, it concluded that the popularity of the books was 'symptomatic of a decline in taste'.[11] James Price, a less trenchant critic, complained that the books were tongue-in-cheek and anti-intellectual and that consequently 'the shortcomings of the James Bond thrillers are just the shortcomings which are likely to result when a certain kind of Englishman sets out to write for a large section of his fellow-countrymen'.[12]

For Umberto Eco, a critic of a very different sort, it was not the qualities of Fleming's writing that mattered (though he admitted that the books provided 'engrossing reading' and admired Fleming's 'highly workmanlike narrative') as it was their structural and ideological mechanisms. Eco argues that at the end of *Casino Royale* (somewhat atypical of the series in that it suggested a degree of psychological realism in characterisation), Fleming 'renounces all psychology as the motive of narrative and decides to transfer characters and situations to the level of an objective and conventional structural strategy'.[13] Thereafter the novels all, to a greater or a lesser degree, conformed to the same narrative structure and conventions. Eco suggests that Fleming's narratives are best understood as a sequence of 'moves' in which the same archetypal characters play out familiar situations: M (Head of the British Secret Service) makes the first move by assigning Bond to a mission of vital national importance; the Villain moves and appears to Bond, usually by attempting to kill him; Bond counter-moves and gives first check to the Villain, usually by besting him in a game that provides a symbolic rattling of sabres before the main confrontation; the Woman moves and shows herself to Bond; Bond seduces or begins the process of seducing the Woman; the Villain captures Bond and tortures him; Bond escapes, conquers the Villain and then convalesces with the Woman, whom he later loses.[14] Within this schemata there are variations – in *Moonraker* and *Goldfinger*, for example, Bond first encounters the Villain before being assigned to investigate him by M – but they do not fundamentally change the narrative. Embedded in the novels, furthermore, are what Eco calls 'play situations': these include a journey sequence (by plane, train or automobile), a meal (described in elaborate detail) and a chase (again often involving cars or trains).[15]

Overlaid on to the narrative structure, moreover, is a set of binary oppositions. These include oppositions between characters (Bond/M, Bond/Villain, Bond/Woman), between ideologies (Free World/Soviet Union, England/non-Anglo-Saxon countries) and between different values (duty/sacrifice, luxury/discomfort, excess/moderation, loyalty/disloyalty).[16] Eco argues that Fleming's novels are Manichaean in that 'he sees the world as made up of good and evil forces in conflict'.[17] In the context of the Cold War, evil tends to be associated with Communism, though the megalomaniac villains whom Bond encounters also represent a throwback to the world of the imperialist thriller. Fleming's veritable gallery of grotesques – Le Chiffre, Mr Big, Sir Hugo Drax, Dr No, Goldfinger, Ernst Stavro Blofeld, Scaramanga – would have been familiar to anyone versed in the stories of Edgar Wallace and Sax Rohmer. A recurring metaphor of the books is the idea of the villain as a dragon – Drax's name in German, we are told, means dragon (*drache*), while in *You Only Live Twice* Bond's mission is 'to enter this Castle of Death and slay the Dragon within' – whereas Bond adopts the mantle of St George: 'Bond sighed wearily. Once more into the breach, dear friends! This time it really was St George and the dragon. And St George had better get a move on before the dragon hatched the little dragon's egg he was now nesting so confidently' (*Goldfinger*).[18]

Tony Bennett has modified Eco's structuralist analysis by arguing that the Bond novels can be understood through a series of narrative codes which regulate the relationships between characters. He identifies three such codes – the 'sexist code', the 'imperialist code' and the 'phallic code' – that are recurrent throughout the stories. The 'sexist code' regulates relations between Bond and the heroine. The heroine is usually out of place, either sexually, in the sense that she is initially resistant to Bond (such as Vesper Lynd in *Casino Royale*), or ideologically, in the sense that she is in the service of the villain (Solitaire in *Live and Let Die*, Tatiana Romanova in *From Russia, with Love*), or both

(Tiffany Case in *Diamonds are Forever*, Pussy Galore in *Goldfinger*). Bond's seduction of the heroine therefore serves an ideological purpose in that he 'repositions' her by putting her into her 'correct' place: 'In thus replacing the girl in a subordinate position to men, Bond simultaneously repositions her within the sphere of ideology in general, detaching her from the service of the villain and recruiting her in support of his own mission.'[19] The 'imperialist code' regulates the relations between Bond and his allies, who are usually loyal colonial or pro-British characters (such as Quarrel in *Live and Let Die* and *Dr No*, and Kerim in *From Russia, with Love*) who defer to Bond and are in a subordinate power relationship towards him. And the 'phallic code' regulates the relationship between Bond and M, a symbolic father-figure who endows Bond with power and authority (his 'licence to kill'), and between Bond and the villain, who threatens Bond with emasculation through torture. This process is enacted quite literally in *Casino Royale* where Le Chiffre whips Bond's genitals with a cane carpet-beater.

It was content like this that led to the charges of 'sadism' levelled against Fleming by critics such as Johnson and Bergonzi. Yet the (perceived) sadism and violence of Fleming's novels is different from, say, that of Micky Spillane's Mike Hammer, thuggish protagonist of a series of pulp thrillers during the 1940s and 1950s to whom Bond was sometimes compared. Fleming's Bond, unlike Hammer, does not enjoy inflicting violence on others and, betraying a sense of chivalry that his critics seem to have missed, never raises his hand to a woman. In *The James Bond Dossier* Kingsley Amis defended Fleming against his critics. Amis conceded that there were occasional lapses (he cites the fight between gypsy girls in *From Russia, with Love* 'full of progressive nudity and breast-biting and clear invitations to the reader to have a good time') but averred that, overall, the stories 'distil what for me is legitimate violence and horror'. The notorious torture sequence in *Casino Royale*, he argued, 'has two closely related effects. It makes us feel admiration and sympathy for the hero and fear and hatred for the villain ... To have pulled Bond's hair and given him a lot of lip instead would have been ineffective, upon both Bond and the reader.'[20]

David Cannadine has placed the hostile reaction of some critics to Fleming's work in historical context by arguing, persuasively, that their hostility was influenced by the fact of Britain's 'decline'. Cannadine points out that the publication of *Casino Royale* coincided with the coronation of Queen Elizabeth II – 'a retrospectively unconvincing reaffirmation of Britain's continued great-power status' – whereas the last novel, *The Man with the Golden Gun*, appeared in 1965, the year of Winston Churchill's funeral, an event that represented 'not only the last rites of the great man himself, but was also self-consciously recognised as being a requiem for Britain as a great power'.[21] The débâcle of the Suez Crisis in 1956 and the hurried 'retreat from empire' between 1957 and 1965 rudely drove home the lesson that Britain's imperial power was diminishing, while exclusion from the Common Market when French President Charles De Gaulle vetoed Britain's application in 1963, left Britain isolated in Europe and increasingly dependent on the patronage of the United States. There was a strong critique (on the right as well as the left) that Britain's decline as a world power was a consequence of declining moral standards at home. The Bond novels, with their emphasis on sex and conspicuous consumption, were seen by some as visible symptoms of this decline.

Fleming's novels, in fact, are equivocal about changes in British society. On the one hand their social politics are conservative in the extreme. Bond's England, as Amis suggests, is 'substantially right of centre'.[22] Thus *The Times* is 'the only paper Bond ever read' (*From Russia, with Love*) and his mental image of his country is 'a world of tennis courts and lily ponds and kings and queens, of London, of people being photographed with pigeons on their heads in Trafalgar Square' (*Dr No*). Bond's attachment to the past is signalled by his choice of car (a 1930s Bentley) and his sentimental affection for the old five-pound note, which had been 'the most beautiful money in the world' (*Goldfinger*). Bond dislikes the consequences of social change: he takes an instinctive dislike to a taxi-driver whom he considers 'typical of the cheap self-assertiveness of young labour since the war' (*Thunderball*) and believes that homosexuality is 'a direct consequence of giving votes to women and "sex equality"' (*Goldfinger*). Bond is characterised as 'a patriotic sort of chap' (*You Only Live Twice*) and, as the title of the twelfth book attests (*On Her Majesty's Secret Service*), is cast in the role of defender of Queen and Country. The stories are replete with assertions of national pride and with references to decline: 'If foreign gangsters think they can get away with this kind of thing they'll decide the English are as soft as some other people seem to think we are' (*For Your Eyes Only*). The penultimate novel, *You Only Live Twice*, responds directly to the narrative of decline when Bond is charged with an impossible mission by Tiger Tanaka of the Japanese Secret Service, who has 'formed an unsatisfactory opinion about the British people since the war' and suggests that social change 'is sapping at ever-increasing speed the moral fibre of the British'. Bond's impassioned reply – 'England may have been bled pretty thin by a couple of World Wars, our Welfare State politics may have made us expect too much for free, and the liberation of our Colonies may have gone too fast, but we still climb Everest and beat plenty of the world at plenty of sports and win Nobel Prizes' – reveals both his patriotism and a High Tory perspective towards decolonisation and social change.

On the other hand, however, the Bond books embrace other aspects of social change. Fleming is at some pains to portray Bond as a modern, even classless, hero. He differs from the clubland heroes of the pre-war thriller in that he is not a gifted amateur – the Drummond and Hannay stories give the impression that crime-fighting is another form of 'sport' to be fitted in between rubbers of bridge and hearty games of rugger – but a ruthless professional assassin: 'It was his profession to kill people. He had never liked doing it and when he had to kill he did it as well as he knew how and forgot about it. As a secret agent who held the rare double-O prefix – the licence to kill in the Secret Service – it was his duty to be as cool about death as a surgeon' (*Goldfinger*). Bond, a middle-grade civil servant who 'liked anonymity', exemplifies what historian Harold Perkin called 'the rise of professional society', one that 'is structured around career hierarchies rather than classes, one in which people find their place according to trained expertise and the service they provide rather than the possession or lack of inherited wealth or acquired capital'.[23] Bond does not belong in the cosy clubland world of previous heroic archetypes ('Doesn't look the sort of chap one usually sees in Blades') and is aware 'that there was something alien and unEnglish about himself' (*Moonraker*). The most frequent description of Bond is 'cruel'. As Price observed: 'It is the fact of his not being a gentleman – both in this sense and in the chivalric meaning of the word – which immediately differentiates him from Buchan's Richard Hannay.'[24]

It can be argued that the charges of 'Sex, Snobbery and Sadism' levelled against Fleming by his critics demonstrate their own unease with social change. Cannadine suggests that 'while some critics saw his work as an unpleasant embodiment of reality, others acclaimed it as a welcome escape'.[25] The perceived snobbery of the books arises from Bond's obsession with brand-name consumer goods (his Rolex

Oyster Perpetual wristwatch, for example) and his expensive tastes in food and alcohol. Rather than being included for the simple snob-value that some critics have alleged, however, Bond's brand-name trappings can be seen in the context of a country which had recently emerged from years of austerity and rationing and which, during the 1950s, was beginning to enjoy the affluence promised by glossy magazines, television advertising and Hollywood. 'Despite recurrent economic crises,' Arthur Marwick asserts, 'the reality for the vast majority of British people was that at last the country seemed to have emerged into the kind of high-spending consumer society long familiar from American films.'[26] Bond's lifestyle may seem rather excessive, but part of the cultural project of the books was that they offered a fantasy of high living and conspicuous consumption in a society emerging from austerity. Hugh Gaitskell, a friend of Fleming's wife Anne, summarised their appeal thus: 'The combination of sex, violence, alcohol and – at intervals – good food and nice clothes is, to one who leads such a circumscribed life as I do, irresistible.'[27] For male readers in particular, the Bond novels provided for the gratification of sensual desires, whether they be focused on fast cars, food, drink, women, or all of those. One critic described Fleming's style as 'the technique of the erotic distraction'. His stories were written for the total stimulation of the reader, encouraging the reader to share by proxy in Bond's sexual encounters and fast driving. Andrew Bear argues that Fleming 'managed to write his sensual titillation into the very texture of his stories, and this is what can be called the technique of the erotic distraction – the Fleming Effect itself'.[28]

The attitude towards sex in the novels is an extension of this effect. The novels again reflected the *Zeitgeist*: they need to be understood in the context of a period when British society was gradually breaking free from the prurient Victorianism which had, depending on one's point of view, acted as either a straitjacket or a safety-valve for the past century. Although the 1960s are generally seen as the 'permissive society', changes in sexual attitudes can be traced back into the 1950s. As Christopher Booker observed in his classic survey of the period, *The Neophiliacs*:

> ... the new prominence of sex in the late Fifties was not just a concern with the realities of sex; even more, it was a preoccupation with the idea of sex, the image of sex; the written word, the visual image, the image that was promulgated in advertisements, in increasingly 'daring' films, in 'controversial' newspaper articles

and 'frank' novels; the image purveyed by the strip-tease clubs and pornographic shops that were springing up in the back streets of Soho and provincial cities; and the image that, mixed with that of violence, was responsible in the years after 1956 for the enormous boom in the sales of Ian Fleming's James Bond stories.[29]

One of the charges made against Fleming was that his books amounted to a sort of pornography, a view apparently endorsed by the author's own remark that 'the target of my books ... lay somewhere between the solar plexus and, well, the upper thigh'.[30]

Michael Denning suggests that 'the James Bond tales can rightly be seen as an important early form of the mass pornography that characterizes the consumer society, the society of the spectacle, that emerges in Western Europe and North America in the wake of post-war reconstruction'.[31] It is symbolic that the publication of the first Bond novel came in the same year as the launch of *Playboy*, the first mainstream pornographic men's magazine. It was not until the 1960s that the links between Bond and *Playboy* were institutionalised when the magazine serialised some of the later stories, in addition to running photo-features on starlets from the Bond films, but long before there was an evident parallel between Bond's sexual behaviour and the *Playboy* ethos of easy, free, open sexuality. The type of pornography represented by *Playboy* was not so-called 'hard core' (meaning the graphic depiction of sexual acts) but rather 'soft core' (a term usually used to refer to representations of women in various stages of undress including full nudity). Fleming's descriptions of his female characters tend to construct them as erotic objects: the physical characteristic most frequently described are their 'fine', 'firm' or 'splendid' breasts. They often appear wearing a swimsuit (such as Tracy in *On Her Majesty's Secret Service*) or underwear (Tiffany Case in *Diamonds are Forever*, Jill Masterton in *Goldfinger*); sometimes they are naked when Bond meets them (Tatiana Romanova in *From Russia, with Love*, Honeychile Rider in *Dr No*).

It has sometimes been argued that the Bond 'girls' represent a liberated femininity in so far as they are characterised as independent and wilful. Domino Vitali, for example, is 'an independent girl, a girl of authority and character ... She might sleep with men, obviously did, but it would be on her terms and not on theirs' (*Thunderball*). There are occasions, moreover, when Bond's life is saved by the heroine (*Diamonds are Forever*, *Thunderball*) and when the heroine has skills or knowledge that help Bond accomplish his mission (*Moonraker*, *Dr No*). Against this, however, must be set the sexist, even misogynistic, attitude towards women that Bond (and by extension Fleming) displays. Bond regards women as being 'for recreation' (*Casino Royale*) and his views on what women really want from sex would be enough to leave some feminists apoplectic with rage: 'All women love semi-rape. They love to be taken. It was his sweet brutality against my bruised body that had made his act of love so piercingly wonderful' (*The Spy Who Loved Me*); 'Be rough with me. Treat me like the lowest whore in creation. Forget everything else. No questions. Take me' (*On Her Majesty's Secret Service*). The rather *outré* names that Fleming adopted for his heroines – Vesper Lynd, Solitaire, Gala Brand, Tiffany Case, Honeychile Rider, Pussy Galore, Kissy Suzuki, Mary Goodnight – should, however, probably be taken as nothing more than an elaborate joke.

The early Bond novels were also very much products of the historical and ideological conditions of the Cold War. They are characterised by an explicit anti-Communism that may also have upset critics on the left. In all but one of the books written during the 1950s (from *Casino Royale* to *For Your Eyes Only*) Bond's enemy is either Soviet or Soviet-backed (the one exception is *Diamonds are Forever* in which Bond combats American gangsters). The enemy is usually a member of SMERSH (a contraction of *Smiert Spionam* – 'Death to Spies') and the conspiracy is directed either against Britain specifically or the West more generally. However, in the ninth book, *Thunderball*, published in 1961, Fleming distanced Bond from the Cold War (Bond reflects that 'with the cold war wearing off, it was not like the old days') and introduced a new antagonist in the form of SPECTRE (Special Executive for Counter-Intelligence, Terrorism, Revenge and Extortion), which was apolitical in so far as it was not motivated by ideology but was a freelance organisation dedicated to the acquisition of wealth and power through terrorism. This ideological shift within the novels is usually interpreted as a reflection of a mild 'thaw' in the Cold War after the anti-Communist paranoia of the 1950s: Eco observes that Fleming 'ceased to identify the wicked with Russia as soon as the international situation rendered Russia less menacing *according to the general opinion*'.[32]

Even within the Cold War narrative of the early Bonds, however, there is evidence of some moral equivocation. *Casino Royale* is significant in this regard in that, for the first and only time, Bond reflects critically on the nature of his profession. *Casino Royale* suggests a critique of the old-school thriller in which spying was a 'game': Bond learns that the game is being played in deadly earnest. Le Chiffre tells Bond (before torturing him nearly to death) that 'the game of Red Indians is over, quite over. You have stumbled by mischance into a game for grown-ups and you have already found it a painful experience.' Bond's treatment at the hands of Le Chiffre causes him to doubt, albeit temporarily, the morality of his profession – reflecting that 'this country right-or-wrong business is getting a little out of date' and 'I'm wondering whose side I ought to be on'. *Casino Royale* is also significant in that, for the only time in the series, it transpires that the woman for whom Bond has fallen is a double agent. Published only two years after the defection of British intelligence officers Guy Burgess and Donald Maclean in 1951 – both had been Soviet moles – the revelation that Vesper Lynd is 'a double, working for Redland' invested the novel with a topicality less evident in some of the later stories. 'What raised *Casino Royale* out of the usual run of thrillers,' writes Fleming's biographer Andrew Lycett, 'was Ian's attempt to reflect the disturbing moral ambiguity of a post-war world that could produce traitors like Burgess and Maclean.'[33]

This theme, anticipating the existential stories of internal treachery and deceit by Len Deighton (*The Ipcress File*) and John le Carré (*Tinker, Tailor, Soldier, Spy*), was absent from later novels, however, in which the assertion of British power became a paramount objective. Britain is presented as being in the front line of the Cold War in *Moonraker* (in which Drax, backed by the Soviets, attempts to destroy London with a nuclear missile) and *From Russia, with Love* (a SMERSH conspiracy to discredit the British Secret Service by killing Bond in a compromising position). In the latter story the British Secret Service is described as 'the most dangerous and [that] which we would most wish to damage' – an ironic view given the extent of Soviet penetration of the British intelligence services at the time. Indeed, *From Russia, with Love* seems like nothing less than a highly programmed attempt to restore the reputation of Britain's intelligence community at a time when it had been severely compromised.[34]

Bennett and Woollacott suggest, furthermore, that 'Bond can be read as a hero of the NATO alliance'.[35] The first novel appeared a few years after the formation of the North Atlantic Treaty Organisation (NATO) in 1949 and shortly before the end of the Korean War (1950–53). Bond is assisted by NATO allies, most usually by an American, Felix Leiter of the Central Intelligence Agency (CIA), who appears in six of the

books. The professional and personal friendship between Bond and
Leiter represents the 'special relationship' that has supposedly existed
between Britain and the United States since the end of the Second
World War, though in a quaint reversal of the real balance of power
it is the American Leiter who is the subordinate partner to the British
Bond. As Amis astutely observes:

> The point of Felix Leiter, such a nonentity as a piece of char-
> acterization, is that he, the American, takes orders from Bond,
> the Britisher, and that Bond is constantly doing better than he,
> showing himself, not braver or more devoted, but smarter, wittier,
> tougher, more resourceful, the incarnation of little old England
> with her quiet ways and shoe-string budget wiping the eye of great
> big global-tentacled multi-billion-dollar-appropriating America.[36]

In this respect the ideological project of the Bond novels is to redress
the decline of British power and to construct an imaginary world in
which the *Pax Britannica* still operates.

The power relationship between Britain and America represented in
the novels is significant when it comes to an evaluation of the first
screen adaptation of a Bond story. Given that the literary and cultural
roots of James Bond are to be found in the specifically British genre
of the imperialist spy thriller, it may be rather surprising that Bond's
first screen incarnation was in a very different idiom. In 1954 Fleming had sold the television rights for his first novel to the American
television network CBS (Columbia Broadcasting System) for $1,000.[37]
On 21 October 1954, CBS broadcast a one-hour adaptation of *Casino
Royale* as part of its weekly thriller anthology *Climax!* Long thought to
have been 'lost', like so much live television drama of the time, *Casino
Royale* has since been 'rediscovered' when a telerecording of the original
broadcast came to light in the 1980s.[38] Although dismissed as a curio
by most commentators on the grounds that it is so different from the
much more successful incarnation of James Bond in the cinema, *Casino
Royale* is nevertheless worthy of attention, not only for the fact that it is
the first Bond 'film' (albeit a telefilm) but also for the way in which it
offers an alternative to the more familiar cinematic version of Bond.

Climax! was one of the dramatic anthology series which proliferated
on American television during the mid-1950s. Before filmed series with
recurring characters became dominant towards the end of the decade,

the usual form of television drama was the live, self-contained play. Sponsored by the Chrysler Corporation, and broadcast on Thursday evenings at 8.30 p.m., *Climax!* focused on stories of adventure and action, often adapted from well-known thrillers. Its first broadcast, on 7 October, was an adaptation of Raymond Chandler's *The Long Goodbye*, starring Dick Powell as Philip Marlowe (Powell had previously played Marlowe in RKO's *Murder, My Sweet*, a film version of Chandler's *Farewell, My Lovely*, in 1944). The third *Climax!* presentation was *Casino Royale*, based on what host William Lundigan described, with some exaggeration, as 'the best-seller by Ian Fleming'. (An American hardback edition of *Casino Royale* was published by Macmillan in 1954, but had excited little interest.) The book was adapted by Antony Ellis and Charles Bennett. The latter had been a regular collaborator with Alfred Hitchcock between 1929 and 1940, working on the screenplays of *Blackmail* (adapted from his own play), *The Man Who Knew Too Much*, *The 39 Steps*, *Secret Agent*, *Sabotage*, *Young and Innocent* and *Foreign Correspondent*. It was produced by Bretaigne Windust, a theatre producer who had turned his hand to film and television, his best-known film as a director being the Humphrey Bogart crime thriller *The Enforcer*. American actor Barry Nelson, best known for his starring roles on Broadway, was cast as James Bond. While an American Bond marked a substantial departure from the novel, the casting of the other two principal parts was more propitious. Hollywood starlet Linda Christian was certainly the right physical type for a Fleming heroine: beautiful, elegant and cool. The master stroke, however, was the casting of Peter Lorre as Le Chiffre. A veteran of German, British and American cinema, Lorre had first made his mark playing the psychopathic child-murderer in Fritz Lang's *M*, had been well used by Hitchcock in *The Man Who Knew Too Much* and *Secret Agent*, and had then carved out a niche as a character actor in Hollywood, including highly memorable appearances in *The Maltese Falcon*, *Casablanca* and *The Mask of Dimitrios*. By the time of his appearance in *Casino Royale*, the once slightly-built Lorre had ballooned in weight to such a degree that his short, bulky physique made him the perfect visualisation of the villain Fleming had described.

While the telecast of *Casino Royale* is necessarily condensed from the novel, and has been adapted to meet the logistics of live television production with a minimum of sets (interiors only) and no costume changes, it maintains Fleming's basic plot. The main difference is that Bond is an American agent, referred to as 'card-sense Jimmy Bond'.

The production begins with someone taking pot shots at Bond outside the front door of the casino as he arrives. As in the novel, Bond has been sent to beat Le Chiffre at baccarat. Le Chiffre is referred to as the 'chief Soviet agent for this area – controlled by Leningrad through Paris', thus locating the television *Casino Royale* within the Cold War context of the early novels. Le Chiffre needs to make up some eighty million francs that he has embezzled from the funds of the French Communist Party. Bond makes contact with Clarence Leiter (Michael Pate) of the British Secret Service. He also finds that his old girlfriend Valerie Mathis is now with Le Chiffre. (In the novel the heroine had been called Vesper Lynd; René Mathis was an agent of the Deuxième Bureau, the French Secret Service.) The following evening Bond plays baccarat against Le Chiffre and, after a long drawn-out game that swings both ways, he wins. Bond survives an assassination attempt by one of Le Chiffre's henchmen armed with a gun disguised as a walking stick (an incident from the novel). He converts his winnings into a cheque, which, as in the novel, he hides behind the number plate on the front of his hotel room door. Whereas in the novel the girl had been kidnapped and Bond had given chase in his car, here Le Chiffre and his men simply arrive at Bond's room, along with Valerie, whom Le Chiffre has discovered is an agent of the Deuxième Bureau. The notorious torture scene from the novel is changed to Bond bound in the bathtub of his hotel suite while Le Chiffre pulls out his toenails with pliers. But Bond escapes while Le Chiffre and one of his heavies are searching the room. Bond knocks out the heavy, takes his gun and shoots Le Chiffre, who collapses in a chair. Le Chiffre recovers, gets to his feet and threatens Valerie with a razor blade. Bond shoots him and this time kills him, before collapsing in Valerie's arms.

The James Bond fan culture has little time for the television *Casino Royale*. Steven Jay Rubin considers it 'feeble', while Barnes and Hearn describe it as 'a creaking adaptation of the story'.[39] Such dismissive judgements seem more than a little unfair, however, for if judged on its own terms rather than in comparison to the films, *Casino Royale* stands up very well indeed. In the first place, quite apart from any intrinsic merits, it is a historically valuable example of a particular kind of television drama production. This apart, the telecast itself has a particular aesthetic quality of its own: with its spare, economical narrative, its necessarily claustrophobic sets, its precise and fluid camera movement and its effective use of close-ups at heightened moments of tension, it is more successful than any of the films have ever been in capturing the mood and suspense of the original novel. Two sequences in particular stand out, as they do in the book: the baccarat game and the torture scene. The baccarat game, while inevitably condensed from the novel, still takes up fully seven minutes of screen time, gradually building the tension by its insistent pans and cuts between the silent, smirking Le Chiffre and an increasingly tense and agitated Bond (Nelson repeatedly frowns, sighs heavily and rubs his brow) as the game drifts away from him. And the torture scene is quite harrowing, with the camera, at Bond's eye-level in the bathtub, looking up at the menacing figure of Le Chiffre, Lorre's sheer physical bulk dominating the frame. While the act itself is not shown, for obvious reasons, the reaction shot on the contorted faces of Bond and Valerie gives a vivid indication of the pain he is suffering. Although the narrative ends with Bond and Valerie together, not with her suicide as in the novel, it is still something less than a conventional happy ending. It is, in short, more bleak and downbeat than the films, and certainly does not warrant Peter Haining's remark that 'the whole production had an element of comedy about it'.[40]

The most significant difference from the novel, obviously, is that Bond has become an American agent. The Americanisation of Bond – and, at the same time, the Anglicisation of Leiter – symbolically reverses the power relationship of the novel. But while making Bond an American may offend the purists, it is entirely explicable (and, dare one say, acceptable) in its own terms. Given that *Casino Royale* was made by an American television company for American audiences, then it is perfectly understandable that the hero should be an American. The telecast can be seen as an attempt to assimilate Bond into the American 'hard-boiled' tradition – which Fleming himself declared was his model for the character. The American paperback edition of *Casino Royale*, published in 1955 and retitled *You Asked for It*, featured a 'pulp' cover with a semi-naked pouting girl in a highly suggestive pose. At this time, moreover, James Bond had not yet developed into the cultural phenomenon that he was later to become. Bond simply did not exist in the popular consciousness at this time, certainly not in America. Unlike today, when Bond is regarded all over the world as a quintessentially British hero, for American television viewers in 1954 there was no pre-determined association of Bond as being British.

For all its merits, however, *Casino Royale* is more interesting in hindsight, given knowledge of what James Bond was later to become, than it was for either critics or public at the time. Critical reaction focused on the violent and unpleasant aspects of the story. *Daily Variety*, for example, expressed concern whether it was suitable viewing for children:

> Violence, gunplay, gambling and other dark deeds associated with Continental spy rings is tied here with Chrysler's 'Forward Look', and providing further ammunition for crusaders against grisly crime in the early evening hours while the small fry is still wide-eyed and setside. The dose is a heavy one, with torture thrown in to intensify the melodramatics. Even the elders might have found it a little strong to take.[41]

'The torture scene', the reviewer went on, 'was hideous enough without the actual horror instrument being shown at its grisly work.' While on one level this provides another example of how Bond in various forms has been criticised for violence, on another level the reaction also needs to be seen in the light of concerns arising in America about the depiction of violence on television. These concerns (to which the *Variety* reviewer alludes) grew during the 1950s as television crime drama became more and more violent, reaching an apogee of sorts with ABC's *The Untouchables*, which ran from 1959 to 1963 and which is often held to be, for its time, the most violent series shown on television.

Casino Royale remained a one-off in Fleming's attempt to interest television and film producers in James Bond. In 1958 he was involved in negotiations with CBS about a possible television series. Fleming wrote treatments for thirteen episodes, and made some suggestions about how Bond should be played. He was particularly concerned about there not being 'too much stage Englishness' in the series: 'There should, I think, be no monocles, moustaches, bowler hats, bobbies or other "Limey" gimmicks … no blatant English slang, a minimum of public-school ties and accents, and subsidiary characters should generally speak with a Scots or Irish accent.'[42] Fleming's aversion to 'stage Englishness' is interesting in so far as *The Avengers*, a British television series which began a few years later, would consciously highlight bowler hats and other 'Limey gimmicks' in asserting its Englishness in contrast to the many American crime series of the time. The James Bond television series did not proceed beyond the development stage, so Fleming used several of the treatments he had prepared as the basis for the short-story collection *For Your Eyes Only*.

What the television *Casino Royale* represents, ultimately, is an alternative direction that Bond may have taken but in the event did not. It should be regarded neither as a mere curio nor as a failure but rather as an attempt to adapt Bond for a different idiom and cultural context. For all its Americanisation, it remains the most 'authentic' adaptation of a Fleming novel. And for that reason, if no other, it deserves to be better known than it is.

Bond's eventual transition to the cinema has its origins in the 1950s. The process needs to be understood in relation to the industrial and cultural contexts of the British film industry and its relationship with Hollywood. The Bond films represent a unique marriage between British cultural capital and American dollars that is rooted in the historical circumstances of their original production arrangements. For this reason we need to consider the state of both the American and the British film industries in the 1950s.

The 1950s was a decade of transition for the US film industry following the landmark decision by the Supreme Court in 1948 that vertical integration gave the major studios an unfair advantage in exhibiting their films and that consequently they should be required to divest themselves of their cinema holdings. One consequence of this decision, coupled with a decline in cinema audiences from the late 1940s, was a shift away from the bread-and-butter films on which the studios had hitherto relied and towards a 'blockbuster' mentality in which the studios concentrated on producing fewer but bigger films. This trend, coupled with the increasing importance of the international market which accounted for about half of the film industry's revenues, caused some producers to migrate abroad. Overseas production was attractive for several reasons, primarily economic in that labour costs were lower in Europe and US producers could benefit from subsidies from European government legislation designed to encourage investment in domestic production industries. Hollywood, through the machinations of its overseas trade organisation, the Motion Picture Export Association, became highly adept at circumventing this legislation by having its films produced overseas by nominally British, Italian or German companies. By the 1960s these 'runaway productions' accounted for almost half of all American features.[43]

Britain became particularly attractive to American producers in the 1950s and 1960s: production costs were cheaper, there were tax breaks for overseas artistes who made their permanent home in Britain and there was a pool of technicians without any of the language obstacles of other European countries. American producers also found that they could benefit from the Film Production Fund (commonly known as the Eady Levy), introduced in 1950 as a means of subsidising film production through an additional tax on ticket sales that was paid to producers and distributors in proportion to the box-office receipts of their films. To qualify for the Eady Levy a film had to be produced by a British-registered company, shot in a studio in Britain or the Commonwealth and with 75 per cent of the labour costs paid to British workers.[44] The Eady Levy, according to Bond producer Albert R. Broccoli, 'was the carrot that induced American production to come here'.[45] Broccoli and his partner Irving Allen had set up Warwick Pictures in Britain in 1952 and, backed by Columbia Pictures, produced eighteen films over the next nine years, specialising in war and adventure films such as *The Red Beret* (1953), *Hell Below Zero* (1954), *Cockleshell Heroes* (1955), *Safari* (1956), *Zarak* (1957) and *Killers of Kilimanjaro* (1959). According to screenwriter Richard Maibaum, Broccoli had considered filming the Bond books in the mid-1950s:

> In 1956 or 1957, when I was in England writing for Cubby and Irving Allen, Cubby gave me two of the James Bond books to read. I read them and liked them enormously. Cubby was very excited, too, but Irving Allen didn't share his enthusiasm. So Cubby put them aside. It's my personal opinion now that that was a wise thing to do, because with the censorship of pictures that existed then, you couldn't even have the minimal sex and violence that we eventually put into the pictures. They just wouldn't have been the same.[46]

Broccoli was not the only producer to show an interest in the Bond books. As early as 1954 Sir Alexander Korda, the flamboyant Hungarian-born producer who had become one of the leading British movie moguls, read a proof of *Live and Let Die*. He claimed to have found it exciting, telling Fleming that 'I really could not put it down until I had finished it', but added that he did not think it would transfer well to the screen as 'the best stories for films are always the stories that are written specially for films'. Fleming, nevertheless, was excited by Korda's interest and replied that his next novel, *Moonraker*, would make better film material: 'It is an expansion of a film story I've had in mind since the war – a straight thriller with particularly English but also general appeal, set in London and on the White Cliffs of Dover, and involving the destruction of London by a super V-2, allowing for some wonderful film settings in the old Metropolis idiom.'[47] No further interest was forthcoming from Korda, however. In 1955 the American actor John Payne was involved in negotiations for an option on *Moonraker*, which broke down after complicated wrangling about rights between Fleming's British and American agents. *Moonraker* was also touted to the Rank Organisation, which bought an option on the film rights but did not persevere any further. It is unlikely that Bond would have met the criterion of 'wholesome' British films that Rank's managing-director, John Davis, saw as the cornerstone of his production strategy.[48]

Victor Saville, another veteran of the British cinema, also claimed to have recognised the potential of the Bond novels. Saville, backed by United Artists, had acquired the rights to Micky Spillane's Mike Hammer novels and had produced two films: *I, the Jury* (1953) and *Kiss Me Deadly* (1955). Saville saw Bond as a natural successor to Hammer:

A few years later, I went to United Artists and proposed buying *Dr No*, the first [*sic*] James Bond book … I thought the books would be a good follow-up to the Spillane pictures. The new management of United Artists had been successful and whether they had become too fat and rich, I cannot say, but my proposal was turned down by all except one of the executives, Max Youngstein, who liked the proposition. The fact that the James Bond pictures, a few years later, became a bonanza for United Artists is neither here nor there, for I am quite sure I would not have made them as well as the producers of the series – indeed, not in the same class. I could never have spent such large sums of money on what, in my book, is such indifferent and characterless writing.[49]

Like Maibaum, Saville pointed to censorship as an obstacle at this time, averring that 'it was necessary to walk carefully' and that the two Mike Hammer films 'came nowhere near the sex and violence of the books'.

A rather more significant initiative in the late 1950s was the development of a film project based on an original Bond story. In 1958 Fleming was introduced through his friend Ivar Bryce to Kevin McClory, an Irishman who was involved in the film industry as an associate producer and who had been foreign location director for Mike Todd's production of *Around the World in 80 Days* (1956). Bryce had co-produced, and financed, McClory's first film as a director, *The Boy and the Bridge* (1959), a whimsical fable about a small boy who runs away from home and hides in the ramparts of Tower Bridge. Fleming and McClory worked on various screen treatments during 1959, with McClory particularly keen on setting the film in the Bahamas so the production would be eligible for the Eady Levy. On 1 October 1959 the trade paper *Kinematograph Weekly* announced that McClory was developing 'an underwater adventure story with the working title of *James Bond of the Secret Service* ... from an original script by Ian Fleming. It will be shot in colour and in a wide-screen process – either Todd-AO or Technirama.'[50] Fleming's interest in the project waned as the financial and logistical problems inherent in such an ambitious undertaking mounted. McClory continued working on the story with British screenwriter Jack Whittingham, the title being changed to *Longitude 78 West*, but was unable to raise the finance to make the film. As he had done several times before, Fleming used the story of the aborted project as the basis for his next book, *Thunderball*. However, McClory and Whittingham objected to this and launched legal action against Fleming. In March 1961 they issued a writ alleging breach of copyright and petitioned the High Court to issue an injunction to prevent publication of the novel. The injunction was refused, but the legal action was to drag on for over two years.

The protracted dispute over *Thunderball* – McClory was eventually awarded the film rights and claimed further intellectual rights to the invention of SPECTRE – would hang like a spectre of its own over the Bond film series. The story of how Albert R. Broccoli and Harry Saltzman came together to produce the Bond films has been told at length elsewhere, so there is no need here for anything more than a reminder of the salient facts.[51] Early in 1961, Fleming sold an option on the available Bond titles (excluding *Casino Royale*) to Saltzman, a Canadian producer based in Britain. Saltzman had been co-founder, along with director Tony Richardson and playwright John Osborne, of Woodfall Films, the company which produced most of the key British 'new wave' films of the late 1950s and early 1960s such as *Look Back in Anger* and *Saturday Night and Sunday Morning*, but had left the company due to creative differences with his partners. Saltzman was unable to raise the financial backing to produce the Bond films and his option had almost expired when Broccoli entered the scene. Broccoli, following the end of his partnership with Irving Allen, had renewed his interest in the Bond books and, learning that Saltzman had an option but no finance, suggested a partnership. They approached Columbia Pictures and asked for $1 million to produce either *Thunderball* or *Dr No*, but the studio baulked at the proposed budget. 'They saw it as just a low-budget film and wanted us to consider making it for $300–400,000,' Broccoli said later. 'I said the cheapest film we'd made for Columbia at Warwick had been *The Red Beret* and that had cost $700,000 and made eight million worldwide.'[52] But Broccoli convinced Arthur Krim, one of the chief executives of United Artists, to give them a sympathetic hearing. On 20 July 1961 *Kine Weekly* announced that 'Saltzman's project with Albert Broccoli to film the Ian Fleming spy-thriller books is maturing nicely. They have clinched a deal with United Artists for 100 per cent financial backing and distribution of seven stories which will be filmed here and on foreign locations.'[53]

The deals concluded in the summer of 1961 were complicated, but would provide the production arrangement for the Bond films for decades to come. Broccoli and Saltzman went into partnership and set up Eon Productions (supposedly standing for 'Everything Or Nothing') to make the films. Another company, Danjaq (from the names of Broccoli and Saltzman's wives, Dana and Jacqueline), was set up to control the copyright of the films. United Artists agreed to provide the finance and distribute the films, which were to be based at Pinewood Studios in Britain with a predominantly British crew. In this way the producers would be eligible for a subsidy from the Eady Levy. The budget for the first film, which it was decided would be *Dr No* due to the on-going legal dispute over *Thunderball*, was set in the region of $800–900,000, though in the event the negative cost came in at slightly more than that. Fleming, for his part, would not be involved in the production but would receive a fee of $100,000 per film plus a percentage of the profits.

The question to be asked here is why was it that United Artists, which in the late 1950s had rejected Saville's proposal to film the Fleming novels, changed its mind only a few years later? There are several possible explanations. The first is that United Artists had opened a production office in London in 1961 under George H. Ornstein, who had a (limited) degree of autonomy from the company's New York headquarters. The Bond films should be seen as part of UA's British production strategy that also included *Tom Jones* (1963), director

Tony Richardson and writer John Osborne's 'swinging' adaptation of Henry Fielding's eighteenth-century novel, and the Beatles films *A Hard Day's Night* (1964) and *Help!* (1965). Another reason, certainly, is that Broccoli had a proven track record of producing successful action films. In this context it is significant that the production team for *Dr No* included two stalwarts from Warwick Pictures, director Terence Young (*The Red Beret, Safari, Zarak*) and writer Richard Maibaum (*The Red Beret, Cockleshell Heroes, Zarak, Killers of Kilimanjaro*). It should also be considered that sales of the Bond novels were already increasing before the films: combined paperback sales had increased over sixfold between 1958 (when UA turned down Saville) and 1961 (when they backed Broccoli and Saltzman). The popularity of the books was seen as an important factor in the box-office appeal of the films. The *Motion Picture Herald*, for example, declared in its review of *Dr No*: 'The vast numbers of people in this country, not to mention overseas, who have read avidly, hungrily and expectantly every story of intrigue and excitement written by Ian Fleming … form a wide, waiting and ready audience for the first of the films based on the James Bond stories.'[54] And, finally, it was in March 1961, only a few months before Broccoli and Saltzman approached UA, that an article in *Life* magazine had revealed that *From Russia, with Love* was one of President Kennedy's favourite books. Fleming's (and Bond's) stock had never been higher than at this moment.

The production of the Bond films also needs to be seen in the context of what the film historians Kristin Thompson and David Bordwell refer to as the 'upscaling' of genres. Genres such as the western, the musical and the historical epic were at the forefront of Hollywood's obsession with blockbusters during the 1950s and 1960s, but other genres that had previously been regarded as essentially low-budget fare, including horror, science-fiction and thrillers, also benefited from the trend to lavish A-class production values on B-movie scripts. With the exception of films by prestigious 'name' directors like Alfred Hitchcock, thrillers were widely regarded as nothing more than B-movie fodder. This was especially the case for series films about the adventures of detectives, secret agents and other crime-fighters, which tended to be produced on the lowest budgets. Characters such as Bulldog Drummond, the Saint and Dick Barton all featured in series films during the 1930s and 1940s which usually occupied the bottom half of a double bill. Drummond was the one thick-ear hero who had appeared in something approximating an A-class feature film – Ronald Colman had played Drummond in a successful early talkie, *Bulldog Drummond* (1929), produced by Samuel Goldwyn, and in a polished sequel, *Bulldog Drummond Strikes Back* (1934) – but thereafter the character was relegated to supporting-feature status in a series of British and American films in the 1930s.[55] RKO Radio Pictures produced eight films based on Leslie Charteris's Saint stories during the late 1930s and early 1940s with Louis Hayward, George Sanders and Hugh Sinclair all impersonating the 'Robin Hood of Modern Crime'.[56] Perhaps the nearest equivalent to James Bond was a British radio character who made the transition to the cinema in the late 1940s. *Dick Barton – Special Agent* was an action-packed thriller serial that ran between 1946 and 1951. Barton was comparable to Bond in several ways: he was a 'special agent'; his adventures were characterised by action and chases rather than cerebral detection; and he had his own distinctive theme tune, 'The Devil's Gallop', a whirlwind of furious strings, blaring horns and clashing cymbals, which perfectly captured the pace and urgency of the serial. Three low-budget movies were made by Hammer Films – *Dick Barton – Special Agent* (1948), *Dick Barton Strikes Back* (1949) and *Dick Barton at Bay* (1950) – in which the low-life spivs and racketeers of the radio stories were replaced by more sensational villainy including a vengeful ex-Nazi mad scientist planning to unleash a cholera epidemic against Britain (*Dick Barton – Special Agent*), a disaffected aristocratic 'fellow traveller' with totalitarian ambitions (*Dick Barton Strikes Back*) and an East European conspiracy to destroy British aircraft with a death ray (*Dick Barton at Bay*).[57] The Dick Barton trilogy was among the last flowering of the low-budget thriller series. In the 1950s television proved that it could do the same sort of thing even cheaper and by the end of the decade the B-movie was on its last legs. Terence Young, who directed three of the first four Bond films, made the point that the Bond stories were the sort of material usually associated with Hollywood's 'Poverty Row'. 'Well, when you analyse it, and this is no disrespect to Ian, they were very sophisticated "B"-picture plots,' Young said. 'If someone tells you, "A James Bond film", you'd say, "My God, that's for Monogram", or Republic, who used to be around in those days. You would never have thought of it as a serious "A" film.'[58]

The demise of the B-movie, however, combined with the trend towards fewer films, helped to bring about the circumstances in which Bond could flourish as A-feature material. As the studios cut back on their production programmes, and with more riding on individual films, each production had to be more distinctive: hence even routine genre films became more expensive and were made with higher production values. 'The effect of amplifying B-film material was perhaps most visible in the rise of the big-budget espionage film,' aver Thompson and Bordwell, citing Hitchcock's *North by Northwest* (1959) as an example of this trend before declaring that 'the catalyst for genre upscaling was Ian Fleming's fictional British agent James Bond'.[59] The Bond films, in this context, mark the transition of the spy thriller from the netherland of the B-movie to the glossy, big-budget world of the A-feature.

Here it is useful to consider the relationship between Bond and *North by Northwest*, not only because Hitchcock's film was part of the same process of genre upscaling but also because Fleming had evidently seen it: he mentions the film in *Thunderball*.[60] *North by Northwest* is essentially an Americanised reworking of the sort of spy story that Hitchcock had made his own in his British films of the 1930s, particularly *The 39 Steps* (1935). Both films feature innocent bystanders caught up in a web of conspiracy and intrigue and who find themselves hunted by both the police and the real criminals; both are narratives of flight and pursuit in which the hero travels across the country; both reduce plot explanation to a minimum through their elusive 'MacGuffin' (Hitchcock's term for the object that all the fuss is about); and both feature the same three character types of debonair leading man (Robert Donat, Cary Grant), cool blonde heroine (Madeleine Carroll, Eva Marie Saint) and outwardly respectable villain (Godfrey Tearle, James Mason). *North by Northwest* is infused with a certain moral ambiguity about the Cold War: learning that the heroine has been sent to sleep with the villain to learn his secrets, Grant's character Roger Thornhill is outraged with the American intelligence chiefs ('If you fellows can't lick the Vandamms of this world without asking girls like her to bed down with them and fly away with them and probably never come back, perhaps you ought to learn to lose a few cold wars'). Like the Bond stories, however, its main influence would seem to be the sensational lineage of the thriller with its fast-moving narrative and spectacular action sequences. As James Naremore writes:

> At the level of generic conventions, for example, *North by Northwest* is symptomatic of a transitional moment in the evolution of spy fiction: it draws many of its best effects from an extensive (and

mostly British) tradition of narratives about international intrigue to which Hitchcock himself had been a major contributor; at the same time it predicts certain features of the sleekly commodified James Bond films that followed in its wake.[61]

To what extent might *North by Northwest* be described as a proto-James Bond film? With its glossy visual style, its witty dialogue and its spectacular set pieces such as the famous crop-duster sequence and the climax on the presidential heads of Mount Rushmore (albeit reconstructed in a studio), there is certainly much in Hitchcock's film that is comparable to the Bond movies. It constructs a very similar consumerist and sexual fantasy world. Cary Grant's character is a successful Madison Avenue advertising executive whose handsome good looks and slightly dangerous charm make him irresistible to women. At one point Grant and Eva Marie Saint travel on the Twentieth Century Limited from New York to Chicago, a refined setting where they eat brook trout before making love. Grant's seduction of her – she is the villain's mistress who is now working as an agent for the American government – might be seen as a partial working through of the process of 'ideological repositioning' which Bennett identifies in the Bond narrative. On a visual level, the sleek, modernist set design of the film, exemplified by the villain's mountain-top eyrie with its angular beams and large windows, anticipates Ken Adam's sets for the Bond films. Finally, it also has, in Cary Grant, a suave, suited hero who moves through the twists and turns of the plot with a bemused and slightly detached air. Indeed, Broccoli sounded out Grant about the possibility of playing James Bond: 'He had the style, the sophistication and, in fact, had been born in Britain. He also happened to be a Bond aficionado. But he said no.'[62]

Robin Wood, as we have seen, compared the early Bonds unfavourably with *North by Northwest*, arguing that Hitchcock's film was 'thematically organic' and displayed a level of psychological depth that demanded it be taken seriously, whereas 'the self-mocking aspect of the Bond films is merely a very shrewd means of permitting the spectator to indulge any penchant for sadism and sexual "kicks" he may have without any accompanying discomfort'.[63] Yet, in terms of narrative construction, the Bond films adopted what might be described as a 'Hitchcockian' structure. Maibaum admitted that he followed Hitchcock's advice in writing the Bond films:

Hitchcock once said to me, 'If I have 13 "bumps" I know I have a picture'. By 'bumps', he meant, of course, shocks, highpoints, thrills, whatever you choose to call them. From the beginning ... Mr Broccoli and Mr Saltzman, the producers, and myself have not been content with 13 'bumps'. We aim for 39. Our objective has been to make every foot of film pay off in terms of exciting entertainment.[64]

Young, similarly, felt that the success of the Bond movies owed much to their fast pacing and kinetic style: 'One wanted the films to have a very slick quality. We wanted to make them as sophisticated as we could, and above all I gave the picture [Dr No] an enormous sense of pace, in fact, it changed styles of filmmaking.'[65] Although Young was never slow to claim credit for the style of the Bond films, the contribution of editor Peter Hunt should not be underestimated. Hunt's editing broke some of the rules of conventional film 'grammar', for example by cutting in the middle of pans and not always cutting on matching action – a style that was to be influential on television action series in the 1960s. The narration of the Bond movies bears comparison with the style of the comic strip – exemplified by the 'James Bond' strip drawn by John McClusky which ran in the *Daily Express* between 1957 and 1963 – in which information has to be conveyed quickly and as far as possible by the visuals alone. The short shot lengths of the Bond films, particularly in the action sequences with their close-ups of fists, feet and guns thrust into the frame, are filmic equivalents of the panels of the comic strip.

This chapter has considered the various contexts of Bond: the cultural politics of Fleming's stories, the first screen adaptation that relocated Bond in a different idiom and the contexts of the film industry in the late 1950s and early 1960s that facilitated the production of the first films. The Bond film series, of course, has long since extended beyond the original texts in which Bond first appeared. While the novels remain rooted in the social and political context of the 1950s, the films have responded to changing industrial and cultural circumstances in order to maintain their position at the forefront of popular film culture. In order to demonstrate how the Bond film series has negotiated changes in the film industry, and how it has developed in response to broader social and cultural changes, it becomes necessary to analyse the history of the series on a film-by-film basis.

2

Snobbery with Violence:
Dr No, From Russia with Love,
Goldfinger

The first three James Bond films – *Dr No* (dir. Terence Young, 1962), *From Russia with Love* (dir. Terence Young, 1963) and *Goldfinger* (dir. Guy Hamilton, 1964) – may be grouped together in various ways. They are the closest of all the films to the snobbery-with-violence ethic of the British spy thriller in general and the work of Ian Fleming in particular. While later films deviated further and further from the books, the first three Bond movies all bear a close enough resemblance to their literary originals to be considered as genuine adaptations of Fleming. Furthermore, it was during these three films that the generic formula of the Bond series was established. The narrative structure and film style were developed over the course of these three to the extent that by the time of *Goldfinger*, regarded by many as the best film of the entire series, all the now familiar ingredients were squarely in place. In an economic context, moreover, the box-office success of the films snowballed. The success of *Dr No* took all but the film-makers themselves by surprise, but it was quickly surpassed by *From Russia with Love* and *Goldfinger*, each of which was the biggest attraction of its year in Britain, breaking all existing box-office records. The critical reception of the films was mixed, but, while *Dr No* passed some critics by, the next two films were sufficient to convince even those who demurred that, whatever they thought of the films themselves, Bond had emerged not only as the most popular screen hero in memory but also as a cultural phenomenon of the first order.

In order to understand the impact which the early Bond movies made, particularly in Britain, it is necessary to consider them in the context of the film culture of the time. The 1950s has generally been characterised as the 'doldrums era' of British cinema, the dull decade between the 'golden age' of the 1940s and the vibrant, new, youth-oriented film culture of the 'swinging sixties'. The dominant genres of 1950s British cinema – the war film, the comedy, the crime thriller – are widely regarded as backward-looking and unimaginative. In 1957, for example, Lindsay Anderson lamented 'the rather tepid humanism of our cinema', which he considered was 'snobbish, anti-intelligent, emotionally inhibited, wilfully blind to the conditions and problems of the present, dedicated to an out-of-date, exhausted national idea'.[1] It was also a decade when cinema-going as a social habit was in decline: annual cinema admissions fell from some 1,365 million in 1951 to 500 million by 1960.[2] And, although some British films were very successful, this has to be set against the fact that Hollywood movies continued to dominate British screens.   *Frankenstein*

Towards the end of the 1950s, however, there were signs of a revival in the fortunes of British cinema. The popular success of Hammer's *The Curse of Frankenstein* (1957), particularly in overseas markets, paved the way for a cycle of colourful, full-blooded Gothic horror films which became synonymous with the studio's name. Despised by the critical establishment for their sensational subject matter and visceral excess, the Hammer horror films were, for a decade or more, successful at the box-office, winning the popular acclaim of increasingly youth-dominated audiences. In Peter Cushing's Baron Frankenstein and Christopher Lee's Count Dracula, Hammer created two of the great anti-heroic characters of British cinema, whose defiance of authority and social convention in the pursuit of perverse science (Frankenstein) and lustful desire (Dracula) might be seen, in retrospect, to anticipate the emergence of the sub-cultures of the 1960s which celebrated personal gratification and sexual licentiousness. The amorality of the Hammer 'heroes' has drawn comparison to James Bond. To quote Robert Murphy: 'Cushing's Frankenstein, sexually active and almost Bond-like in his casual use (and disposal) of women, sets a tone altogether new to the horror film and to British cinema.'[3] There was a significant difference, however, in that whereas the Bond films were to be thoroughly modern in their foregrounding of technology, the Hammer horrors were usually set safely in the past.   *The new wave of in British cinema*

If Hammer represented the commercially successful but critically disreputable end of British cinema in the late 1950s and early 1960s, the 'new wave' films of the same period occupied the other end of the spectrum: critically acclaimed, serious and respectable cinema with the emphasis very much on realism and social relevance. The core of new wave films is relatively small – *Look Back in Anger* (1959), *Room at the Top* (1959), *The Entertainer* (1960), *Saturday Night and Sunday Morning* (1960), *A Taste of Honey* (1961), *A Kind of Loving* (1962), *The Loneliness of the Long Distance Runner* (1962), *Billy Liar* (1963) and *This Sporting Life* (1963) – but, taken together, they are usually held to have brought a new vitality and social awareness to British cinema. Most of these films were adapted from the work of the so-called 'angry brigade' of dramatists (John Osborne, Keith Waterhouse, Shelagh Delaney) and the novels of the 'northern realists' (John Braine, Alan Sillitoe, David Storey); they utilised the talents of a new generation of younger, naturalistic actors (Albert Finney, Tom Courtenay, Alan Bates, Richard Harris); and they were characterised by the gritty realism of their visual style, by their stark black-and-white photography, and by their use of natural lighting and real locations, most often in the back streets, canals and workshops of grim northern industrial towns. They were also rather more frank in their acknowledgement of class divisions and their treatment of sex (most of them were awarded an 'X' certificate) than had hitherto been common in British cinema.

While not denying the importance of the new wave in British cinema history, it must be considered that it was relatively short-lived, flowering and disappearing within the space of four or five years. Certainly by 1963, there were strong indications that the tides of critical and popular taste had turned. Lindsay Anderson's *This Sporting Life*, generally regarded as the last of the new wave films, had a mixed press and was a commercial failure, prompting Sir John Davis, managing director of the Rank Organisation, which had financed it, to observe that the days of this new type of realist drama had come to an end. 'I do feel that independent producers should take note of public demand and make films of entertainment value,' he told the Rank Theatre Division's Annual Showmanship Luncheon in December 1963. 'The public has clearly shown that it does not want the dreary kitchen sink dramas.'[4] Although Davis's comments were probably inspired as much by the reluctance of the major cinema circuits to show 'X'-certificate films, the timing of the speech is significant in that *From Russia with Love*, which surely exemplified the sort of 'entertainment value' which he mentioned, had recently broken circuit records for the Rank-owned Odeon cinemas.

It is tempting, though perhaps a little too simplistic, to suggest that the impact of the James Bond films arose from a film culture in which popular taste was already turning against the new wave. To some extent, of course, this is probably true, and it is reflected in the career trajectory of Harry Saltzman, who left Woodfall Films in 1960, declaring in hindsight that he was tired of social realism. 'All the films were designed to show how the other half lives, but for God's sake, we *are* the other half,' he later said. 'I thought it was time to go back to big entertainment and I saw in the Bonds the bigger than life thing.'[5] Terence Young, director of *Dr No*, endorsed this view. 'It fitted the mood of the people, anyway in Britain,' he told *Films and Filming* in 1967. 'I think people were getting tired of the realistic school, the kitchen sinks and all those abortions.'[6]

Obviously, with their far-fetched plots, exotic foreign locations and colourful visual style, the Bond films created a fantasy world which was far removed from the kitchen sink realism of the new wave. If, as Arthur Marwick suggests, *Room at the Top* 'could have been photographed to illustrate certain passages in Hoggart's *The Uses of Literacy*', then the Bond films, as Jeffrey Richards remarks, were the equivalent of 'colour supplement chic'.[7] Yet for all these differences in style, it is possible to trace some thematic links between new wave cinema and the Bond films. In certain respects the character of Bond can be compared to Joe Lampton, the protagonist of *Room at the Top*. Lampton (Laurence Harvey) is a northern working-class hero with a chip on his shoulder and a burning ambition for money and status: what he wants is 'a clerk's dream – a girl with a Riviera tan and a Lagonda'. James Bond, it might be argued, is Joe Lampton's fantasy *alter ego*. The glossy, materialist world of the Bond films is what Lampton aspires to. In the persona of Sean Connery, Bond has all the abrasiveness of Lampton, but he inhabits a very different world of elegant Mayfair clubs and Whitehall offices. He enjoys social mobility, has money and social status without having been born into the privileged classes, has plenty of girls with a suntan and a sports car, and, moreover, can indulge his sexual appetite without

Bond films represent a fantasy that entices most dissimilar to the films at the time.

having to marry any of them. 'In terms of ideology, the Bond films were not escapist aberrations,' remarks Sarah Street. 'Bond's globetrotting and proven success with women reveals another, fantasy aspect of the social realist films' masculine nightmare of being trapped in the provinces with a wife and family.'[8]

There is a thematic link of sorts, therefore, between the Bond films and the new wave, suggesting that the success of the early Bond movies should not be attributed solely to their stylistic differences from the social realist films. Nor were the Bond movies the only non-realist genre of the 1960s: horror films, pop musicals and 'Swinging London' films also foregrounded fantasy and escapism. In this sense the Bond films, again, were not an aberration, but rather the most extreme manifestation of a trend towards colourful fantasy in 1960s British cinema after the sober black-and-white aesthetic of the 1950s.

So why did the Bond films make such an extraordinary impact? Young thought that *Dr No* was 'the most perfectly timed film ever made'. 'I think we arrived [in] not only the right year, but the right week of the right month of the right year,' he said.[9] But while this might be sufficient to account for a one-off success, it does not explain the phenomenal and on-going success of the Bond series. The reason why the early Bond films were so successful in Britain is tied to deeper, longer-term developments in film culture and the film industry. There are two inter-related factors which, it seems reasonable to suggest, provided the conditions in which the Bond movies could make the impact they did. The first is that they offered a very different entertainment pattern from anything else in popular cinema at the time. The second is that at a time when cinema attendances were in decline, the Bond films succeeded in tapping the diverse constituents of an increasingly fragmented cinema audience.

That the Bond films stood out from the rest of popular cinema can be demonstrated by considering the type of films which had been most successful at the box-office in the years immediately preceding their arrival. Although precise box-office statistics are not available for this period, the trade press provided annual surveys of the top attractions, which, if inevitably somewhat impressionistic, were regarded within the trade as a reliable guide to which films had been most successful.[10] What the trade press surveys between 1955 and 1960 reveal is that British audiences preferred big-budget Hollywood productions alongside smaller-scale home-grown products. The most successful Hollywood movies of the late 1950s and early 1960s included biblical/historical epics (*The Ten Commandments, Ben Hur*), adventure spectaculars (*Around the World in 80 Days*), musicals (*The King and I, South Pacific*) and westerns (*The Big Country, The Magnificent Seven*). Taken together, this would seem to indicate a preference for widescreen, colour spectaculars with high production values and big-name stars. At the same time, however, certain British genres also did very well domestically, particularly war films (*The Dam Busters, Reach for the Sky, The Bridge on the River Kwai, Dunkirk, Sink the Bismarck!*) and comedies (especially the 'Doctor' series, which had started with *Doctor in the House* in 1954, and the 'Carry On' series, starting with *Carry On Sergeant* in 1958). Most of these films were concerned with peculiarly British themes and subject matter. Certainly in the case of the 'Carry On' films (*Carry On Nurse* was *Kine Weekly*'s 'biggest box-office attraction' of 1959) they were rooted in an indigenous cultural tradition of low-brow, vulgar comedy which appealed uniquely to British audiences. The Bond films, therefore, filled a gap in the prevailing film culture in that they combined a particularly British generic tradition (the spy thriller) with the sort of production values, colour and spectacle more usually associated with Hollywood movies.

It was realised at the time that the Bond films did not fit easily into the existing generic profile of popular cinema. Veteran trade journalist Josh Billings, in his annual survey of the box-office winners for *Kine Weekly* in 1962, seemed unsure precisely how to account for *Dr No*. Selecting the Cliff Richard musical *The Young Ones* as the top money-maker ('typically English light entertainment put over with tremendous zing'), he identified *Dr No* as the 'second biggest winner', but was unsure how to categorise it, describing it rather uneasily as 'a bizarre comedy melodrama'.[11] Anecdotal evidence for the popular appeal of the Bond films is provided by future James Bond star Timothy Dalton: 'The first Bond movie I saw was *Dr No*, in my local cinema in a place called Belper in Derbyshire. I must have been about 13 or 14 years old … The only movies we'd seen were war pictures, or drawing room comedies, or westerns, and here was something right up to date and really terrific.'[12] Dalton's comment is particularly interesting in that he emphasises Bond's appeal for youth audiences, a point which is linked to the second factor in explaining the movies' success.

The 1950s had witnessed not only the decline of the regular cinema-going audience, but also the start of the various processes whereby the cinema audience became more fragmented. It was not only the rise of television which drew audiences away from the cinema. The regular cinema-goers of earlier decades now had homes and families of their own, while post-war youth had other leisure interests, particularly rock'n'roll, which competed with the cinema for their patronage. By the late 1950s the family audience for films was dwindling, while teenagers and young adults comprised the majority of cinema-goers. The film industry, in Britain as in America, tried to adapt to the changing composition of its audience by making films aimed at particular groups. One manifestation of this was the emergence of the pop musical. British youth audiences responded in particular to Bill Haley and the Comets (*Rock Around the Clock*), Elvis Presley (*Jailhouse Rock, King Creole*) and the home-grown British equivalent, Cliff Richard (*Expresso Bongo, The Young Ones, Summer Holiday*). Another manifestation was the horror film, which appealed primarily to a young adult male audience, and which was reflected in the box-office success enjoyed by Hammer in the late 1950s and early 1960s. The Bond films, as Timothy Dalton observes, were modern and up-to-date in a way that other genres such as the war film and the western were not. Their immediacy and contemporaneity, their use of popular recording artistes to perform the title songs, and their calculated inclusion of elements of sex and violence, surely account in large measure for their popular appeal.

The decline and fragmentation of the cinema audience obviously had important consequences for the film industry. From the 1950s, Hollywood had ceased to be the 'film factory' that it had been during the 1930s and 1940s, when each of the major studios produced about fifty films a year which, taken together, would ensure an overall profit. Instead, the tendency was to concentrate on producing fewer but bigger films intended to reap individual profits. This was the origin of the 'blockbuster' syndrome: the production of big-budget, high-profile films which it was hoped would prove spectacularly successful at the box-office. The Bond films arrived at precisely the moment when the British film industry was beginning to follow the pattern established by Hollywood. As Bill Altria, replacing Josh Billings as *Kine Weekly*'s chief reviewer, observed in 1963: 'The really big pictures – big at the box-office that is – are attracting larger audiences and more money to cinemas then ever before, but the run-of-the-mill films, the type that only a year or so ago were the bread and butter of the business, are barely yielding a crust.'[13] Following *Dr No*, which was something of a surprise success, all the Bond films were treated by producers, distributors and exhibitors alike as 'big' films which had great box-office potential. *From Russia with Love*, Altria observed, was 'a natural', and by the time of *Goldfinger* it was taken for granted that the Bond film would be the top money-maker of the year. Within a very short space of time, the Bond series had established itself as an annual institution of the British film industry.

The quite extraordinary success of the Bond movies in the early 1960s was due, therefore, to changes both in film culture and in the film industry. Far from being a mere accident of timing, the impact of the Bond films arose from a combination of circumstances and trends which had been on-going for some time. But what of the films themselves? What was the formula which proved so successful? And what were the narrative and stylistic ingredients which established the Bond series virtually as a new genre in its own right?

Terence Young liked to give the impression that the style of the films came together almost by accident. 'I don't think when I took on *Dr No* I had a very clear conception of what I was going to do,' he said. 'The original Ian Fleming story was diabolically childish, something straight out of a Grade B thriller ... The only way I thought we could do a Bond film was to heat it up, to give it a sense of humour, to make it as cynical as possible.'[14] Childish it may have been, but what is most remarkable about the adaptation of *Dr No* from page to screen is just how cinematic Fleming's novel actually was. In part this was due to the fact that, like *Thunderball*, the origins of *Dr No* lay in a screen treatment. In 1957 Fleming had been approached by budding producer Henry Morgenthau III (son of the wartime US Treasury Secretary) to devise a treatment for a television series based on the adventures of an American secret agent, variously referred to as *Commander Jamaica* or *James Gunn, Secret Agent*. Fleming's story revolved around an on-going battle between the titular hero and his enemy Dr No, 'an international freelance spy of Chinese–German extraction', who attempted to sabotage an Anglo-American missile test station in the Caribbean. The projected series failed to materialise, but Fleming used the basic storyline for his sixth Bond novel.[15]

Dr No has Bond investigating the disappearance of Commander Strangways, the British Secret Service Head of Station in Jamaica. He is assisted by loyal Cayman Islander Quarrel (who had previously appeared in *Live and Let Die*), while attempts are made to kill Bond with poisoned fruit and with a deadly tropical centipede which is left in his hotel bed. Bond pursues a link to Dr No, a Chinese German who owns a guano (bird dung) refinery on the island of Crab Key. Bond and Quarrel sail out by night to the island, where they meet Honeychile Ryder, a wild, beautiful young woman diving for valuable sea shells who tells them Dr No has a dragon. They are hunted by Dr No's men: Quarrel is killed by the 'dragon' (a marsh-buggy armed with a flamethrower), while Bond and Honeychile are captured and taken to Dr No's headquarters. Dr No, a scientific mastermind backed by the Russians, is using a specially developed radio beam to interfere with American test rockets launched from a nearby base on Turks Island. Bond endures a horrifying obstacle course, involving crawling through a series of small ducts and tunnels, a cage of tarantulas and finally plunging into the sea where he faces a giant squid. But he negotiates it successfully, kills Dr No by burying him under a pile of guano and makes his escape with Honeychile.

Of all Fleming's books, *Dr No* attracted most criticism for its 'sex, snobbery and sadism'. Unlike the previous novel, *From Russia, with Love*, which had been a taut, suspenseful espionage story, *Dr No* is closer to the world of Edgar Wallace and Sax Rohmer with its megalomaniac criminal mastermind and its fast-paced narrative with the emphasis on action rather than exposition. The science-fiction elements were to be developed in the film, which, nevertheless, is a reasonably faithful adaptation of Fleming's story.

According to the stories which circulate about the preparation of *Dr No*, however, this was not always the case. 'We had at one time, I think, five different scripts on *Dr No* including one in which Dr No was a monkey,' Young recalled.[16] Several writers worked on the film, and it is difficult to ascertain who made the most significant contributions. 'The prolific pen of Wolf Mankowitz has been signed by Harry Saltzman and "Cubby" Broccoli to do the screenplay of *Dr No*, first of the James Bond series which the producers are making for United Artists,' *Kine Weekly* reported in July 1961.[17] Mankowitz was a British writer, author of several novels including *A Kid for Two Farthings* (which he had adapted for the screen in 1955) and screenwriter of British films including Hammer's *The Two Faces of Dr Jekyll* (1960), the Peter Sellers comedy *The Millionairess* (1961) and the science-fiction drama *The Day the Earth Caught Fire* (1961). According to Richard Maibaum, however, he had already been working on a Bond script before Mankowitz came on board:

> *Thunderball* was actually the first; we decided it was the one to start
> with. I'd finished a first draft, and then Kevin McClory jumped
> up with a lawsuit against Ian Fleming ... So we put *Thunderball*
> aside until that was settled and decided to do *Dr No*. I was then
> in London, after having finished the first draft of *Thunderball*, so
> I began to write *Dr No* with Wolf Mankowitz. Cubby and Harry
> didn't like our first treatment, so Wolf bowed out; and I went on
> to do the first draft of the screenplay. Later, after I left, a novelist
> named Aubrey [*sic*] Mather (Jasper Davis is his real name) did
> some work with a girl playwright, Joanna Harwood.[18]

Young gave a slightly different account again of the completion of the
script, saying that he polished it up with his script girl: 'That's how this
girl, Joanna Harwood, who was my continuity girl on a previous picture,
got in it with me. We took a room at the Dorchester Hotel and we
worked day and night.'[19] On the titles of the film itself, the screenplay
is credited to Maibaum, Harwood and Berkeley Mather (whose name
is misspelt as 'Berkely').

While the various contributions by the different writers may be
impossible to disentangle, it seems likely that Maibaum and Mankowitz
between them were most responsible for the final shape of the story.
The 'fourth draft screenplay', dated 12 December 1961, bears both
Maibaum's and Mankowitz's names.[20] It follows the general storyline
of the novel and transposes many scenes directly: the opening with the
three 'blind' beggars who gun down Strangways, Bond's interview with
M and his re-equipping with a new gun (a Walther PPK 7.65-millimetre
instead of the old Beretta .25), the night-time canoe expedition, the first
appearance of the girl on the beach, the battle with the marsh-buggy
and Quarrel's death, and the scene where Bond and his companion
are wined and dined by Dr No while he lectures them on the nature
of power. The main changes made in the screenplay were due to the
need to flesh out the story, rather than alter it in any drastic way. So,
for example, as this was to be the first film of a series, a scene was
fashioned to introduce James Bond to the audience: this takes place
in a London gambling club (perhaps deriving from the introduction
of Fleming's Bond in *Casino Royale*), where Bond meets and flirts with
Sylvia Trenchard over a game of baccarat. Sylvia (whose surname in the
film is Trench) was an additional love interest who was not in the novel,
suggesting that even from the beginning the film-makers intended to

increase the number of sexual partners for Bond. The screenplay also lengthened the section of the story in Jamaica before Bond and Quarrel set out for Dr No's island. Bond's American colleague Felix Leiter, who does not appear in the novel, was written into the screenplay, and the character of Miss Taro, Dr No's spy inside Government House, was developed to provide another sexual encounter for Bond. An incident alluded to in the novel whereby Bond learns that his car, being driven by someone else as a decoy, has been caused to crash, was developed into a chase sequence with Bond at the wheel of his car pursued by a hearse which tries to force him off a mountain road. The script also changed the centipede in Bond's bed to a tarantula. When Bond and Quarrel arrive on Crab Key, the screenplay follows the novel quite closely until the climax, though the girl whom Bond and Quarrel encounter is known simply as Honey rather than Honeychile and has her own personal grudge against Dr No, whom she believes responsible for the death of her marine zoologist father. The object of Dr No's 'toppling' radio beam are now American space rockets launched from Cape Canaveral – a topical touch in so far as there had been a number of misfires in the early days of the American space programme. Bond's ordeal in Dr No's obstacle course is simplified, the episode of the giant squid is omitted, and instead of having Bond kill Dr No by burying him under a pile of guano, the screenplay substituted a fight to the death between Bond and the doctor in the reactor room ('Dr No is tearing and slashing with his claws. Bond's suit and headpiece are now in tatters and fall away, finally disclosing him'). Honey's ordeal from the book, wherein she is staked out in the path of giant crabs, was omitted from the screenplay, though such a scene would later be filmed.

While most of the differences between novel and screenplay were fairly cosmetic, reflecting the necessity of a different structure and tempo for a film, one particularly significant alteration was made at this stage which was to determine the future direction of the Bond series. Whereas in the novel Dr No's operations were backed by the Russians, in the screenplay he became a member of SPECTRE. Given that Maibaum had previously worked on a screenplay of *Thunderball*, the novel in which Fleming had introduced SPECTRE, this change may well have been his idea. The draft screenplay of *Dr No* contained more details about SPECTRE than does the finished film:

BOND: With your sort of disregard for human life you can only be working for the East.

DR NO (*contemptuously*): East? West? Points of the compass, Mr Bond. Each as brutishly stupid as the other. *I* work for SPECTRE.

BOND: Spectre? Never heard of them ... and I thought I knew all the nuts.

DR NO: Special Executive for Counter-Intelligence, Terrorism, Revenge and Extortion.

BOND: They sound a pleasant bunch. (*He looks round and shrugs.*) Albeit a little theatrical ... if this is their headquarters.

DR NO: Headquarters? Don't talk like a fool, Bond. Or are you trying to make me lose my temper? No, this is not their head-quarters. Crab Key is but a microcosm of the organisation, syndicate, call it what you will. Do you think that the diversion of a few miserable rockets is the be-all and end-all of our efforts?

BOND (*looking at him levelly*): I'm calling your bluff. What is?

DR NO (*after slightest pause, looking at him levelly*): Ultimate Control ... Complete ... All-Powerful ... of the world ... and beyond.

BOND looks at him for a further few minutes in silence. Then throws his head back with a shout of laughter.

BOND: I see. Doctor, I said 'nuts' just now. I apologise for the coarseness of my speech. The psychiatric term, I believe, is paranoia ... illusions of grandeur.

The reference to SPECTRE's long-term ambitions suggests that from the beginning the film-makers anticipated there would be more screen adventures to follow.

The introduction of SPECTRE, as various commentators have suggested, marked an important ideological shift which differentiated the films from the books. Bennett and Woollacott argue that 'the primary impetus for this ideological readjustment came from the requirements of the film industry'.[21] The films were deliberately de-politicised and detached from the Cold War background of the novels, a point which is made explicit through Dr No's reference to East and West as nothing more than 'points of the compass'. The argument that this de-politicisation accounts for the success of the Bond films in the international market-place, however, seems a spurious one given that other successful films

– including Hitchcock's *North by Northwest* – had made direct reference to the Cold War. And it should also be borne in mind that in adopting the SPECTRE formula, the films were still following the narrative strategy established by Fleming himself with *Thunderball*.

Dr No introduced most of the generic ingredients that have come to define the Bond films. These can be identified at various levels, including narrative structure, visual style and characterisation. In the first place, *Dr No* encapsulates the narrative formula which was to be followed in most other Bond movies: a villainous conspiracy is plotted; Bond is assigned by M (played by Bernard Lee) to investigate; Bond travels abroad and meets up with allies; various attempts are made to kill Bond; Bond seduces a woman in the service of the villain; Bond meets 'the girl' who is destined to be the principal heroine; an ally meets a grisly death; Bond and the girl are captured by the villain and taken inside his headquarters; the villain reveals his plot to Bond; Bond then foils the plot, kills the villain and escapes with the girl.

While, on the surface, this may seem nothing more than a *Boy's Own* adventure story, at a deeper level certain ideological structures are apparent. Most obviously, Bond functions as an agent of British imperialism. This is more explicit in *Dr No* than in the later films, due in large measure to the Jamaican colonial settings, including Government House and the Queen's Club. Some commentators, indeed, regard it as a reactionary film. Raymond Durgnat posits a reading which dismisses the notion of Bond as a modernising hero and instead stresses the racial undertones in the representation of British imperialist ideology:

Whatever Brand X critics may have written, Bond isn't just an Organization Man, but a rigid jingoist, almost loveably archaic. If you have forelocks, prepare to touch them now, in fond farewell to the Edwardiana in modern drag lovingly panoplied forth in the first half of *Dr No* (1962) as Bond glides along the Establishment's Old Boy Net. The British Raj, reduced to its Caribbean enclave, lords it benevolently over jovial and trusting West Indians and faithful coloured police-sergeants, the Uncle Toms of Dock Green. We might almost be back with Lieutenant Kenneth More on the North-West Frontier. Meanwhile out on Crab Key lurks Dr No, last of the war lords, whose 'chigro' minions ... blend of the Yellow Peril and the Mau-Mau, battle it out with his English co-anachronism.[22]

Durgnat can be the most idiosyncratic of writers, but it is hard not to agree with his interpretation here. The film does seem explicitly racist, not only in the characterisation of its villains (all Chinese or black, with the exception of Anthony Dawson's Professor Dent), but also in the diminution of the character of Quarrel: in the novel treated by Bond with respect, but in the film little more than a lackey ('Fetch my shoes', Bond orders him at one point) played in stereotypical eye-rolling fashion by John Kitzmiller. Bond's intervention in Jamaica saves this colonial outpost from the potentially subversive threat of a sinister secret organisation – a reaffirmation of white, British superiority at a time when, in reality, Britain was beating a hasty retreat from empire (Jamaica became independent on 6 August 1962).

On another level, however, Bond can be seen as more than just the last imperial hero. As Britain reluctantly faced up to the decline of its power in the 1950s, the conviction grew among British politicians and diplomats that the country could still play a role on the world stage through its 'special relationship' with the United States. In *Dr No*, Bond functions as an index of Anglo-American relations. The threat is directed at American space rockets, but as the interference originates in the Caribbean the Americans have passed the investigation over to the British ('You Limeys can be pretty touchy about trespassing,' remarks Jack Lord's Felix Leiter). It is Bond, rather than Leiter, who sails out to Crab Key ('it's my beat'). At the end of the film Leiter turns up on a Royal Navy motor launch with a detachment of Royal Marines (a scene not in the Maibaum–Mankowitz screenplay). But Bond has already saved the day: 'Where were you when I didn't need you?' he asks Leiter, thus reasserting his ability to sort out the crisis without American help. American involvement, therefore, is marginal and is legitimised through co-operation with the British. In reality, of course, the Americans have rarely shown such deference to the remnants of British colonialism in the Caribbean, a fact dramatically demonstrated in 1983 by their military intervention in the Commonwealth island of Grenada following a Marxist coup – against the wishes of the British government. In the Bond films, as in the novels, the 'special relationship' was rather more equal than *realpolitik* would allow.

But if *Dr No* harks back to the glories of Britain's imperial past, why was the film received as something so fresh and new? The answer lies not in the narrative ideology of the film, but in its visual style. *Dr No* established the look of the Bond films with its glossy surface and highly detailed *mise-en-scène*. The film is at pains to distance itself from the sober, restrained visual style which was so prevalent in British cinema, especially through its insistence on colour. Everything in *Dr No* emphasises colour, from the pop-art title sequence – a kaleidoscope of brightly coloured dots which flash on and off in rapid succession, suggesting that the film is going to be fast, fun and frenetic – to the high-definition Technicolor cinematography which creates a travel brochure image of Jamaica, all sunshine and bright primary colours. The titles were designed by graphic artist Maurice Binder who also devised the iconic image – the silhouetted figure of Bond seen through a gun-barrel turns and fires at the camera – that would become the trademark motif of the series. The image recalls the gun fired at the audience at the end of *The Great Train Robbery* (1903). The visual style of the film is enhanced by its distinctive sound, especially the energetic signature melody with its twanging electric guitar and strident brass. 'The James Bond Theme' is always credited to Monty Norman, though it was a more up-tempo arrangement by John Barry that was used in *Dr No* and the subsequent films. There is only one disappointingly slack and old-fashioned sequence: the car chase, with its repeated shots of two cars driving along the same piece of road and its highly obvious back-projection, is reminiscent of so many B-movie thrillers.

The most distinctive aspect of the look of the Bond films, however, has always been their set design. *Dr No* provides an early indication of the complex design work of Ken Adam which was to become one of the distinguishing features of the series. In his designs for *Dr No*, Adam employs different styles, contrasting the traditional with the exotic. Bond is introduced in the refined surroundings of an elegant London gambling club (supposedly 'Les Ambassadeurs' in Park Lane), while his briefing takes place in M's reassuringly traditional office, with its wood panels, naval paintings and leather-bound furniture. Dr No's lair, by contrast, mixes Adam's characteristically modernist aesthetic with designs which are strongly reminiscent of the cinema of German Expressionism. Perhaps the most visually striking set in the film is the eerie chamber where Professor Dent (Anthony Dawson) receives his orders from the voice of the unseen Dr No: with its grey walls, low ceiling and a large grille which casts cross-patterned shadows over the floor, the design foregrounds visual style over narrative logic and marks the moment at which the film breaks decisively from any pretence of realism. Adam's *tour de force*, however, is Dr No's bizarre underground dining room, with its Gothic candelabras and an aquarium built into the wall, a set which locates Dr No visually in the lineage of criminal masterminds such as Fritz Lang's Dr Mabuse. Finally, the atomic reactor room, all gantries and banks of instruments, is the first of the futuristic science-fiction sets which would become increasingly familiar in later films.

As well as establishing the narrative formula and style, *Dr No* also introduced the basic character types of the Bond series. The most important of these, of course, is Bond himself. Connery's performance in *Dr No* did much to define Bond's screen persona. Introduced in a sequence which both parodies and pays homage to the classic Hollywood star build-up – Young is said to have modelled it on Paul Muni's appearance in *Juarez* (1939) – Connery displays remarkable confidence in his first major starring role. '*Dr No* effectively marked the end for the kind of arid stardom that actors like Leslie Howard had epitomised, and in which Britain had persistently traded,' writes Andrew Rissik. 'It declared a whole tradition obsolete, a tradition that had associated chivalry with polite vowels and a decorous repression of passion, overt sexuality and any real kind of spontaneous physical action.'[23] Although trailers for the early films described Bond as 'the gentleman agent with a licence to kill', he had less in common with the traditional image of the English gentleman hero personified by actors like Ronald Colman, Robert Donat and David Niven, than he did with the rugged masculinity, physical presence and virile sexuality more often associated with American stars such as Clark Gable or Gary Cooper. Connery (whose ability as an actor has consistently been under-rated by critics) should be credited with having established a new style of performance: a British screen hero in the manner of an American leading man. In *Dr No*, admittedly, his interpretation of Bond is not yet complete: the rough edges are still apparent, some of the polish is lacking. He gives the impression of being on edge; there is an abrasiveness in his performance, demonstrated in his exchanges with other actors where he is often curt and impatient. There are early indications, however, of the snobbery which was such an essential part of the Bond character. This is best exemplified in the dinner sequence when Dr No orders his guards to take Honey away and Bond picks up a champagne bottle as a weapon. 'That's a Dom Perignon '55, it would be a pity to break it,' Dr No remarks, to which Bond replies, 'I prefer the '53 myself' – both a snobbish assertion of his superior taste in champagne, and an indication that he is not taking the situation entirely seriously.

Along with the snobbery, of course, goes the violence. Few spy thrillers, with the notable exception of Hitchcock's *Secret Agent* (1936), had ever focused on the secret agent's role as assassin. *Dr No* included one important sequence which defined the nature of Bond's job as a professional killer. The Maibaum–Mankowitz screenplay introduced a scene in which Bond waits for Professor Dent at Miss Taro's apartment (Miss Taro herself having already been handed over to the police). Scene 135 in the screenplay is as follows:

> FIGURE *glances round – sees bedroom door ajar – creeps over – listens – pushes door gently open – peers round door – sees barely visible dark forms under sheet –* KICKS DOOR OPEN *– raises gun and fires four times into forms (silenced 'coughing' shots which done properly can sound horrible).*
>
> BOND (*out of darkness*): Good evening ... Professor.
>
> *The room springs to life as light goes on.* BOND *is seated in chair, one leg over the arm – left hand on table light switch – Walther in right.* DENT *swings on* BOND, *snarling. Two 'plunks' are drowned in roar of* BOND*'s unsilenced gun. The* PROFESSOR *does* NOT *stagger forward – he spins backwards as if somebody has kicked him in the chest – slamming up against a flimsy Chinese table and crushing it as he collapses. He rolls right over on to his back ... brings his legs up under his chin in an agonised convulsion ... shoots them straight out ... and then lies still.*
>
> BOND *rises and crosses to him. He doesn't need to examine him closely – he knows exactly where he's hit him – right between the two nipples. He blows fumes away from his gun and replaces it carefully in shoulder holster. He then goes to bed where we see two interlaced 'forms' are bolster and pillow. They are ripped by shots – (charred round edges of holes) – and feathers are scattered.* BOND *takes up phone and dials. His eyes are hard.*

The description of Dent's death is graphic enough in the screenplay, though as the scene is played in the film Bond is even more cold-blooded. Dent fires six shots into the bed, whereupon Bond, holding a silenced pistol, switches on the light and orders him to drop the gun. As Bond quizzes Dent, the professor pulls the rug on which he has dropped his gun towards him with his foot, apparently unnoticed by Bond, and then suddenly picks the gun up, only to find that it is empty. 'That's a Smith and Wesson – and you've had your six,' Bond says coldly. He then shoots Dent in the chest, with the professor spinning around as in the script to lie face-down on the floor, whereupon Bond fires another bullet into his back. Whereas in the script Bond had killed Dent while the professor was shooting at him, in the film it is a cold-blooded act because Bond knows Dent's gun is empty. The additional shot which Bond fires into the dead man's back is unnecessary, therefore gratuitous. The scene was controversial and apparently caused some problems with American film executives. 'That caused a lot of heartache; United Artists were not happy about it,' said Young.[24]

Dr No also established the prototypes for the Bond villain and the Bond girl. Joseph Wiseman's Dr No, with his expressionless face and monotone 'voice of doom' delivery, set the standard for all the later megalomaniacs bent on world domination. And Ursula Andress's celebrated appearance, walking out of the ocean wearing a clinging white bikini – Young thought it 'the greatest woman's entrance in a picture'[25] – established the enduring visual image of the 'Bond girl'. The film follows the novel in introducing Honey in a voyeuristic manner whereby Bond gazes at her before she is aware that she is being watched. Indeed, the sequence can be seen as a textbook example of certain feminist theories of the representation of women in mainstream cinema. Laura Mulvey has argued that women function as fetishised 'objects of to-be-looked-at-ness'. Visual pleasure in the cinema, she suggests, is linked to an explicitly male point-of-view, in which women are objects of the male gaze, providing sexual stimulation not only for the male protagonist, but also for the male spectator through the way in which filmic narration identifies with the male point-of-view.[26] While this interpretation of the ideological processes of mainstream cinema has since been modified by other writers, the Bond films do lend credence to Mulvey's thesis. Indeed, the predominance of the male gaze is institutionalised: in the screenplay Honey's first appearance is described from Bond's point-of-view ('Bond's Eyeline ... What He Sees'). That women in the Bond films were there purely for decoration is reinforced in so far as Andress (along with other early Bond girls Eunice Gayson, Daniela Bianchi, Shirley Eaton, Tania Mallet and Claudine Auger) was dubbed; denied her own voice, the girl is, literally, reduced to the level of an object only to be looked at.[27]

As the first of the James Bond films, the reception of *Dr No* is worth considering in some detail. The critics were divided, with the film finding admirers and detractors among both the popular and the quality press. What most critics recognised from the outset, however, was that it was likely to be the first of a series of screen adventures for Fleming's hero. Many accepted it as undemanding entertainment and believed it was likely to be successful on that basis. One of the film's biggest admirers was Dilys Powell, one of the two 'Sunday ladies' (along with C. A. Lejeune) who had dominated middle-brow British film journalism for over two decades. She compared it favourably to the classic days of British Hitchcock, and considered that the humour hit just the right note:

> Efficiency: perhaps that doesn't sound high praise for *Dr No*, but I mean it as high. The first of the James Bond films (I trust there will be others) has the air of knowing exactly what it is up to, and that has not been common in British thrillers since the day when Hitchcock took himself off to America. The jokes (one of them, a beauty, has been buzzing round London all the week) are tossed away with exactly the right carelessness. The excitements have a right little skin-crawling effect, but they aren't over-emphasised; the hair's-breadth escape from the ambush is handled with the nonchalance proper to agent 007; all in the day's work, now for the next, please.[28]

The joke which most amused the critics, incidentally, was that a painting which Bond notices in Dr No's headquarters was Goya's portrait of the Duke of Wellington, which had recently been stolen from the National Gallery – the first of many such topical references in the films.

Other critics, however, were less enthusiastic. The *Monthly Film Bulletin* thought that it did not stand comparison even to lesser Hitchcock or Lang:

> Once the cluttered preliminaries are out of the way – for instance the film is obviously destined to be the first of a James Bond series, so M must be glimpsed at his London desk – the story proceeds in traditional thick-ear fashion from vamps and violent death to the fitting grandeur of a final holocaust. One by one Bond's enemies are rendered brutally *hors-de-combat*, while Bond himself survives tarantulas and cliff-side car collisions at the expense of little more than a few bruises and a lot of perspiration. And yet strangely enough excitement, and humour, and the glamour of corruption, are all rather lacking. Just as, say, *The 1,000 Eyes of Dr Mabuse* seemed to wander anachronistically through the motions of once splendid (and why not still?) devices that Lang no longer retained much apparent faith in, *Dr No* misses the genuine sadistic, sybaritic

relish attributed to Fleming's novels, and the narrative invention of even second-rate Hitchcock. Something really new is needed, if not in the incidents then in the telling of them. Terence Young's direction has pace but little real vigour; the tortures and the killers are comparatively tame, nowhere near bizarre enough; the women, apart from Dr No's ultra-polite Chinese receptionist, are sexless and dull; and Sean Connery is such a disappointingly wooden and boorish Bond that the script's touches of grim humour go for less than they need.[29]

Ian Cameron, in the *Spectator*, was rather more abrupt: '*Dr No*: no, no. Too inept to be as pernicious as it might have been. Costly gloss flawed by insidious economy on girls. Superannuated Rank starlet tries to act sexy. Grotesque.'[30]

Just as they were divided on the film itself, the critics were also split on how suitable Connery was for the role of Bond. Derek Hill, himself no fan of the Bond character, thought he was 'played with exactly the right mixture of strong-arm fascist and telly commercial salesman by Sean Connery'.[31] *The Times* compared the screen Bond unfavourably with Fleming's Bond, opining that 'it is doubtful whether either his admirers or his detractors will recognize him' on the grounds that he exhibited an 'Irish-American look and sound, which somehow spoils the image'. It reserved judgement on Connery, suggesting that 'perhaps Mr Sean Connery will, with practice, get the "feel" of the part a little more surely than he does here'.[32] Many critics, confronted with Connery's Scots burr, clearly had some difficulty in placing his accent, which was widely described as Irish-American.

Other critics were less concerned with how appropriate Connery was to play Bond than with the question of whether Bond was an appropriate character to transfer to the screen at all. 'I find it disturbing that we should be offered as a hero – as someone we are supposed to admire – a man whose methods and morals are indistinguishable from those of the villains,' said Thomas Wiseman in the *Sunday Express*.[33] Nina Hibbin, film critic of the communist *Daily Worker*, saw in *Dr No* evidence of all the snobbery-with-violence ethics that other left-wing critics had found so repulsive in the novels. She disliked its 'sinister racialist implications', considered it 'a brutalised film' and thought it even nastier than the Hammer horrors (which she also disliked): 'It doesn't wallow, as horror films do, in blood and torture and slow death. It goes a stage further – by asking you to take such things for granted, playing for a laugh whenever the sardonic Mr Bond makes a new joke.'[34] Hibbin was to be the most outspoken critic of the early Bond movies, but hers was by no means an isolated voice. Richard Whitehall of *Films and Filming* compared Bond to Mike Hammer, the thuggish Red-bashing American private eye created by Mickey Spillane and brought to the screen in a couple of low-budget thrillers, *I, the Jury* (1953) and *Kiss Me Deadly* (1955):

> There hasn't been a film like *Dr No* since ... when? The Mickey Spillane thrillers of the middle 'fifties? *Dr No* is the headiest box-office concoction of sex and sadism ever brewed in a British studio, strictly bath-tub hooch but a brutally potent intoxicant for all that. Just as Mike Hammer was the softening up for James Bond, so Bond is the softening up for ... what? A fascist cinema uncorrupted by moral scruples? The riot of a completely anarchist cinema? *Dr No* could be the breakthrough to something ... but what? At one point Bond nonchalantly fires half a dozen shots into the *back* of a helpless opponent – the British cinema will never be the same again.[35]

It was, Whitehall considered, 'the perfect film for a sado-masochistic society', and he even went so far as to compare it to Michael Powell's notorious *Peeping Tom* (1960), which had drawn howls of outraged protest from the critics. He believed it should have been given an 'X' certificate, and wondered why the British Board of Film Censors had let it through with only an 'A'. 'Oh, Trevelyan, art thou sleeping in Soho?' he asked. 'This is surely one of the X'iest films imaginable, a monstrously overblown sex fantasy of nightmarish proportions.'

For all the criticisms levelled against its sex and violence, however, *Dr No* had been passed by the BBFC with nothing more restrictive than an 'A' certificate, and was therefore considered appropriate for general audiences in a way that horror films, with their sensationalist crimes and visceral gore, and new wave films, with their adult discussion of sexual issues, were not. BBFC secretary John Trevelyan said that he had discussed the representation of sex and violence in the Bond films with the producers and they had agreed what was necessary for the films to be suitable for an 'A' certificate:

> When we had the first of these films, *Dr No*, I had a discussion

with Harry Saltzman and we agreed that since he intended to make a series of these films we should aim to get them all suitable for the 'A' category since 'X' certificates would reduce his viewing audiences. These films were essentially fantasies, Bond being the 'Superman' of the 1960s who could not only get all the girls to bed without any difficulty but could escape from any perilous situation, using violence and being quite callous about it even to the point of joking about it. The agreement resulted in keeping the sex to a reasonable level, but we had some problem with the violence and in most of the films we asked for some modifications. We were anxious to avoid anything that was realistic or nasty. It is of course arguable that by doing this we were encouraging people to avoid facing up to the realities of violence by making them laugh when Bond killed an enemy and made a joke about it. However, although I have some sympathy with this argument, I think our category decision was right.[36]

While clearly sensitive to the criticisms of the films, Trevelyan believed that their fantasy aspect had the effect of rendering the violence less realistic. It would seem that, as was his policy, Trevelyan had consulted with the producers to avoid any conflict between them and the BBFC over the content of the Bond films. It is unclear, however, whether the script of *Dr No* had been presented for pre-production scrutiny by the BBFC (a procedure which film-makers were encouraged to follow, though it was not compulsory), or whether the film had been viewed by the censors in a rough cut.[37]

Ian Fleming's own opinion of the first James Bond film, publicly at least, was that it was good, though not as good as the novel. 'Those who've read the book are likely to be disappointed, but those who haven't will find it a wonderful movie,' he told the press. 'Audiences laugh in all the right places.'[38] As with his novels, however, he had to endure the scorn of his wife's *literati* friends who thought it low-brow and vulgar. Evelyn Waugh described the première of *Dr No* as a 'preposterous event' and thought the film itself 'was totally fatuous and tedious, no mystery, not even erotic'.[39]

Dr No opened at the London Pavilion on 5 October 1962 and was soon reported to be attracting large and enthusiastic audiences.[40] By chance, it happened to be showing in cinemas during the period of the Cuban Missile Crisis, which was at its height in the fourth week of

October, and it is quite possible that international events, and the very real danger of nuclear war between the Superpowers, created the sort of atmosphere in which a film about the 'toppling' of American space rockets acquired a sudden topicality. As one recent commentator has observed: '*Dr No* was not the most extravagant of Bond novels, but it was surely the most timely in its concern with a malevolent island despot and secret missile base in the Caribbean.'[41] Coincidentally, it was also in October 1962 that arguably the greatest Cold War spy thriller opened in America. John Frankenheimer's *The Manchurian Candidate* bears some comparison to the Bond movies through its brainwashed assassin, sinister orientals and bruising karate-fight, though Frankenheimer's black-and-white film creates a much more claustrophobic atmosphere of conspiracy and paranoia than any of the Bonds have ever achieved.

By the time *Dr No* was released in America in May 1963, it would no longer have benefited from the topicality which the Cuban Missile Crisis had engendered. Its critical reception was again mixed. Some reviewers admired it as undemanding hokum. Bosley Crowther, the senior film critic of the *New York Times*, thought it a 'lively, amusing picture' which 'is not to be taken seriously as realistic fiction or even art ... It is strictly a tinseled action-thriller, spiked with a mystery of a sort. And, if you are clever, you will see it as a spoof of science-fiction and sex.'[42] But others were less enthusiastic. *Time* magazine was particularly disparaging, considering that the filmic Bond would disappoint fans of the books: 'Is it possible to make a good movie out of a James Bond thriller? Fleming fans probably won't take *No* for an answer.'[43] The American trade press, however, were unanimous that the film was an excellent box-office prospect. And, given that by the time *Dr No* opened in America the second Bond film had already gone into production, the trade journalists knew there would be more to follow. 'There is every reason to suppose, and expect, that Harry Saltzman and Albert R. Broccoli, the producers, have here the first of what could become the most successful series of films of its kind since the happy days of the Charlie Chan pictures and the Thin Man films,' declared the *Motion Picture Herald*, adding that 'the film is said already to have recouped its negative cost in its initial engagements in England and on the Continent alone'.[44]

In the long term, of course, the predictions of success for the series were to be fulfilled, but what is sometimes overlooked is that *Dr No* itself was not especially successful, initially at least, at the American box-office. According to the *Hollywood Reporter*, by 1976 the total domestic

(North American) rentals amounted to $6.4 million, a healthy total in itself, but one which includes several profitable re-releases as well as the all-important first run, and certainly one which pales in comparison with the $15.7 million of foreign rentals.[45] United Artists, Broccoli recalled, 'expressed some doubt that they could sell a picture in the major US cities with "a Limey truck driver playing the lead"'.[46] *Dr No* was not accorded the prestigious, high-profile release that came to characterise later Bond films. It was released in what was traditionally a 'low' season; in New York it played at only a few locations (the Astor Theater on Broadway and several cinemas on the East Side); and across the country it was generally shown in smaller neighbourhood movie theatres and at the drive-ins, where it did reasonable business through good word-of-mouth. Although Bond would eventually conquer America, the films' success in that market did not come about immediately.

It was the British and European success of *Dr No*, therefore, which allowed for the production of a second James Bond film. *From Russia with Love* was budgeted at $1.9 million (twice the cost of *Dr No*). The choice of this particular novel as the second film has often been attributed to the fact that President Kennedy had named it as one of his ten favourite books in an article for *Life* magazine, so therefore the title already had a degree of public recognition and kudos from Kennedy's endorsement. But this seems an unlikely explanation given that the *Life* article had been in March 1961, a full two years before the start of production on *From Russia with Love*, and also before production had started on *Dr No*. A more likely explanation for the decision to make *From Russia with Love* the second film was that it offered the opportunity to exploit Bond's popularity in Europe: it is the most 'European' of all the films in its content and style.

From Russia, with Love is one of Fleming's strongest stories, a richly detailed and tightly plotted narrative of intrigue and suspense. The plot concerns SMERSH's plan to destroy the reputation of the British Secret Service by luring its most celebrated agent to a humiliating death. SMERSH concocts a plan whereby a Russian cypher clerk in Istanbul claims that she has fallen in love with Bond from a photograph, and that she is willing to defect if Bond will personally come to rescue her. The bait for the trap is a brand-new 'Spektor' cypher machine. The first third of the novel details the planning of the trap by SMERSH, whose personnel include chess master Kronsteen, the notorious Rosa Klebb, Head of Operations and Executions, and the chief executioner

Donovan 'Red' Grant. Bond duly travels to Istanbul, where he teams up with Darko Kerim, Head of the Turkish Section. Bond meets the girl, Tatiana Romanova, who steals the cypher machine from the Russian Embassy, and along with Kerim they make their getaway on the Orient Express. Kerim is killed by a Russian security man, while Bond is successfully deceived by Grant, masquerading as British agent 'Captain Nash'. Grant reveals that he is to kill Bond and Tatiana, leaving their bodies together on the train, but Bond gets the better of Grant and kills him. Arriving at the Ritz Hotel in Paris, Bond finds Rosa Klebb waiting, disguised as an old woman. Bond overpowers her and hands her over to the French authorities, though not before she has managed to kick him with a poisoned steel spike concealed in her shoe.

The screenplay of *From Russia with Love* was again a collaborative venture, though Richard Maibaum would seem to have had the greatest input. Maibaum said that another distinguished thriller-writer was involved in the early stages:

> On *From Russia with Love* they had Len Deighton start, and he did about thirty-five pages; but it wasn't going anywhere, so they brought me in. I did the screenplay and got a solo credit on it. Joanna Harwood got an adaptation credit, because she worked some with the director, Terence Young, and made several good suggestions. I was a little put out that she was given an adaptation credit because I didn't think she deserved it, but there are always politics in these things.[47]

While the screenplay followed the general narrative structure of the novel, there were again some changes to the details of Fleming's story. The most important of these, as in *Dr No*, was the substitution of SPECTRE for SMERSH as the principal villains of the piece. Klebb, Kronsteen and Grant all become agents of SPECTRE (Klebb having recently defected), and the character of Blofeld – the head of SPECTRE introduced by Fleming in *Thunderball* – was written in to the story. The lengthy planning sequence in the first third of the book was condensed, though Maibaum added two new scenes. The first of these was an opening where Grant stalks 'Bond' through a 'Renaissance Garden' and kills him ('Bond', of course, turns out to be another man entirely). The second was a scene to introduce Blofeld, which took place on the SPECTRE yacht – described in the screenplay as 'a large, beautiful boat similar to one owned by a well-known Greek shipping tycoon', suggesting an intriguing real-life model for a Bond villain. Maibaum also opened up the last quarter of the story, adding two more action sequences following Bond's fight with Grant on the Orient Express – a helicopter attack and a motorboat chase – before the final confrontation between Bond and Klebb, which now took place in Venice rather than Paris.[48]

Broccoli later nominated *From Russia with Love* as his favourite Bond movie, 'as I feel it was with this film that the Bond formula and style were perfected'.[49] Many Bond aficionados share Broccoli's view, but it seems rather odd that he should have considered the formula and style to have been perfected in *From Russia with Love* when the film is compared to all the others in the series. The second Bond movie, indeed, adopts a different narrative structure and exhibits a different visual style than the films which came before or after it. What this illustrates is that at this early stage of the series the Bond formula was not yet absolutely fixed: variations were possible, other directions could be explored, the generic evolution was not an entirely linear process. *From Russia with Love* is the nearest of all the films to a 'straight' espionage story, which has resulted in it being claimed as the most 'realistic' Bond film within the fan culture. While it is hardly realistic in comparison to, say, *Saturday Night and Sunday Morning*, it certainly eschews the science-fiction trappings that had been foregrounded in *Dr No* in favour of a less spectacular espionage narrative. The set pieces are still there, of course, but the conspiracy in *From Russia with Love* is a relatively small-scale affair by Bond standards, and the threat is directed more against Bond personally than against the whole of civilisation as we know it. Many of the incidents in the film – the secret meetings between spies, the exchange of recognition codes, the train journey, the problem of a border crossing – are standard narrative devices of spy fiction. Unlike the later films, where such generic clichés would be parodied, here they are played entirely straight. *From Russia with Love*, therefore, represents not so much the perfection of the Bond formula as an aberration from it, an excursion into a more traditional sort of spy story which was not to be repeated.

From Russia with Love is the most political of the early Bond movies. Partly this is due to the title, with its specific resonances within the spy genre. Although the film is at great pains to stress that SPECTRE is playing Britain and the Soviet Union off against each other for its own gain, nevertheless it is not as completely detached from the ideological context of the Cold War as *Dr No* had been. For the first two-thirds of the film, Bond believes that he is up against the Russians, and the film draws explicitly upon Cold War tensions. Klebb only has to have Grant kill a Russian agent in order to ignite those tensions ('Who can the Russians suspect but the British? The Cold War in Istanbul will not remain cold very much longer'). The fact that another enemy is behind the conspiracy does not mean that the incidents in the film – a pitched battle between Kerim's gypsy associates and their Bulgar enemies, the assassination by Kerim and Bond of the agent Krilencu, and Bond's raid on the Russian Embassy – are devoid of any political meaning of their own. In locating part of its action in Cold War conflict, *From Russia with Love* again represents a deviation from the usual narrative formula of the films. Not until the 1980s was the Bond series to refer so explicitly to the Cold War as its political background.[50]

For all its political content, however, there is a sense in which *From Russia with Love* is the most old-fashioned of the Bond films. In particular, the Orient Express sequence is a link to the past, its steam locomotive and elegant Pullman carriages harking back to the refined days of continental travel in refined luxury before the advent of the jet airliner. The setting, in fact, is reminiscent of 1930s fiction, from Graham Greene's *Stamboul Train* (1932) and Agatha Christie's *Murder on the Orient Express* (1934) to Hitchcock's film of *The Lady Vanishes* (1938), which, if not actually on the Orient Express, nevertheless is set on a train in a vaguely defined Middle Europe. The Orient Express sequence, moreover, which takes up almost a quarter of the film, exhibits a quaintly dated style of narration with its montages of engine wheels and speeding carriages superimposed over a map which charts the train's progress through the Balkans. The old-fashioned look of the film is also apparent in its visual style, which eschews the technological modernism of *Dr No* and instead foregrounds authentic locations (Istanbul, Venice) and elegant interiors. Penelope Gilliat observed that the chess tournament 'seems to be being played in somewhere like the Doge's Palace in Venice'.[51] It may be significant in this respect that *From Russia with Love* was designed not by Ken Adam, but by Syd Cain, who had been the art director on *Dr No*.

The distinctly old-fashioned look of *From Russia with Love* is one of the factors which makes it stand out among the films, but there are many other reasons why it is so highly regarded by aficionados. Connery looks much more at ease, with the nervous, edgy quality he had shown in *Dr No* replaced by a relaxed, wry performance of subtle wit and style. It was in *From Russia with Love* that his interpretation of Bond really took shape, acquiring the exterior polish to complement the hardness. Altogether it is the most perfectly cast of the films, with Lotte Lenya (Klebb), Robert Shaw (Grant) and Pedro Armendariz (Kerim) all turning in memorable performances. Lenya, widow of composer Kurt Weill and star of G. W. Pabst's film of *The Threepenny Opera* (*Die Dreigroschenoper*, 1931), is the perfect visualisation of Fleming's toad-like lesbian villainess who terrifies Tatiana (Daniela Bianchi) and tries to kick Bond to death with her poisoned shoe-spikes.

From Russia with Love is also the most atmospheric and suspenseful of the films. The pre-title sequence, as 'Bond' is stalked by Grant through moonlit, ornamental gardens, is an eerie, almost dreamlike piece of visual story-telling which Young said he modelled on Alain Resnais's *Last Year at Marienbad* (*L'Année dernière à Marienbad*, 1961): a deliberate reference to European art cinema which establishes the very European style of the film. The sequence in the San Sofia Mosque recalls Hitchcock's habit of using famous landmarks as atmospheric background for important scenes, while the helicopter sequence, as many critics remarked, seemed to have been borrowed directly from *North by Northwest*. On a rather different level, *From Russia with Love* also included the first of the instances of inter-textuality that were to become increasingly common in the series in later years. In this instance it takes the form of a visual in-joke: the escape route from Krilencu's hideout is disguised by a giant billboard advertising the film *Call Me Bwana* – a Bob Hope–Anita Ekberg comedy produced by Broccoli and Saltzman between the first two Bond movies.

The snobbery-with-violence ethos is again much in evidence. Only in a Bond film could a villain give himself away by his choice of red Chianti to accompany grilled sole ('Red wine with fish – that should have told me something,' Bond remarks). In this instance, snobbery is followed immediately by violence as Bond and Grant fight to the death in a confined train compartment. What makes the Bond–Grant confrontation so effective is that in the sequence preceding the actual fight Grant has held the upper hand, holding Bond at gunpoint, while Bond desperately tries to trick Grant into opening his booby-trapped attaché case (primed with a tear-gas canister ready to explode). A long drawn-out suspense sequence is therefore followed by an explosion of violent mayhem as Bond and Grant grapple with each other, exchanging blows, bouncing off the walls and doors of the compartment, a frenzy of movement and noise, before Bond kills Grant with his own garotte. Unlike most movie fight sequences, which were often filmed in long takes, the Bond–Grant struggle is a montage of fast shots, with hand-held cameras being used to cut into the screen space and exaggerated sound effects emphasising the violence. The potential of using sound in this way was not unique to Bond films, however, for in the same year Lindsay Anderson had used non-naturalistic sound to great effect in the rugby-scrum sequences of *This Sporting Life*.

From Russia with Love also furthers the voyeuristic tendencies that had been evident in *Dr No*. Indeed, the act of looking is central to the narration: Bond's first glimpse of Tatiana is the sight of her legs through a periscope hidden beneath the Russian Embassy; Klebb and Grant film Bond and Tatiana making love through a one-way mirror in Bond's hotel suite; and they are again filmed by tourists with a cine-camera at the end of the film. Furthermore, the film explicitly presents the female body as a fetishised erotic object. Thus, the main title sequence (designed in this instance by Robert Brownjohn) presents the cast and credits by superimposing them on the body of a belly-dancer. And one sequence in particular foregrounds the female body as erotic spectacle: the catfight between two gypsy girls, which occurs immediately prior to the Bulgars' attack on the gypsy camp. The two combatants, both skimpily dressed (one in green, the other in red – the visuals again emphasise primary colours), claw and scratch viciously at each other, while Bond, Kerim and the other gypsies sit and watch. The girl-fight is irrelevant to the main narrative; the purpose it serves is entirely for the erotic gratification of the spectators (both the characters in the film who are watching and the spectator in the cinema).

From Russia with Love was released in Britain in October 1963 to immediate popular acclaim. Whereas *Dr No* had opened at the London Pavilion, the second Bond movie was premièred at the Rank Organisation's flagship cinema, the Odeon, Leicester Square, where it broke the house record by taking £14,528 in its first week. 'The Most Sensational Business in the History of the Film Industry', trumpeted *Kine Weekly*.[52] It went on to become not only the biggest box-office attraction of the year in Britain, beating *Tom Jones* and *The Great Escape*, but also the highest-grossing film hitherto released in the country. The producers were now sufficiently confident of their franchise that the end credits of *From Russia with Love* could declare: 'The End ... Not Quite the End.

James Bond will return in the next Ian Fleming thriller, *Goldfinger*.' Thus
began the tradition of naming the next film at the end of the current
one – and, moreover, the process whereby Broccoli and Saltzman began
planning for the long-term future of the Bond series.

The critics lined up much as they had for *Dr No*. The trade and
popular press were ecstatic, and their enthusiasm was again shared by
several of the more middle-brow critics. John Coleman of the *New
Statesman* liked the cinematic Bond because he thought it downplayed
the violence of the books and added a sense of humour:

> *From Russia with Love* is the new James Bond instalment and hilari-
> ously maintains the disinfecting [*sic*], larky tone of its predecessor.
> Two gypsy girls scrap (rather tamely), poisoned knives sprout from
> the toes of villains' boots, and a gun is ominously aimed at Bond's
> privates by Robert Shaw's assassin – 'homicidal maniac, splendid
> material', as the principal of a murder college points out. These
> screen doings-over of the Fleming books certainly have their small
> hints of real nastiness. But the interesting thing is that what has
> forcibly to become explicit on the screen is a hundred times milder
> than the horrible imaginings stimulated by Mr Fleming's elliptic
> pages: better yet it tends to come out funny. Terence Young and
> his screenwriter, Richard Maibaum, give Bond some nice laconic
> cracks to round off the surreal events of his working day. A bad
> man crawls out between Ekberg's lips on a giant hoarding and is
> picked off through telescopic sights. 'She should have kept her
> mouth shut,' drawls Bond. Mr Young's direction is still hazy when
> it comes to simple exposition, and Lotte Lenya's impersonation
> of evil old Rosa Klebb disappoints, but a genuine filmic sense
> animates the fantasy – from a blinding pre-credit sequence in the
> grounds of that school for murder on to the final, literal flare-up.
> There's even a death-dealing helicopter – and thank you, Hitch-
> cock, Losey, and all who flew in her before.[53]

Coleman, therefore, acknowledged the debt which the film owed to
others, while emphasising its filmic and visual qualities and recognising
it for the 'fantasy' it was.

Other critics again questioned the morality of Bond. 'We tend to
get the movie heroes we deserve, and I suppose nowadays that means
James Bond,' said Thomas Wiseman. 'He is very much a figment of
our times, the arch exponent of pop fascism ("licensed to kill"), the

patriot-libertine, always ready to seduce a pretty spy for his country.'[54] And Nina Hibbin thought the film was 'sick', again detecting unpleasant undertones in that 'although the film appears to be sending up the cloak-and-dagger tradition, in reality (along with its predecessor *Dr No*) it is building up a tradition that is far more vicious'.[55]

The American release of *From Russia with Love* again followed on some six months after it had been shown in Britain. North American rentals of $9.9 million were an improvement on its predecessor, helped by a slightly wider release, though they were still only half the $19.5 million of foreign rentals (as a rule of thumb most movies make roughly the same amount of money in the North American market as in the rest of the world). Interestingly, the American critics were divided over the balance between the straight thriller and comic elements of the film. The *Esquire* critic was disappointed: 'A comedown after *Dr No*, whose brisk parody here slackens into a queasy compromise with the real thing that tries to have it both ways and so fails to have it either way.'[56] But Hollis Alpert in the *Saturday Review* suggested that 'Terence Young ... has now learned how to balance the thriller and the spoof qualities about equally, and the blend results in a superior kind of entertainment'.[57]

Whether audiences accepted it as a straight thriller or regarded it as a comedy is impossible to say, but what is certain is that *From Russia with Love* was sufficiently successful in the international market for United Artists to put up a budget for the next film which exceeded the combined cost of the previous two. It seems reasonable to suggest that, just as the choice of *From Russia with Love* as the second film had probably been made to consolidate Bond's popularity in Europe, so the choice of *Goldfinger* for the third film represented a strategy whereby the producers hoped to establish Bond in the American market. The setting of *Goldfinger* is predominantly American, and the conspiracy is directed against America.

Goldfinger was the seventh Bond novel, coming after *Dr No*, and maintains that book's trend towards fantastic and highly improbable plots. Like *Dr No*, what at first appears to be a relatively trivial matter turns out to be a grandiose criminal conspiracy. Bond first encounters Auric Goldfinger by chance in Miami, where he stops over while returning from an assignment in Mexico, and exposes him for cheating at cards. Back in London, Bond is assigned by M to investigate Goldfinger, a gold broker by trade, whom the Bank of England suspects of smuggling gold bullion, and whom M suspects of being the 'foreign banker' of SMERSH. It transpires that Goldfinger's ambitions extend far beyond smuggling: backed by the Russians, he plans to rob the US gold bullion depository at Fort Knox, having disabled the military defences by poisoning the local water supply. Bond is captured by Goldfinger but manages to leak details of the plan to the authorities, who ambush Goldfinger's train when it arrives at Fort Knox. It is one of the most implausible of Fleming's plots – literal-minded critics pointed out that the sheer weight of gold bullion involved would make the plan impossible from the start – but this is partly mediated by the detailed description of small details and incidents, particularly the celebrated high-stakes round of golf during which Bond successfully out-cheats Goldfinger.

Richard Maibaum was once again employed to write the screenplay, though this time he had a different collaborator. Paul Dehn was the film critic of the *News Chronicle* who also worked occasionally as a screenwriter, his credits including the Boulting Brothers' *Seven Days to Noon* (1950) – for which he jointly won an Academy Award – and, later, two film adaptations of John le Carré novels, *The Spy Who Came in from the Cold* (1965) and *The Deadly Affair* (1966). According to Maibaum: 'On *Goldfinger* I did a first draft. Harry Saltzman didn't like it, and he brought in Paul Dehn, a good writer, to revise. Then Sean Connery didn't like the revisions, and I came back to do the final screenplay. That was the first time that happened: where I was followed by someone and then called back to finish up.'[58]

There was also to be a different director. Terence Young, who started pre-production work, decided instead to direct *The Amorous Adventures of Moll Flanders* (1965), a bawdy costume romp in the mould of *Tom Jones*. Guy Hamilton, who had originally been offered *Dr No*, took the director's chair. 'I'd enjoyed the previous two films, but felt there was a real danger of Bond becoming Superman; consequently there would be no suspense in whatever predicaments were dreamt up for him,' Hamilton said later. 'So we concentrated on the villains; Bond is only as good as his villains.'[59]

For many aficionados, *Goldfinger* is the best of the Bond films. John Brosnan, for example, writes:

> *Goldfinger* represents the peak of the series. It is the most perfectly realized of all the films ... It moves at a fast and furious pace,

but the plot holds together logically enough (more logically than the book) and is a perfect blend of the real and the fantastic. It is full of sly humor but the humor doesn't detract from the excitement as it does in the more recent Bonds. It is also the most visually attractive of the films; the central theme of gold seems to pervade every scene, giving it a distinctive motif that the other films have lacked.[60]

Goldfinger again illustrates that the generic development of the Bond series was not a linear process. It is closer to *Dr No* than *From Russia with Love* in that it foregrounds the science-fiction and technological trappings of the plot and marks a return to a grand conspiracy which Bond foils at the last possible moment. It is, however, slicker and more polished than *Dr No* – made possible by a larger budget, not to mention the increasing confidence of the film-makers with their formula – and also contains more humour.

As with the two preceding films, *Goldfinger* follows the basic storyline of the novel but makes some significant changes in the detail. One of these can be read as a direct response to some of the criticisms made of the novel. Bond, having overheard Goldfinger (Gert Frobe) briefing the American gangsters whom he has lured into collaborating with him, and who believe that his intention is to 'knock off' Fort Knox, makes the same point that several critics had of the novel. 'I've worked out a few statistics of my own,' Bond remarks. 'Fifteen billion dollars in gold bullion weighs ten thousand five hundred tons. Sixty men would take twelve days to load it on to two hundred trucks.' However, it is then revealed that Goldfinger's plan is not to rob Fort Knox, but rather to explode an 'atomic device' inside it in order to contaminate the bullion supply of the United States. The film therefore not only addressed the criticisms made of Fleming's original story, but it also allowed a more exciting finale in which Bond has to race against time to defuse the bomb. A similar plot device had been used in *Seven Days to Noon*, in which a mad scientist threatens to blow up London.

Another significant change is that whereas in the novel Goldfinger was a member of SMERSH, in the film his 'Operation Grand Slam' is backed by Communist China. The character of Mr Ling (Burt Kwouk) is explicitly referred to as a 'Red Chinese agent', and it is his government which has provided Goldfinger with the atomic bomb. The detonation of the bomb inside Fort Knox therefore has a dual purpose. As Bond observes: 'They get what they want – economic chaos in the West – and the value of your gold increases many times.' The substitution of Red China for the Soviet Union as the 'enemy' behind Goldfinger is intriguing. On one level, it continues the narrative strategy of detaching the Bond films from the context of the Cold War (defined in this sense as the political and diplomatic conflict between the Western powers and the Soviet bloc, not the People's Republic of China). On another level, it reflects growing fears in the West over the growth of Chinese military strength. It was entirely coincidental that in October 1964, a month after *Goldfinger*'s British release and shortly before its American release, China exploded its first atomic bomb; but it is reasonable to assume that the nuclear threat posed in *Goldfinger* would have a certain topicality, particularly in America, whose security and economic stability was threatened.

What is most remarkable about *Goldfinger* is that, for a Bond film at least, there is relatively little conventional action in it. There is the pre-title sequence, in which Bond blows up a semi-military installation somewhere in Latin America and has a punch-up with a heavy in his hotel room which culminates in the assailant being electrocuted in a bath ('Shocking, positively shocking,' Bond observes wryly). There is a car chase around Goldfinger's Swiss factory; a brief struggle between Bond and one of Goldfinger's Korean guards as Bond escapes (temporarily) from his imprisonment at Goldfinger's Kentucky stud farm; and a light-hearted tussle between Bond and Goldfinger's accomplice Pussy Galore (Honor Blackman), which really constitutes the foreplay to Bond's seduction of her. Other than that, it is not until the raid on Fort Knox, and Bond's fight with Goldfinger's manservant Oddjob (Harold Sakata), that the film sustains an extended action sequence of the sort which had proliferated in *From Russia with Love*.

However, the relative dearth of action is compensated for by greater visual excess. Hamilton's direction is less abrupt than Young's, and the camera moves around more freely. There are more extravagant touches, and a tendency towards bizarre visual jokes: in the first shot a seagull bobbing on the water turns out to be a disguise fixed to Bond's head, while shortly afterwards he removes his wetsuit to reveal an impossibly dry, immaculate white tuxedo underneath, nonchalantly placing a red carnation in the buttonhole. As Brosnan observes, the visual style of the film emphasises the colour gold. The main titles (again designed by Robert Brownjohn) are presented around the body of a golden girl, on which images from the film are projected as the title song is belted out, with customary gusto, by Shirley Bassey. This anticipates a scene shortly later in the film where Bond, having seduced Goldfinger's assistant Jill Masterson, is knocked unconscious and awakes to find her laying face down on the bed, dead, covered in gold paint. The scene is celebrated within the Bond fan culture as one which ensured actress Shirley Eaton her moment of screen immortality, but it has disturbing undertones of necrophilia: Bond, and the spectator, are invited to gaze at the near-naked and very dead body of the girl, which nevertheless is presented as a sort of erotic spectacle through the fetishistic covering of gold paint. It is a scene which stands out in what, otherwise, is a more light-hearted and humorous film than its two predecessors.[61]

Goldfinger foregrounds technology and gadgetry to a greater extent than even *Dr No*, indicating the direction which the series was to take thereafter. The publicity discourse emphasised the technological modernity of the film. An official press release made much of the industrial laser which Goldfinger employs, first to threaten Bond and later to effect his entry into Fort Knox, declaring that it was 'a scientific device so new that only a minority of the general public have even heard of it' and that its use in the film 'is sure to give the laser its greatest international publicity as a scientific development of great power and worth in the modern world'.[62] At one point Bond finds himself spread-eagled beneath the laser which is burning its way through a table of solid gold. The scene plays, obviously, on male castration anxiety as the beam slowly creeps up between Bond's legs. But it also provides a modern, up-to-date variation on an old cliché. In the novel Bond had been threatened by a circular saw, a situation familiar from the old cliff-hanger serial melodramas. Maibaum explained why this was changed for the film: 'Vividly depicted on the screen, however, we were sure audiences would find the episode old-fashioned, hackneyed and ridiculous. What to do? We substituted an industrial laser beam, a development as fresh as tomorrow, for the antiquated circular saw.'[63] However, not all commentators approved of the change, which was seen by some as an unnecessary display of technology for its own sake rather than serving a logical narrative purpose. G. B. Zorzoli, for example, wrote that whereas the circular saw of the novel was 'sufficiently simple and efficacious within the grasp of everyone', in the film 'a laser is employed in an entirely gratuitous exhibition'.[64]

The other gadget that played an important role in *Goldfinger* was

Bond's modified Aston Martin DB5. Unlike some of the later films, where gadgets are used for comic effect, in *Goldfinger* the car still serves a logical narrative purpose: Bond uses its radar to tail Goldfinger across Switzerland and employs its other devices during the chase around Goldfinger's factory. Suspense arises from the audience knowing the gadgets the car is equipped with and waiting for the moment when Bond will use them, particularly in the case of the ejector seat; there are several teasing shots of Bond's hand on the gear lever before he finally presses the button inside and ejects his unwanted passenger through the roof. The car, as Vittorio Bonicelli argued, represents a particular type of fantasy for the male spectator:

> The best invention of the film is the automobile: its destructive power belongs to the realm of dreams. The medium of the auto-mobile, the metropolitan man who secretes at the wheel, hour by hour, his daily neurotic moods and then relieves himself in nightmares thronged with mechanical riches finds in *Goldfinger* the ideal instrument for his fantastic vendetta. This car wields, in fact, supreme power upon the road: the destruction at will of all other vehicles; the sadism (or the sado-masochism?) of exercising itself upon [the] bodywork and tyres of its enemies.[65]

The destructive power of the gadgets at Bond's disposal was to become an ever-more central aspect of the films, though in *Goldfinger* the car does not quite have the 'supreme power' which Bonicelli attributes to it, as the chase finishes with Bond crashing and being captured.

It was with *Goldfinger* that Ken Adam's designs for the films really came into their own. His interior of Fort Knox is a visual *tour de force*: rejecting any notion of authenticity (gold is so heavy that it can only be stored in small piles), Adam created a massive multi-storey set in which gold ingots are stacked forty feet high behind chrome bars. The gleaming, highly polished set exhibits the modernist aesthetic of the Bond visual style to perfection, emphasising once again the fantasy world of Bond's adventures. It also creates a marvellous arena for the fight between Bond and Oddjob. Unlike the Bond/Grant confrontation, which took place in a confined setting, the Bond/Oddjob fight utilises all the space available as the combatants circle around each other, and Bond is thrown across the smooth metal floor before electrocuting his opponent.

The representation of women in *Goldfinger* is again indicative of the ideological processes of popular cinema. Janet Thumim provides a useful summary of the very limited scope which the film allows for its female characters:

> In line with other films popular at the sixties box office there are relatively few women to be seen on the screen in *Goldfinger* (after the initial pan around the borders of the Miami swimming pool). Even fewer have any significant narrative function ... Tilly, Jill and Pussy follow each other as 'partners' to the central male character, James Bond. But what is interesting ... is the other narrative traits which these three women have in common. The actions of all three are motivated by a very limited view of self interest and are highly susceptible to male influence, and they are all suggested to be incompetent in at least one narratively crucial skill. Jill is working for Goldfinger because, as she tells Bond, 'he pays me' but is easily persuaded by Bond to change sides. Tilly is trying to avenge her sister's death but her incompetence with a gun leads to Bond's capture and her own death. Pussy is supposed to be a competent pilot and a trustworthy accomplice to Goldfinger, yet it is Bond who takes over at the end of the film when she panics as the punctured plane loses altitude.[66]

In fact, Tilly Masterson does not become a sexual partner for Bond, whereas both Jill Masterson and Pussy Galore do. This is explicable in terms of the ideological role which women play in the Bond narrative: Jill and Pussy both work for Goldfinger, and Bond needs to seduce them in order to 'reposition' them on the side of right, whereas in Tilly's case there is no need to do so as she has already sided against Goldfinger.

Thumim also suggests that with Pussy Galore's Flying Circus – the pulchritudinous female pilots who spray nerve gas over Fort Knox – 'the implication of lesbianism is thrown in for good measure'. 'It is curious,' she continues, 'that at a time when legal attitudes towards male homosexuality were finally being liberalised there should be this (admittedly minor) "backlash" against female homosexuality.' Yet the film is not so much of a 'backlash' against lesbianism as the novel, in which Fleming's overt heterosexism had been writ large. Both Tilly and Pussy were lesbians in the novel; the former remained resistant to Bond and was killed, the latter succumbed to him and survived. For the film all references to Tilly's lesbianism have disappeared, and there is only the briefest hint of it with Pussy ('You can skip the charm,' she tells Bond. 'I'm immune'). As played by Honor Blackman, there is no denying that Pussy Galore has more to offer as a character than the bland personalities of the usual Bond starlets. Blackman's performance owes much to her already established persona as the leather-clad judo expert Cathy Gale in *The Avengers*, often claimed as the first 'feminist' heroine on television. Even so, Graham Rye's claim that 'Pussy Galore was a reflection of the more liberated and self-sufficient women of the Sixties' is rather overstating the case.[67]

The release of *Goldfinger* in Britain was marked by an outbreak of 'Bondmania' on a massive scale. When it premièred at the Odeon, Leicester Square, on 17 September 1964, there was nearly a riot outside the cinema. One trade columnist who attended the première wrote: 'Never in 25 years of première-going have I experienced anything like it; rounds of applause, hoots of good-natured laughter.'[68] The film broke the house record for the Odeon, Leicester Square (previously set by *From Russia with Love*), taking £32,874 in its first fortnight, and went on to become the highest-grossing film released in Britain. Such was the public's appetite for Bond that a re-release of *Dr No* at the same time also proved hugely popular.

Critics responded to the enormous popularity of the Bond films in different ways. Nina Hibbin was still the most vociferous anti-Bond critic, and she launched a broadside against *Goldfinger* that was even more vitriolic than her reaction to the previous two:

> The cult of James Bondism is a vicious one, a symptomatic sickness of the age, and the latest in the film series is well in the mould of its predecessors, *Dr No* and *From Russia with Love*. Bondists are expected to shriek with laughter even before the first victim is kicked in the guts or battered against a wall. They must gurgle with relish whenever their nonchalant hero, created by the late Ian Fleming, rolls a girl he's hardly met and certainly hates into the nearest bed. Above all, they must be ready (as soon as they are given the magical wisecrack signal) to roll in the aisles as a man is electrocuted and disintegrates in a flame-coloured flash. ...
>
> But this is all one vast, gigantic confidence trick to blind the audience to what is going on underneath. The constantly lurking viciousness, and the glamorisation of violence – they are real enough. So, too, are the carefully timed peaks of titillation and the

skilfully contrived sensationalism – they're real, too. The racialism (inscrutably smiling villains of Oriental countenance), the cold-war implications of the plot – they are not in the film for a joke. All this is the underlying menace of the film which gives the laughter a dangerous and sinister ring.[69]

Hibbin's attack was directed as much against the fans who could laugh along with Bond as it was at the film itself, exhibiting a characteristic contempt for the audiences whom she believed had been taken in by the subterfuge of the film.

Hibbin's criticisms were rejected by Penelope Houston, the editor of *Sight and Sound*, who thought that *Goldfinger* 'perfects the formula' and 'assumes a mood of good-humoured complicity with the audience' that was the key to its popular appeal. Houston's response demonstrates how the critical establishment, as represented by the most prominent intellectual film journal of the time, was coming to realise that the enormous success of the Bond movies required that they should be taken, if not altogether seriously, then at least as significant and prominent artefacts of popular culture. Typically, for a serious critic used to a diet of European art cinema, Houston found it necessary to try to compare the Bond films, however tangentially, to other, preferred styles of film-making, and she found a parallel for their light-hearted playing with filmic conventions in the French *Nouvelle Vague*: 'There is an assumption – which you find, at quite the other end of the spectrum, in the Godard films – that we all know the clichés and can have a little fun with them.' The reason for the success of the Bond films, she argued, was that they so perfectly caught the mood of the times. For the same reason, she believed, the moment of the films would soon pass:

> In a few years the films will seem dated by their assumptions as much as by the lines of their cars, or by Pussy Galore's extravagantly leathery wardrobe. At the moment, however, and for the moment, it's all sufficiently here: 'the brassy, swinging, ungallant taste of the Sixties', to quote Penelope Gilliat. Ian Fleming's Bond could still be considered – was in fact considered by Mr Bergonzi – in terms of the ethics of Richard Hannay. The screen's Bond is at once the last of the clubland buccaneers and the first of the joke supermen. The transformation has earned the film-makers their place in the annals of popular taste. One must give the sociologists best and admit that *Goldfinger* really is rather a symbolic film.[70]

Houston's article marks one of the first serious attempts to place the Bond films in their social and cultural context, relating them to the attitudes and fashions of the early 1960s, though her belief that they would quickly become out of date was less prescient. As so often, sociological reasons are advanced for the success of popular entertainments, suggesting that the extraordinary degree of their success must be due to something more than just the films themselves, that it is somehow rooted in the *Zeitgeist*, the mood of the times which the films reflect. Whether this simply was the case, or whether, as has been argued, the impact of the early Bond movies was due in some measure to more long-term developments in the British film industry and film culture as a whole, there is no denying that by 1964 the phenomenon of 'Bondmania' had well and truly arrived.

3

Bondmania: *Thunderball, Casino Royale, You Only Live Twice, On Her Majesty's Secret Service*

The first three James Bond films introduced, developed and refined the generic formula of the series. If, as so many commentators have suggested, *Goldfinger* is the archetypal Bond film in terms of its narrative structure and balance of thriller, science-fiction and comedy elements, then the generic formula had already achieved its most perfect form. 'Between them, the first three movies had more or less covered all the variations that were possible,' observes John Brosnan; 'after *Goldfinger*, the producers were faced with the problem of what direction to take.'[1] The direction which the official series was to take was defined over the course of the next three films: *Thunderball* (dir. Terence Young, 1965), *You Only Live Twice* (dir. Lewis Gilbert, 1967) and *On Her Majesty's Secret Service* (dir. Peter Hunt, 1969). These three films belong together as a group in much the same way that *Dr No, From Russia with Love* and *Goldfinger* are a group. Collectively, they represent the trend towards longer running times, bigger budgets and ever more spectacular set pieces which have become a *sine qua non* of the Bond series. Whereas the first three films had been reasonably tight and well-structured narratives, the second three were longer, looser and more episodic. In production terms, while the first three films had been released at annual intervals, from *Thunderball* onwards the Bond series settled into a long-term release pattern whereby a new film would appear at roughly two-yearly intervals. At a time when imitations of the Bond films proliferated – and the mid-1960s were the heyday of gimmicky spy extravaganzas which sought, with varying degrees of success, to cash in on the popularity of 007, including a spoof version of *Casino Royale* in 1967 – the Bond producers sought to differentiate the genuine article by making it ever more spectacular and expensive, and by extending the time between each film, thus ensuring that the audience was ready and waiting each time a new Bond film was released.

The mid-1960s was the time when 'Bondmania' was at its height. On one level this is exemplified by the increasing box-office success of the films. *Goldfinger* far surpassed the box-office figures of the first two films, taking some $23 million in North America and $26.6 million in the rest of the world: its total worldwide rentals of over $49 million were almost as much as the combined rentals of *Dr No* and *From Russia with Love*. These figures were quickly surpassed, however, by *Thunderball*, which achieved domestic rentals of $28.6 million and foreign rentals of $27.8 million: its total worldwide rentals of over $56 million were the most for any Bond film until *The Spy Who Loved Me* in 1977. Given the effect of inflation and increased ticket prices since 1965, however, *Thunderball* is probably the most successful Bond film in real terms. Following the high point of *Thunderball*, the next two films showed evidence of a falling-off in Bond's box-office appeal. Even so, the $44 million worldwide rentals of *You Only Live Twice* were still extremely good at a time when more and more Hollywood movies were failing to recoup their production costs. It was not until *On Her Majesty's Secret Service* that a Bond movie could be said not to have lived up to box-office expectations: its worldwide rentals of $24 million were disappointingly low, less than *From Russia with Love* though still more than *Dr No*.[2]

It was the release of *Goldfinger* that marked the emergence of 'Bondmania' as a truly international phenomenon. Unlike the first two films, which had been released in smaller movie theatres and drive-ins across the United States, *Goldfinger* was chosen by United Artists as its major Christmas release. It opened on 22 December and premièred in prestigious locations, such as Grauman's Chinese Theatre in Hollywood, where, according to one commentator, 'lines of eager ticket buyers formed for blocks on opening day and afterward, this enthusiastic reception being duplicated all over the country'.[3] 'The success of *Gold-finger* was such', wrote another, 'that in one cinema in New York one showing followed another day and night, and the management imposed an interval only to sweep away from the auditorium the remains of popcorn which had reached a depth of several inches.'[4] *Goldfinger* was the film which firmly established Bond in America – and in other markets which had hitherto been resistant. In France, for example, where the Bond cult had not really taken off as it had elsewhere in Western Europe, it was *Goldfinger* which made the breakthrough. '*Goldfinger* has hit Paris like a thunderbolt,' the British press reported early in 1965. 'Only two weeks after this latest James Bond epic was launched here it is already creating cinematic history.'[5] The film broke box-office records at Parisian cinemas, and there were reports of thousands of cinema-goers queueing in the 'biting cold' and being prepared to sit in the aisles to see it. Nor was the Bond cult confined to North America and Europe. 'There seems to be no geographical limit to the appeal of sex, violence and snobbery with which Fleming endowed his British secret agent,' *Time* magazine declared in June 1965, reporting that in Tokyo 'the queue for *Goldfinger* stretches half a mile', while in Beirut 'even Goldfinger's hat-hurling bodyguard, Oddjob, has become a minor hero'.[6]

The spectacular box-office returns of the Bond films in the mid-1960s were made possible, to some degree, by the release strategy adopted by United Artists and Eon Productions. An unusually large number of prints were used worldwide – some 1,100 in the case of *Goldfinger*[7] – so that the film could be seen as widely and as quickly as possible. This practice is now commonplace for Hollywood block-busters: the saturation of thousands of screens on the all-important opening weekend, which is regarded in the industry as the make-or-break time as to whether or not a movie is going to be a hit. This strategy means that a film maximises the effectiveness of pre-release publicity, benefits from word-of-mouth, and also reduces the interest payable on the money invested in the film by accelerating the rate of box-office returns. *Thunderball*, for example, earned back its production and distribution costs after only seven weeks in the North American market. It surpassed *Goldfinger*, which was 'withdrawn from domestic release to make way for *Thunderball*', despite being shown in fewer movie theatres. 'There are several reasons for the bigger, faster *Thunderball* grosses, the most obvious being that Agent 007's popularity has continued to build,' remarked Vincent Canby in the *New York Times*. 'Also, because of the success of the earlier films, the distributor has been able to get a larger share of the receipts and the theaters, in turn, have in many cases been charging higher admission prices.'[8]

However, the box-office success of the Bond films in the 1960s tells only part of the story. 'Bondmania' was not confined to the reception of the films themselves; it was a phenomenon which permeated into the wider realms of popular culture more generally. *Time* observed that 'James Bond has developed into the biggest mass-cult hero of the decade'.[9] In Italy, where Bond was known colloquially as 'Mr Kiss Kiss Bang Bang', the youth magazine *Ciao Amici* described him as 'the most popular personality of 1965'.[10] Bond's penetration of other areas of cultural production was evident at many levels: *Playboy* began running photo-spreads of Bond starlets; 'golden girl' Shirley Eaton appeared on the cover of *Life* magazine in September 1964; the title song of *Goldfinger* performed by Shirley Bassey reached number eight in the US singles charts, and the soundtrack LP went to number one; toy manufacturers produced James Bond toys; the Galeries Lafayette in Paris opened a 'James Bond Boutique' selling 007 cufflinks and shirts; and an Australian lingerie manufacturer even launched a range of women's underwear with the slogan 'Become fit for James Bond'. Furthermore, sales of the Bond novels reached their peak in the mid-1960s, as Pan produced paperback tie-ins with images from the films on the covers, though, as Bennett and Woollacott have shown, 'the effect of the films in this period was to revivify the market for the Bond novels *as a whole*. It was as an *integrated set*, rather than as individual titles, that the Bond novels sold over this period.'[11] In France, meanwhile, the publishers Plon sold 480,000 copies of the first four novels in French translation in three months during the summer of 1964, while *Dr No* was serialised in *France-Soir*.[12]

How is the phenomenon of 'Bondmania' to be explained? Various reasons have been advanced to account for the enormous popularity of the Bond films, and for the widespread currency of the figure of Bond as a popular cultural icon, at this time. Given the quite extraordinary success of the films, it seems rather too simplistic to suggest, as the trade press did, merely that they exhibited in full measure the sort of entertainment value that cinema-goers wanted. This may be true, but it is hardly adequate as an explanation. In order to account for the outbreak of 'Bondmania', it is necessary to consider the films, and particularly the character of Bond as he was portrayed therein, in the wider context of the society and culture of the 1960s. For, just as Ian Fleming's Bond was very much a product of the social and political conditions of Britain in the 1950s, so the cinematic Bond was a product of the social and political conditions of the 1960s.

On one level, the Bond films need to be seen within the context of the cultural regeneration which many commentators identified as taking place in Britain in the mid-1960s. This is most frequently expressed through the label of 'Swinging London', from the title of an article in *Time* in April 1966, though, as Arthur Marwick shows, similar views were also being expressed in a range of French and Italian magazines at the same time.[13] There was a perception that British society had suddenly thrown off its shackles and that, led by the newly emergent youth cultures, a more hedonistic, liberated, 'swinging' spirit had taken its place. Historians have since questioned whether this was the case – processes of change were gradual and on-going, while for many people the 1960s did not bring about the new freedoms they were popularly supposed to have done – but what is important in considering the impact of the Bond movies is the perception by contemporaries that Britain had become a more open, liberal, even permissive society. One sign of the 'new' Britain was the Labour government of Harold Wilson, elected in 1964 after a generation of Conservative rule, which gave the impression of being modern and meritocratic rather than old-fashioned and class-bound. But a more significant manifestation of different attitudes and behaviour was to be found in the new international prestige enjoyed by British popular culture. It was a popular culture led by pop music, and pre-eminently by The Beatles, but it also included new trends in fashion (especially the mini-skirt and the designs of Mary Quant), a new generation of attractive and sexy film stars with international appeal (Sean Connery, Michael Caine, Julie Christie, Terence Stamp), and films which featured hedonistic and sexually liberated characters such as *Tom Jones* (1963), *Darling* (1965) and, of course, James Bond. The Bond films need to be seen, therefore, as one component of a new British popular culture in the 1960s which emphasised youth, sex appeal and modernity. This line of argument is taken further by Bennett and Woollacott:

> More particularly, in the context of 'swinging Britain', Bond provided a mythic encapsulation of the then prominent ideological themes of classlessness and modernity, a key cultural marker of

the claim that Britain had escaped the blinkered, class-bound perspectives of its traditional ruling elites and was in the process of being thoroughly modernised as a result of the implementation of a new, meritocratic style of cultural and political leadership, middle class and professional, rather than aristocratic and amateur.[14]

This is, of course, an interpretation which is based entirely on the Bond films, illustrating that the screen Bond had a different cultural meaning and significance to Ian Fleming's Bond.

In certain other respects, too, the Bond films reflected, mediated and even defined some of the distinguishing characteristics of the 'cultural revolution' of the 1960s.[15] In the first place, it was a decade in which technology and technological progress came to the fore. In America, Kennedy had used the metaphor of the 'new frontier' to describe any kind of technological innovation, particularly in respect of the expansion into space, while in Britain Wilson spoke of 'the white heat of science and technology'. The Bond films, from *Goldfinger* onwards, contributed to the obsession with technology by fetishising it. This aspect of the films was commented upon by numerous critics, including Richard Mallet of *Punch*, who pointed out how smoothly everything always worked on the screen:

> Watching the new James Bond film, *Goldfinger*, one can't help feeling that this time the gadgets have really taken over. Particularly in the second half of the film, there seems to be hardly a scene that does not involve the operation of some beautifully made, photogenic mechanical or electronic device. (Always, by the way, the *smooth* operation; a bit of grit in the works now and then would radically alter the course of the story).[16]

Mallet suggested that 'the gadgets, like everything else, are used above all to arouse laughter'. But in fact much of the technology displayed on the screen was authentic: the laser in *Goldfinger*, the Bell jet-pack and underwater camera in *Thunderball*, the autogiro and rocket-firing guns in *You Only Live Twice*, were all real technological innovations.

The 1960s is also perceived as the decade of 'permissiveness', which Marwick defines as 'a general sexual liberation, entailing striking changes in public and private morals and ... a new frankness, openness, and indeed honesty in personal relations and modes of expression'.[17] This openness and honesty concerning sexual relationships had been evident in Fleming's novels in the 1950s, and to some extent the films were actually rather more coy in their presentation of sex. There is, for example, no full nudity in the Bond movies. 'Nudity would destroy Bond's career,' Broccoli once observed. 'His image must be clean cut. We can't risk offending his massive family audience in any way.'[18] That having been said, Bond's various sexual encounters are illustrated in the films, albeit with due restraint, and on average he has more girlfriends per film than he did in the books. Bond is the perfect hero for the permissive society: hedonistic, sexually active, progressing from one girl to the next and treating them with the same casual indifference he shows towards the gadgets supplied to him by Q. The only occasion on which Bond has a more serious and romantic relationship is in *On Her Majesty's Secret Service*, wherein he marries the heroine – thus proving that even the most committed bachelor would make an exception for Diana Rigg.

The representation of women in the Bond films has been the subject of some debate. On the one hand, the films have been criticised for being overtly sexist, for presenting women as little more than disposable playthings for the dominant male hero. Certainly in the films of the 1960s it is hard to disagree with this charge. Most of the women's roles are fairly two-dimensional, with the Bond girls generally having a less active role in the narrative, and less interesting character traits, than they had in Fleming's original stories. Women are commodities, to be consumed by Bond and then discarded, often meeting grisly ends. As for the Bond starlets themselves, acting ability was an optional extra. With the exceptions of Honor Blackman and Diana Rigg, who both had established acting careers outside the Bond series, none of the Bond girls of the 1960s had much to offer beyond their obviously pulchritudinous charms, and, other than Ursula Andress, none of them achieved lasting stardom after their stint in 'Bondage'. The Bond starlets represented a *Playboy* male-fantasy image of female sexuality: well-scrubbed, big-breasted, long-haired and sexually available. The criteria for casting them would appear to have been their physical attributes: a story persists that Julie Christie was turned down for the role of Domino in *Thunderball* because the producers thought her breasts were too small.

On the other hand, the publicity discourse around the Bond girls suggested they were modern, liberated, independent women. Claudine Auger, a former Miss France who was preferred to Julie Christie for

Domino in *Thunderball*, considered that her character was 'the ultimate in modern, emancipated woman'. Of the Bond girls, she said: 'They can live without a man doing everything for them because they are independent. They like to decide their future destinies for themselves. They are highly sexual – but only with men worth their loving. They are free, you see, completely free. I may be married, but I feel I am like this. I am free. I always have been. I always will be.'[19]

Terence Young put forward a similar view: 'They are women of the nuclear age, freer and able to make love when they want to without worrying about it.'[20] Clearly this is a rather limited view of what constitutes freedom for women. It can be argued, indeed, that it represents a very male-oriented view of female behaviour in so far as women are free only in the sense of being able to have sex without having to get married or make a long-term commitment, which is presumably what many men wanted of them anyway. In this sense, the Bond films of the 1960s reflect the greater sexual freedom experienced by women during the decade but also embody an inherent contradiction of that freedom. As Marwick asks, 'was this sexual liberation for women, or simply enhanced liberation for men, a grand occasion for the even more ruthless sexual exploitation of women?'[21] Given that most of the Bond starlets would perform the obligatory photo-shoot for *Playboy* to coincide with the release of the films (and, indeed, were often contractually required to do so), it may be that they had rather less freedom than Claudine Auger believed.

To some extent, therefore, the impact of the Bond movies can be related to the various ways in which they reflected certain aspects of the 'cultural revolution' of the 1960s. A rather different explanation for their success, especially in America, has been advanced in a speculative essay by an American writer, Drew Moniot. 'Bond's success was probably due to the formula aspects of his series and the culturally relevant messages conveyed by the formula,' Moniot writes, '007 actually had a great deal in common with the American moviegoer of the Sixties.'[22] Moniot draws on Charles Reich's 1970 book *The Greening of America*, which had suggested that in the 1960s the American Dream had been destroyed by the rise of the 'corporate state', which created a social climate controlled by a hierarchical, mechanical, dehumanised, supremely powerful organisation that was indifferent to the rights and interests of the individual. Moniot draws a parallel between the notion of the corporate state and Bond's principal enemy in the films of the

1960s, the international crime syndicate SPECTRE. If, as Reich argued, the general mood of America in the 1960s was one of growing disenchantment with the corporate state, then the Bond films, Moniot suggests, struck a chord because they offered the possibility of the individual turning against the organisation: 'Thus the 007 fan, vaguely sensing a loss of identity and worth in the age of the corporate state, could vicariously experience a certain sense of triumph and relief when Bond struck a blow against SPECTRE.'[23] It is an intriguing argument, but ultimately unconvincing. Moniot admits that Bond himself is very much an organisation man, and that the secret service for which he works might itself be seen as another manifestation of the corporate state. The theme of the individual against a machine-like organisation was hardly a new idea in the 1960s, evidenced by Chaplin's *Modern Times* (1936). And the argument does not take account of the fact that, while the Bond films were popular in America, on a purely fiscal level they were that much more successful in markets outside America.

It was a sign of the success of the Bond series, and of the extent of 'Bondmania', that the mid-1960s witnessed a sudden upsurge in gimmicky secret agent movies which tried to copy the Bond formula. The film industry had initially proved slow to respond to the success of the Bond films and there had been relatively few other spy thrillers, and none in the style of the Bonds, between *Dr No* and *Goldfinger*. Indeed, the only film during this time which might be said to imitate the Bonds in any way was *Carry On Spying* (1964), an entry in the long-running British comedy series which spoofed the espionage film in general and the Bond movies in particular. However, it was in the wake of *Goldfinger*, and more particularly of *Thunderball*, that the floodgates opened and cinema screens were inundated with a glut of Bond spoofs and imitations. Hollywood made several attempts to get its own rival secret agent series off the ground, with mixed results. James Coburn starred as super-cool, super-stud, super-spy Derek Flint in the enjoyable *Our Man Flint* (1965) and its sequel *In Like Flint* (1967). The advertising for *Our Man Flint* emphasised Flint's Americanness, presenting him explicitly as an American alternative to James Bond.[24] Broccoli's former partner Irving Allen produced a series of four reasonably amusing spoofs adapted from Donald Hamilton's Matt Helm books, starring Dean Martin as the lazy, droopy-eyed, girl-chasing secret agent: *The Silencers* (1966), *Murderer's Row* (1966), *The Ambushers* (1967) and *The Wrecking Crew* (1969). In addition, there were no fewer than eight feature films derived from episodes of the television series *The Man from U.N.C.L.E.* which were released theatrically outside the United States.[25] In Britain, meanwhile, Bulldog Drummond was resurrected and updated to the 1960s by the producer–director team of Betty Box and Ralph Thomas. Richard Johnson, who had been one of those considered for the role of Bond, played Drummond in *Deadlier than the Male* (1966) and *Some Girls Do* (1969). The mid-1960s were the high-point of the spy craze in British cinema: *The Liquidator* (1965), *Where the Spies are* (1965), *The Quiller Memorandum* (1965), *Modesty Blaise* (1966), *Where the Bullets Fly* (1966), *Hammerhead* (1968) and *Assignment K* (1968) were among the many spy films made at this time. Harry Saltzman himself produced a trilogy based on the novels of Len Deighton – *The Ipcress File* (1965), *Funeral in Berlin* (1966) and *Billion Dollar Brain* (1967) – starring Michael Caine as Cockney spy Harry Palmer (the character had been nameless in the books) who was very different from James Bond. Along with *The Spy Who Came in from the Cold* (1965), based on the John le Carré novel, the Deighton trilogy represented a more realistic trend within the spy thriller which probed the seedier side and the moral uncertainties of espionage, eschewing the glamour and sophistication of the Bond movies for a shadowy world in which no one is to be trusted and treachery and deceit are everywhere.

British and American spy movies, however, were far outnumbered by the proliferation of derivative, low-budget European efforts to cash in on the success of the Bond franchise. From France, Spain and especially Italy there was a wave of 'spaghetti' spy movies which, like European westerns, became ever-more gimmicky and bizarre in their attempts to outdo the genuine article.[26] A coup of sorts was accomplished with *Operation Kid Brother* (1967), a dire spoof starring Sean Connery's brother Neil as the younger brother of agent 'zero zero', with a supporting cast familiar from the authentic Bonds (Bernard Lee, Lois Maxwell, Daniela Bianchi, Adolfo Celi, Anthony Dawson). So many Italian films used the '007' label that United Artists issued the following warning: 'Only James Bond, the character from the novels by Ian Fleming, can be agent 007 ... Warning is given to all Italian companies which, exploiting the success achieved by agent 007, have distinguished the leading figures in their films by the same numerals.'[27]

The official Bond series, meanwhile, differentiated itself from its rivals and imitators by becoming more expansive and more expensive. The snowballing success of the films, particularly *Goldfinger* and *Thunder-*

ball, was such that United Artists could provide Eon with much larger budgets than most other producers enjoyed. Thus, the negative cost of *Thunderball* was $5.5 million, rising to $9.5 million for *You Only Live Twice*. The $6 million budget of *On Her Majesty's Secret Service* was as much as the negative costs of the first three films combined. Taken together, these films are an intriguing if ultimately slightly unsatisfying trilogy which collectively represent a trend towards longer and more episodic narratives.

The novels on which these three films were based form a trilogy in which Bond, like Bulldog Drummond before him, fights several 'rounds' against his arch enemy Ernst Stavro Blofeld. The order of the stories was different, however, in that *Thunderball* was published in 1961, *On Her Majesty's Secret Service* in 1963 and *You Only Live Twice* in 1964. (Another novel, *The Spy Who Loved Me*, had been published in 1962, though this was a minor story which did not really have anything to do with the 'Blofeld trilogy'.) The different order in which they were filmed, with *You Only Live Twice* preceding *On Her Majesty's Secret Service*, had significant implications for the continuity of the films.

Thunderball concerns a SPECTRE plot to blackmail Britain and America by hijacking two nuclear bombs and threatening to destroy a major city unless a huge ransom is paid. Although Blofeld is the mastermind behind the conspiracy, it is his second-in-command Emilio Largo who is in charge of the operation. As so often, Bond happens upon the conspiracy by chance after a run-in with Count Lippe at a private health farm, where he has been sent by M following his latest medical report. Lippe turns out to be a SPECTRE operative charged with posting the ransom demands to the prime minister and the American president; he tries to kill Bond but is himself liquidated by a SPECTRE assassin. As the worldwide hunt for the stolen bombs gets under way, Bond is assigned to the Bahamas, where he investigates Largo and seduces Largo's mistress, Domino, whose brother has been bribed by Largo to hijack the aircraft carrying the bombs. Bond is assisted by Felix Leiter and by the US Navy, who intercept the team of SPECTRE frogmen in the process of transporting one of the bombs. A fierce underwater battle ensues, in which Bond saves Leiter's life and is then saved himself by Domino, who shoots Largo with a harpoon-gun.

On Her Majesty's Secret Service begins a year later with Bond having been assigned to track down Blofeld, who it is revealed had escaped capture at the end of *Thunderball*. Bond has found no trace of his quarry and is tired of the assignment, which he considers routine police work, to such an extent that he is contemplating resignation. Driving through France he meets the Comtesse Teresa di Vincenzo, otherwise known as Tracy, a girl who seems hell-bent on killing herself, and with whom he makes love after bailing her out in a game of baccarat. The next day Bond is abducted by two gunmen who take him to see Marc-Ange Draco, head of the Union Corse (the Corsican Mafia), who turns out to be Tracy's father. In return for what Bond has done for his daughter, Draco provides him with information that Blofeld is in Switzerland. Blofeld is pressing his claim to the aristocratic title of Comte de Bleuville in order to buy himself a new identity. Bond, posing as Sir Hilary Bray from the College of Arms, travels to Blofeld's isolated mountain-top retreat in Switzerland, ostensibly an allergy clinic where the 'count' is engaged in medical research using twelve girls as guinea-pigs. When Bond's identity is discovered he is forced to make his escape on skis, and is rescued by Tracy who had been told by her father where to find him. Blofeld is planning biological warfare, using the twelve girls as unwitting germ carriers, but Bond and Draco's men return and destroy his headquarters before the plan can come to fruition. Bond, meanwhile, has fallen in love with Tracy, and the two of them marry, but driving away from the wedding their car is machine-gunned by Blofeld and Tracy is killed.

You Only Live Twice begins with Bond, grief-stricken after Tracy's death, on the verge of a nervous breakdown. Sir James Molony, neurologist to the British Secret Service, recommends that Bond should be given a near-impossible mission that will involve a supreme call upon his talents in order to jolt him out of his despair. M sends Bond on a semi-diplomatic mission to Japan to try to persuade the Japanese to make some intelligence secrets available to the British. Bond meets Tiger Tanaka, Head of the Japanese Secret Service, who agrees to make the material available if Bond in return will perform a 'favour' by assassinating one Dr Shatterhand, a foreigner who lives in a medieval castle on the southern island of Kyushu. Shatterhand has a 'garden of death', with the castle grounds full of poisonous plants and animals which attracts many Japanese to commit suicide there. When Bond sees a photograph of Shatterhand he recognises Blofeld, but keeps the information to himself. Bond trains as a ninja and lives in a Japanese fishing village while preparing for the mission. One night Bond swims out to the castle and enters it, but is captured. He is savagely beaten, but finally kills Blofeld in vicious hand-to-hand combat before escaping from the castle on a helium balloon and falling into the sea. Back in Britain Bond is presumed dead, and his obituary is published in *The Times*, but it turns out that he is alive, though suffering from amnesia, and is being cared for by Kissy Suzuki, a Japanese girl who is in love with him. One of Fleming's most accomplished novels, *You Only Live Twice* is really an allegorical story of Good and Evil told on an epic scale.[28]

Thunderball, of course, had been the subject of an on-going legal dispute between Fleming and Kevin McClory. The court case was resolved at the end of 1963. It was accepted that Fleming had acted in good faith in writing *Thunderball*, but that in future editions of the book an additional credit would be added to the effect that the novel was 'based on an original screen treatment by Kevin McClory, Jack Whittingham and Ian Fleming'. McClory disclaimed any further interest in the novel, but was awarded the screen rights to the story. McClory lost no time in announcing 'plans to make a film featuring the character of James Bond at an early date'.[29]

In the event, McClory did not produce his own rival Bond film, but instead came to an agreement with Broccoli and Saltzman that they would produce *Thunderball* together. Accordingly, McClory is credited as the producer of the film, with Broccoli and Saltzman as executive producers. To all intents and purposes, however, *Thunderball* fits into the Eon production ideology and bears the unmistakable stamp of the series' producers. McClory's own contribution would seem to have been minimal, though according to Steven Jay Rubin 'he had rewritten his script a dozen times and had covered every foot of the Bahamas, searching for possible locations'.[30] The screenplay for *Thunderball* was written by Richard Maibaum and John Hopkins, and Terence Young returned to direct.

Thunderball defined the direction which the Bond series was to take thereafter. 'Here Comes the Biggest Bond of All!', declared the posters. The official publicity discourse emphasised the size and scale, describing it as 'the most ambitious and lavishly-mounted of all the Bond films'.[31] It was the first of the series to be made in the widescreen process Panavision, and the first with a running time in excess of two hours. However, the scale and length of the film works against the narrative structure, so that rather than being a relatively tightly constructed thriller along the lines of the first three movies, *Thunderball* is an episodic narrative with a long middle section in which one action sequence follows another without significantly advancing the plot. Furthermore, much of the action takes place underwater, which in Young's view slowed down the tempo of the film. It was to be the last Bond that Young directed, and he did not rate it as highly as his other two:

> I really honestly don't know why I did *Thunderball*. I don't particularly like it. ... It was very successful, but to my mind all that underwater stuff was anti-James Bond, because it was slow motion. People swim slowly and you couldn't have them going very fast; we undercranked some of the shots and they looked ridiculous – the water was wobbling around so much it suddenly became stupid. On the whole, I would say it's not my favourite picture by a long way. It's a very efficient picture, but already the hardware was creeping into the stories.[32]

There are also more continuity errors in *Thunderball* than most Bond movies, particularly noticeable in the underwater battle when Bond's diving mask changes colour.

The narrative ideology of *Thunderball* exemplifies perfectly Bennett and Woollacott's notion of Bond as a hero of the NATO alliance. This is inscribed in the text itself, in so far as SPECTRE's threat is explicitly directed against NATO: Blofeld describes it as 'our NATO project', while Largo (Adolfo Celi) states that 'Our intention is to demand a ransom from the North Atlantic Treaty powers of two hundred and eighty million dollars, a hundred million pounds.' The nuclear bombs are stolen from a NATO training flight (albeit that it is a British Vulcan bomber which is hijacked) and the search for them is conducted jointly by the chief NATO allies, Britain and America. Like *Dr No* and *Goldfinger*, America is threatened – the target is Miami – and Bond works with his CIA colleague Felix Leiter. But, as in *Dr No*, the location (the Bahamas) is in the British Commonwealth, and Leiter functions as little more than a 'yes' man. Unlike *Dr No*, however, where the overtones of British colonialism were very apparent, *Thunderball* does not feature any of the apparatus of colonial government (other than a passing reference to the islands' governor, whose authority is required when Bond wants a power cut at Largo's residence, Palmyra). The climax symbolises Anglo-American collaboration: the frogmen who intercept the SPECTRE squad belong to the US Navy, while it is the Royal Navy which pursues and destroys Largo's yacht.

On another level, *Thunderball* offers an interesting commentary on the notion that one of the assumptions underlying the Bond narrative is that Bond must seduce the heroine in order to 'reposition' her ideologically. In so far as the main girl, Domino, is Largo's mistress, then this process can be seen to be enacted in Bond's pursuit and seduction of her. However, it is made clear that Domino herself is aware of what is happening. In one scene Bond and Domino meet at a secluded beach and make love. Afterwards, Bond reveals to Domino that her brother is dead, and that he has been killed by Largo, in order to enlist her help in finding the bombs. 'So that is why you make love to me,' Domino remarks. Therefore she realises that Bond has deliberately set out to seduce her in order to further his mission, though, having thus been repositioned, Domino becomes a willing accomplice, to the extent, as in the novel, of killing Largo herself. A more direct challenge to Bond's ability to convert women to his side through the sheer force of sexual magnetism is provided by the character of SPECTRE assassin Fiona Volpe (Luciana Paluzzi). Bond has sex with Fiona in the knowledge that she is an enemy agent, but immediately afterwards finds himself captured by her heavies. When taunted by Fiona about his vanity ('Vanity, Mr Bond? Something you know so much about'), Bond reveals that he knew who she was all along and that sex was merely part of his job ('My dear girl, don't flatter yourself. What I did this evening was for king and country. You don't think it gave me any pleasure, do you?'). Fiona's reply challenges the very notion of ideological repositioning: 'But of course, I forgot your ego, Mr Bond. James Bond, who only has to make love to a woman and she starts to hear heavenly choirs singing. She repents and then immediately returns to the side of right and virtue. But not this one!' Fiona thus refuses to be repositioned – the first instance in the Bond films of a woman whose allegiance proves stronger than Bond's sex appeal. Bond shrugs and quips 'Well, you can't win them all' – thus showing that he too is aware of what is entailed in the seduction/repositioning process. But if Fiona's refusal to be repositioned seems, on the face of it, a more progressive and independent character trait for a Bond girl, the film reasserts its sexist code by quickly killing her off. In the ideology of the films, any woman who resists Bond is problematic and needs to be disposed of: Fiona, pursuing the wounded Bond to the 'Kiss Kiss Club', is shot in the back by a bullet intended for him.

The form and style of *Thunderball* build on the innovations of the earlier films. The cinematography is bright and colourful, the set design extravagant and detailed. There are the usual topical references, such as the revelation that SPECTRE was paid a 'consultation fee' for the British Great Train Robbery. Snobbery and violence again go together. Thus, in the pre-title sequence, Bond realises that the 'widow' at a funeral he has just attended is really a man in disguise ('My dear Colonel Boivoit, I don't think you should have opened that car door by yourself') and there follows a furious fight in which Bond and his opponent manage to demolish most of the furnishings in the drawing room of an elegant French chateau. Opinions differ over this fight sequence. Pfeiffer and Lisa describe it as 'ferociously staged, and well choreographed and edited', whereas Barnes and Hearn consider it 'overcranked' (whatever that means).[33] Some of the action seems to have been slightly under-cranked (meaning that the camera is slowed down so that when projected at normal speed the action is faster). Peter Hunt's editing makes the fight more stylised: several cuts do not match precisely on the action, so that the combatants change position or are suddenly back on their feet after being knocked down. Rather than being 'mistakes', this style of action editing should be seen as a stylistic innovation on Hunt's part that was to find its fullest expression in the only Bond film he directed, *On Her Majesty's Secret Service*. The jumpy, discontinuous, disorienting editing style accelerates the tempo of the fight sequence and accentuates the sensation of violence, particularly when accompanied by loud sound effects and strident music. This technique is also employed in the fight between Bond and Largo's men in the speeding hydrofoil at the end of the film, where the fast editing emphasises the impact of fists and bodies, the 'shock' of the slight discontinuities in the cutting making the violence seem more real than it actually is. While these two protracted punch-ups effectively 'bookend' the film, the most visually impressive action sequence in *Thunderball* is the underwater battle between SPECTRE and US Navy frogmen which has an aesthetic quality all of its own. Despite Young's reservations about underwater filming, the sequence manages to be fast and exciting, and is choreographed with the precision of an Esther Williams underwater ballet. With the combatants identified by the colour of their wetsuits (the US frogmen in bright orange, the SPECTRE team inevitably in black), the battle becomes a montage of writhing bodies, harpoons and oxygen bubbles, with the fast cutting overcoming the relative slowness of the underwater movement. It is also quite remarkably violent: some thirty men are killed within the space of seven minutes, and there are numerous shots of harpoons having pierced masks and bodies (though there is no blood – a reminder of the non-realistic, cartoonish style of violence in the Bond movies).

Thunderball was released in both Britain and America at the end of 1965. While the popular and trade press were as enthusiastic as ever, there were signs in Britain that some of the more middle-brow critics were beginning to tire of the formula aspects of the series, and their response was not as wholeheartedly enthusiastic as it had been for *Goldfinger*. The film critic of *The Times* wrote:

> *Thunderball* does show alarming signs that the series is going to seed. The plot, which after all is what keeps most of us watching between the set-pieces, has been thinned out at times almost to vanishing point, and the sexiness of the sexy scenes and the violence of the violent scenes correspondingly stepped up. But here this film's makers run into the law of diminishing returns: each time Bond ends up in bed with another glamorous young woman, or someone else is transfixed with a harpoon, strangled with a telephone cord, or drowned by having his airpipe cut, the effect becomes less surprising, titillating, or exciting.[34]

Nina Hibbin, oddly enough, thought that *Thunderball* 'isn't quite so vicious as the others'. 'It hasn't, thank goodness, any racialist overtones,' she wrote. 'Life and women are still as cheap as ever, but its deaths aren't so grisly, its sex is less in earnest, and its sadistic joke lines are more subdued.'[35]

Some American critics were rather more enthusiastic than their British counterparts. Bosley Crowther included it among his ten best films of the year. 'Here is the ultimate achievement of scenic excitements and melodramatic spoof in the series of James Bond movies,' he wrote. 'It combines a delightful hyperbole with the serio-comic twists of science-fiction, some amusing adumbrations on sex and always a cinematic satire of the contemporary culture of the hero comic strips.' Crowther considered, furthermore, that Bond had 'a much better sense of humor than he has shown in his previous films' and that accordingly *Thunderball* was 'the best of the lot'.[36]

It had originally been intended to make *On Her Majesty's Secret Service* the next film in the series, following the order of the books, and Saltzman had been scouting locations in Switzerland in the summer of

1965 while *Thunderball* was still in production.[37] In the event, production logistics worked against that and it was decided to make *You Only Live Twice* instead. In the meantime, however, a potential problem had emerged in the form of a rival Bond film which was in production at the same time as *You Only Live Twice*.

The screen rights for *Casino Royale*, which Fleming had sold to producer Gregory Ratoff in 1955, had been acquired from Ratoff's widow by Charles K. Feldman, a former showbusiness lawyer and talent agent who had become a producer with films including *The Seven Year Itch* (1954) and *What's New Pussycat?* (1965). Feldman had apparently intended to make a 'straight' film version of the novel, but having been unable to secure the services of Sean Connery, and sensibly realising that the public would be unlikely to accept anyone else in the role of Bond, he decided instead to make *Casino Royale* the spy spoof to end all spy spoofs. Backed by Columbia Pictures and filmed in conditions of great secrecy at no fewer than three British studios (Shepperton, Pinewood and Borehamwood), *Casino Royale* was far from being another cheapskate imitation in the manner of the Italian '007' movies. The range of talents involved was impressive. The stellar cast comprised Peter Sellers, Ursula Andress, David Niven, Orson Welles, Joanna Pettet and Woody Allen, supported by a host of international 'guest stars' including Deborah Kerr, William Holden, John Huston, Charles Boyer, George Raft and Jean-Paul Belmondo. Five directors were credited (John Huston, Kenneth Hughes, Val Guest, Robert Parrish and Joseph McGrath) and three writers (Wolf Mankowitz, John Law and Michael Sayers), and there were uncredited contributions from many others, including Billy Wilder, Ben Hecht and Joseph Heller, the author of *Catch 22*. However, the production was hampered by constant rewrites and by the erratic behaviour of Sellers, and ended up going months over schedule and way over budget. The final negative cost was $12 million, more than any of the official Bond films had cost. *Casino Royale* was finally released in April 1967, two months before *You Only Live Twice*.

'It's too much for one James Bond,' declared the posters. The main joke of *Casino Royale* – such as it is – is that nearly everyone in the film is known as 'James Bond 007'. The beginning of the film at least has the germ of an interesting idea. With the secret services of Britain, America, Russia and France having been decimated by an unknown enemy, their chiefs unite to persuade Sir James Bond (Niven), 'the greatest spy in history', to come out of retirement to meet the crisis. 'The true, one and only, original James Bond', is how M (Huston) describes him, and he is played by the actor who had been Fleming's preferred choice for the role. The film posits the notion that Bond is the embodiment of the noble spy of yesteryear, clean-living and appalled by the decadence of his modern-day namesake. 'In my day spying was an alternative to war,' he remarks, 'and the spy was a member of a select and immaculate priesthood, vocationally devoted, sublimely disinterested – hardly a description of that sexual acrobat who leaves a trail of beautiful dead women like blown roses behind him.' This other James Bond – by implication Sean Connery's – was given the name and number after the real Bond retired because, as M tells him, 'it was essential that your legend be maintained – without a James Bond, oh-oh-seven, no-one would respect us'. Sir James is contemptuous of the new generation of 'joke-shop spies' with their gadgets and hidden weapons – another veiled reference to the official Bond series – and rejects the materialism of the modern world, 'including an Aston Martin complete with lethal accessories'. This Bond, like Fleming's, drives a vintage Bentley.

The rest of the film, however, does not develop this interesting premise. The actual plot of *Casino Royale* defies description; it is really more a series of separate incidents than a coherent narrative. Sir James does indeed come out of retirement when M is killed in a freak accident, and discovers a conspiracy by an organisation called SMERSH – a collective of beautiful women – to besmirch his reputation. Bond resists the advances of SMERSH agent Lady Mimi (Kerr), posing as M's widow, and avoids being killed by exploding flying ducks and a booby-trapped milkfloat. Taking over as head of the secret service, Bond decides to confuse the enemy by designating all remaining agents 'James Bond 007'. He seeks out Mata Bond (Pettet), his daughter by Mata Hari, and sends her on a mission to Berlin to infiltrate SMERSH headquarters. Meanwhile, cardsharp Evelyn Tremble is also recruited by fashion designer and occasional spy Vesper Lynd (Andress) to challenge Le Chiffre (Welles) at baccarat. The various plot strands come together at Casino Royale, where it turns out that the evil mastermind behind SMERSH, Dr Noah, is really none other than Bond's nephew Jimmy Bond (Allen), who suffers from an acute inferiority complex in the presence of his uncle, and whose plan is to remove all men over four feet six tall, thus making himself the tallest man alive in a world populated by beautiful women.

Critical judgements are irrelevant with a film like *Casino Royale*. Robert

Murphy considers it one of those films 'which ought to be shipped to a desert island and screened continuously to those responsible for them'.[38] For Clive Hirschhorn, it is 'a self-indulgent mess – an inferior Monty Python sketch stretched way beyond its limits'.[39] There are, to be fair, one or two good visual jokes, mainly in the cinematography of Jack Hildyard, with additional photography by future director Nicolas Roeg. In Berlin, for example, the 'red side' literally is red, while Mata Bond's journey through SMERSH headquarters, all sloping walls and uneven staircases, is an amusing spoof of the visual style of German Expressionism. The psychedelic dream sequence in which Le Chiffre tortures Tremble with columns of bagpipe-playing Scots Guards is the most surreal moment in a surreal film. The climax – which some-how includes cowboys and Indians, Frankenstein's Monster, the French Foreign Legion and the Keystone Kops, not to mention George Raft accidentally shooting himself with a backward-firing gun – is a mad parody of generic clichés which anticipates the free-for-all ending of Mel Brooks's *Blazing Saddles*. But these are isolated moments in a film that is an overlong, confusing, disjointed, messy extravaganza, cinematic proof of the maxim that too many cooks spoil the broth. It is very far from being an authentic Bond movie, and as a spoof it is nowhere near as funny as the much less ambitious *Carry On Spying*. 'While Sean Connery and the original James Bond associates will not lose much sleep over this joshing of their goldmine pictures, *Casino Royale* may easily find a profitable audience among those who see in it the ultimate in hectic screen spy gimmickry,' predicted *Variety*.[40] And, astonishingly, it was quite successful at the box-office, with rentals of $17 million, suggesting either that audiences liked this kind of crazy comedy, or that it rode the wave of 'Bondmania' in anticipation of the real article.

You Only Live Twice opened with posters declaring 'Sean Connery IS James Bond', just so there could be no confusion with Feldman's spoof extravaganza. Some of the British critics had wondered how the film-makers would adapt this particular novel given that it featured a grieving Bond on a personal vendetta against Blofeld; the solution was simply to discard Fleming's story entirely, keeping just the location and the character names. With Maibaum unavailable on this occasion, Roald Dahl was employed to write the screenplay. Dahl – a British writer of Norwegian parentage, famous for his children's stories – was a curious choice, as he had no previous experience as a screenwriter and admitted to having seen only one of the Bond films, 'the one with the crazy motorcar'. He had, however, known Ian Fleming, and was to be employed by Broccoli to adapt Fleming's *Chitty Chitty Bang Bang* (1968), presumably on the strength of his own children's fiction. In an amusing interview for *Playboy*, Dahl recounted how Broccoli and Saltzman had told him that 'You can come up with anything you like so far as the story goes', but that he was under strict instructions not to alter either the character of Bond or 'the girl formula':

'So you put in three girls. No more and no less. Girl number one is pro-Bond. She stays around roughly through the first reel of the picture. Then she is bumped off by the enemy, preferably in Bond's arms.'

'In bed or not in bed?' I asked.

'Wherever you like, so long as it's in good taste. Girl number two is anti-Bond. She works for the enemy and stays around throughout the middle third of the picture. She must capture Bond, and Bond must save himself by bowling her over with sheer sexual magnetism. This girl should also be bumped off, preferably in an original fashion.'

'There aren't many of those left,' I said.

'We'll find one,' they answered. 'Girl number three is violently pro-Bond. She occupies the final third of the picture and she must on no account be killed. Nor must she permit Bond to take any lecherous liberties with her until the very end of the story. We keep that for the fade-out.'[41]

While this was not strictly the formula followed in the previous four films, Dahl was to adhere to it very closely in his screenplay for *You Only Live Twice*.

Very little of the novel was retained for the film. The title, of course, refers to Bond's apparent death, but whereas in the novel he is assumed dead after the completion of his mission, the film begins with him apparently being shot dead in Hong Kong. Bond is buried at sea, but the shrouded body is collected by frogmen who take it on board a Royal Navy submarine where it turns out that Bond is not dead after all: his 'death' has been a ruse to put his enemies off the track. While Fleming's plot was discarded, however, Dahl's screenplay reworked numerous narrative elements from preceding Bond films. The basic premise is that SPECTRE is trying to start World War Three by intercepting both American and Russian space capsules in orbit. The interference with the space programme, directed from a secret head-quarters (SPECTRE's interceptor rocket which 'swallows' the capsules is launched from inside a volcano), reworks the science-fiction theme of *Dr No*. The policy of deliberately exacerbating Cold War tensions recalls *From Russia with Love*. When the American capsule is intercepted, the Americans naturally suspect the Russians: 'My government sees this as nothing less than a blatant attempt to gain complete and absolute control of space itself,' says the American representative at a secret summit meeting, warning that any future interference will be regarded as an 'act of war'. The British, for their part, are not convinced that the Russians are behind it all, though their suggestion that the interceptor vehicle may have come down somewhere in Japan is dismissed by the Americans. As in *Goldfinger*, it is implied that Red China is secretly behind the conspiracy; although not named, as in the earlier film, the official representatives seen negotiating with Blofeld, and who have provided SPECTRE with the space equipment, are of oriental appearance, and the dialogue makes clear that their government is paying SPECTRE to trigger a war between the Superpowers. 'In a matter of hours, when America and Russia have annihilated each other, we shall see a new power dominating the world,' Blofeld (Donald Pleasence) remarks towards the end of the film. In suggesting, however obliquely, that Red China was behind the conspiracy, *You Only Live Twice* can be placed within a trend in films of the late 1960s which identified China rather than the Soviet Union as the main Communist threat to the West. For example, the science-fiction film *Battle Beneath the Earth* (1967) had the Chinese using a giant laser to tunnel underneath America, while the spy thriller *The Most Dangerous Man in the World* (1969) had Gregory Peck as a scientist sent on a mission to China with a bomb implanted in his skull. The demonification of China at this time was almost certainly a reaction to the so-called 'Cultural Revolution' of Chairman Mao Tse-tung, as well as, in the longer term, a reflection of aggressive Chinese foreign policy in Tibet and on the Indian border.

Dahl's screenplay not only departs from the novel; it actually offers a complete ideological reordering of it. Thus, whereas the novel betrays some markedly anti-Japanese sentiments and seems morbidly concerned with the Japanese obsession with suicide, the film by contrast emphasises the modernity of Japan, especially its technological expertise. Made at a time when Japanese corporations were at the forefront of technological innovation, particularly in the manufacture of electronic consumer goods, the film foregrounds a plethora of ingenious gadgets, from miniature television monitors to rocket-guns. 'How's that for Japanese efficiency?' Tiger Tanaka (Tetsuro Tamba) asks after a car pursuing Bond has been lifted off the road by a helicopter equipped with a huge magnet and dropped into the sea. 'Just a drop in the ocean,' Bond replies, impressed.

As well as the very different representation of Japan, the film also mocks the ideology of national identity which characterised the novel. Fleming's original is an explicitly patriotic story in which Bond represents Britain on a symbolic level: in undertaking a special mission, Bond proves that Britain is not the second-rate power that the Japanese believe it has become and thus reaffirms its world power status. The screen Bond, however, parodies the values which the literary Bond stood for, mocking his notions of patriotism and duty. 'The things I do for England!', Bond remarks at one moment, but rather than being engaged on a deadly mission to prove that his country is still a great nation, he is at the time cutting away the dress straps of villainess Helga Brandt (Karin Dor). It is a highly ironic comment: the arduous task which Bond undertakes for his country is making love to a beautiful woman.[42] Indeed, the film seems to be implying that the patriotic code underlying the novels is redundant, an illustration of how the films modernised the image of Bond in a manner more suited to the irreverent popular attitudes of the 1960s.

For all these interesting points, however, *You Only Live Twice* is a poorly constructed, episodic, meandering film in which one incident follows on from another without much sense of narrative development. At times the film seems to resemble a travelogue of Japan – it is very attractively photographed by Freddie Young, the Oscar-winning cinematographer of David Lean's *Lawrence of Arabia* and *Doctor Zhivago* – in which the story has been written to suit the locations. Ken Adam's set design is as impressive as ever, particularly in the huge SPECTRE base, and the climactic battle in which Japanese ninjas attack it is exceptionally well staged by director Lewis Gilbert. And John Barry's score is one of his finest efforts, a sweeping melody with full orchestra which perfectly captures the atmosphere of the oriental locations. However, as Bosley Crowther observed, the film 'is evidently pegged to the notion that nothing succeeds like excess. And because it is shamelessly excessive, it is about a half-hour too long.'[43] As in *Thunderball*, gadgets and technology are foregrounded at the expense of characterisation. Bond's autogiro 'Little Nellie' is an amusing touch which makes for a visually impressive aerial dogfight, but, unlike the car chase in *Goldfinger*, there is little suspense as Bond mechanically uses its various weapons to destroy the four helicopters which attack it. Connery gives the impression of going through the motions, which in a sense he was, as he had already announced his intention of giving up playing James Bond.

When it became apparent that Connery was serious about not continuing, the producers faced the problem of finding another actor to fill his shoes. A much-publicised worldwide search for a new James Bond finally settled on George Lazenby, a thirty-year-old Australian model whose acting experience was limited to carrying crates of chocolate in television commercials as 'Big Fry'. Lazenby won the part because of his tall, athletic physique and his ability to stage realistic fight sequences – he broke stuntman Yuri Borienko's nose during his screen test – while Peter Hunt, who was to direct *On Her Majesty's Secret Service*, was confident that he could counter Lazenby's lack of experience in the cutting room. Hunt had long harboured ambitions to direct. He was keen to put his own stamp on the film, particularly in downplaying the gadgets that had featured so prominently in the previous three. Upon the film's release, Hunt elaborated his idea of the 'new' Bond:

> The James Bond films set the trend for tongue-in-cheek spy spoof movies and, as we know, they were fantastically successful. But there have been so many imitators – not all of them very good by any means – that we were in danger of imitating our imitators.
>
> We could have stuck to exactly the same formula, but we preferred to progress. Besides, *On Her Majesty's Secret Service* is better without the gadgetry and paraphernalia. It is a marvellous adventure story, with Bond surviving by his own physical skill and ingenuity, and at the same time it is a genuine love story, with 007 falling in love and marrying for the very first time. ...
>
> I am more convinced than ever, now that the picture has been completed, that the choice of George Lazenby as Bond was right. With Lazenby, we revert to the concept of Bond implicit in Ian Fleming's books. The essence of Bond is a young man who has an inherent sexual assurance – which was the predominant thought in my mind during the search for the new 007.[44]

However, the relationship between Lazenby and the film-makers was strained and *Secret Service* was to be his one and only appearance as Bond.[45]

In all sorts of other respects, too, *On Her Majesty's Secret Service* is the odd-one-out in the Bond series. Like *From Russia with Love*, it does not fit into the overall direction the series was taking, illustrating once again that the evolution of the generic formula of the Bond films was not a linear process. Ever since *Goldfinger* the series had been moving further and further into the realms of technological fantasy, but *Secret Service* bucks this trend by downplaying the gadgets and hardware to focus on story and characterisation. Whereas *You Only Live Twice* had completely discarded Fleming's plot, *Secret Service* is the closest of all the films to its original source. 'As a novel I think it's the best of them and the one we had to do the least with to make a good motion picture script,' said Richard Maibaum, who received a solo credit for the screenplay. 'It was a solid novel, more of a serious effort than most of his books, which are really one hundred pages of brilliant exposition and then some good, swift action.'[46] Again, however, this fidelity to the original is out of step with the direction of the series as a whole in so far as the films which followed during the 1970s were to become completely removed from Fleming. The fidelity of *Secret Service* even extends to the downbeat ending, in which Bond marries Tracy only to see her killed by Blofeld (actually, in the film it is Blofeld's accomplice and mistress Irma Bunt who fires the fatal shots). This makes *Secret Service* unique as the only Bond film with an unhappy ending, which probably accounts as much as any other factor for its relatively less successful performance at the box-office. As Molly Haskell said in *Village Voice*: 'If you like your Bonds with happy endings, don't go.'[47]

The film follows the novel very closely indeed. There are some changes, of course, but they actually improve the narrative structure of the film rather than detracting from it, as had been the case in the two previous efforts. Whereas in the novel Bond had contemplated resignation because he thought hunting Blofeld was routine police work, in the film he threatens resignation when M takes him off the case ('But sir, Blofeld's something of a must with me'). Bond's courtship of Tracy (Diana Rigg) is more protracted than in the book, conducted through a romantic montage sequence. There is a new sequence in Bern in which Bond breaks into the office of a Swiss lawyer to find proof of a link with Blofeld, who is claiming his aristocratic title ('Bleauchamp' rather than 'Bleuville'), during which Bond uses his only gadget of the film, a combined safecracker and photocopier that is lifted up to the office window by crane. Bond's masquerade as Sir Hilary Bray proceeds much as it does in the book, though his meeting with Blofeld (Telly Savalas) does not make strict narrative sense due to the films having been made in a different order (in the novel it is the first time Bond and Blofeld come face to face, but on screen they had already met in *You Only Live Twice*). Blofeld discovers Bond's masquerade and informs him of his plan, which is the distribution of 'virus omega', a sterility drug. Unless his demands are met, he will proceed with 'the systematic extinction of whole species of cereals and livestock all over the world'. Bond's escape from Piz Gloria is more protracted in the film, with a succession of chase and fight sequences. As in the book Bond is rescued by Tracy, but in the film she is captured by Blofeld and taken back to Piz Gloria, which provides a more logical motivation for Draco (Gabriele Ferzetti) to lead a helicopter attack on Blofeld's base.

The main problem confronting the film-makers was how to introduce the new James Bond to the audience. An idea that Bond would have plastic surgery to alter his appearance and thus disguise him from his enemies was quickly discarded.[48] Instead, *On Her Majesty's Secret Service* adopts a quite innovative narrative strategy for introducing Lazenby, through a series of textual references which playfully acknowledge the presence of the new lead actor while at the same time maintaining continuity with previous films. Thus, at the end of the pre-title sequence in which Bond has prevented Tracy from drowning herself and has had a vicious fight with two heavies on the beach, only for Tracy to run off and leave him holding her shoes, Lazenby remarks 'This never happened to the other fellow' – a line which makes the audience complicit in the changeover of leading man, therefore potentially disarming those who would be unwilling to accept anyone other than Connery in the role. But while the film itself acknowledges that Lazenby is *not* Connery, it is at great pains to show that Lazenby *is* James Bond. Thus, when he pinches Miss Moneypenny's bottom, her response is 'Same old James – only more so!' The opening titles establish continuity within the Bond series by including images of heroines and villains from the five previous films; this continuity is later reinforced in a scene where Bond empties his desk and takes out props from earlier films (Honey's knife-belt from *Dr No*, Grant's watch-garotte from *From Russia with Love*, the miniature underwater breather from *Thunderball*), while on the soundtrack there is a brief reprise of the theme music from those films. Lazenby's introduction, therefore, was carried out in a manner which maintained continuity with the earlier films, suggesting that while the actor may change, James Bond himself remains constant.

As for Lazenby himself, opinions are divided on his performance. Alexander Walker points out that casting a complete unknown did not help, but that in any case Lazenby was faced with an almost impossible act to follow: 'Another actor who had "paid his dues" in the same sort of adventure genre as the Bonds might – just *might* – have graduated to the prime role: but the public resented being asked to accept someone who had neither earned his right to be a contender, nor possessed enough distinctiveness of his own to dim the memory of his predecessor.'[49] But Lazenby's performance is actually quite assured for someone with no previous acting experience. Physically he looks the part, his on-screen movement combines athleticism with an arrogant swagger, and he manages to convey the snobbery of the character (for example in identifying Beluga caviar 'from the *north* Caspian'). Although his lack of experience is evident in some of the lengthy dialogue scenes, it also, paradoxically, has the effect of making his Bond a more believable character. Whereas Connery's Bond had become a heroic superman, Lazenby's Bond comes across as vulnerable and consequently more human. This is especially evident in the scene at the skating rink, where an exhausted Bond (he has just skied down a mountain and fought off two of Blofeld's men in a highly physical brawl) hides from his pursuers and appears to have reached the end of his tether – whereupon Tracy appears to rescue him.

For all the reservations about Lazenby, however, *On Her Majesty's Secret Service* is one of the richest and most interesting Bond films. It is, for example, the most explicitly patriotic film of the series. Whereas *You Only Live Twice* had mocked Bond's duty to his country ('The things I do for England!'), *Secret Service* emphatically reasserts the patriotic code of the literary Bond. Partly this is due to the special resonances of the title, and partly it is due to the film's fidelity to the book. Bond's patriotism and sense of duty are constantly asserted by references to 'Her Majesty's Secret Service', and just to reinforce the point a framed reproduction of Annigoni's portrait of Queen Elizabeth II is displayed prominently on the wall of his office. The setting of the College of Arms, and the role which heraldry plays in the story, further emphasises history and tradition.

The themes of patriotism and monarchy also operate on a visual level. The title sequence features silhouettes of women, one of whom bears the trident and shield of Britannia, against a Union Jack which is squeezed through an hour-glass. The figure of Britannia is a visual representation of the ideology of national identity constructed by the film (in which the Queen is symbolically at the head of things), while the motif of the hour-glass suggests that time is running out for Britain. Only Bond can save Britain, which he does by turning back the clock – literally, in so far as the titles show the silhouette of Bond hanging on to the hands of a giant clock which are turning anti-clockwise. (The image could also be read as illustrating Bond's desire to turn the clock back in order to save Tracy's life.) The picture of the Queen on Bond's office wall also serves a symbolic function in the narrative by figuring prominently in the *mise-en-scène* at two key moments. After he has dictated his resignation to Moneypenny, there is a shot of Bond's face reflected in the glass of the picture as he raises a hip flask and says, 'Sorry, ma'am', before taking a swig. Later, when Bond is telephoning Draco to arrange the unsanctioned raid on Blofeld's headquarters, he turns his head and looks over his shoulder at the picture. At moments which question Bond's relationship to the secret service, therefore, the image of monarchy reminds him of his duty.

On Her Majesty's Secret Service is unique in that for the first and only time in the series Bond experiences a conflict of interests between love and duty. The relationship between Bond and the girl is mapped on to the relationship between Bond and his country. Bond's love affair with Tracy performs an ideological role very different from his sexual conquests in any of the other films: rather than the girl being repositioned, it is Bond who finds his allegiance being called into question. At first, Bond sees his courtship of Tracy as a way of furthering his mission in that he wants to extract information from her father concerning Blofeld's whereabouts. This is information which Draco is prepared to give only on a personal basis ('I wouldn't tell Her Majesty's Secret Service, but I might tell my future son-in-law'). But when Bond realises that he has fallen in love with Tracy, and proposes to her, love and duty no longer go together. Unlike in the novel, where Bond intends to stay in the secret service, in the film he accepts, apparently quite willingly, that he will have to 'find something else to do'. When Tracy is captured by Blofeld, Bond's personal interests conflict with his job. M informs him that the United Nations has agreed to meet Blofeld's demands – an amnesty for all past crimes and official recognition of his title 'when he retires into private life' – and that no action is to be taken. M refuses to sanction a rescue mission for Tracy despite Bond's protests ('This department is not concerned with your personal problems'). Bond therefore turns to Draco, head of a criminal organisation, to mount the raid on Piz Gloria. When Bond marries Tracy, and thus accepts a new life outside the secret service, narrative logic demands that Tracy will have to be killed in order that Bond can return to the service for the next film.

On Her Majesty's Secret Service therefore provides a rather more important role for the girl than any of the other films. Although introduced in a typically voyeuristic manner – Bond observes her through a telescopic lens as she walks along a beach – Tracy is no mere 'object of to-be-looked-at-ness'; she performs an active role in the narrative, rescuing Bond when he is cornered at the skating rink, and actually causing Bond to rethink his profession. Tracy's greater narrative importance necessitated a break from tradition for the film-makers in selecting an established actress to play her, which would also help to counterbalance the inexperience of Lazenby. The casting of Diana Rigg was propitious in that, like Honor Blackman before her, she was an established action heroine, having succeeded Blackman as John Steed's female partner in *The Avengers*. Rigg's popular image from her role as Emma Peel was that of a sophisticated, intelligent young woman who was capable of looking after herself in a fight – an image which *Secret Service* refers to when she fights and kills Grunther (Yuri Borienko) at the film's climax. While the role of Tracy challenged the traditional role assigned to the girl in the Bond films, the more usual characterisation of Bond girls as passive playthings is also represented by the 'patients' at Blofeld's 'clinic'; inevitably, Bond seduces two of them during his masquerade as Sir Hilary Bray.

It is not only in its narrative ideologies that *On Her Majesty's Secret Service* is so unique within the Bond series. It is the most attractively photographed of the films, with more attention seeming to have been given to visual composition than usual; this is particularly evident in the pre-title sequence on a Portuguese beach at sunrise and in the panoramic Swiss snowscapes where lines of skiers suddenly appear silhouetted against the white mountains in a manner that recalls Anthony Mann's *The Heroes of Telemark* (*Secret Service* was the only Bond assignment for cinematographer Michael Reed). The dramatic use of landscape is matched by the soaring heights of John Barry's score, which ranges from an insistent, minimal, instrumental title track to a gentle romantic ballad, 'We Have All the Time in the World', movingly performed by Louis Armstrong. The use of this song, which complements the romantic montage illustrating Bond's courtship of Tracy, is comparable to the use of 'Raindrops Keep Falling on My Head' in the same year's *Butch Cassidy and the Sundance Kid* (Hal David wrote the lyrics for both). The editing style of the film is also noticeably different. As Alexander Walker observes:

> Above all, the direction of Peter Hunt – an editor on earlier Bond films – brought a cutting-room crispness to every set-up, though even he was not able to truncate a film that feels as if it is ending four times before it actually does so. John Glen, not only this film's editor, but its second-unit director (and later a Bond director in his own right) gave *O.H.M.S.S.* a completely different feeling from any earlier Bonds. Using the discontinuity of a cartoon strip (what would soon be called a 'video clip'), he made fist-fights look like the splitting of the atom, had blows boomeranging in from off-screen and bodies flying apart as if released from a spring-clip.[50]

The editing style of *Secret Service* marks the fullest extent of the techniques which Hunt had been developing in the earlier films. The fight sequences are stylised, kinetic and extremely physical, employing jump cuts and other disorienting devices to jar the spectator, and loud, exaggerated sound effects to accentuate the sensation of violence. And the chases, particularly the protracted ski–car–ski sequence in which Bond escapes from Blofeld's men, are most impressively staged and filmed. Unlike some of the later films, where a chase would be introduced gratuitously, often for comic effect, in *Secret Service* they serve a narrative purpose – the urgency of Bond's escape so that he can contact London and inform them of Blofeld's plan – and Bond has to rely on his strength and wits rather than gadgets.

How did the critics react to the 'different' James Bond film? Although it is generally assumed that *On Her Majesty's Secret Service* was not as well received as the Connery films had been, and that Lazenby was universally panned for his performance, in fact this was not the case. Reactions to the film and to Lazenby himself were mixed, though no more so than they had been for Connery and *Dr No*. Derek Malcolm considered that 'it's quite a jolly frolic in the familiar money-spinning fashion – not a penny spared on production values, smart direction from Peter Hunt, and a shrewd eye kept throughout on the well-worn mixture of sex, violence, thrills and laughs'. But he was less charitable towards Lazenby, whom he thought 'looks like a Willerby Brothers clothes peg and acts as if he's just come out of Burtons short on credit'.[51] David Austen in *Films and Filming*, by contrast, was less harsh on Lazenby – 'It's true that he doesn't have quite the right voice, nor does he parade the trappings of pseudo-sophistication with quite the same ease as his predecessor, but he does tackle the unenviable task with commendable vigour and apparent good humour' – and more critical of the film which, despite the impressive stunts and pyrotechnics, was showing signs that the formula was becoming rather worn:

> Peter Hunt directs the whole thing with an appropriately simplified comic-strip style, the wildly exaggerated fight sound effects being the film's equivalent for POW, ZOCK and ARGHHH. And there's been no penny-pinching on the stunt work. The set pieces – a ski chase gun-battle, a stock car race on ice, an avalanche, a fight on a runaway bobsled, and the explosive climax on a mountaintop – are all crowded into the second half; but while being agreeably spectacular they generate little real tension, since, like Fleming's books, all this action follows so predictable a pattern. But now, as with *Carry On* films, you're bound to know whether you like these things or not; if you do, you'll be pleased to learn that the end credits promise, yet again, that Bond will return.[52]

Austen's reference to the 'Carry On' films, scorned by the critical establishment, is a sure sign of his estimation of the place of the Bond movies in film culture.

One significant difference in the reception from the earlier films, however, was that the trade press, which hitherto had been enthusiastic about the series, was rather less keen on the new Bond. 'The appearance of a new Bond coincides, maladroitly, with a story less gloriously fantastic than its predecessors,' opined Marjorie Bilbow of *Today's Cinema*. 'Without the way-out weapons and weirdly designed vehicles the plot is exposed as a run-of-the-mill adventure in which any adequately athletic performer could take the leading role. This critic, for one, did not approve of the decision to do away with the gadgets and gimmicks.' While Bilbow thought that 'George Lazenby makes a tough, hard-hitting hero with plenty of man appeal', she added that he 'gives no hint of the tiger beneath the man about town skin that was the key to Bond Mark I's fascination for the female section of the audience'. For all her reservations, however, she still observed that 'the action of the last hour or so is superlatively exciting and as a result the film should do excellent business'.[53]

The American critics were also divided about Lazenby, though most of them were impressed by the production values and visual excitement of the film. Pauline Kael found the new Bond 'quite a dull fellow' and added that 'the script isn't much either', but thought that Hunt was 'a wizard at action sequences, particularly an ethereal ski chase that you know is a classic while you're goggling at it, and a mean, fast bobsled that is shot and edited like nothing I've ever seen before'. 'I know that on one level it's not worth doing,' she added, 'but it sure has been done brilliantly.'[54] Kael, therefore, was one of those critics who found the Bond movies essentially trivial, but nevertheless fun. Of the trade papers, *Variety* opined that the film-makers 'have packed so much break-neck physical excitement and stunning visual attractions into *On Her Majesty's Secret Service* that the initial disappointment of George Lazenby replacing Sean Connery as James Bond is almost forgotten by the film's climax'.[55] The *Hollywood Reporter* was the most fulsome in its praise for the new Bond, declaring that the series was 'revitalized' by the presence of Lazenby, who 'brings new youth and humor to a role which had begun to look and act tired'.[56]

However, the North American rentals of *On Her Majesty's Secret Service* were a disappointing $9.1 million, substantially less than the previous three films. It may have been that audiences were put off by the unhappy ending, or simply that they did not want to see anyone other than Sean Connery as James Bond. Some commentators, however, advanced deeper sociological reasons for the apparent decline in Bond's popularity. 'Bondmania', it seemed, had run its course. An article by one such critic in the *New York Times* in February 1970 suggested that the Bond films had suddenly become relics of the past. What had seemed fresh and exciting earlier in the 1960s had become outmoded by the end of the decade: the Bond films had failed to keep pace with the great social and cultural upheavals of the late 1960s, particularly the emergence of the various counter-cultures to whom James Bond now seemed a square and old-fashioned figure. The writer A. Marks admitted to being 'disturbed by the lavish violence which had previously amused so much', especially in the aftermath of the civil disorders of 1968–69, the assassinations of Martin Luther King and Robert Kennedy, and 'the useless obscenity of death in Vietnam'. The spectre of the Vietnam

War blurred straightforward distinctions between good guys and bad guys. Complaining that Bond was 'intellectually fraudulent', the writer implied a parallel between Bond and the American military on the one hand, and SPECTRE and the Vietcong on the other:

> Spectre – that diabolical world organization of sin and corruption – seems less corrupt than Bond himself, not to mention his heartless superiors who license 007 to kill. Meanwhile, the enemy is an enigma. We aren't told why we must hate the enemy, but only that we must at all costs HATE the enemy. But it doesn't work. We are enlightened young men and women who have learned the importance of *knowing* the enemy – and we have learned to know him well in real life. In fact, we are downright intellectual about the enemy. And we aren't buying any hate propaganda; so the evil that lurks behind the guillotine shadows of childhood doesn't frighten the activist-oriented kids of the seventies. We don't get our jollies from sitting in dark theaters and hating prescribed enemies.[57]

But this polemic against the Bond movies provides a less than convincing argument for the relative failure of *Secret Service*. In the first place, straightforward escapist movies with 'prescribed enemies' continued to be popular: *Where Eagles Dare* (1969), a *Boy's Own*-style comic-book war adventure which owed much to the Bond movies in its kinetic action sequences and foregrounding of stunts and pyrotechnics, was one of the biggest box-office winners of the year. And, furthermore, the argument that the violence of the Bond movies was too disturbing for audiences who had witnessed the real thing is very unconvincing given the popularity in the late 1960s of American films such as *Bonnie and Clyde* (1967), *The Dirty Dozen* (1967) and *The Wild Bunch* (1969), all of which surpassed the Bonds in their graphic depiction of violence.

And, in fairness, it has to be said that *On Her Majesty's Secret Service* was not the outright failure that has generally been assumed. While its worldwide rentals of $24 million were just over half those of *You Only Live Twice*, this was a disappointment only in comparison to the other Bond movies, for it was still among the most successful films of the year. Its perceived failure, however, along with the fact that Lazenby made no more Bond movies, has led to the film being unfairly neglected and under-valued. For obvious reasons the producers were not interested in promoting Lazenby, and the film itself came to be treated as something of a poor relation to the rest of the series. Unlike the other films, which were continually and successfully reissued, *Secret Service* was not shown very frequently in revival houses. When it was first shown on American television in 1976 it was screened in a truncated version in two parts as a filler before the soap opera *Rich Man, Poor Man*. And when the Bond films were successfully released on home video, the Sean Connery and Roger Moore films were privileged whereas a full version of *Secret Service* was only belatedly made available. In retrospect, however, the reputation of *Secret Service* has grown, particularly within the Bond fan culture, to the extent that many aficionados – the present writer included – number it among their favourite Bond films.[58]

4

Bond in Transition: *Diamonds are Forever, Live and Let Die, The Man with the Golden Gun*

The perceived failure of *On Her Majesty's Secret Service* was to have highly significant consequences for the future direction of the Bond series. The films which followed during the 1970s were to be very different in style. The three Bond movies of the early 1970s – *Diamonds are Forever* (dir. Guy Hamilton, 1971), *Live and Let Die* (dir. Guy Hamilton, 1973) and *The Man with the Golden Gun* (dir. Guy Hamilton, 1974) – mark a transitional phase in the development of the series. Most obviously, they facilitated the transition from one star to another: Sean Connery, who was lured back to the series for *Diamonds are Forever*, then gave way to Roger Moore for *Live and Let Die*. Unlike Lazenby, Moore proved to be a successful replacement, to such an extent, indeed, that he carried the series on throughout the 1970s and into the mid-1980s, making a total of seven Bond films. On another level, the films of the early 1970s are transitional in that they offered various strategies by which the Bond series attempted to reinvent itself and keep pace with changing popular tastes at a time when many critics were saying loudly that in style and outlook it belonged to the 1960s. Taken together, these films mark a decisive shift away from the more character-driven and less gadget-oriented story of *On Her Majesty's Secret*

Service, turning once again in the direction of gimmicky plot devices, technological fantasy and comedy. Finally, they also mark the point at which the series abandoned any fidelity to the Ian Fleming originals, opting instead for screen stories which used only Fleming's titles and character names.

The change from one star to another inevitably affected the style of the Bond films, particularly at the level of performance. Roger Moore was an established television star from the adventure series *The Saint* and *The Persuaders!*, in both of which his persona had been that of the charming, debonair, international playboy. Moore lacked Connery's brawn and physicality, and did not have the same grace of movement on screen, but what he brought to the role was greater polish and sophistication. Moore was two years older than Connery, but looked younger. 'Roger Moore is 45. I predict he could now be playing James Bond into his fifties,' one critic remarked, presciently, after the actor's series debut.[1] Alexander Walker provides a useful, if somewhat impressionistic, comparison of Connery and Moore:

> The contrast between the two stars was piquant – it was the substitution of the head prefect for the school bully. Moore looked such an essentially *nice* lad; Connery had brought with him a hint of macho relish. The retiring Bond had learnt to wear his wardrobe as if he had grown into it; the new man at first carried *his* with the slight self-consciousness of someone in uniform. Connery was a hairy man, though the growth was mainly on his chest; Moore was a smooth man, and his growth appeared at first glance to be mainly on his scalp. Both men, in their different ways, were virile specimens – and patriots. Roger would have gone all out to win the race for the school; so would Sean, but probably by nobbling his competitor in the locker room.[2]

The main difference, however, was that Moore's forte was light comedy and that his style of performance was more geared towards innuendo and self-mockery than Connery's had been. Both could deliver the Bond one-liners with aplomb, but whereas Connery's had a sardonic wit, Moore's humour was broader and delivered with an even greater wink at the audience. Whereas Connery's one-liners had been used to mitigate violent situations by making a joke about them – such as the occasion in *Thunderball* where he shoots a villain with a spear-gun (what in reality would be a very nasty death) and remarks 'I think he got the point' – Moore's one-liners were delivered in such a way as to suggest that the violence was all a joke to begin with. Thus, in *Live and Let Die*, he disposes of the villain Tee-Hee, who has a metal claw for his right arm, by throwing him out of a moving train in such a way that the arm itself is left behind. 'Just being disarming, darling,' Moore tells his female companion, effectively 'disarming' the violence by suggesting that it is all unreal anyway.

It is fashionable to regard Moore as a 'bad' actor: the former Brylcreem boy who became the king of eyebrow-acting. This is a tendency reinforced by his own self-mocking attitude towards his profession, though in fact, as with stars such as Cary Grant, his performance style is such that the technique is completely hidden. Official publicity suggested that Moore was closer to Fleming's conception of Bond than Connery had been – though as the same claim was also made for both George Lazenby and Timothy Dalton it should perhaps not be taken too seriously. Certainly there are some traits of Moore's Bond – his preference for safari suits and flared trousers, the Cuban cigars which he smokes in his first two films – which reflect the actor rather than the role. His interpretation of Bond was not to the taste of all Bond fans, or even all members of the production team, including Richard Maibaum:

> In a strange way, some people like Roger better than Sean. I certainly don't. I think Roger does very well. He's suave, witty, and so forth, but as far as I'm concerned, he has a dimension of disbelief. He does what I consider unforgivable: he spoofs himself and he spoofs the part. When you start doing that, the audience stops laughing. *Just play the part.*
>
> The most important thing in the Bond pictures is a pretence of seriousness. If your leading man doesn't really appear to believe in what he is doing as either an actor or a character, that will count against the performance's effectiveness.[3]

Maibaum also complained that because Moore did not look as tough as Connery, the scripts had to be tailored accordingly to toughen up his image: 'We knew Roger was not a rough, tough guy like Sean. So, we deliberately gave him things to do that would make him tougher.'

For all that it was not to everyone's liking, however, Moore's performance style was perfectly in tune with the direction the series was taking at the time. Although some commentators have criticised the

Moore films for overplaying the humour, this is to ignore a trend which was already becoming apparent before he joined the series. It was not the arrival of Moore which turned the Bond films in the direction of comedy, but rather the perceived failure of *On Her Majesty's Secret Service*, which had played the action straight and featured a serious love interest. Following *OHMSS*, and until the return to a slightly more serious style in the 1980s, the Bond series became ever more tongue-in-cheek, with elaborate stunts and set pieces usually being concluded with a joke. Action sequences were often played for laughs: all the three films under consideration in this chapter featured chases which invariably ended up with pursuing police cars being involved in multiple pile-ups. Gimmicks and visual jokes became more pronounced, but at the expense of narrative logic and characterisation. The Bond films of the 1970s became more outlandish: visual spectacle, fantastic technology, and increasingly bizarre narrative situations were the order of the day.

The direction which the films took also resulted in them moving further away from Ian Fleming. When *Diamonds are Forever* was under development in 1970, one United Artists executive is reported to have remarked that 'for its annual one hundred thousand dollar fee, the Fleming estate was giving us a few nice characters, ten per cent of a usable plot and a great Fleming title'.[4] The trend towards screenplays which bore little or no resemblance to the Fleming originals might be seen, again, as a reaction to the lukewarm reception of *On Her Majesty's Secret Service*, which had been the closest of all the films to its literary source. Some commentators lamented that the essence of Fleming's Bond had now been lost. George Melly regretted that 'all links with Fleming's cunning exploitation of male fantasy in the fifties and sixties, the realism of technical detail masking the absurd omnipotence of the central figure, have long gone', though he qualified it in so far as 'on the credit side it means that Fleming's dubious morality – the sex, sadism and snobbery as Paul Johnson once categorised it – have vanished too, and good riddance'.[5] It was not only the social context that had changed since the 1950s, moreover, but also that the films' insistence upon technological fantasy meant that they inevitably left Fleming further behind. 'A few Fleming fans will no doubt regret that the films now have to be played strictly for the gags and special effects: but at this distance from the books it is the least incongruous approach,' remarked Christopher Hudson in the *Spectator*.[6]

In other respects, too, the early 1970s was a key transitional moment for the Bond series. The wave of 'Bondmania' had passed; Bond was no longer the cultural phenomenon of the day, but rather, as Bennett and Woollacott have argued, an 'institutionalised ritual'. The Bond films continued to be popular, but the image and character of Bond no longer permeated into the wider realms of popular culture as it had done during the 1960s. Sales of the novels decreased from their mid-1960s peak, and, whereas at the height of 'Bondmania' all the novels had sold well, in the 1970s it was more usually the case that the appearance of a new film would stimulate sales of that particular title (despite the fact that the films themselves now bore so little relation to the originals). Bennett and Woollacott suggest, furthermore, that 'the ideological and cultural concerns to which the figure of Bond resonated had become somewhat less vital, assessed in relation to the changing configuration of British popular culture as a whole'.[7] During the 1960s the Bond films had been one of the elements in the renaissance of British popular culture, but by the 1970s they represented almost the last remnant of that cultural renaissance. The Beatles had broken up, 'Swinging London' had ceased to swing, and there was a sense of what Christopher Booker described as an 'unwelcome explosion into reality'.[8]

For the British film industry, this explosion into reality took the form of facing up to the withdrawal of American finance, following Hollywood's economic crisis at the end of the 1960s. After profligate expenditure on costly extravaganzas which failed to recoup their costs – including not only British-made films such as *Half a Sixpence*, *Goodbye Mr Chips*, *Battle of Britain* and *Cromwell*, but also Hollywood's own self-made disasters like *Doctor Dolittle*, *Star!*, *Hello Dolly* and *Darling Lili* – there was a period of fiscal retrenchment. The Bond series, indeed, was the only major exception, as United Artists continued to provide financial backing for Eon Productions at a time when it, along with the other Hollywood majors, was curtailing its operations in Britain. For British cinema, as for British society as a whole, the 1970s is often regarded as a moribund period in which there was precious little in the way of either cultural innovation or economic success. Whereas the 1960s had given rise to a new, vibrant, youth-oriented film culture which had produced films which succeeded in both artistic and commercial terms, the 1970s has generally been characterised as a time of stagnation. Alexander Walker wrote that British cinema 'looked like the country itself: it had a residual energy, but in the main was feeling dull, drained, debilitated, infected by a run-down feeling becoming characteristic of

British life'.[9] There were precious few of the international successes on the scale of *Tom Jones*, *Alfie* or *Darling* which had brought such prestige to British cinema in the 1960s. In contrast, the most prolific British movies of the early 1970s were low-budget, low-brow comedies made solely for the domestic market: adaptations of television sitcoms, the ailing 'Carry On' series, and blue sex comedies.

The Bond films, which a decade earlier had symbolised the youthful, hedonistic, liberated spirit of the 'swinging sixties', now came to be regarded as a comfortingly old-fashioned ritual. Some critics, indeed, believed that the ideology of the Bond films remained rooted in the 1960s. 'As long as they keep on making James Bond films, the 1960s will never die,' John Russell Taylor remarked in 1973.[10] Vincent Canby thought that *Diamonds are Forever* was 'a nostalgic journey down memory lane' which 'recalls the moods and manners of the sixties (which, being over, now seem safely comprehensible)'.[11] That such opinions should be expressed about both Moore's and Connery's films (Taylor's comment was made in his review of *Live and Let Die*) is significant in that it suggests the differences between the two stars were less important than the overall style of the films.

And what of the place of the Bond movies in film culture? Here, too, there is evidence of significant changes in the ways in which the Bond movies were perceived, and how they perceived themselves in relation to the rest of popular cinema. In the first place, the hostility with which some critics had greeted the early Bond films had entirely disappeared. Critical opprobrium was now reserved for films like Sam Peckinpah's *Straw Dogs* (1970) and Stanley Kubrick's *A Clockwork Orange* (1971), in comparison to which the violence of the Bond movies seemed very tame and unrealistic indeed.[12] A decade earlier some critics had complained about the sex and violence of the early Bond movies, but now they were widely regarded as family entertainment. As George Melly said of *Live and Let Die*: 'With the school hols in the offing, at least 121 minutes can be filled without any effort at all.'[13]

The Bond series found itself having to negotiate the changing nature of popular cinema in the early 1970s. Bennett and Woollacott suggest that the Bond series 'reorganised its cultural associations by referring it to more influential genres within the contemporary cinema'.[14] From Hollywood, for example, there came a new wave of tough law-and-order thrillers with violent heroes who operated both within and outside the law. Foremost among these was Clint Eastwood's rogue cop Harry

Callaghan in *Dirty Harry* (1971) and its sequels *Magnum Force* (1973) and *The Enforcer* (1976); the vigilante alternative was personified by Charles Bronson in *Death Wish* (1974). Films such as these typically featured lone heroes engaged in an urban war against low-life villains, and their content was extremely violent – far more so than the Bond movies. While the Bond series, made for the mainstream family audience, did not set out to compete directly with 'R'-rated (in Britain 'X'-certificate) films like *Dirty Harry* and *Death Wish*, it did have to take the new-style action thrillers into account. Bennett and Woollacott identify a 'law and order' inflection in *Diamonds are Forever* and *Live and Let Die*: in both films Bond works in America alongside the CIA. (In reality the CIA was forbidden by law from operating inside the United States, though here the Bond films unwittingly reflected Nixon's improper domestic use of the Agency.) A more direct influence can be identified at the climax of *Live and Let Die* when Bond discards his usual Walther PPK in favour of a Smith and Wesson .44 Magnum, a massive long-barrelled handgun which was the weapon of choice of Eastwood's 'Dirty Harry'. It might be argued that this was one of the ways in which the films attempted to 'toughen up' Roger Moore's image through the gun's association with male machismo.

Although a relatively minor point in itself, the fact that Bond on one occasion adopted the weapon associated with another screen hero was indicative of how the Bond series had been overtaken by other trends in popular cinema. Whereas in the 1960s the Bond films had started trends – exemplified by the vogue for gimmicky spy movies in the middle of the decade – by the 1970s they seemed to be following trends which had been started elsewhere. So, for example, *Live and Let Die* may be seen as an attempt to cash in on the so-called 'blaxploitation' cycle of the early 1970s, while *The Man with the Golden Gun* features a martial-arts sequence which recalls the kung-fu craze of the time. As one critic remarked: 'It was only a matter of time before kung fu caught up with James Bond. And vice versa.'[15]

In the case of *Diamonds are Forever*, the inspiration which the film-makers sought came not so much from other areas of popular cinema as from the successful pattern established by earlier films in the Bond series itself. Fleming's fourth novel had featured Bond investigating a case of diamond smuggling in which he followed the pipeline to America, travelling from New York to Las Vegas and coming up against a group of American gangsters known as the Spangled Mob. The film of *Diamonds are Forever*, however, owes more to *Goldfinger* than it does to the original novel. *Goldfinger* was the film which had firmly established the Bond formula and which had marked the series' breakthrough in the American market. *Goldfinger*'s Guy Hamilton returned to the director's chair, while the locations for *Diamonds are Forever* were again predominantly American. The desire to rework the earlier film even extended as far as bringing back the same villain. Maibaum said that in his first treatment for *Diamonds are Forever*, Bond was going to come up against Goldfinger's twin brother, a shipping magnate who is black-mailing the world with a giant laser mounted on a supertanker. 'This fellow is supposed to say to Bond at one point, "Oh, my brother Auric – mother always said he was a bit retarded." We were going to cast Gert Frobe again, but it didn't work out.'[16] The diamond-smuggling plot of the original novel was to be maintained in so far as Maibaum had discovered that the first laser beam was generated through a diamond, and Goldfinger would be stockpiling them to build his super-laser. But Maibaum's first treatment was rejected and the producers brought in Tom Mankiewicz, son of screenwriter Joseph L. Mankiewicz and nephew of Herman Mankiewicz (Orson Welles's co-writer on *Citizen Kane*) to revise it. The shooting script of *Diamonds are Forever* bears Mankiewicz's name only, though on the film's titles the screenplay is credited jointly to Maibaum and Mankiewicz.[17] Goldfinger is gone, and Bond's enemy is once again Blofeld. The plot device of stockpiling diamonds to manufacture a powerful laser is maintained, but instead of it being mounted on a supertanker it is launched into space (the idea of a supertanker was to return in *The Spy Who Loved Me*). Blofeld has taken over the identity of a reclusive billionaire whom no one has seen for three years – widely said to have been based on Howard Hughes – and is using his business and industrial empire for cover. Blofeld has also undergone plastic surgery, and has several doubles of himself in order to throw Bond off the scent – thus reworking an idea that Maibaum had considered using for *On Her Majesty's Secret Service* to explain Bond's new appearance.

Bond might have had another new appearance in *Diamonds are Forever*, for with George Lazenby out of the picture the producers had been obliged to look again for another leading man. American actor John Gavin, whose best-known film roles had been as Janet Leigh's boyfriend in Hitchcock's *Psycho* and as the young Julius Caesar in Stanley Kubrick's *Spartacus*, was actually signed to a holding contract.

But United Artists were worried about introducing a new leading man after the disappointment of *OHMSS*, and decided that Connery must be brought back, whatever the cost. United Artists president David Picker personally negotiated the one-picture contract that earned Connery a place in the *Guinness Book of Records* as the (then) highest-paid actor in the world: a straight fee of $1.2 million (which Connery donated to his Scottish International Educational Trust charity), 10 per cent of the gross receipts, and an undertaking from United Artists to back two films of the actor's choice. In the event only one film was made as a result of this agreement: *The Offence* (1972), directed by Sidney Lumet, in which Connery played a police sergeant who beats up a suspected child molester and has a nervous breakdown after the man dies in custody. It is one of Connery's best performances, as far removed from his Bond image as could be imagined.

'*Diamonds are Forever* revealed a Connery who was now packing flab as well as a Walther PPK,' writes Alexander Walker. 'His style resembled an elder statesman of espionage with an implanted pace-maker.'[18] Returning to the role at the age of forty-one, Connery was heavier in build and greying at the temples, but his relaxed, droll performance drew much praise from critics who responded enthusiastically following the disappointment of Lazenby. 'Connery's thickened figure is all to the good, contributing solidity to his imposture [*sic*], as well as a slight weariness which is usefully evident when two young women give him a savage drubbing at bare-handed combat,' remarked *Esquire*'s Thomas Belger.[19] Connery's performance is very much in tune with the style of the film, which emphasises bizarre narrative situations and foregrounds the comic elements: Bond almost being cremated at a funeral parlour, Bond using a piton-gun to climb around outside his hotel while clad immaculately in a black dinner jacket, and Bond being knocked around by two athletic women called Bambi and Thumper. The film even sends up the myth of Bond as superman. When Bond kills one heavy and switches his own wallet for the dead man's, Tiffany Case (Jill St John) is incredulous: 'You've just killed James Bond!' she exclaims. 'Is that who it was? Well, it just goes to show nobody's indestructible,' Connery replies with comic irony. Indeed, Connery's performance in this film prefigures Roger Moore's interpretation of Bond in that he is sending up both the role and himself. The emphasis on comedy, however, is rather at odds with the ending of the previous film.

In narrative, as well as style, *Diamonds are Forever* marks a complete change from *On Her Majesty's Secret Service*. There are no references to the death of Bond's wife (such references would, however, feature in some of the Roger Moore films), and no obvious burning desire for revenge on Bond's part in his confrontations with Blofeld (Charles Gray). In the pre-title sequence Bond tracks down Blofeld and (apparently) kills him in a pit of burning sulphur, but even when Bond says, 'Welcome to hell, Blofeld', it is done with a self-satisfied smirk rather than vengeful relish. M reminds Bond curtly that Blofeld is dead and tells him 'the least we can expect from you now is a little plain, solid work'. It is almost as if *Diamonds are Forever* sets out to erase the memory of Lazenby and *OHMSS*, taking up the Bond story from the time when Connery left the series. Thus, when Sir Donald Munger (Laurence Naismith) asks, 'You've been on holiday, I understand. Relaxing, I hope?', and Connery replies, 'Oh, hardly relaxing, but most satisfying', the film is referring to his 'holiday' from the series and, by implication, to the four non-Bond films – *Shalako*, *The Molly Maguires*, *The Red Tent* and *The Anderson Tapes* – that he made in the interim.

Diamonds are Forever also represents a significant departure from the ideology of national identity that had been constructed in *OHMSS*. Whereas the previous film had emphatically restored the patriotic code of the novels and had been nothing if not explicit in its foregrounding of the motifs of monarchy and country, *Diamonds are Forever* suggests that such ideologies are redundant. 'Surely you haven't come to negotiate, Mr Bond? Your pitiful little island hasn't even been threatened,' taunts Blofeld – a remark which clearly suggests that Britain is a country of little significance in world affairs. As in *Goldfinger*, the threat is directed against America – Blofeld intends to destroy Washington, DC – and Bond's role is to act virtually as a surrogate American hero, with the American military lending support in the climactic destruction of Blofeld's headquarters.

Diamonds are Forever is by far the most camp of the Bond films. 'Camp' itself is virtually impossible to define: originally a term used to describe any form of excessively affected, theatrical or ostentatious behaviour, it is now more often used to refer explicitly to stereotyped homosexual behaviour and mannerisms. All the Bond films are camp in the broader sense of the word, but *Diamonds are Forever* is camp in a more specific sense. 'Camp', according to Jack Babuscio, 'is a way of poking fun at the whole cosmology of restrictive sex roles and sexual identifications which our society uses to oppress its women and repress its men.'[20] Charles Gray's performance as Blofeld, with his affected voice and mannerisms which almost amount to an impersonation of Noël Coward, even down to the cigarette holder, is very camp indeed – especially in a scene where Blofeld appears in drag. The most obviously camp aspect of the film, however, is the characterisation of Blofeld's homosexual assassins Mr Wint and Mr Kidd (Bruce Glover and Putter Smith). In the novel Wint and Kidd had been a pair of unpleasant, vicious killers, but the nastiness of their characters is downplayed in the film to the extent that they function as comic relief rather than representing any real physical threat. Their homosexuality is displayed openly when they are shown holding hands and in Wint's jealous glance when Kidd remarks that 'Miss Case is very attractive – for a lady'; the campness is most evident in Wint's exaggerated mannerisms and his habit of spraying himself with perfume.

In other respects, too, *Diamonds are Forever* foregrounds ostentation and excess. Hamilton's direction emphasises the glitzy colours and gaudy decor of the Las Vegas location, highlighting the excesses of the central character: Bond, in his white tuxedo, cuts a distinctive figure in the midst of the casually dressed clientele of the Whyte House casino. In an ironic reflection of the artificiality of Las Vegas, so many things in the film turn out to be fake: Blofeld's doubles, the diamonds which Bond smuggles in for the villains, the circus sideshow in which a girl supposedly turns into a gorilla, the cat which Bond kicks to determine which is the real Blofeld ('Right idea Mr Bond'; 'But wrong pussy'); even what appears to be the landscape of the moon turns out to be a mock-up at a space research centre. Narrative development takes second place to visual spectacle, and there is an emphasis on the gratuitous destruction of property and vehicles. This is most pronounced in the car chase sequence – itself derivative of the squeal-and-slither chases of *Bullitt* (1968) and *The French Connection* (1971) – in which half a dozen police cars crash into each other as they pursue Bond's red Mustang around a parking lot and through the streets of Las Vegas. Indeed, other than a violent punch-up in a lift which recalls the train fight of *From Russia with Love* in its use of a confined space, most of the action sequences in *Diamonds are Forever* are played for laughs, none more so than when Bond makes his escape from the Whyte Laboratories installation in the Nevada desert in a cumbersome moon buggy.

How was *Diamonds are Forever* received? The critics universally welcomed Connery back into the fold, and most found it an improvement

on its immediate predecessor. The *Monthly Film Bulletin* thought it the
most enjoyable in the series since *Goldfinger*.

> Although – or perhaps because – its plot is an unashamedly thin
> excuse for a colourful assortment of suspenseful set-pieces (an
> acrobatic car chase, Bond's near death in a crematorium, his cliff-
> hanging ascent of a Las Vegas skyscraper), the latest Bond film
> impresses as probably the most efficient and enjoyable since *Gold-
> finger*. The style has become genuinely distinctive, shaped partly
> by Connery's idiosyncratic hero with his impeccable grooming
> and throwaway innuendoes, partly by Ken Adam's highly inven-
> tive set designs. Connery proves again that he is irreplaceable as
> Bond, handling the script's most worn *double entendres* like a master
> ('There's something I want you to get off your chest,' he purrs
> to a bikini-clad girl on a beach); while Adam's surrealistic designs
> for Blofeld's sumptuous penthouse apartment and Bond's hotel
> suite (a sunken bath whose walls encase a miniature aquarium) lift
> the film into a Langian world of high-class espionage. *Diamonds
> are Forever* shares some of its predecessors' faults – the women,
> for all their exotic names, are so many *Playboy* mannequins, Guy
> Hamilton's direction is energetic but somewhat lacking in style,
> and the fascist elements of the Bond image still seem obnoxious
> (especially since Blofeld's rather appealing aim in holding Washing-
> ton to ransom is to secure world disarmament). But the action
> set-pieces remain as watchable as ever, and the whole tone of
> the film improves, as in *Goldfinger*, with the makers' confidently
> tongue-in-cheek approach.[21]

The review, by Nigel Andrews, exemplifies one of the narrative ambiguities of *Diamonds are Forever* in that it is never spelled out precisely
what Blofeld's demands are. Although he tells Dr Metz (Joseph Furst)
that their mutual aim is disarmament, it would seem that this is the
story he has spun to enlist Metz's assistance (he is an expert in laser
refraction). Willard Whyte (Jimmy Dean) tells Bond that Blofeld intends
to hold 'an international auction – with nuclear supremacy going to
the highest bidder'.

Diamonds are Forever marked a return to the box-office heights of the
Bond films of the mid-1960s. Its worldwide rentals were $45.7 million,
of which $19.7 million came from the North American market – over
twice as much as *On Her Majesty's Secret Service*.[22] While most critics

attributed this to the return of Connery, some advanced more sociological reasons to explain the film's success. Only two years earlier the
New York Times had suggested that Bond was out of date at the end
of the 1960s, but another journalist in the same newspaper now argued
that the Bond films provided just the sort of nostalgia that the weary
and disillusioned America of the early 1970s was crying out for:

> *Diamonds are Forever* stands to make about a zillion dollars, and
> nostalgia of an especially piercing sort will have a lot to do with
> it. Simply, the Bond brand of escapist fantasy – to a world where
> the two eternal verities are money and power and the two foregone
> conclusions are violence and sex – scratches an itch, and it's an
> itch that nothing else in the emotionally torpid Nixon era can
> reach as directly. Bond is as authentic an article of the sixties as
> Fred Astaire was of the thirties, and the issue of 'quality' hardly
> seems germane. I don't imagine many of the thousands of people
> who rushed to see *Diamonds are Forever* when it opened paused en
> route to check the reviews. They just rushed.[23]

While some critics thought the film provided escapism from the
problems of the present – Vietnam and Cambodia abroad, and violent
incidents at home such as the Kent State University shootings and
the Attica prison revolt – others argued that *Diamonds are Forever* had
caught the mood of American cinema-goers not because it offered a
nostalgic escape into the past but because it offered a commentary
on contemporary issues and concerns. Andrew Sarris, the influential
film critic of *Village Voice*, suggested that the film successfully brought
the Bond series up to date 'because it demonstrates how to enrich an
established genre by digging deeper into the sociological subconscious
of its audience'. He continued:

> Actually, the major positive virtues of the movie seem to originate
> from the cockily contemporaneous screenplay ... which manages
> to relate to recent headlines without being oppressively relevant
> to the in-depth continuations on the back pages. This process can
> be described as having your cake and throwing it like a custard
> pie. Thus, we get tantalizing glimpses of the Howard Hughes
> empire with its invisible emperor, the ecological nightmare of oil
> rigs off the California coast, spoofs of moon men and their dune
> buggies, Russian nuclear subs and Red Chinese nuclear missiles, a

Los Angeles mortuary out of 'The Loved One', jokes about the
dullness of Kansas as nuclear target and about the deterioration
of Great Britain into a third-rate power.[24]

Sarris added that 'the writers haven't missed a topical beat, even with
the villains, one pair representing the gays, and another representing the
man-hating branch of women's lib'. It is an interesting socio-political
reading of the film by a critic more renowned for his advocacy of the
auteur theory, though intriguingly Sarris said that his favourite Bond
movie was *On Her Majesty's Secret Service*. What the review indicates,
however, is that some critics recognised how the film-makers were
deliberately trying to keep the Bond series up to date through topical
references and plot devices which had some contemporary relevance,
even if they were hardly used in a serious way.

The argument that *Diamonds are Forever* was successful because it
reflected certain contemporary concerns is rather more convincing than
the view that it succeeded simply because it provided a nostalgic return
to the heyday of the 1960s before the impact of Vietnam and social
unrest had been felt. Throughout the 1960s, indeed, the most successful Bond films had enjoyed topical relevance, whether intentional or
unintentional: the relative failure of *On Her Majesty's Secret Service* might
be explained in part by the fact that it had less obvious contemporary
relevance than some of the others. The strategy of topicality can
certainly be seen in the choice of *Live and Let Die* as the next film in
the series, which was in response to a particular cultural and industrial
phenomenon of Hollywood at the time – the hugely successful but
short-lived cycle of black exploitation films of the early 1970s.

Approximately one-quarter of regular American film-goers in the late
1960s and early 1970s were black.[25] The size and importance of the
black audience was illustrated by the box-office success of a cycle of
cheaply made genre movies featuring relatively unknown black actors
which proliferated between 1970 and 1973. Unlike earlier films with black
stars which had explored the issue of racism in a well-intentioned and
thoughtful way, and which were made for a general audience, such as
In the Heat of the Night (1967) and *Guess Who's Coming to Dinner* (1967),
the 'blaxploitation' movies were made primarily for the black, urban
audience, and downplayed racial issues in favour of action-based narratives with heavy doses of sex and violence. The film which is often
taken to represent the start of the cycle is *Cotton Comes to Harlem* (1970),

based on the novel by black crime writer Chester Himes, and the most successful of the blaxploitation films which followed were private-eye and crime thrillers: *Shaft* (1971), *Shaft's Big Score* (1972), *Superfly* (1972), *Slaughter* (1972), *Black Gunn* (1972) and *Shaft in Africa* (1973) were among the more commercially successful of a glut of similar and inevitably derivative films. Richard Roundtree and Jim Brown were the foremost stars who came to prominence as a result of blaxploitation, though the distaff side was represented by Tamara Dobson in *Cleopatra Jones* (1973) and *Cleopatra Jones and the Casino of Gold* (1975) and by Pam Grier as *Foxy Brown* (1974).

Live and Let Die was the obvious choice for the Bond film-makers if they wanted to exploit the success of the blaxploitation cycle in that it was the book which most readily lent itself to a black theme. Fleming's second novel had Bond assigned to investigate the smuggling of seventeenth-century gold coins between the Caribbean and America – treasure which had been seized by the pirate Bloody Morgan and thought lost. The smuggling is traced to Mr Big, a black American gangster who is a member of SMERSH and who is using the treasure to finance Soviet operations in the United States. Mr Big, who was born in Haiti, uses voodoo to ensure the loyalty of his henchmen. Bond travels to New York and, along with Felix Leiter, goes to the Harlem nightclub where Mr Big's headquarters are. Bond meets Mr Big, who is accompanied by Solitaire, a beautiful young white woman who 'can divine the truth in people' and whom he dominates through fear. Bond kills several of Mr Big's men and escapes. He is contacted by Solitaire, who wants him to free her from Mr Big, and the two of them travel to Florida on the Silver Meteor. In Florida, Solitaire is recaptured and Leiter is seriously injured when he is thrown into a shark tank by one of Mr Big's henchmen, The Robber, whom Bond subsequently kills. Bond then follows Mr Big to Jamaica and swims out to the Isle of Surprise where Mr Big's yacht is moored. Bond is captured and, together with Solitaire, is dragged over a coral reef by Mr Big, but Mr Big is killed when his yacht is blown up by a limpet mine previously attached to its hull by Bond.

Although the novel was freely adapted by Mankiewicz, slightly more of Fleming's original plot remained than in *Diamonds are Forever*. When three British agents are killed – one at the United Nations in New York, one in New Orleans, and one on San Monique, a small island in the Caribbean – Bond is assigned to investigate. The villain is now

[handwritten marginal note:] Want to attract blacks

Protect USA one Dr Kananga (Yaphet Kotto), the prime minister of San Monique, who is manufacturing heroin for distribution in the United States. At first it seems that Kananga is in league with Mr Big, but it turns out that the two are one and the same. Kananga's plan is to create a nation of drug addicts by flooding the United States with free heroin and thus putting all his rivals out of business, after which he will have a monopoly in its supply. The film maintains most of the locations of the novel (New York and the Caribbean, though it substitutes Louisiana for Florida), but most of the narrative incidents and action sequences have been invented for the film. Richard Maibaum, who was not involved this time, did not approve of the storyline. 'It was about nothing, a lousy cooking-some-dope-somewhere-in-the-jungle movie,' he said. 'That's not Bond at all. To process drugs in the middle of a jungle is not a Bond caper.'[26]

To what extent can *Live and Let Die* be placed within the context of blaxploitation? In the first instance, the film is not in itself a blaxploitation picture, given that its hero is a white male and that it is set only partly in a black *milieu*. The producers probably hoped that by making some nods to the cycle of black action movies they would attract some of the audience for those films, but a Bond movie still needed to have broad-based audience appeal. Commercial imperatives, therefore, dictated that the film could not stray too far into blaxploitation territory for fear of alienating the mainstream, predominantly white audience. For example, Mankiewicz's original idea that Solitaire should be played by a black actress was vetoed.

By the time *Live and Let Die* was released in the summer of 1973, the blaxploitation cycle had almost run its course anyway. What the film does is to borrow and renegotiate some of the themes and motifs of blaxploitation within the narrative formula of the Bond series. The result, however, is a rather uneasy tension within the film between the use of these themes and motifs on the one hand and the stereotyped representation of black characters as villains on the other. The sequence where Bond goes to Harlem, for example, places him in the *milieu* of blaxploitation as he is captured by flamboyantly dressed gangsters with a nice line in irreverent dialogue ('Names is for tombstones baby. You all take this honky outside and waste him'). Bond's excursion into Harlem makes him look foolhardy, even foolish: he is easily spotted and *black* tailed ('Can't miss him – it's like following a cue ball'), and is chided by black CIA agent Strutter (Lon Satton) for 'that clever disguise you're wearing – white face in Harlem. Good thinking, Bond.' In contrast to the colourful and flamboyant gangsters, Bond comes across as square and old-fashioned – a white man out of place at a time when the coolest and hippest screen hero was Richard Roundtree's John Shaft. But while Bond may seem out of place in Harlem, he does still best the villains at every opportunity, thus reasserting the supremacy of the white hero.

The script itself makes only scant reference to the fact that the villains are black, but at a deeper level the narrative ideology of the film does betray its racist undertones. This is especially evident in the relationship between Bond, Solitaire and Kananga. On one level, of course, Bond's seduction of Solitaire (Jane Seymour), who is in the power of the villain, represents the process of ideological repositioning that had been enacted so often before. But it also represents a different sort of repositioning in that, for the first time in the series, it is made explicit that the heroine is a virgin. Solitaire has the power to predict the future, but knows that she will lose it once she has known 'earthly love'. Kananga, who relies on Solitaire's mystical power, informs her that she will lose it only when he decides, and, moreover, that he will be the one to take it away. Bond effectively tricks her into sleeping with him: knowing that she believes in Tarot cards, he uses a deck stacked with cards representing 'The Lovers' to persuade her they are destined to become lovers themselves. After the act, Bond misinterprets Solitaire's mood as disappointment at her first sexual experience ('Cheer up, darling, there has to be a first time for everyone'), but she is actually more concerned that she has lost her power and that Kananga will kill her because she is no longer of any use to him. Later, when Kananga learns that she has lost her virginity to Bond, he strikes her in fury and shouts hysterically that 'I myself would have given you love – you knew that!' In ideological terms, therefore, there is a racial dimension overlaid on the repositioning of Solitaire in that she is 'saved' from losing her virginity to the black villain by losing it first to the white hero. The film thus embodies one of the oldest themes of white culture: the resistance to miscegenation between black men and white women, which is invariably presented in terms of the black male representing a violent sexual threat to the white woman. In its attitude towards miscegenation, however, the film contrives to have its cake and eat it: while sex between a black man and a white girl is beyond the pale, Bond is allowed a sexual encounter with a black woman, Rosie Carver (Gloria Hendry), albeit that she turns out to be working for Kananga and is quickly killed off. In this sense, there is an undeniable racist subtext to the film, and it was to be noted by a number of critics.

In other respects, *Live and Let Die* develops many of the themes and characteristics of *Diamonds are Forever*, particularly in its virtual Americanisation of Bond: much of the film is again set in America, the threat is directed against America, and Bond is assisted by Leiter and the CIA. It also resembles its predecessor in its comical action sequences and its evident delight in gratuitous displays of destruction. In *Live and Let Die* there are no fewer than four chase sequences which involve some form of vehicular destruction: Bond at the wheel of an out-of-control car on a busy New York freeway; Bond escaping from the San Monique police in an old double-decker bus, during which he slices the top off driving under a low bridge; Bond escaping from Mr Big's heavies at an aerodrome, during which he slices the wings off an aeroplane; and a lengthy speed boat chase through the Louisiana bayous which results in numerous boats and several police cars being written off. 'Personally, I can't get too much of machines smashing each other to smithereens,' declared John Coleman, suggesting that some critics, at least, enjoyed the aesthetic of destruction which had now come to characterise the Bond films.[27] This element of the films might be seen to prefigure the successful *Smokey and the Bandit* (1977), a chase comedy starring Burt Reynolds in which narrative complexity is reduced to the level of one spectacular car crash after another. *Smokey and the Bandit* also borrowed from *Live and Let Die* the characterisation of a dim-witted redneck southern lawman. Sheriff J. W. Pepper (Clifton James) proved so popular with audiences and critics that he was to be brought back in *The Man with the Golden Gun*.

At the level of visual style, however, *Live and Let Die* differs from *Diamonds are Forever*. Both of Moore's first two films reverted to the standard aspect ratio, which had not been used since *Goldfinger*, rather than using Panavision – an odd decision given that the appeal of the Bond films was based so much on their visual spectacle, which was undoubtedly enhanced by the widescreen process. Like *From Russia with Love*, *Live and Let Die* does not have the 'epic' feel of other Bond films, due largely to the absence of any lavish interiors in the Ken Adam style: production designer Syd Cain favours real exteriors above studio sets. It was also the first Bond film for which John Barry did not write the music, though the score by former Beatles producer George Martin, and the title song written and performed by Paul McCartney and Wings, are both among the best of the series, using a mixture of rock and reggae motifs in place of Barry's more familiar orchestral compositions, effectively matching the music to the locations (Harlem, New Orleans, the Caribbean).

Live and Let Die is very much a transitional film in the Bond series, its main purpose, of course, being to introduce the new star. But the film does, intriguingly, explore other narrative possibilities, particularly through the introduction of a supernatural theme. 'Somewhere at the back of the script is an ingenious idea about fates and furies, the Tarot cards being intended to guide Bond's actions more closely than he'd care to admit,' observed Philip Strick; 'while the curious encounters with Baron Samedi suggest a chunk of plot that nobody finally cared to face up to.'[28] Tarot cards are used as a linking motif through the first half of the film. Each of the main characters is linked to one of the cards: Solitaire is 'The High Priestess', Rosie is 'The Queen of Cups' (a treacherous, deceitful woman), and Bond is 'The Fool' – a highly significant motif in that critics were coming increasingly to regard the films as comedies. The voodoo theme is maintained from the novel, particularly through the character of Baron Samedi (Geoffrey Holder) who appears both as one of Kananga's henchmen and as a performer in a dance routine. Although Samedi is killed when Bond knocks him into a coffin full of poisonous snakes, he reappears just before the end credits perched on front of the train on which Bond and Solitaire are travelling to New York. Inexplicable in narrative terms, this is the only explicitly supernatural moment in the Bond series which elsewhere, for all its implausibility, is insistent on rationality.

The critical reception of *Live and Let Die* was mixed. Most reviewers made the point that the Bond films had now become action comedies rather than action thrillers, a tendency reinforced by the performance of the new star. 'Roger Moore has none of the gravitas of Sean Connery,' said Christopher Hudson, '... but he does fit slickly into the director's presentation of Bond as a lethal comedian let loose in a world of thuggish buffoons who are a little slower on the punch-lines'. 'As a matter of fact,' Hudson added, 'Guy Hamilton, after two mediocre films, has brought the Ian Fleming sequence back into top gear with as fast-paced and snappily entertaining piece of claptrap as we have a right to expect.'[29] But other critics felt that the film's attempt to reflect cultural trends had fallen flat. 'And if *Live and Let Die* does break new ground – perhaps it hopes for topicality by having all its villains black – the advantages in terms of newsworthiness are nuanced by characterisation nearer to *Porgy and Bess* than to *Shaft*,' opined John Russell Taylor. 'Will James Bond live on in the 1970s? Not much further, if this episode is anything to go by.'[30]

It was the racial elements of the film which drew most comment, and which proved most controversial. In America the film was attacked for its alleged racial bias, with Richard Schickel of *Time* magazine sarcastically labelling Bond 'the Great White Hope' and describing the film itself as 'the most vulgar addition to a series that has long since outlived its brief historical moment – if not, alas, its profitability'. He went on:

> As for Bond's new character as a racist pig, there is a dubious rationale for it. Through the years he has kicked and chopped his way through most of the other races of man, so it could be argued that it is just a matter of equal rights to let blacks have their chance to play masochists to his pseudo-suave sadist. Not surprisingly, this strained justification fails to relieve the queasiness *Live and Let Die* induces. Why are all the blacks either stupid brutes or primitives deep into the occult and voodooism? Why is miscegenation so often used as a turn-on? Why do such questions even arise in what is supposed to be pure entertainment?[31]

However, charges of racism were rejected by Dilys Powell, who thought that 'the blacks are the true heroes of the latest fantasy on an Ian Fleming theme' and who offered a reading of the film which was precisely the opposite of Schickel's:

> Racist? Nonsense, unless you mean anti-white racialism, for it is true that the film is slanted against the incompetence of the whites, who let the blacks run rings around them and so far as I can see would founder without trace if it were not for our old friend James Bond. As you were – our new friend: this time we have Roger Moore in the role.
>
> It is the blacks, though, whom one watches most eagerly. I know they are generally designated as the enemy in the film (not always: Bond is glad of a hand from a black CIA man in New York, and he would never have got to the sinister Caribbean island without his faithful black boatman). But such charming enemies,

so well-mannered, sometimes so pretty (don't you find the black decoy played by Gloria Hendry more appealing than the statuesque Tarot-card dealer played by Jane Seymour?). Clever too: such ingenious methods of disposing of a body (look out for the coffin in New Orleans), so startling a variety of man-traps, such perfection of communication: if they tail James Bond they tail him not with taxis (taxis are old hat) but with telephone calls to every street corner.[32]

Opinions differed, therefore, over the representation of the black villains. What is most intriguing about these reviews is that American and British critics could put forward such different, indeed diametrically opposed, interpretations of the same film – which says rather less about the film itself than it does about the prevailing racial attitudes of the two countries at the time.

In hindsight, however, *Live and Let Die* seems less offensively racist than it does merely dated. The colourful costumes and slang dialogue of the gangsters, redolent as it is of the blaxploitation cycle, dates the film at a precise historical moment in the early 1970s. The style and idiom of black cinema have since changed dramatically from those represented by blaxploitation, evidenced by the films of directors such as Spike Lee and Robert Townsend. And, while it is hard not to agree with Schickel's observations about the stupidity of the black villains in *Live and Let Die* – Powell's review reads more like an apologia – this is perfectly in line with the characterisation of villains in other Bond movies, and indeed in popular action cinema generally. In other words, they are stupid because they are villains, not because they are black.

The racist undertones which some critics detected in *Live and Let Die* did not damage its performance at the box-office. With worldwide rentals of $48.7 million it actually made slightly more than *Diamonds are Forever*, though when the figures are broken down it took less in North America ($15.9 million) and more overseas ($32.8 million). This represented the biggest ratio difference between domestic and foreign earnings for any film in the series since *Dr No*. But the overall success of the film suggested that audience acceptance of Moore was great enough to sustain the series. In order to consolidate him in the role, Moore's second Bond film was produced quickly and released at the end of 1974, the first time that Bond films had been released in successive calendar years since the mid-1960s.

The Man with the Golden Gun had been Fleming's last full novel, and was not one of his best. The book begins with a bizarre oedipal situation in which Bond, presumed dead at the end of *You Only Live Twice*, returns to London and immediately tries to assassinate M in his office. It turns out that Bond, suffering from memory loss, had travelled from Japan to Russia, where he had been recognised by the Russians and brainwashed. After Bond's memory has been restored, M gives him the opportunity to redeem himself by terminating the career of Francisco Scaramanga, a Cuban-based gunman who has been responsible for the death of several British agents. Scaramanga is known as 'the Man with the Golden Gun' because he uses a gold-plated Colt .45 revolver with gold bullets. Bond travels to Jamaica, where he traces Scaramanga to a brothel where he is staying with a group of other gangsters. Bond insinuates himself into Scaramanga's entourage – it is implied that Scaramanga, who is thought to be homosexual, finds him attractive – and learns that Scaramanga is involved in sabotaging the Jamaican economy and smuggling drugs into the United States. When Bond's real identity is discovered there is a gunfight on a speeding train, which is derailed by an explosion. Bond follows Scaramanga into a swamp and kills him.

Given that Caribbean locations had been used in *Live and Let Die*, the film version of *The Man with the Golden Gun* changed the location to the Far East: Macao, Hong Kong and Thailand. In certain ways the film is an improvement on the novel, with the character of Scaramanga upgraded from a fairly run-of-the-mill hoodlum to the world's foremost assassin, whose price is $1 million per hit. Mankiewicz originally envisaged the relationship between Bond and Scaramanga as a reworking of that between hero and villain in the classic western *Shane* (1953), and veteran heavy Jack Palance, who had played the sadistic Wilson to Alan Ladd's morally righteous Shane, was considered to play Scaramanga, though in the event the role went to Christoper Lee. In hindsight it is hard to imagine Palance as Scaramanga: his brand of screen villainy was roughly sinister, whereas Lee's was smoothly sinister and much more in keeping with the character of a highly paid, sophisticated killer who, like Bond, enjoys the best things in life. However, the screenplay was revised by Maibaum after Mankiewicz pulled out following a disagreement with director Hamilton, and for some reason it was deemed necessary to introduce an extra layer of plot in which Scaramanga has stolen a device capable of harnessing the sun's energy and is planning on cornering the world market in solar power. This was a topical theme at the time due to the world oil crisis brought about when the Arab nations of OPEC (Organisation of Petroleum Exporting Countries) put an embargo on oil export due to the Yom Kippur War. Britain was particularly hard hit, as the oil crisis came at a time when there was also a growing shortage of coal but before the North Sea oil and gas fields had come on line. There was a massive cut in energy supplies, the price of oil increased fourfold and consequently there was huge inflationary pressure on the economy and the worst balance-of-payments deficit (some £1.5 billion in 1973) hitherto recorded. The result, in the words of historian Kenneth Morgan, was an 'intensified feeling of national weakness, even impotence, prevalent throughout the nation in the wake of the oil crisis and the inflationary explosion as never before'.[33]

Grafting the solar-energy plot on to the duel between Bond and Scaramanga does not work entirely successfully in *The Man with the Golden Gun*, which, despite many outstanding individual moments and a splendid villain, is overall one of the less satisfying Bond films. It is fundamentally structurally flawed in that it contains two lines of narrative which are only tangentially and coincidentally linked. On one level there is the topical solar energy theme, or what might be termed the public plot. Bond has been assigned to track down a missing solar energy expert who has perfected the 'solex agitator', which offers a way of solving the energy crisis. The solex is the 'MacGuffin' of the film, much of which features the device passing from one person to another. On another level there is the private plot concerning the relationship between Bond and Scaramanga, which is far more interesting ideologically. The main threat is a personal one directed against Bond in that Scaramanga wants to fight him in a duel to the death ('You see, Mr Bond, like every great artist I want to create an indisputable masterpiece once in my lifetime – the death of double-oh seven, *mano a mano*, face to face'). Scaramanga admires Bond to the extent that he has a wax effigy of him in the bizarre shooting gallery where he tests his skills against his prey. There is none of the implied homosexuality of the novel; rather, Scaramanga sees himself and Bond as professional equals. One scene, where Scaramanga entertains Bond to lunch before their duel, perfectly encapsulates one of the key ideological themes of the Bond series: the notion of Bond as a servant of the Crown. Scaramanga taunts Bond by mocking his allegiance to Queen and country ('You work for peanuts – a hearty well-done from Her Majesty the Queen and a pittance of a pension. Apart from that, we are the same'). Thus the monarchical authority underlying Bond's profession is alluded to once again. Bond's reply asserts the official and moral legitimation for his own actions which differentiate him from Scaramanga ('When I kill it's on the specific orders of my government, and those I kill are themselves killers'). Following this interesting rehearsal of ideologies, however, the duel between Bond and Scaramanga is quite a tame affair, with Bond eventually killing his foe by posing as his own effigy – a moment which gave critics of Moore's acting an obvious source of amusement. Moreover, the flawed structure of the film is such that the duel, which should have been the climax, is followed by a boring and redundant sequence in which Bond has to retrieve the solex device from Scaramanga's solar energy plant before it blows up.

The flaws in the narrative structure of *The Man with the Golden Gun* are exacerbated by a constant tension between the serious and comic elements in the film. It does not seem sure whether it is intended as a straight action thriller or as a comedy thriller, resulting in an uneasy combination of the two. There are some thematically interesting ideas which are not fully developed. The film invokes the association of the gun with the phallus, an idea which has become widespread due to the popularisation of Freudian psychoanalytical theory. This is evident not only in the blatant lyrics of the title song ('He has a powerful weapon, he charges a million a shot'), but also in the scene where Scaramanga, after killing a victim, caresses the face and lips of his mistress Andrea (Maud Adams) with the barrel of his recently discharged golden gun. But, like the supernatural theme of *Live and Let Die*, the phallic symbolism and fetishism of *The Man with the Golden Gun* is not explored any further. On a political level, the film once again alludes to Britain's decline – secret service headquarters in Hong Kong are located, rather symbolically, on the submerged wreckage of the liner *Queen Elizabeth* – and again suggests that Red China is a threat lurking in the background: Scaramanga's island is in Chinese territorial waters, where he lives rent-free in return for doing his landlords 'the occasional favour'. But elsewhere, the psychoanalytical and political aspects of the film are diffused by its insistence on broad comedy. The chase sequences verge on slapstick; heroine Mary Goodnight (Britt Ekland) is characterised as a scatter-brained bimbo in a bikini; the character of J. W. Pepper makes an irrelevant return as a loud-mouthed American tourist in Thailand; and there are some excruciating puns on oriental names which might be considered racist (character names like Hai Fat and Chu Mee, not to mention a wine called Phu Yuck). The tradition of physically bizarre villains in the Bond series, moreover, is spoofed by the character of Scaramanga's manservant Nick Nack (Hervé Villechaize): the name may recall Oddjob, but as he is a midget he presents no credible physical threat to Bond with the result that, like Wint and Kidd in *Diamonds are Forever*, he functions mainly as comic relief. In comparison to the characterisation of Nick Nack, Scaramanga's own physical peculiarity of having three nipples – the source of some fairly obvious humour ('A fascinating anatomical titbit'; 'I think he found me quite titillating') – seems positively tasteful.

The Man with the Golden Gun is also highly derivative of other films. As visually impressive as Peter Murton's design for Scaramanga's hall of mirrors is, the sequences in the shooting gallery are strongly reminiscent of the famous climax of Orson Welles's *The Lady from Shanghai* (1948), though they are rather less suspenseful. And, just as *Live and Let Die* had been influenced to some extent by blaxploitation, so too *The Man with the Golden Gun* imitates another popular phenomenon of the early 1970s, namely the kung-fu craze. Martial-arts films emerged in Hong Kong and Taiwanese popular cinema in the late 1960s, though their international breakthrough came in the early 1970s with the emergence of the superbly athletic Bruce Lee as the kung-fu hero *par excellence* in films like *The Big Boss* (1971), *Fist of Fury* (1972) and *Game of Death* (1973). The kung-fu films, which bore some resemblance to Japanese *samurai* films, reduced narrative to a virtually non-existent level while foregrounding action as spectacle, their fight sequences choreographed with the precision of a complex dance routine and having an almost balletic quality of their own. The most successful, internationally, was the Hollywood-backed *Enter the Dragon* (1973), starring Bruce Lee, John Saxon and Jim Brown as secret agents on a mission to break up a gang of white slavers and drug dealers operating from a fortress on a Chinese island; the frenetic climax is among the most spectacular exhibitions of martial-arts fighting ever put on the screen. With Bond travelling to the Far East in *The Man with the Golden Gun*, it was inevitable that, given the success of kung-fu cinema at the time, the film would incorporate a martial-arts sequence. At one point Bond finds himself a prisoner in a karate school where he is forced to fight the star pupil, which he does reasonably capably, but once again an action sequence ends up being played for comedy. Thus, in a spoof of one of the conventions of kung-fu cinema in which the high-kicking heroes would take on dozens of opponents at the same time, Bond is saved from the entire assembly of the karate school by two teenage schoolgirls who chop and kick their way through the opposition.

The narrative and structural flaws of *The Man with the Golden Gun* go a long way towards explaining its rather lukewarm reception. It was the least successful film in the series since *On Her Majesty's Secret Service*: its worldwide rentals amounted to $37.2 million, but only $9.4 million of that came from the North American market. The overwhelming critical response was that the Bond formula was looking tired, despite the usual high production values. 'Guy Hamilton, the most experienced Bond director of them all, goes through his paces once again with admirable stoicism and occasional flair,' said Derek Malcolm. 'But he can't disguise the fact that the script is just about the limpest of the lot and that Roger Moore as 007 is the last man on earth to make it sound better than it actually is.'[34] Tom Milne found it 'sadly lacking in wit or imagination' and observed that it had resorted to imitations of other films: 'This series, which has been scraping the barrel for some time, is now through the bottom and tarting up a silly story about a stolen energy device with depressing borrowings from Hong Kong kung-fu movies, not to mention more depressing echoes of "Carry On" smut.'[35] Some critics even suggested that the Bond series had run its course, or at least that it should be given a rest. According to Jay Cocks in *Time*:

> Although the final screen credits promise that Bond will return in *The Spy Who Loved Me*, it is time to retire him. He should be packed off to a sanitarium, where he can give his liver a rest and wait in leisure for his moment to come again. Right now, Bond has been around too long to be fresh, but not long enough to qualify as a genuine antique.[36]

Clearly there was a feeling that the series had run out of steam, that it had become predictable and derivative. But, although there would be a slightly longer than usual gap until the release of the next film, Bond was not to be retired, and indeed would return in the late 1970s with all his popular appeal restored.

5

Keeping the British End Up:
The Spy Who Loved Me, Moonraker

*T*he *Spy Who Loved Me* (dir. Lewis Gilbert, 1977) and *Moonraker* (dir. Lewis Gilbert, 1979) marked the return of the Bond series to the popular acclaim which it had enjoyed during the 1960s. *The Spy Who Loved Me*, which was the first Bond movie to be produced by Broccoli alone following his split with Saltzman in 1975, earned total worldwide rentals of $80 million, over twice as much as *The Man with the Golden Gun*, of which some $24 million came from North America. These figures were surpassed by *Moonraker*, which earned total worldwide rentals of $87.7 million, of which $33 million came from North America.[1] When converted to estimated wordwide grosses, these figures approximate to $186 million for *The Spy Who Loved Me* and $203 million for *Moonraker*.[2] While these increased figures were due in no small measure to the effect of inflation, they still represent a significant upturn in Bond's box-office fortunes following the relatively disappointing performance of *The Man with the Golden Gun*. Taking inflation into account, *Moonraker* was probably not quite as successful as *Thunderball* had been, but its total grosses were the biggest for any of the Bond films until *GoldenEye* in 1995.

For all the popular success of these films, however, it was not a stable time for the film industry or for the Bond franchise itself. Alexander Walker considers that the mid-1970s marked 'the lowest point in British film-making' and 'the lowest, most shameful nadir of film industry fortunes'.[3] Cinema attendances continued to decline, while the number of British feature films produced per year fell dramatically from an average of between seventy and eighty during the 1960s, and between eighty and ninety in the early 1970s, to sixty-four in 1976, forty-two in 1977, and fifty-one in 1978.[4] Most British productions were low-budget comedies and 'sexploitation' films made for the domestic market – *Confessions of a Window Cleaner* (1974), for example, was the most successful British film of its year – though there were still a handful of big-budget films aimed at the international market such as *Murder on the Orient Express* (1974), *The Eagle Has Landed* (1976), *Shout at the Devil* (1976) and *The Wild Geese* (1978). At a time when there were numerous expensive flops, most notoriously the spectacular failure of Lord Lew Grade's $34 million production *Raise the Titanic!* (1980), the continuing international success of the Bond series came as welcome relief for the British film industry.

The production base of the Bond series in Britain had substantial economic benefits for both the series' producers and the film industry. In 1974 it was estimated that the Bond films had drawn over £3 million from the Eady Levy.[5] Given that the Eady money was distributed among eligible producers on the basis of box-office takings, it amounted, in effect, to a subsidy for commercial success. At the same time, however, the Bond films were big-budget productions which invested in British personnel and facilities. At a time when British studios were faced with serious under-employment and loss of revenue due to the sudden decline in production – Elstree, for example, halved its workforce in 1975 – the presence of the Bond series had become increasingly important to Pinewood. As *Screen International* reported in August 1976: '*The Spy Who Loved Me* has taken somewhat longer than the average Bond film to get to the production stage – as many people in the film industry will have noticed, not least the management of Pinewood Studios, which rather depends on the Bond pictures these days to absorb some of the studio's own costs.'[6] Pinewood had even greater reason to be thankful, for in 1976 Eon Productions invested some £400,000 in the construction of a new silent stage, then the biggest in the world, when it was realised that existing stages would be too small to accommodate the massive sets planned for *The Spy Who Loved Me*. Opened by former Prime Minister Sir Harold Wilson on 5 December 1976, the '007 Stage' was a permanent stage (unlike the volcano set built for *You Only Live Twice*) which could be rented out to other producers.

However, the future of the Bond series at this time was not as stable as the investment in the '007 Stage' would seem to suggest. For all the popular success which the films enjoyed, there were a number of problems. For one thing, there was a dramatic increase in production costs in the late 1970s. Whereas the previous three films had all cost around $7 million, the negative cost of *The Spy Who Loved Me* was $13 million. This was due mostly to inflation, though it also reflected the series' return to the scale of visual spectacle and level of production values which had characterised the mid-1960s films, following the relatively low-key style of Roger Moore's first two films. Broccoli hinted to the trade press that *The Spy Who Loved Me* might be a make-or-break film for the series: 'Hopefully, we'll reach that if the picture is successful. If it isn't, we've had it, that's all – you roll the dice and that's it.'[7] But while *The Spy Who Loved Me* was almost twice as expensive as each of the three films before it, *Moonraker* was over two-and-a-half times as expensive as *The Spy Who Loved Me*, with a negative cost of $34 million.

Moonraker was also the first Bond movie not to be based at Pinewood Studios. Although *Screen International* had suggested in 1976 that Broccoli 'feels it would be sacrilege to take Bond elsewhere', by early 1977 (before the completion of *The Spy Who Loved Me*) it was being rumoured that future Bond films might be lost to Britain.[8] Early in 1978 it was announced that *Moonraker* would be made in France. Broccoli was highly critical of the circumstances which had forced him to abandon, albeit as it happened only temporarily, the British production base, complaining, with much justification, that he had been making films in Britain since the early 1950s. 'I made pictures, stayed during the industry's trials and tribulations and invested a great deal of money,' he said. 'But now "they" are turning people out.'[9] 'They' were the Callaghan government, which had increased tax to such an extent that it not only affected Broccoli personally, who moved back to California after living for twenty-five years in Britain, but also made the production of a film on the scale of *Moonraker* prohibitively expensive. In the event, *Moonraker* was filmed at three major French studio complexes – Epinay, Billancourt and Boulogne – with only the special effects work carried out at Pinewood.

The rising costs of production were not the only problem which the Bond series faced in the late 1970s. There had been difficulties over the screen adaptation of *The Spy Who Loved Me*, the rights for which had been granted on the condition that only the title could be used, and not the story. The novel of *The Spy Who Loved Me* had been an experiment in which Fleming varied the usual Bond formula. It was written as if from the point of view of a woman, Vivienne Michel, who once had a liaison with James Bond. Vivienne leaves England after two disappointing love affairs and, after a series of travels, ends up at a motel in New York State where she is offered a job running it. However, it turns out that the owner is involved in an insurance scam, and two gangsters, Horror and Sluggsy, arrive with the intention of burning the motel down. They are about to assault Vivienne when James Bond arrives, entirely by chance (it is later explained that the episode occurs after *Thunderball* when Bond is engaged in tracking down the fugitive Blofeld). Bond kills the two gangsters, spends the night with Vivienne and leaves in the morning.

'It is true that Fleming forbade the film adaptation of *The Spy Who Loved Me*, but that was no excuse for attaching the title to a very unFlemingian hotchpotch,' remarked Anthony Burgess.[10] Intriguingly, Burgess himself had at one stage been commissioned to write a screenplay for *The Spy Who Loved Me*, which was to feature the relationship between Bond and a female Russian spy, though his treatment was rejected. Other writers involved at one stage or another included John Landis and Stirling Silliphant, while Guy Hamilton was once again slated to direct until he withdrew and was replaced by Lewis Gilbert.[11] Richard Maibaum wrote a screenplay reintroducing SPECTRE, which had been absent from the most recent films, and which began with a new, radical group of terrorists 'comprised of everyone from the Red Brigade to the Weathermen' taking over SPECTRE headquarters:

> They level the place, kick Blofeld out, and take over ... They're a bunch of young idealists. In the end, Bond comes in and asks, 'All right, you're going to blow up the world. What do you want?' They reply, 'We don't want *anything*. We just want to start over – the world is lousy. We want to wipe it away and begin again. So, there's no way we can be bribed.'
>
> I never had Stromberg – or whomever the hell it was in that movie – or that interminable thing that went on in the tanker.[12]

This treatment was turned down, according to Maibaum, because 'Cubby thought it was too political. So many young people in the world support those people that we would have scrambled sympathies in the picture.'

A rather more plausible explanation for doing away with Maibaum's plot, however, was that at the time of pre-production on *The Spy Who Loved Me* Broccoli was involved in a legal dispute with Kevin McClory. McClory, who was planning to produce his own rival Bond film in the mid-1970s, based on the treatments he had developed with Fleming in 1959, now claimed that the organisation SPECTRE had been his brainchild and that Eon Productions were not entitled to use it at all. In order to avoid protracted legal problems which might further delay production of the film, Eon decided to remove all references to SPECTRE from *The Spy Who Loved Me*. The final shooting script was by Christopher Wood, hitherto best known as writer of the 'Confessions' films; on the film itself Maibaum and Wood share the writing credit.[13]

'It's the Biggest. It's the Best. It's Bond – and B-E-Y-O-N-D', declared trailers and posters for *The Spy Who Loved Me*. It is a film in which size and spectacle are everything. The series returned to the widescreen Panavision process and to the massive Ken Adam sets that had been absent since *Diamonds are Forever*. The villain has not one but two headquarters: an ocean research laboratory called Atlantis, which rises from beneath the sea on spider-like legs, and an ocean-going supertanker. The cinematography of Claude Renoir (nephew of the great French director Jean Renoir) emphasises the 'epic' (in the sense of size) canvas against which the action takes place by constantly showing human beings who are dwarfed by the physical environment around them. This is evident not only in the studio sets, but in the real locations, which obviously were chosen for the visual possibilities they offered: the Pyramids, the Temple of Karnak and the Valley of Kings. The film juxtaposes the ancient and the modern: the dusty, crumbling edifices of Ancient Egypt are contrasted with the smooth, metallic modernity of Atlantis. In plot terms, *The Spy Who Loved Me* returns to the countdown-to-doomsday theme that had been absent from Roger Moore's first two Bond outings. There is also an emphasis on ever more elaborate and visually exciting technological gadgetry, ranging from Bond's rocket-firing ski-stick to his sleek Lotus Esprit sports car which transforms into a submersible.

The foregrounding of visual spectacle is established from the beginning of the film with the justly celebrated pre-title sequence in which Bond, pursued by a KGB hit squad, skis off the side of a vast precipice and free falls into space, whereupon a parachute (inevitably decorated with a Union Jack) opens above his head. Widely regarded as one of the most spectacular stunts in cinema history, it was to have a pronounced effect on the future development of the series in that whereas the pre-title sequences of previous films had generally featured punch-ups (*Goldfinger*, *Thunderball*) or atmospheric scene-setting (*From Russia with Love*, *The Man with the Golden Gun*), the trend hereafter was to use the pre-title sequence as an excuse to display a stunt of an ever more spectacular and excessive nature. Following the sheer audacity of the parachute stunt, the theme song 'Nobody Does It Better', performed over the main titles by Carly Simon, reaffirms Bond's status as the premier movie action hero. (It might also be read, of course, as a statement of Broccoli's ability to produce the series alone following his break with Saltzman.)

Its sheer size and spectacle make *The Spy Who Loved Me* the perfect illustration of the 'Bondian' production ideology in which everything has to be the 'biggest' and the 'best'. The film was not only expensive, it was deliberately intended to look expensive as well; it follows in exemplary measure the old adage of putting the budget on the screen. There are other ways, too, in which it can be seen, rather like *Goldfinger*, as one of the definitive Bond movies in which all the required ingredients are in place. As a genre film, it is a compendium of the narrative formulae and conventions of the entire series. The source for the film is not Fleming, but rather all the previous Bond movies themselves. '*The Spy Who Loved Me* is basically an anthology of all the Bond films that have gone before,' writes John Brosnan. 'It's as if Broccoli and his team deliberately set out to take a number of the more memorable set-pieces and remake them, even bigger and more spectacular.'[14] Brosnan identifies ingredients such as a ski chase (*On Her Majesty's Secret Service*), a train fight (*From Russia with Love*, *Live and Let Die*), Bond's modified sports car (*Goldfinger*), and an underwater battle (*Thunderball*), as reworking tried and trusted elements from other films in the series. At the level of plot, the closest resemblance is to *You Only Live Twice*, significantly also directed by Lewis Gilbert, in that it revolves around a criminal megalomaniac with his own private army who intends to destroy the world by causing the United States and the Soviet Union to destroy each other in a nuclear war. Stromberg (Curt Jurgens), a shipping magnate and 'one of the richest men in the world', has perfected a submarine tracking system which he uses to hijack British and Russian ballistic missile submarines. With Stromberg's own crews in place, the submarines are then sent out to fire missiles at

Moscow and New York and thus trigger mutual nuclear annihilation. The climax again recalls *You Only Live Twice* in that Bond releases the imprisoned submarine crews who battle against Stromberg's men for control of the tanker, and Bond must break into the fortified control room before the submarines can launch their missiles.[15]

However, there is another film which invites comparison to *The Spy Who Loved Me*, and which reaffirms the generic links between the Bond series and the British imperialist spy thriller. There are some intriguing plot similarities between the tenth Bond spectacular and the relatively less well-known *Q-Planes* (1939), directed by American Tim Whelan. This was one of the eve-of-war cycle of spy thrillers which the British cinema produced in 1939 (others included *The Four Just Men*, *Traitor Spy*, *Spies of the Air* and *The Spy in Black*) and which were seen, both at the time and in hindsight, as reflecting the increased international tensions of the time. A polished and entertaining thriller which, like the Bond films, combines both action and comedy, *Q-Planes* also anticipates several of the specific plot devices of *The Spy Who Loved Me*. Thus, while *The Spy Who Loved Me* revolves round the mysterious disappearance of nuclear submarines, which transpire to have been hijacked by a supertanker equipped with a tracking system, *Q-Planes* revolves around the mysterious disappearance of secret prototype bomber planes, which transpire to have been hijacked by a salvage ship equipped with a radio-beam which cuts out the engines and radios of the aeroplanes. The planes are picked up by crane and concealed in the hold of the ship, called the *Viking*, just as in *The Spy Who Loved Me* the tanker *Liparus* opens its bows to capture the submarines which are then concealed inside. The *Viking* belongs to a 'foreign power' which is unnamed but which, given the political situation at the time, is surely meant to be Germany. There are two hero-figures in *Q-Planes*: test pilot Tony McVane (Laurence Olivier) and secret service agent Major Hammond (Ralph Richardson). Hammond, an eccentric character who wears a homburg and always carries a rolled umbrella (seen by some commentators as a satiric allusion to Neville Chamberlain), was said by Patrick Macnee to have been the inspiration for his performance as John Steed in *The Avengers*. Although he is the most memorable of the characters, it is the more conventional hero-figure McVane who is involved in the action at the film's climax. His plane is intercepted by the enemy ship but, in another anticipation of *The Spy Who Loved Me*, McVane frees the imprisoned crews of the other planes who take over the ship after an exciting battle. The similarities between the two films may be coincidental, but they are sufficient to show that *The Spy Who Loved Me* should be seen not merely as a compendium of all the other Bond movies, but also as part of a generic lineage of the British spy film which extends back to the 1930s.

In identifying the similarities between *The Spy Who Loved Me* and other films, both Bond and non-Bond, however, that is not to say that *The Spy* itself has nothing new to offer. Indeed, the film rings some changes on the underlying ideologies of the Bond films which makes it particularly important in the overall development of the series. Tony Bennett's reading of the narrative, while seeing it essentially as a re-working of the 'SPECTRE genre', also suggests that it has a particular meaning and relevance in the political context of the late 1970s when fears about nuclear proliferation threatened to undermine the fragile détente in the Cold War:

> Indeed, bearing no relation to the novel from which it derives its title, the film is in a sense the perfection of the SPECTRE genre, although SPECTRE is never mentioned, inasmuch as Stromberg's ransom plan is applied indiscriminately to East and West, playing upon the tensions which subsist beneath détente, Stromberg himself being presented to us as a personification of the irrational forces which permanently threaten the delicate balance of peaceful coexistence. In this sense, particularly at this precise moment in history, Bond's adventures take on a new significance inasmuch as it is through his endeavours that the ever impending world crisis which threatens the world with calamity is averted. The world is led to the brink of nuclear holocaust, and back again. It is thus by effecting a purely imaginary resolution of real social contradictions, which are themselves misrepresented in the form of the fantastic and the grotesque, that the Bond films attain their ideological effect.[16]

Bennett's reading is useful, though flawed in so far as it overlooks the modifications which *The Spy Who Loved Me* makes of the 'SPECTRE genre'. While *The Spy* may have started out as a SPECTRE film, there is a significant difference between it and, say, *Thunderball* or *You Only Live Twice*. The purpose of SPECTRE's acts of terrorism and threats of nuclear destruction had always been extortion and blackmail. In *The Spy Who Loved Me*, however, Stromberg's ambition is to destroy the world so that he can create a new social order. He is not, as Bennett suggests, holding the world to ransom, a point made explicit when he scoffs at Bond's notion to name his price for not firing the missiles: 'You are deluded, Mr Bond. I am not interested in extortion. I intend to change the face of history. … Today civilisation as we know it is corrupt, decadent. Inevitably it will destroy itself. I am merely hastening the process.' In this sense, the character of Stromberg maintains some links to Maibaum's idea of a group of idealists who want to destroy the world and start all over again. The grotesque element which Bennett identifies is to be found in the fact that Stromberg has webbed hands, thus maintaining the Fleming tradition of physical deformity in the Bond villains.

There are other ways, too, in which *The Spy Who Loved Me* modifies the ideological structures of the Bond series. While previous films had mostly detached themselves from the Cold War by focusing instead on supra-national villains, with the occasional hint of Red China lurking in the background, *The Spy* actually moves the Bond series for the first time towards a positive ideology of détente. It is not merely suggesting that the threat to civilisation does not come from the Eastern bloc; it actively promotes the idea that East and West should work together to combat the threat which Stromberg poses to both sides. Thus, after a few initial skirmishes, Bond teams up with his Russian opposite number, Agent Triple X, to investigate the disappearance of their submarines. 'We have entered a new era of Anglo-Soviet co-operation,' declares General Gogol (Walter Gotell), head of the KGB. As so often, the Bond films were slightly ahead of their time in prefiguring warmer Anglo-Soviet relations during the mid-1980s when Prime Minister Margaret Thatcher famously said of Soviet Premier Mikhail Gorbachev that 'I think we can do business together'.

The role accorded to Britain in this new world of détente is a central one. *The Spy Who Loved Me* once again reverses the trend of preceding films (particularly *Diamonds are Forever*) by placing Britain at the forefront of the world stage. The film presents Britain as a power of equal status with America and the Soviet Union. It could be argued, indeed, that *The Spy* is an allegory of the international alliance of the Second World War in which the 'Big Three' (Britain, Russia and America) combine to defeat the common threat presented by an enemy which is hostile to all their ways of life. In this reading Stromberg represents Hitler: a power-crazed megalomaniac with his own private army (Stromberg's men have uniforms and insignia not unlike the SS) who is intent upon genocide on a massive scale. The allegory extends further: Britain is the first power to become involved (the first submarine to be hijacked is British); it enters into an uneasy alliance with Russia just before the halfway point; and the Americans are the last to join in. Indeed, it is not until the last third of the film that there is an American presence, in the form of a submarine with the highly symbolic name of USS *Wayne* – a reminder of the iconic All-American who virtually single-handedly won Hollywood's Second World War. The big battle on board the *Liparus* has British, American and Russian crews fighting side by side under Bond's leadership – the 'Big Three' united through the efforts of the British. If Stromberg represents Hitler in this reading, then Bond must surely represent Churchill. It is a fanciful reading, perhaps, though an irresistible one given that the film constructs its own version of the wartime Grand Alliance.

Bond =
Churchill

In all, the patriotic code of the Bond series is at its most strongly evident since *On Her Majesty's Secret Service*. When Bond is called away from a romantic liaison with a blonde in the pre-title sequence, he responds to her plea, 'But James, I need you!', with the line 'So does England!' (delivered in this instance without any discernible irony). The Union Jack parachute which saves Bond following his ski jump is a reminder of British pluck and ingenuity, and the motif of the flag is carried through into the title sequence where it figures prominently, as it had in *OHMSS*. The most obvious explanation for this renewed degree of patriotic display in *The Spy* is that it was released in the year of Elizabeth II's Silver Jubilee, a focus for pageantry and expressions of national pride at a time of increased economic problems and rising unemployment. On another level, the naval motifs of *The Spy* – Bond is seen for only the second time in his Royal Navy uniform, while the end credits are presented over shots of naval vessels and helicopters – is a reaffirmation of British maritime power at a time when it had recently been involved in a so-called 'cod war' with Iceland.

Perhaps the most significant modification in the narrative ideologies of *The Spy Who Loved Me*, however, is that it marks the point at which the centre of narrative interest in the Bond films switches from the relationship between Bond and the villain to the relationship between Bond and the girl. The difference in this respect to the immediately preceding film is quite pronounced: whereas in *The Man with the Golden Gun* it was Scaramanga who had been Bond's professional equal, in *The*

Spy it is the heroine Major Anya Amasova who is his opposite number in the KGB. In a broader sense, it would probably be fair to say that in most of the earlier films the most memorable characters had always been the villains (Dr No, Rosa Klebb, Grant, Goldfinger, Oddjob, Largo, Blofeld) whereas most of the heroines had been little more than eye-catching adornments. From *The Spy* onwards, however, the villains were to become ever more bland and colourless, whereas slightly more interesting roles would be written for the heroines. Generally supposed to have been a response to the criticisms levelled at the Bond films for their sexism, *The Spy* provided the most prominent role for a heroine since *OHMSS*. According to actress Barbara Bach, Anya was 'really not one of Bond's girls so to speak. She's in the film doing her own bit ... Most of the girls in the Bond films have just been merely beautiful girls that you know have small parts and come in and go out. Anya stays from the beginning to the end.'[17] Certainly Anya is more cool-headed and capable than the feather-brained heroines of early 1970s films such as Tiffany Case or Mary Goodnight. Her introduction is a neat reversal of audience expectations: when a call goes out for Agent Triple X, it is not the handsome, hairy-chested Bond-like man who answers but rather the woman in bed with him. However, it would be stretching the point to suggest that Anya is in any serious way a 'liberated' or even 'feminist' heroine. Bach was still cast for her physical charms rather than her acting ability, and ultimately her character is subordinated to Bond, both professionally and sexually: feminism may have been on the upsurge in the 1970s, but it met its match with James Bond.

What is important, however, is not so much the characterisation of the Bond girl as the symbolic role she plays in the narrative. The relationship between Bond and Anya represents on a personal level the ideology of détente which underlies the narrative strategy of *The Spy Who Loved Me*. As Stromberg remarks when Bond arrives at Atlantis to rescue Anya: 'Well, well, well, a British agent in love with a Russian agent – détente indeed.' The thawing of the Cold War – already alluded to in the title sequence in which a line of bare-breasted goose-stepping Russian female soldiers fall like dominoes when pushed over by Bond – is played out through the love scenes between Bond and Anya in which they make repeated references to 'shared bodily warmth'. There is also a more personal dimension to the relationship: halfway through the film Anya discovers that it was Bond who killed her previous lover and vows to kill Bond herself when the mission is over. Thus the personal and public lines of narrative are much more successfully integrated than they had been in *The Man with the Golden Gun*. In the end love (or sex) overcomes ideology: Anya inevitably relents and the film ends in the conventional fashion.

The ending of *The Spy Who Loved Me* is symbolic on several levels. Bond and Anya have escaped from the sinking Atlantis in an escape capsule which is picked up by a Royal Navy vessel. Their superiors – M, Gogol and the British Minister of Defence (Geoffrey Keen) – peer in through the window of the capsule and interrupt their moment of passion. When the minister demands, 'Bond, what do you think you're doing?', Bond's reply (the last line of the film) is 'Keeping the British end up, sir'. The comment may be interpreted in several ways. Most obviously, it is a sexual innuendo in that Bond is keeping his own end up (maintaining an erection) with Anya. In another way, it is reasserting Britain's position in world affairs in that Bond, as ever, is on top of the situation. And on a different level again, it could be read as a comment on the role which the Bond films themselves were playing in keeping the British end up in the international film market at a time when very few British films were being made, let alone proving successful at the box-office.

In various ways, therefore, *The Spy Who Loved Me* redefines the narrative ideologies of the Bond series. In other ways, too, it develops what had gone before, particularly through a slightly different style of humour. Inter-textuality – which may be defined as the ways in which a text resembles and explicitly borrows from others – had been a feature of the Bond series almost from the beginning, but it became more pronounced with *The Spy*, which makes numerous, obviously deliberate references to other films. For some reason there are several references to the epic films of David Lean: Anya's music-box-cum-radio plays the love theme from *Doctor Zhivago* (the Boris Pasternak novel was banned in the Soviet Union at the time), and later Bond and Anya set off walking across the desert to the music from *Lawrence of Arabia*, and spot a boat on the Nile in a scene which recalls a moment in the Lean film. The most obvious filmic reference, however, is the heavy called Jaws (Richard Kiel), a seven feet two inches man-mountain with steel teeth, which refers explicitly to Steven Spielberg's record-breaking 1975 film. The humorous strategy of *The Spy* thus acknowledges the success of other popular movies, while at the same time distancing itself by poking gentle fun at them: the terror of a shark attack so effectively captured in *Jaws* is mocked in *The Spy* when Jaws, having been dumped by Bond in Stromberg's shark tank, bites the shark himself.

The critical reception of *The Spy Who Loved Me* was divided between the popular and trade press on the one hand, which for the most part regarded it as a return to form for the series, and the more serious critics on the other, who were rather less impressed with what they saw as heavily formulaic and derivative entertainment. The veteran trade reviewer Marjorie Bilbow thought it was the best entry in the series for some time, and made some interesting observations on the director's role in making a Bond movie:

> How exhilarating it is to find an old friend in such splendid form, simply bursting with youthful health and vigour. Lewis Gilbert modestly praises everybody but himself when speaking of the team effort that went into making the latest Bond extravaganza such an imaginative variation of the familiar, but it takes the right director to encourage and co-ordinate wayward talents and skills. Without diminishing the excitement-value of the fast-moving action, the comedy is used to particularly good effect ... It's all been done before, of course, but the glory of it is that the old tricks are performed with such cheeky panache that the saucy title of the theme song sums it all up. 'Nobody does it better' than all those who were involved in rejuvenating 007.[18]

The reaction of the more middle-brow critics, however, indicates that, for all it was supposed to be the 'biggest' and the 'best', *The Spy* was widely regarded as being much the same as before. Tim Pulleine in the *Monthly Film Bulletin* was clearly tired of the innuendoes and thought the latest film was little more than a rehash of highlights from the others:

> 'Tell Bond to pull out', says 'M'; cut to 007 in coitus with (anonymous) damsel in a mountain chalet. Responding to the call of duty, Bond polishes off sundry (anonymous) attackers before soaring over a cliff on skis, a Union Jack parachute blossoming over his head. In the ensuing two hours, seaside-postcard smut and comic-strip feats of derring-do continue unabated, suggesting that the makers are being driven to desperate extremes to keep the formula going (having roped in the author of the *Confessions* series for the purpose). Sometimes, however, it is difficult to be certain how deliberate the absurdities are, particularly with a lacklustre,

[handwritten margin note: irony Jaws v Jaws 1975]

clockwork villain like Stromberg, incarnated by all-purpose international guest star Curt Jurgens. The strip-cartoon aspect of the
film extends beyond such running gags as the presence of a super-
human, steel-toothed heavy called 'Jaws', who emerges unscathed
from one lethal hardship after another and drops huge boulders
on his toes in careless moments, and permeates the structure
itself. Narrative coherence has been disregarded (the takeover of
Stromberg's HQ, for instance, looks too easy by half) in favour
of a succession of self-contained set pieces. This might not matter if these were more precisely organised or less derivative of
earlier movies in the series – a train sequence out of *From Russia
with Love*, for instance, and a death-dealing car straight out of
Goldfinger. Indeed, where Ian Fleming's novel offered an attempt
to ring some changes in terms of scale and viewpoint, the film
– bearing no relation to its nominal source – seems to do nothing
more than anthologise its forerunners, and comes out looking, for
all the expensive hardware and location shooting, like a Saturday
serial risen grandiloquently above its station.[19]

The popular reception of the film, however, was extremely favourable,
as it became the second biggest-grossing film of the year behind the
record-breaking space opera *Star Wars*. In Britain, and other territories
where *Star Wars* was not released until 1978, *The Spy Who Loved Me*
was the top box-office attraction of 1977. What was most significant,
however, was that it was successful in America, which had not proved
so receptive to Moore's previous two Bond outings. In an article in the
New York Times, film critic Frank Rich echoed the views of the trade
press in arguing that the Bond films succeeded because they provided
the sort of entertainment value which audiences wanted. 'The continued
appeal of the Bond movies is a real phenomenon – particularly when
you consider what a dated cultural artefact James Bond is,' he observed.
The appeal of the Bond movies, Rich suggested, was one of nostalgia,
'a throwback to a vanished past – a Hollywood past'. 'This movie', he
wrote, 'takes us back to the time when craftsmanship and good humor
were standard fixtures in light film entertainments; it's a movie that
actually fulfills the conventional expectations that an audience brings to
it.' At a time when many contemporary film-makers had lost the ability
to tell uncomplicated stories which did not wallow in sordid realism, or
so Rich believed, the Bond movies were guaranteed crowd-pleasers:

What we really want from big-budget summer films like *The Spy Who Loved Me* are the simple things: a little romance, some visceral thrills, a hell of a ride. These are the goods that the Bond pictures fairly consistently deliver, and if the 007 movies are not as inspired as such blockbuster entertainments as *Star Wars* or *Jaws*, they're more dependable than all the rest. Maybe we no longer need James Bond to defend the honor of the free world, but how lucky we are that he's survived to defend the increasingly endangered traditions of the well-made commercial film.[20]

The comparison to *Jaws* and *Star Wars* is a highly pertinent one, as between them these two films had redefined the expectations of the blockbuster movie and of the audience that existed for it. In 1975 *Jaws* became the first film to return over $100 million rentals in the North American market, while *Star Wars*, released two years later, had staggering domestic rentals of $193 million. Both *Jaws* and *Star Wars* were special-effects-driven movies which foregrounded spectacle over narrative complexity and characterisation, and were accorded nationwide saturation release accompanied by high-profile advertising campaigns.[21] In this sense they exemplified the sort of popular cinema which the Bond series had represented for the last fifteen years. But the difference now was that the films of the new generation of American 'movie brats' personified by Spielberg and Lucas were that much more successful than the Bonds. As successful as *The Spy Who Loved Me* was, it was not on the same box-office plateau as *Jaws* or *Star Wars*.

The success of *Star Wars* in particular had a pronounced effect on the Bond series. In 1977 Broccoli had announced that the next Bond title would be *Octopussy*, and said that the budget 'will return to the seven and a half to eight million dollar range', suggesting, perhaps, that the scale of the film would be smaller than *The Spy Who Loved Me*.[22] The title of the next film had been changed by the time *The Spy* was released: the end credits declared that 'James Bond will return in *For Your Eyes Only*'. Shortly after, however, this was changed again to *Moonraker*. There were two, related reasons for this decision. One was that the success of *Star Wars* brought about a science-fiction boom in the cinema, illustrated by films such as *Superman* (1978), *Alien* (1979), *The Black Hole* (1979) and *Star Trek: The Motion Picture* (1979), which the Bond producers decided to join in by using the only remaining Fleming title which suggested a science-fiction theme. The other reason was that the American space shuttle programme was approaching a stage where the first flights would soon be taking place – in the event the first shuttle launch was in April 1981 – and which thus offered topical possibilities in that space flight had once again caught the public imagination. In Broccoli's words: 'Putting James Bond in orbit brought Ian Fleming into the space age.'[23]

There was, however, very little of Fleming in the film version of *Moonraker*. The third Bond novel, which unusually was set entirely in England, had Bond investigating the millionaire industrialist Sir Hugo Drax. Ostensibly an English patriot, Drax has pledged millions of pounds to build a nuclear rocket, the 'Moonraker', for the defence of Britain, which he has built to his own specifications at his plant in Kent. However, he arouses M's suspicions when, as a member of Blades, he is unmasked as a card cheat. As so often in the books, a relatively trivial incident leads to the unravelling of a great conspiracy. Bond is sent to investigate a death at Drax's plant and discovers that Drax is really a German who harbours an intense hatred of the British and who, backed by the Russians, plans to target the 'Moonraker' at London. For the film, Drax (Michael Lonsdale) became a multi-billionaire who is funding the 'Moonraker' space shuttle programme. When a shuttle on loan to the British government is hijacked, Bond is sent to investigate. It turns out that Drax stole his own shuttle because he needed to use it in his conspiracy, which is to kill off the world's entire population with a deadly nerve gas, launched in capsules from an orbiting space station, while a handful of specially selected astronauts breed a physically perfect new order.

Once again, *Moonraker* illustrates how the Bond films constantly updated and modified their ostensible source material. 'But naturally, the plot had to be up-dated,' the publicity material said. 'For who now in the realms of imaginative fiction would be satisfied with such an unambitious piece of villainy as a nuclear rocket hitting London?'[24] Whereas in the book the threat was directed against England and was motivated by Drax's intense hatred of the English, in the film it is directed against the entire world and is motivated by Drax's obsession with racial purity. Even more so than Stromberg before him, Drax is to all intents and purposes a Hitlerite villain. His astronauts have been chosen according to his own physical criteria (most of them are tall, blonde and Aryan-looking), and, just to make the point explicit, Bond refers to Drax's ambition of creating a 'new master race'. The substitution of a conspiracy with Nazi overtones for the Communist-backed threat of the book demonstrates the ideological flexibility of the Bond films: the forces which threaten the world with destruction do not represent a particular political ideology, but rather an irrational and anarchic threat to civilisation as we know it which may derive equally from left or right.

Moonraker also develops one of the themes of *The Spy Who Loved Me* in providing a narratively more significant role for the Bond girl. If the relationship between Bond and Anya had represented Anglo-Soviet détente, then that between Bond and Holly Goodhead (Lois Chiles) represents the 'special relationship' between Britain and America, with CIA agent Holly as a female equivalent of Felix Leiter. The film mocks Bond's male chauvinism: he is surprised to find that Dr Goodhead is 'a woman' ('Your powers of observation do you credit, Mr Bond,' she replies sarcastically). For the first time in the Bond series, the girl possesses a narratively important skill which Bond does not: she is able to pilot the space shuttle that is necessary for them to reach Drax's space station, and, later, to track and destroy the nerve gas globes. Within the admittedly limited scope of the Bond films, Holly is perhaps the most 'progressive' heroine of the series to date. Having said that, of course, the ending of the film reassigns her to the more traditional female role as sexual partner for Bond. Although it is Holly who pilots the shuttle, her last line is to ask Bond to 'take me around the world one more time', thus reassigning Bond to the dominant role.

Whereas the publicity discourse surrounding *The Spy Who Loved Me* had made much of the 'new' type of Bond girl, for *Moonraker* it was not the characterisation of the heroine that was emphasised but rather the technological hardware. The producers were keen to emphasise that the space technology shown in the film was based on the real thing, and official publicity constantly asserted that *Moonraker* was 'science fact, not science fiction'. This even extended so far as commissioning an article on the making of the film from Eric Burgess, author of many books on space technology and rocket propulsion, who had been a founder of the British Interplanetary Society in the 1930s and was now a contracted author for America's National Aeronautics and Space Administration (NASA). Burgess argued that *Moonraker* should be differentiated from the recent 'spate of fantasies which ignored physical laws but appealed to popular imagination' (he cited *Close Encounters of the Third Kind*, *Star Wars* and *Battlestar Galactica*), and should instead be

considered as one of the rare 'attempts at serious technology forecast-
ing ... into the immediate future based on current technology while
keeping within accepted physical laws' (a tradition which he traced back
to Fritz Lang's *Die Frau im Mond* of 1929 and George Pal's *Destination
Moon* of 1950):

> The Bond series of motion pictures evolved as a natural medium
> for looking at practical aspects of spaceflight. Over the years
> these films developed as motion pictures which aimed at a level
> of credibility even though pushing the imagination beyond what is
> actually being done today (satellites to control Earth, cities beneath
> the seas, mountain top eyries of super scientists, and the like)
> and they thrust toward spaceflight applications in the clandestine
> satellites of *Diamonds are Forever* and *You Only Live Twice*.[25]

Burgess was at pains to point out how 'the producer and director of
Moonraker attempted to achieve space reality'. Thus they used space
suits modelled on those used by real astronauts, and personal propulsion units of a sort which had already been tested in the space station
Skylab; the space shuttles in the film were based closely on the real
thing; and Drax's space station was designed along the sort of lines
which scientists at the time were planning, albeit that it also had to
be 'aesthetically pleasing, functional, and visually suitable for various
camera angles and viewpoints'. Burgess described the special effects and
model work in great detail, pointing out that they 'had to reach new
heights of realism'. Indeed, there is a contradiction running throughout
his essay between the emphasis on how realistic the space hardware
was supposed to be on the one hand, and the artifice that went into
creating the impression of realism on the other. For example, real
laser beams were found not to be bright enough for filming, so they
were created by special effects instead: 'It was much easier to simulate
the lasers, and then they seemed "more realistic".' A better example
of how the Bond films resist categorisation in terms of conventional
notions of realism could hardly be imagined. For all that it might be
based on 'science fact' or 'space reality', *Moonraker* is still essentially a
fantasy film.

Moonraker follows the direction of *The Spy Who Loved Me* in foregrounding visual spectacle above all else. The narrative is reduced
virtually to a travelogue of highly photogenic locations (California,
Venice, Rio de Janeiro) which serve as backdrops for improbable action

sequences. Again there is a juxtaposition between the ancient and the futuristic: Drax's secret shuttle launch silo is hidden in the ruins of an ancient city deep in the Amazonian jungle. With the cost of the film having been offset partly by deals with companies and manufacturers anxious to have their products associated with James Bond, *Moonraker* also exhibits what might be described as an aesthetic of product placement: Christian Dior perfume, Bollinger champagne and Canon cameras are featured prominently. In one sequence, as Bond fights with an assailant in the back of an ambulance driving up a hillside outside Rio, the struggle is intercut with narratively irrelevant shots of the vehicle passing advertising billboards for 7 Up, Seiko watches and Marlboro cigarettes, while the villain ends up careering on a runaway stretcher into the mouth of a stewardess on a giant British Airways advertisement ('We'll take more care of you'). The special effects and model work are very impressive, and the climactic battle in space between Drax's army and US Space Marines, with its criss-crossing laser beams and bodies cartwheeling into space, is at least the equal of any of the other science-fiction blockbusters of the late 1970s. However, the outer space storyline and reliance on visual effects were not to the liking of most critics, who complained that the Bond films were imitating the science-fiction boom with disappointing results. Marjorie Bilbow, who had been so effusive about *The Spy Who Loved Me*, remarked that 'we have been so deluged with films about space flights that journeys and chases in shuttles have not [*sic*] built-in excitement and call for great stretches of directing and screenwriting imagination to be more than run of the mill'. Although she predicted that the film 'will be enjoyed by millions', Bilbow added that, for her own part, 'I shall be glad to see Bond return to terra firma and stay there'.[26]

Other critics simply found *Moonraker* tedious and derivative. 'If the preceding Bond opus, *The Spy Who Loved Me*, rather resembled a conglomerate remake of the series to date, the latest instalment looks like nothing so much as a remake of *The Spy Who Loved Me*,' observed Tim Pulleine. 'In fact, the kind of double vision which has increasingly fogged the Bond pictures, as they have sought to parody an already parodic model, here becomes virtually complete.'[27] At the level of narrative structure, certainly, *Moonraker* is simply a reworking of *The Spy*. Many of the specific incidents are the same: it begins with a hijacking, the pre-title sequence has Bond making a death-defying escape when an attempt is made to kill him (pushed out of an aeroplane, Bond wrests a parachute from one of his assailants after a mid-air tussle), and it ends with Bond and the heroine being caught *in flagrante delicto* by their embarrassed superiors ('I think he's attempting re-entry, sir,' says Q, while the shuttle's onboard camera shows Bond and Holly in a zero-gravity clinch). In between are the usual succession of stunts and set pieces, though most of them lapse into broad comedy. Thus, after escaping from pursuers in his motorised gondola, which then turns into a hovercraft, Bond performs a lap of honour around St Marks Square while tourists stare in astonishment and a pigeon performs a double take. The inter-textual references which had characterised *The Spy* are again in evidence: the entry-code to a secret laboratory is the same tune used to communicate with the aliens in *Close Encounters of the Third Kind*, and Bond, wearing a poncho and sombrero, rides a horse to the strains of Elmer Bernstein's theme from *The Magnificent Seven*. The comic strategy of the film is reinforced by the return of Jaws, who had proved such a popular character in *The Spy*, and whose attempts to kill Bond are so remarkably incompetent that he becomes the comic relief rather than a believable threat. Indeed, the character is softened to such an extent that he is even given a small, short-sighted girlfriend called Dolly. Dilys Powell, for one, found this distasteful: 'I doubt whether the surrender of Jaws (himself, of course, a reference-joke) to the diminutive blonde would have seemed as funny if one didn't remember Frankenstein's Monster encountering the innocent child.' Powell, who had been one of the Bond series' biggest admirers among British critics, found *Moonraker* too disjointed to be thoroughly enjoyable: 'Its two hours could be divided into independent episodes: Bond at the pigeon-shoot, Bond in the velocity-test, Bond attacked from a canal-hearse, or acrobatic in a cable-car, or resourceful with a tropical reptile.' 'In fact,' she added, '*Moonraker* is a serial: it would gratify the desire, common in the silent days, to see all the episodes in one go.'[28]

It is ironic that *Moonraker*, which is generally regarded as one of the most derivative of the Bond series and which critically was among the least well received, actually became the biggest-grossing Bond to date at the box-office. There is no clearer indication of the difference between critical and popular tastes. If judged solely on the basis of popular reception, then *Moonraker* has to be considered a triumph. Like *The Spy Who Loved Me*, it was that rarity in British cinema of the late 1970s, an international box-office hit, proving that the Bond films were indeed 'keeping the British end up' in the international film market. However, the sheer size and scale of *Moonraker* were such that it represented the fullest lengths to which visual spectacle could be taken in the Bond movies. Having sent Bond into outer space, the only direction he could take thereafter was to come back down to earth.

6

Cold Warrior Reborn: *For Your Eyes Only, Octopussy, Never Say Never Again, A View to a Kill*

The direction of the Bond series during the first half of the 1980s once again demonstrates that the generic formula of the Bond films is not permanently fixed, but adapts and modifies itself according to various industrial, political and cultural determinants. The official series continued with three films which belong together as a group in much the same way as *The Spy Who Loved Me* and *Moonraker* belong together as a pair: *For Your Eyes Only* (dir. John Glen, 1981), *Octopussy* (dir. John Glen, 1983) and *A View to a Kill* (dir. John Glen, 1985). The narrative ideologies of these films marked a change of direction after the détente-themed narrative of *The Spy Who Loved Me* in that they relocated Bond, partially at least, within the political and ideological co-ordinates of the Cold War. At the level of visual spectacle, while they maintained the exotic and colourful locations, they downplayed the massive sets of the two preceding films in favour of a slightly less fantastic look in which authentic locations took precedence over futuristic technology. 'It may be that by then we had overworked the sophisticated hardware in our pictures,' Broccoli admitted of *Moonraker*, and that with *For Your Eyes Only* a decision was taken 'to focus more upon character and story than the familiar set-piece fireworks'.[1] And in terms of characterisation, Roger Moore's Bond came increasingly to represent an old-fashioned construction of Englishness, a National Heritage hero whose ageing masculinity is tested by a succession of more assertive and challenging women, culminating with the appearance of Grace Jones in *A View to a Kill*. Another challenge to Moore's Bond came in the form of Sean Connery's return to the role in *Never Say Never Again* (dir. Irvin Kershner, 1983), a one-off production made outside the Eon series which revived debates about who was the 'best' James Bond.

In comparison to the spiralling production costs of the late 1970s, the early 1980s was a period of relative stability in which the negative costs of the Bond films averaged \$28–30 million. The Bond films continued to be among the most successful at the box-office, if not in the same league as the phenomenally successful Spielberg–Lucas spectaculars, including the two *Star Wars* sequels *The Empire Strikes Back* (1980) and *Return of the Jedi* (1983), the Indiana Jones films *Raiders of the Lost Ark* (1981) and *Indiana Jones and the Temple of Doom* (1984), and Spielberg's record-breaking *E.T.: The Extra-Terrestrial* (1982). The total worldwide grosses of the Bond films at this time were \$196 million for *For Your Eyes Only*, \$188 million for *Octopussy* and \$153 million for *A View to a Kill*, figures which look impressive enough on their own but which are put into perspective by the fact that *E.T.* took over \$200 million *rentals* in North America alone (the North American rentals of the three Bond films were, respectively, \$26.5 million, \$34 million and \$25.3 million). Yet for a series that was now twenty years old, the fact that the Bond films were still consistently successful at the box-office was a considerable achievement in its own right. It was in markets outside North America that the Bond films performed best, with their international grosses generally being between two to three times their North American figures.[2]

The British film industry during the early 1980s was undergoing one of its periodic revivals following the doldrums of the 1970s. The critical and commercial success of *Chariots of Fire* (1981), a dramatisation of the real-life stories of British athletes Harold Abrahams and Eric Liddell who won gold medals at the 1924 Paris Olympics, won the Oscar for Best Picture in 1982 and prompted screenwriter Colin Welland to declare optimistically 'The British are coming!' What *Chariots of Fire* also heralded was a cycle of period costume pictures which have subsequently been labelled 'heritage' films. The film-makers most associated with this cycle of films are the producer–director team of Ismail Merchant and James Ivory, responsible for films such as *Heat and Dust*

(1983), *A Room with a View* (1986), *Maurice* (1987), *Howards End* (1992) and *The Remains of the Day* (1993). These films, and those like them by other hands, represent the critically respectable 'quality' end of British cinema and need to be seen in terms of a long tradition of literary adaptation encompassing films such as David Lean's *Great Expectations* (1946) and *Oliver Twist* (1948) and even Cecil Hepworth's *Comin' Thro' the Rye* (1923). They are characterised by their adaptation of classic literature (particularly E. M. Forster), by their highly pictorialist visual style which foregrounds sites of national heritage (Oxbridge, country houses), and by their narrative concern with the upper classes. The heritage films were popular with 'art house' audiences in Britain and America, and as such they exported a traditionalist and Anglocentric construction of national identity to overseas audiences.

While the Bond series was not itself part of the heritage cycle, it was at this moment that the films began to draw upon the sort of visual motifs which asserted their Englishness more explicitly than ever before. In *Dr No* Fleming had evoked the picture-postcard image of London, though the films had hitherto steered away from using such imagery. Indeed, there are remarkably few indicators of the London location of secret service headquarters before the 1980s: the most subtle is the first shot of *On Her Majesty's Secret Service* (missing from some prints) in which Big Ben can be seen reflected in the brass wall-plate of 'Universal Exports (London) Ltd.', the cover-name for the secret service.[3] In the early 1980s, however, the sequence of Bond's briefing with M would be preceded by an exterior shot of the building in which a visual signifier of location features prominently: a red double-decker bus in *Octopussy*, a mounted horse guard in *A View to a Kill*. The purpose of these images is to say to audiences 'this is London': snapshots which could have been lifted straight from a postcard. It is yet another indication of how the Bond series had changed since the 1960s: once seen as an embodiment of progressive modernisation, they had now come to represent a heritage industry construction of British culture.

'With the retreat of the Cold War,' writes Sarah Street, 'the Englishness of Bond betrays a concern to insert a comforting national stereotype (particularly with Roger Moore's Bond) into a world which is increasingly governed by international forces and threatened by an unidentified enemy.'[4] But while in the films of the early 1980s the ageing Moore does indeed represent a 'comforting national stereotype', the Cold War was far from being in retreat at this time. Indeed, Cold War tensions assumed a greater narrative significance in the Bond films of the early 1980s than at any other moment in the series' history. Even in *From Russia with Love* the Russians had been secondary villains and latent Cold War antagonisms were exacerbated by an even more sinister, initially unknown enemy. However, *For Your Eyes Only* is based around a contest between Bond and a Soviet-backed villain for possession of the 'MacGuffin', thus resurrecting Bond as a cold warrior and reassigning him to an ideological role he had not performed since the novels of the 1950s. Dissident and renegade Russian villains also featured in both *Octopussy* and *A View to a Kill*, in which the peaceful co-existence of East and West is shown to be under threat from extremists on the Soviet side.

How is the renewed foregrounding of Cold War tensions in the Bond series at this time to be explained? While it is difficult to make straightforward causal links, it seems reasonable to relate the modified ideological structures of the films to changes in the international political climate. Although the Cold War had never really gone away, tensions had not been especially acute since the Russian invasion of Czechoslovakia in 1968. Indeed, the 1970s had seen a mild thaw, which the Bond films reflected through the détente-themed narrative of *The Spy Who Loved Me*. But dormant tensions came to the surface again through events such as the Russian invasion of Afghanistan in 1979, the American boycott of the 1980 Moscow Olympics (and the tit-for-tat Russian boycott of the 1984 Los Angeles Games), and the suppression of the Solidarity trade union in Poland in the early 1980s. The proliferation of medium-range nuclear missiles in Europe (American Cruise and Pershing missiles were stationed in Britain and West Germany from 1983) further increased East–West tensions. This period coincided with the election of strongly right-wing governments in Britain and the United States, under Margaret Thatcher and Ronald Reagan respectively. Aggressive anti-Communist rhetoric was part of the ideological platform of both Thatcherite and Reaganite foreign policy: Reagan famously referred to the Soviet Union as an 'evil empire'. This hawkish climate was reflected in a spate of aggressively nationalistic Hollywood films, including the hysterically paranoid *Red Dawn* (1984) in which a Soviet-Cuban invasion of the USA was defeated by a group of American teenagers, and the brutal *Rambo: First Blood, Part II* (1985) in which Sylvester Stallone's musclebound killing machine returned to Vietnam to rescue forgotten American prisoners and single-handedly decimated the North Vietnamese and Russian armies.

While there were no Red-bashing films as such in British cinema, there was much evidence of a more hawkish and nationalistic mood. Even before the Falklands War of 1982, this was exemplified by events such as the terrorist siege of the Iranian Embassy in London, which was ended in dramatic fashion by the SAS (Special Air Service). Margaret Thatcher wrote in her memoirs: 'Wherever I went over the next few days, I sensed a great wave of pride at the outcome ... we had sent a signal to terrorists everywhere that they could expect no deals and would extort no favours from Britain.'[5] This bullish mood was perfectly captured in the blatantly exploitative action film *Who Dares Wins* (1982), which dramatised a terrorist take-over of the American Embassy in London and its storming by the SAS. With its unequivocal anti-terrorist message and its celebration of ruthless, clinical military force, *Who Dares Wins* is surely one of the most ideologically right-wing tracts ever produced by the British cinema. While the Bond films did not resort to the jingoistic extremes of *Who Dares Wins* or to the nihilistic aggression of *Rocky* or *Rambo*, they did nevertheless reflect the mood of the times in that they exhibited a tendency towards the foreign policy agendas of Thatcherism and Reaganism.

The new direction of the Bond series in the 1980s was indicated by *For Your Eyes Only*, in which the production team made a conscious decision to steer away from the technological futurism and massive visual spectacle of *Moonraker*. 'That kind of production design isn't really in the nature of this story, and I don't think there would be any point in building super-grand sets just so people can walk around in front of them,' director John Glen said, distancing himself from the preceding Lewis Gilbert films. Interestingly, the film which Glen compared it to was the one generally supposed to have been a failure: 'I think the best way of describing it is as more of a straight thriller; the one closest to it might be *On Her Majesty's Secret Service*. It's a bit of a throwback in the sense that the emphasis is back on people rather than gadgets.'[6] The Bond film which *For Your Eyes Only* most closely resembles, however, is *From Russia with Love*, in that it is a straight espionage thriller set entirely in Europe in which the Cold War provides the political background to the plot. It is also the closest of the latter-day Bond films to Ian Fleming, drawing on characters and incidents from two short stories, 'For Your Eyes Only' and 'Risico'. The character of the heroine Melina (Carole Bouquet), whom Bond meets when she sets out to track down and kill the men who murdered her parents, is derived from 'For Your Eyes Only', while the characters of rival smugglers Kristatos (Julian Glover) and Columbo (Topol) are taken straight from 'Risico'. Although the original Fleming stories were over twenty years old, and the most recent films had increasingly distanced themselves from their ostensible source materials, several films in the 1980s (*For Your Eyes Only, Octopussy, The Living Daylights*) were to return to specific incidents in Fleming as their starting point, while expanding them into broader and more contemporary narratives.

The main line of narrative in *For Your Eyes Only* is located squarely within the geopolitical co-ordinates of the Cold War in that the struggle for possession of the 'MacGuffin' takes place in Europe between Bond and a Soviet-backed villain. A British spy ship equipped with a device known as ATAC (Automatic Targeting Attack Computer), which can be used to transmit coded orders to Polaris missile submarines, is sunk accidentally off the Albanian coast. The British government fear the Russians getting their hands on the device because in the event of war they could use it to order British nuclear submarines to launch their missiles against British cities. For the first time in the Bond series the principal villain is working for the Soviet Union: Kristatos is a freelance operative who is sympathetic to the Russians – General Gogol refers to him as 'our usual friend in Greece' – while one of his associates, an East German biathlon champion called Kriegler, is a KGB assassin. The détente theme of *The Spy Who Loved Me* is reversed in so far as Gogol, an uneasy ally in *The Spy*, now assumes the role of Cold War enemy. The fragility of détente is underlined at the end when Bond, facing Gogol and a Russian gunman, throws the ATAC off a cliff where it is smashed to pieces. 'That's détente, comrade,' Bond remarks. 'You don't have it – I don't have it.' Gogol departs with a wry chuckle and a gesture which suggests that, while this may be the end of one incident, the larger war goes on.

The presence of Gogol is an example of how the Bond films at this time maintained continuity with their predecessors (Walter Gotell as the KGB chief was a recurring character in every film from *The Spy Who Loved Me* to *The Living Daylights*). *For Your Eyes Only* also refers back explicitly to other films, particularly *On Her Majesty's Secret Service*. In doing so it establishes a link between the past and the present of the Bond series which has significant implications for the interpretation of the Bond character. Up to this point in the series Bond had remained basically the same age, generally assumed to be permanently in his late thirties. *For Your Eyes Only*, however, is suggestive of an older hero. The textual evidence for this is to be found in the opening shots, where Bond is seen laying flowers in an English country graveyard where the headstone reads 'Teresa Bond. 1943–1969. Beloved wife of James Bond. We have all the time in the world'. The scene was written, apparently, when the producers thought Roger Moore might not make the film, and was devised to introduce a new lead actor by providing a point of identification with the series' past. What is unusual, however, is not that the film refers back to Bond's wife (this had already happened once in *The Spy Who Loved Me* and would occur again in *Licence to Kill*), but that it should do so in such a temporally precise way. The dates on the gravestone place the Bond of *For Your Eyes Only* as being twelve years older than the Bond of *OHMSS*. Assuming that Bond is usually taken to be in his late thirties, then the Bond of *For Your Eyes Only* would therefore be approaching fifty. In this sense, the film brings Bond roughly in line with Roger Moore's own age (he was fifty-three when the film was released) and works better for Moore than it would likely have done for a younger, incoming actor.

Another link to the past is provided by the ensuing pre-title sequence, unrelated to the main narrative, in which Bond's helicopter is hijacked and flown by remote control by an old enemy who intends to crash it in order to kill him. Although not referred to by name, this man is clearly meant to be Blofeld: he is a bald man in a neck brace and a wheelchair who strokes the white cat which the films had introduced as a prop for the character of Blofeld from his first appearance in *From Russia with Love*. A line from the script which is not in the finished film – 'Good afternoon, Mr Bond. I thought we should celebrate the tenth anniversary of our last meeting' – makes it even more obvious that the man is meant to be Blofeld, who had last appeared in *Diamonds are Forever* in 1971.[7]

Yet at the same time as establishing these links with the series' past, *For Your Eyes Only* also stresses its contemporaneity. The film locates itself explicitly in Thatcher's Britain through a number of topical references which, unusually for the Bond films, refer specifically to the government of the day. Occasionally in previous films there had been references to 'the prime minister', but always in anonymous terms which did not specify any particular person. In *For Your Eyes Only*, however, there are several direct references to Mrs Thatcher herself. In a film which on the whole eschews the excessive parody of some of the 1970s Bonds, Thatcher is the subject of several in-jokes which play upon the novelty of Britain's first woman prime minister, and particularly on her famous reputation as the 'Iron Lady'. Thatcher's legendary ability to intimidate her male Cabinet colleagues is illustrated when the Minister of Defence is shown to be afraid of her ('She'll have our guts for garters'). And Thatcher herself appears in the fade-out joke, which is rich in ideological and gendered meanings. The prime minister has been put through to Bond on a phone-link from the kitchen at 10 Downing Street, in order to congratulate him personally on the successful completion of his mission. Even when placed in a traditionally domestic feminine role (she is preparing a meal), Mrs Thatcher is shown to exercise authority over men (she slaps the wrist of husband Denis when he tries to steal from the salad bowl). Her message of congratulation asserts in the strongest terms notions of patriotism and duty ('Your courage and resourcefulness are a credit to the nation'). However, she is unaware that she is speaking not to Bond, who has gone swimming with Melina, but rather to Melina's parrot Max. When the parrot squawks 'Give us a kiss', Mrs Thatcher pats her hair and, clearly flattered, says 'Really, Mr Bond!' Even the fearful Iron Lady, therefore, resorts to feminine gestures when propositioned (or so she thinks) by Bond. A further, culturally specific reference is that Mrs Thatcher and Denis are portrayed by impressionist Janet Brown and comedian John Wells, who were well-known in Britain for their impersonations of the Thatchers.

While Mrs Thatcher becomes the butt of a typically Bondian sexual joke, in other respects the film follows the trend of its immediate pre-decessors in again providing a more prominent role for the Bond girl. The public and personal lines of narrative are neatly interwoven: Bond's mission to retrieve the ATAC and Melina's desire to avenge the death of her parents bring them together in the common objective of destroying Kristatos. Melina is not a professional secret agent, like the heroines of the two previous films, but she is no mere damsel in distress. She is shown to be competent and resourceful, dispatching sundry villains by means of a crossbow. The film's allusion to classical mythology ('Greek women, like Elektra, always avenge their loved ones') places her within a tradition of determined and vengeful women which has a long cultural history. Indeed, the narrative importance accorded to Melina's desire for revenge is such that it takes precedence over the romance between Bond and herself. Co-writer Richard Maibaum was not happy with the way the relationship was handled, suggesting that the underlying idea was missed: 'The whole idea was that the great lover James Bond can't get to first base with this woman because she's so obsessed with avenging her parents' death. Nothing was ever done with it. It was as if the director didn't feel there was a love story there at all.'[8] Marjorie Bilbow, however, thought Bond's relationship with Melina made a welcome change from the usual sexual shenanigans. 'I perceived, with relief, that his use 'em and dump 'em treatment of his women has been whittled down to a much more likeable selectivity and some caring,' she said. 'In fact, the film as a whole is nothing like as old-hat sexist as the image put over in the graffiti-attracting posters.'[9] The posters for the film, which featured a shapely pair of woman's legs shown from behind with the smaller figure of Bond between them, attracted much criticism from militant feminist groups, and it is part of Bond folklore that they were censored on some American university campuses.

Most critics responded favourably to this back-to-basics Bond after the overblown extravagance of *Moonraker*. *Variety* offered a particularly favourable review, opining that it was 'one of the most thoroughly enjoyable of the 12 Bond pix despite the fact that many of the usual ingredients in the successful 007 formula are missing this time out'. The review continued that 'all the action has been staged with an expertise and excitement unusual even for this exceptionally well produced series' and considered that '[the] entire film is probably the best-directed since *On Her Majesty's Secret Service*, as John Glen, moving into the director's chair after long service as second unit director and editor, displays a fine eye and as often as not keeps more than one thing happening in his shots'. For once, a Bond film 'benefits from [the] presence of a truly sympathetic heroine, fetchingly played by Carole Bouquet, who exhibits a humanity and emotionalism not frequently found in this sort of pop adventure and who takes a long time (the entire film in fact) to warm up to Bond sufficiently to jump into the sack with him'. What the reviewer found most praiseworthy, however, was the way in which the film-makers had kept the Bond franchise fresh by offering some variations on the usual formula:

> After all these years, producer Albert R. Broccoli and his writing cohorts, Richard Maibaum and Michael G. Wilson, are certainly entitled to play around with their standard formula a bit if they feel like it, and some of the variations here seem like deliberate

attempts to counter what one has come to expect from these efforts.

After a smashing helicopter prolog, next action set piece is a super car chase. This time, however, Bond isn't driving his super-charged sports car, but Bouquet's tin can 2CV Citroen thereby proving his own value rather than that of his vehicle.

M is gone, due to Bernard Lee's death; Bond doesn't make his first feminine conquest until halfway through the picture; there's no technology introduced by Q which saves the hero in the end; no looming supervillain dominates the drama; Bond's bons mots are surprisingly sparse, and the fate of the whole world isn't even hanging in the balance at the climax. But the fact that these omissions don't matter much just proves the durability of the basic premise and leading character, and absence of some of them even proves somewhat refreshing, for a change.

Ultimately, the more basic prosaic nature of the weapons and villainy here brings Bond closer to the 'real world', if such a thing was ever on view in this series, than any of the pix since *From Russia with Love*, which remains the Bond film par excellence for most devotees. It's a terrific, nonstop romp, and only those exclusively into Bondian hardware should be disappointed.

To boot, [a] final throwaway scene featuring Margaret Thatcher lookalike Janet Brown will have Britons, particularly, rolling in the aisles.[10]

What this review proves more than anything else is that critics identified subtle changes and modifications in the generic formula of the Bond series and, in this particular case, approved. Furthermore, the favour with which *For Your Eyes Only* was greeted, following the lukewarm critical reaction to *Moonraker*, suggests that the producers were more receptive to critics' views than perhaps they would care to admit. Their decision to bring Bond back down to earth won critical plaudits, at least from the trade and popular press.

Octopussy reworks the themes and narrative ideologies of *For Your Eyes Only*. It is even more directly rooted in Cold War conflicts and equally topical in its references; once again narrative interest focuses on the relationship between Bond and the heroine rather than Bond and the villains; and it is again suggestive of an older Bond. Furthermore, as in *For Your Eyes Only*, incidents from two Fleming short stories ('Octopussy' and 'The Property of a Lady') are worked into the plot. The film has Bond travelling to India to investigate a jewellery smuggling operation run by Kamal Khan (Louis Jourdan), an exiled Afghan prince, and Octopussy (Maud Adams), a fabulously wealthy woman who lives on an island populated exclusively by beautiful girls. Bond discovers that, unbeknown to Octopussy, Kamal is in league with a senior Russian military commander, General Orlov (Steven Berkoff), who plans to use the Octopussy Circus (front for the smuggling pipeline) to smuggle an atomic bomb across the border from East to West Germany and explode it on an American air force base.

In terms of structure, *Octopussy* falls somewhere between the taut espionage narrative of *For Your Eyes Only* and the expansive travelogue of *Moonraker*. Much of the film is set in India, a location which was chosen not merely for the visual possibilities which it offers. *Octopussy* also needs to be seen in the context of a cycle of British films and television series of the early 1980s which showed a fascination with India. ITV's *The Jewel in the Crown* (a dramatisation of Paul Scott's 'Raj Quartet'), Channel 4's *The Far Pavilions* (made by Goldcrest Films and based on M. M. Kaye's novel), and films such as Merchant-Ivory's *Heat and Dust*, Richard Attenborough's *Gandhi* (1982) and David Lean's *A Passage to India* (1984) can be placed within the heritage genre in so far as they were all narratives of Britain's imperial past. But whereas they all adopt a critical perspective towards British rule in India, *Octopussy* is set in a present where Anglo-Indian relations are uncomplicated by racial or political problems. The film presents a tourist's view of India in which there is no indication of the poverty and social distress ex-perienced by millions of the sub-continent's inhabitants. Instead, the India of *Octopussy* is one of colourful bazaars, luxurious hotels and sumptuous palaces. The casino, where Kamal plays a retired English major at backgammon while turbaned waiters attend the predominantly white European clientele, is a throwback to the culture of the Raj. Bond, to all intents and purposes, travels around India like a tourist: at one point he even escapes from Kamal's men, who have been hunt-ing him through the jungle, by clambering aboard a river boat full of camera-clicking American tourists. Bond's reply to the query 'Are you with our group?' – 'No, ma'am, I'm with the economy tour' – might be read as an ironic comment on the relative poverty of British resources (Q has already complained of having no proper facilities in his Indian workshop) in comparison to the wealthy Americans.

For all that the greater part of the film is set in India, however, the conspiracy plot in *Octopussy* is, like *For Your Eyes Only*, rooted in the geo-political situation in Europe. It is here that a structural flaw in the film becomes very evident: while Kamal Khan is the most prominent of the villains, it is General Orlov who fulfils the more important ideological role. Early in the film, Orlov opposes disarmament talks between the Warsaw Pact and NATO, reminding his colleagues of the Eastern bloc's overwhelming superiority in conventional forces which he forecasts could over-run Western Europe in five days. He asserts that NATO would not dare resort to using nuclear weapons in retaliation ('The West is decadent and divided. It has no stomach to risk our atomic reprisals. Throughout Europe, daily, demonstrations demand unilateral nuclear disarmament'). The film reflects the military and political circum-stances of the time. It was military reality that the Warsaw Pact had such overwhelming superiority in conventional forces that the NATO forces stationed in West Germany would probably not have been able to hold a full-scale invasion. And there were loud calls for unilateral disarmament in the West. In Britain, for example, the Campaign for Nuclear Disarmament (CND), which had waned in influence since its heyday in the early 1960s, received a fresh stimulus from the station-ing of American nuclear missiles in Britain. In 1981 both the Labour Party and the Trades Union Congress passed motions in favour of unilateral nuclear disarmament at their annual conferences, while one of the most notable protest movements of the early 1980s was the series of demonstrations by women at Greenham Common air base in Berkshire, where Cruise missiles were to be based.

Although the film makes clear that Orlov is a renegade whose war-mongering ambitions are not shared by the Politburo – the chairman, who with his huge bushy eyebrows resembles the recently deceased Soviet leader Leonid Brezhnev, declares that 'World Socialism will be achieved by peaceful means' and states that 'our military role is purely defensive' – all the same it reinforces the notion that the Soviet Union represents a threat to the West. The ideological impetus behind Orlov is underlined by the giant portrait of Lenin which dominates the wall of the conference chamber where he makes his blustering speech. The film suggests a difference of opinion between politicians and the military, the latter rejecting diplomacy in favour of armed force (Orlov refers contemptuously to 'a handful of old men in Moscow [who] bargain away our advantage in disarmament talks'). Orlov's motivation would seem to be a combination of ideology and his desire for personal glory – even as he dies he believes he will be seen as 'a hero of the Soviet Union' – and as portrayed by a manically twitching Berkoff, who played a similar part in *Rambo*, he can be seen in the same tradition of hard-line military lunatics in the cinema as Sterling Hayden's General Jack D. Ripper in Stanley Kubrick's *Dr Strangelove* (1963).

Although topicality was always one of the features of the Bond series, *Octopussy* is slightly unusual in that it tackles such a controversial political issue as nuclear disarmament. The film is nothing if not Thatcherite in its unequivocal assertion that the nuclear deterrent, and especially the presence of American missiles in Europe, is essential to the defence of the West. Orlov's plan is to detonate an atomic bomb on a US air force base, which will look like an accident as early warning radar would rule out the possibility of a Russian attack. The catastrophe of a nuclear accident would lead to loud demands for nuclear disarmament that politicians in the West would be unable to resist. The consequences of this are spelled out by Bond, who realises it would leave Europe defenceless against the Red Army ('Europe will insist on unilateral disarmament, leaving every border undefended for you to walk across at will'). It is not an entirely fanciful scenario, and is certainly more plausible than the doomsday plots of *The Spy Who Loved Me* and *Moonraker*. Indeed, a similar plot featured in *The Fourth Protocol* (1987), based on a novel by Frederick Forsyth, in which a Soviet agent (played by future James Bond star Pierce Brosnan) is sent to detonate an atomic bomb at a US air force base in Britain.

While the face of the enemy has changed in the films of the early 1980s, however, the professional code of ethics which Bond stands for remains the same. The meeting between Bond and Octopussy serves an important narrative role, for two reasons. First, it ingeniously incorporates Fleming's original tale into the film as a backstory for the title character. In 'Octopussy' Bond had gone to Jamaica to investigate Major Dexter-Smythe, an army officer who had disappeared after the Second World War with a cache of Nazi gold. Bond listens to Dexter-Smythe's confession, then leaves to write his report; Dexter-Smythe swims out to see his pet octopus, and commits suicide by allowing himself to be stung by a scorpion fish. In the film, Octopussy reveals that Dexter-Smythe was her father (the details of the story are altered slightly to Chinese gold and the Korean War, with Bond tracking him down to Sri Lanka). 'I had hoped that fate would bring us together,' Octopussy tells Bond, but not for revenge, as he assumes, but rather to thank him for giving her father the 'honourable alternative' of suicide. The backstory is again suggestive of an older Bond: given that Octopussy was only a young girl when her father died and, according to the script is now a woman in her early thirties, then this would place Bond as being around fifty.[11]

The second reason why the Bond–Octopussy confrontation is significant is that it again rehearses the ideologies of patriotism and duty. Their exchange recalls similar moments in earlier films, particularly *The Man with the Golden Gun*. Octopussy believes that she and Bond are 'two of a kind', just as Scaramanga had declared 'We are the best'. However, Bond declines Octopussy's invitation to join her organisation ('I'm not for hire'). She scoffs angrily at his sense of duty ('A man of principle ... naturally you do it for Queen and country!') and sets herself apart from him ('I have no country, I have no price on my head. I don't have to apologise to you, a paid assassin, for what I am!'). The crucial difference between *Octopussy* and *The Man with the Golden Gun*, however, is that now Bond's ethic of duty is being mapped on to his relationship with the heroine rather than his relationship with the villain. It is another example of how, by this time in the series, greater narrative importance was being attached to women in the Bond films than to the male villains. However, the ideological potency of the Bond–Octopussy relationship is never really developed; immediately after they argue, Bond kisses her forcefully and she relents. As ever, Bond's irresistible charm is sufficient to convert even a supposedly powerful and intelligent woman like Octopussy into a simpering sex kitten who begs him to 'come back to bed'.

In other respects, *Octopussy* displays some of the parodic humour that had been absent from *For Your Eyes Only*. Thus, in-jokes are back: at one point Bond imitates celebrity animal trainer Barbara Woodhouse in telling a tiger to 'Sit!', and shortly later swings on a vine while letting out a Tarzan-yell. There are some excruciatingly racist jokes ('That'll keep you in curries for a while,' Bond quips as he hands some of his backgammon winnings to his Indian colleague). In an example of the policy of territorial casting that became particularly important in the later Bond films, Bond's amiable assistant Vijay is portrayed by Indian tennis star Vijay Amritraj, the cue for some fairly predictable jokes about backhands. One sequence recalls the gondola in *Moonraker*: pursued by Kamal's men in a three-wheeler taxi, Vijay uses his tennis racket as a weapon, while the watching crowds turn their heads from side to side as if watching a match on centre court.

Critical reaction to *Octopussy* was muted. Nick Roddick, writing in the *Monthly Film Bulletin*, noted 'the usual flurry of lavish sets, ingenious gadgets and inventive stunt work', but felt that the plot was too complicated and overloaded with details. 'The problems start when we get down to the plot, which is more intrusive – and more difficult to follow – than in previous films,' he wrote. '*Octopussy* frequently tends to bog down in explanations, and the impressive array of touristy Indian locations and the string of rather old-fashioned action sequences have a little difficulty in keeping up the pace.'[12]

It may have been that some critics were lukewarm about *Octopussy* because they were awaiting the return of the cinema's original James Bond. Sean Connery had returned to the role after twelve years in the ironically entitled *Never Say Never Again*, a rival Bond film produced outside the official series which for a while looked set to go head-to-head with *Octopussy* at the box-office but which in the event was delayed until later in the year due to post-production problems. *Never Say Never Again* was another instalment in Kevin McClory's persistent efforts to launch his own Bond franchise. After producing *Thunderball* in association with Eon in 1965, McClory, who retained the screen rights to the story, had agreed not to make another film based on the same story for a period of ten years. In the mid-1970s McClory began working on a new Bond film, entitled *Warhead*, with Len Deighton and Sean Connery, who had expressed an interest in the project if he could be involved in the writing and production. However, the storyline – which involved a SPECTRE base in the Bermuda Triangle, an underwater flotilla attacking New York and a climactic battle on the Statue of Liberty – soon ran into litigation when Eon alleged that it went beyond McClory's rights, which were limited to a remake of *Thunderball*. In the face of these legal obstacles, McClory was unable to raise the financial backing to make the film, and, although a film entitled *James Bond of the Secret Service* was occasionally reported to be in development during the late 1970s, it was not until 1981 that the project took on a more definite shape. McClory made an agreement with Jack Schwartzman, a former executive at the television company Lorimar who had left to become an independent producer, whereby Schwartzman bought McClory's rights to the *Thunderball* story. Schwartzman's background as a showbusiness lawyer enabled him to sort through the tangled legal minefield surrounding the project. He rejected the *Warhead* script and hired screenwriter Lorenzo Semple Jr, who had written the tongue-in-cheek remakes of *King Kong* (1976) and *Flash Gordon* (1980), to develop a new screenplay which updated the *Thunderball* story. For all that the new film had to follow the plot of the original to avoid further legal entanglements, Schwartzman denied it was simply a remake:

> The key point for us is that this film has no reference to any other film. And by that I mean that if no other Bond film had been made, this film would not be any different. It has its own story and approach. ... We're happy with the basic plot, which, with its nuclear overtones, holds up very well. But obviously it's not a remake of a film that has already been done.
>
> I think the best way we can compare it is to say was *Heaven Can Wait* a remake of *Here Comes Mr Jordan*? On one level yes, but it existed in its own right as a new film.[13]

Schwartzman also suggested that *Never Say Never Again* was going to be a more 'realistic' type of Bond film:

> The best way to describe how our film will look is rich, grand, even magnificent, but totally realistic. It has a definite 1980s feel, and if Bond were being written about in the Secret Service of now, we reckon that this is roughly how he would behave. He is getting on a bit, and to some extent he's a maverick in that he relies mainly on his wits in a computer age. I think Sean is rather enjoying that side of it. It's funny and a little cynical, but totally believable.[14]

Never Say Never Again survived a last-ditch attempt to block its release, brought at the High Court in London by Fleming's trustees in the spring of 1983, and was released in the autumn.

Although made outside the official series, *Never Say Never Again* deserves to be seen as a genuine Bond film in a way that the spoof *Casino Royale* was not. It contains essentially the same ingredients as the Eon films: an improbable plot, exotic locations, technological hardware and visual excess. The plot is a reworking of *Thunderball* rather than a straight remake. SPECTRE's conspiracy – masterminded by Blofeld (Max Von Sydow, complete with white cat – a motif borrowed from the Eon films) and carried out by Maximilian Largo (Klaus Maria Brandauer) – acquires an added topicality in that it revolves round the hijacking of two American Cruise missiles from Britain, which will be detonated unless each of the member countries of NATO pays a ransom equivalent to 25 per cent of their annual oil purchases. The locations extend beyond those of *Thunderball*, moving from the Bahamas to the South of France and North Africa. There are some novel touches, including a black Felix Leiter (Bernie Casey), though he still functions as nothing more than a 'yes' man, while comic relief is provided by British comedian Rowan Atkinson as our man in the Bahamas. The set design eschews the modernism of Ken Adam; the ancient underground temple where Largo conceals one of the warheads is more reminiscent of *Raiders of the Lost Ark*. However, Schwartzman's assertion that it was 'totally realistic' should certainly not be taken at face value. Indeed, the film itself foregrounds its own improbability: 'Let's think of a more logical explanation,' says M (Edward Fox) when Bond suggests (correctly as it turns out) that the presidential authority required to substitute dummy warheads for real ones may have been accomplished by using a false eye (the authorisation procedure involves a retinal scan).

The most significant difference between *Never Say Never Again* and *Thunderball* is that Bond is now older and semi-retired. The film begins with him clad in military fatigues apparently on a mission to rescue a girl hostage kidnapped by South American terrorists, but it turns out to be a training exercise – and one which Bond fails when the hostage stabs him (the exercise scenario had her brainwashed by her captors). Bond now spends most of his time teaching, and the new, younger M believes he is a relic of the past ('I'll make you no secret I hold your methods in far less regard than my illustrious predecessor did'). But when the missiles are hijacked, M is ordered by the Foreign Secretary to reactivate the Double-O Section. Connery's return to the role is alluded to in one scene which recalls a similar moment in *Diamonds are Forever* in which Connery/Bond is welcomed back into the fold after time away. 'Good to see you, Mr Bond,' says the new Q (Alec McCowen). 'Things have been awfully dull around here. … Now you're on this, I hope we're going to have some gratuitous sex and violence.'

The narrative ideology of *Never Say Never Again* replays that of *Thunderball* in so far as Bond functions principally as a hero of the NATO alliance. It differs from the official films of the same period in that it makes only tangential reference to the Cold War, opting instead to base its ideological operations on the Anglo-American relationship. However, the power relationship between Britain and America has shifted since *Thunderball*; it is American military force alone which provides the backup necessary to defeat Largo's men. There are numerous references to the British Secret Service being financially depleted: M complains of his 'meagre budget', while Q works in a freezing workshop, complains about the lack of spare parts, and is generally gloomy about the austerity regime he has to endure ('If the CIA made me an offer, I'd be off like a shot. Unlimited resources, air conditioning, twenty-eight flavours of ice cream in the restaurant'). But Bond is still able to strike a blow for Britain when he informs an American submarine captain that he knows about the US Navy's latest top-secret gadget 'from a Russian translation of one of your service manuals'.

Never Say Never Again also provides one of the most ordered and thoroughgoing sets of structural oppositions between characters in all the Bond films. The contest between Bond and Largo takes place on two levels: public and private. The public contest is for power, symbolically represented when they play a game known as 'Domination' in which they battle for control of the world – the Bond narrative encapsulated in a computer game. The personal contest is for Domino (Kim Basinger), whom Largo treats as a possession but Bond treats as a woman, the scene of their tango together performing an elaborate sort of seduction ritual. Largo's belief that money buys love is illustrated in his belief that he could not lose Domino to 'an underpaid British agent'; when he discovers this has happened, his reaction is to sell Domino to the highest bidder from among a group of filthy and lascivious Arabs. The opposition between the demure, blonde, blue-eyed, Nordic Domino and the sensual, dark-haired Latin villainess Fatima Blush (Barbara Carrera) is the sort of visual contrast familiar from countless films. Fatima is once again the woman who refuses to be 'repositioned' by Bond, though in contrast to the coolly calculating Fiona Volpe of *Thunderball* she is characterised as psychologically unstable. Holding Bond at gunpoint, she demands that he issue a public statement that she had provided him with 'the greatest rapture' of his life. Any woman who presents such a challenge as Fatima to Bond's masculinity (to underline the point she aims her revolver at his groin) naturally has to meet a grisly end: she is dispatched spectacularly, blown to smithereens by Bond's exploding Union Jack fountain pen.

Critics welcomed Connery's return to the role he had made his own some twenty years earlier, but were more equivocal about the film itself. Inevitably, comparisons were made to the Eon series, which was the yardstick against which any other Bond film would be judged. Philip Strick in the *Monthly Film Bulletin* considered that Connery 'now incarnates more 007 in one raised eyebrow than subsequent claimants have come anywhere near emulating'. The film itself he thought provided just the right mixture of the old and the new:

> Ingeniously reconstructing *Thunderball* ... *Never Say Never Again* has a usefully engaging familiarity which it embroiders and extends: this time, the sharks are electronically motivated, the duel with Largo is on a holographic computer game, it's Bond himself on the rocket-assisted motorbike, and the dance-floor embrace that led to the death of Fatima (previously Fiona) has been replaced by an eradication so thorough that only her smouldering shoes are left.[15]

Variety, however, found the storyline too familiar, remarking that 'a heavy sense of déjà vu hangs over the picture, with few surprises now being possible within the standard format. Given the familiarity of the mission,' the review went on, 'pic's success depends entirely upon the moment-to-moment pleasure it can provide and results here are moderately good, but hardly enthralling'. It complained, furthermore, that '[the] pace is extremely relaxed and [a] running time of 137 minutes proves excessive given pic's lack of anything new to offer'. It suffered in comparison to the Eon films 'from lack of the accustomed accoutrements of the series, such as the Maurice Binder credits and familiar musical theme'. But *Variety* did approve of the casting, considering that 'Klaus Maria Brandauer ... makes one of the best Bond opponents since very early in the series', while reserving most of its praise for Connery himself: 'In fine form and still very much looking the part, he gets knocked around more than Bond is accustomed to and has cut down a bit on both his vices and his quips, but the actor has brought Bond very gracefully, and pleasurably, into middle-age.'[16]

A View to a Kill was to be the swansong for another middle-aged Bond. Roger Moore's seventh film, the fourteenth of the official series, is not highly regarded by aficionados. For Nicholas Anez, it is 'one of the most derivative films in the series with only superficial changes in the story and characterizations. The threadbare script includes the requisite villain, henchman, good girl, bad girl, chase scenes, visual stunts and other familiar elements.'[17] But while *A View to a Kill* is undoubtedly a very flawed film, it is not without its points of interest. It is not as entirely derivative as Anez suggests, and although the narrative construction of the film as a whole is unsatisfying, it does offer some intriguing variations on the usual formula.

Unlike the preceding films, *A View to a Kill* bears no relation to the Fleming story from which it derives its title. 'From a View to a Kill' had Bond investigating the death of a dispatch rider near SHAPE headquarters outside Paris. He discovers an underground Soviet hideout, which is destroyed. The film had Bond investigating the activities of millionaire industrialist Max Zorin (Christopher Walken), who arouses M's suspicions when a Soviet-made microchip, recovered from 002's body in Siberia, turns out to be identical to a new British chip (capable of withstanding electro-magnetic pulse radiation) manufactured by a company recently taken over by Zorin Industries. Zorin – who, it turns out, is the result of a genetic engineering experiment carried out by a Nazi doctor during the Second World War – is now planning to corner the world market in microchips by destroying Silicon Valley, where 80 per cent of the world's microchips are manufactured.

While the action set pieces of *A View to a Kill* are familiar – a pre-title ski sequence (*The Spy Who Loved Me*), Bond's pursuit of an assassin through Paris (recalling the gondola sequence of *Moonraker*), Bond in a stolen fire truck pursued by the San Francisco police (replaying the gratuitous demolition of police cars from *Diamonds are Forever* and *Live and Let Die*) – the plot itself offers some alternative narrative possibilities which are not, however, developed to their fullest extent. Bennett and Woollacott argue that *A View to a Kill* 'shows signs of considerable effort having been made to adjust and renovate the Bond formula in order to accommodate new cultural and ideological concerns'. In this case, however, the adjustments do not work, so that 'the film is caught between a traditional formula which it does not entirely jettison and a new one which it does not fully develop'.[18] The narrative ideologies of *A View to a Kill* are rather more confused than in previous films, offering an uneasy compromise between the Cold War themes of *For Your Eyes Only* and *Octopussy* and the détente narrative of *The Spy Who Loved Me*. On the one hand there are Cold War overtones in the fear that the Soviet Union may catch up technologically with the West. The idea of a microchip that is resistant to electro-magnetic pulse radiation (of the sort that would follow the detonation of a nuclear bomb) associates the film with the technologically advanced 'Star Wars' defence programme initiated in the United States by President Reagan as a counter to the threat of a Soviet missile attack. On the other hand, Zorin's conspiracy is distanced from the ideologies of the Cold War. While his business empire was initially a cover for his activities as a Soviet agent, Zorin now distances himself from his superiors, who disapprove of his unauthorised commercial activities. 'I admit no association – I no longer consider myself a KGB agent,' he informs General Gogol. It is made clear that Zorin's plot to destroy Silicon Valley is his own freelance venture and is not supported by the Soviet Union. Indeed, the KGB are just as keen as the British to find out what Zorin is up to, as Bond discovers when he comes across Pola Ivanova (Fiona Fullerton), a KGB agent and former lover on the same case as himself. There are echoes of *The Spy Who Loved Me* as Bond enjoys an amorous interlude with Pola ('Détente can be beautiful,' she murmurs as they share a spa bath). But here Bond's relationship with a female Russian spy plays only a subsidiary role in the narrative. The main Bond girl is an American geologist, Stacey Sutton (Tanya Roberts), whose father had been one of Zorin's financial victims. In this sense *A View to a Kill*, like *Moonraker*, reaffirms the Anglo-American special relationship as the one most likely to succeed (reflecting perhaps the political and personal friendship between Thatcher and Reagan) rather than opening up the alternative of an Anglo-Soviet alliance as in *The Spy*. Nevertheless, the film ends with a unique gesture towards détente: Gogol offers the Order of Lenin for 'Comrade Bond'. 'I'd have expected the KGB to celebrate if Silicon Valley had been destroyed,' remarks M. 'On the contrary, admiral,' Gogol replies. 'Where would Russian research be without it?' The result, in Bennett and Woollacott's view, is that 'the plot becomes confused and its ideological articulations fuzzy as it zig-zags between the discourse of Cold War and that of détente and, ultimately, distances itself from both of them'.[19]

There is much substance in Bennett and Woollacott's discussion of the confusions and contradictions within the narrative ideologies of *A View to a Kill*, but their argument is less convincing when they come to analyse the nature of the conspiracy plot itself. Their reading is worth quoting at length as an example of how over-theorisation can lead up a blind alley of interpretation:

It is, however, the nature of Zorin's conspiracy which most unhinges the traditional Bond formula. Having manufactured and

accumulated a massive stockpile of micro-chips, Zorin's ambition is to head a syndicate that will dominate the world's micro-electronics market by eliminating its main rival: California's Silicone [*sic*] Valley which Zorin plans to flood by means of an explosion strategically placed to activate the region's major geological fault-lines. While this conspiracy incorporates aspects of the SPECTRE formula, two crucial ingredients are lacking. The first concerns the motivation of the conspiracy. Although there are exceptions – Stromberg in *The Spy Who Loved Me*, for example – the villain is usually motivated by a compound of avarice and a utopian altruism. ... Zorin's motivation, by contrast, is entirely devoid of any ethical rationalisation, no matter how warped or perverted. As a power-hungry industrialist and a psychotic, Zorin has only two ends in view. To express these in terms of the somewhat laboured play that is made with the film's title, his conspiracy is motivated with a view to making a financial killing and 'with a view to a kill' – that is, to the pleasure of witnessing the infliction of pain, suffering and death by observing the destruction of Silicone Valley from an airship. Secondly, the conspiracy is localised in its import. Far from threatening a global catastrophe, it portends merely the end of America's dominance of the high-tech economy and, as a consequence, lacks the broader political and ideological articulations of either the SMERSH or the SPECTRE formulae.[20]

However, this reading fundamentally misinterprets the nature of Bond villainy. In the first place, it is simply untrue to say that the villain is 'usually motivated by a compound of avarice and a utopian altruism'. It is either one or the other: the grand conspiracy of extortion (particularly the SPECTRE films) or the desire to create a new social order (Stromberg and Drax). Furthermore, in arguing that Zorin's conspiracy 'unhinges the traditional Bond formula', Bennett and Woollacott completely miss the point that *A View to a Kill* is essentially a reworking of *Goldfinger*, a film widely regarded as the archetypal Bond narrative. Goldfinger had wanted to destroy Fort Knox so that the value of his own gold would increase; Zorin wants to destroy Silicon Valley so that he can corner the world market in microchips. Goldfinger's 'Operation Grand Slam', like Zorin's 'Project Main Strike', threatens to destroy the American economy (which, far from being localised, would in both cases have catastrophic consequences for the rest of the world). Goldfinger was no less psychotic than Zorin: he had planned to use nerve gas to kill off the local population. The narrative similarities between *A View to a Kill* and *Goldfinger* work on other levels too: both films follow a trajectory from Europe to the United States; both feature Bond working in America alongside the CIA; and both have a shadowy Communist presence lurking in the background (Goldfinger was backed by Red China, Zorin is ex-KGB).

One aspect of *A View to a Kill* which does offer something new, however, is the prominence accorded to its female villainess, Zorin's sidekick/lover May Day. As played by the bizarre pop-singer-turned-actress Grace Jones, May Day is physically strong and expert at martial arts, coming across as a sort of female Oddjob in thigh boots and a black leotard. She was privileged in the advertising campaign for the film: posters featured Bond and May Day standing back-to-back with the question 'Has James Bond finally met his match?' Jones's appearance emphasises the physicality and sexuality of May Day: her lithe body and animalistic gestures (she snarls and snaps her jaws at Zorin as he pins her down following their karate work-out) suggest the grace and aggression of a black panther. Yet May Day is a highly problematic character within the terms of the Bond series: as a dominant woman (and, moreover, a dominant black woman) she represents a challenge to Bond's masculinity which is never properly resolved. When May Day finds Bond in her bed she climbs in with him, but when he leans over to her she roughly turns him over so that she is on top, thus assuming the dominant position and placing Bond in an unaccustomed submissive role. Given that May Day has killed two of Bond's colleagues, the film seems to be moving towards a showdown between her and Bond, which, given May Day's strength and martial arts ability, he would be hard pressed to win. But having offered up this tantalising possibility, the film does not fulfil the expectation it has created. Like Jaws in *Moonraker*, May Day turns 'good' at the end. Just at the moment when it seems that Bond and May Day are about to come to blows, Zorin lets off the explosive charges which cause the mine to flood, oblivious to the fact that May Day and his men are still inside. Thus feeling betrayed by Zorin ('And I thought that creep loved me!'), May Day helps Bond remove the bomb that will blow up the geological lock and flood Silicon Valley. So while May Day may have changed sides, it is not due to the force of Bond's sexual charisma, as had been the case with Pussy Galore in *Goldfinger*, but rather due to her own feelings of betrayal and desire for vengeance against Zorin. In terms of the sexist code of the Bond films, May Day is simply too problematic to be allowed to live. And the more problematic the woman, the more emphatic her death has to be: like Fatima Blush in *Never Say Never Again*, May Day is not merely killed but is blown to pieces by the bomb which she is transporting clear of the mine. But in killing off May Day in this way, the film denies Bond the opportunity of proving his masculinity against her in a straight fight – and, moreover, denies the audience the confrontation which it had seemed to offer. Yet despite this deeply unsatisfactory resolution, May Day remains a far more memorable character than the main Bond girl who, as played by Tanya Roberts, represents a throwback to the worst excesses of 1970s bimboism.

In contrast to the flamboyant and colourful villains, the Bond of *A View to a Kill* comes across as little more than a caricature. Bond's Englishness is foregrounded even more than usual, but it verges on parody: the identities which he adopts – a rich racehorse owner called James St John Smythe, a *Financial Times* reporter called James Stock – are stereotypes straight from the drawer marked 'English types' and redolent of the sort of class distinctions that had been absent from Sean Connery's Bond. Indeed, Roger Moore's performance in this film, to a greater extent than any of his previous outings, relocates the character of Bond in the tradition of the English gentleman hero, thus differentiating himself even further from Connery's rugged Celtic machismo. The stage Englishness of the film is reinforced by Patrick Macnee's cameo as Sir Godfrey Tibbett, the horse-fancier who facilitates Bond's entry to Zorin's stables. Macnee brings to any part the inter-textual association of his role as John Steed, the dandified English gentleman hero of *The Avengers*, and the combination of Moore and Macnee works as a nostalgic reminder of a kind of screen heroism now eclipsed by the likes of Stallone's Rocky and Rambo, Mel Gibson's Mad Max and Arnold Schwarzenegger's Conan the Barbarian. But to add insult to injury, the former John Steed is all too easily killed off by May Day, as if to suggest that his style of heroism is now outdated. Even Bond's legendary status as Britain's foremost secret agent is mocked: when Bond reveals his name to a San Francisco police captain in the time-honoured fashion ('The name is Bond. James Bond'), the reply is: 'And I'm Dick Tracy, and you're still under arrest.' (Although the ensuing chase, to be fair, does restore some of Bond's mythic potency, evidenced by the police chief's memorable line: 'To all units. Intercept murder suspect in stolen fire truck. He may be armed – and he sure is dangerous.')

It was Moore's performance – and, more particularly, the fact that even he was now starting to show his age – that most reviews focused on. As they had done at various moments in the series' past, critics asserted that the formula was looking stale and that an injection of new ideas, and new blood, was becoming necessary if the series was to continue. This view was expressed, for example, by Richard Buskin in *Films and Filming*:

> Although an improbable plot line has always been part and parcel of the Bond films, and one of the key factors behind their continuing success, this time the story fails to convince on any level – the filmmakers evidently having spent less time patching up the holes in the plot than in applying layers of mascara and eye-liner to Roger Moore's face. For the most part, Moore looks tired, and so are many of the corny double entendre jokes (seemingly cribbed from a *Carry On* film script), whilst Tanya Roberts as the damsel in distress provides much glamour but little else. Grace Jones, meanwhile, plays Grace Jones, as she did in *Conan the Destroyer*.
>
> The stunt work, as usual, is absolutely outstanding, but director John Glen has failed to instil the film with the atmosphere reminiscent of the earlier Bond movies. However, the fact that for the first time the closing credits simply promise that Bond will return – without naming a title – hopefully means that the producers are giving much thought to casting a new 007 as well as infusing some much-needed fresh ideas.[21]

Variety's prediction that *A View to a Kill* would not be as successful as recent films and that audience interest would wane – 'Trading on the Bond name, outlook is good for initial business, but momentum is likely to falter, just as the production does'[22] – proved to be accurate in that its box-office was down noticeably from the previous four Roger Moore films. There was a widespread feeling that Moore's tenure had come to an end, which was confirmed shortly after the release of the film when the actor announced that it would be his last Bond movie. Within the space of a little over a year and a half, therefore, both Connery and Moore – who between them had starred in no fewer than fourteen Bond films – had made their last bows in the role. And, according to some critics, it was not before time. 'I think it's time to say farewell to old friends,' said one reviewer at the time of *Never Say Never Again*. 'The earlier movies look increasingly dated, the new ones merely out-dated.'[23] Once again, the Bond series was faced with the task of reinventing itself if it was to continue.

7

Continuity and Change:
The Living Daylights, Licence to Kill

The phrase 'continuity and change' has become one of the clichés of historical scholarship, but it perfectly describes the nature of the Bond series which constantly strives to maintain a balance between familiarity and tradition on the one hand and variation and innovation on the other. The phrase is especially pertinent to the last two Bond films of the 1980s: *The Living Daylights* (dir. John Glen, 1987) and *Licence to Kill* (dir. John Glen, 1989). These two films exhibit processes of continuity and change at several levels. At the level of production they maintain continuity with the films of the early 1980s through the maintenance of the same core personnel (director Glen, screenwriters Maibaum and Wilson), while at the same time marking an important moment of change through the introduction of a new lead actor (Timothy Dalton). And at the level of narrative ideology, *The Living Daylights* exhibits continuity with the three preceding films through its replaying of Cold War themes, whereas *Licence to Kill* represents a complete change of direction in that it dispenses with the Cold War background entirely and provides a new ideological role for Bond by relocating him in the war against the international drugs trade. Indeed, *Licence to Kill* marks the furthest deviation from the generic formula of the Bond series by any of the official films. Its relatively less successful reception might be attributed, in part at least, to the equation between continuity and change being overbalanced in favour of change, to the extent that too many of the expected conventions of the Bond narrative were absent on this occasion.

The casting of a new, younger James Bond naturally impacted on the style of the films. Timothy Dalton had been approached about the role on several previous occasions when Roger Moore had been threatening to leave the series, though he had turned down Broccoli's overtures on the grounds that he thought he was too young to play Bond. When he accepted the role Dalton was forty, and thus the right sort of age to return Bond to his more accustomed permanent late thirties, following the slightly older character implicit in Moore's last three films. With serious acting credentials behind him for both his stage and film work, Dalton was a surprise choice for the role. He had often been compared to the young Laurence Olivier, on account of his chiselled, dark, brooding looks which were not unlike Olivier's in his 1930s matinée idol days. Official publicity once again suggested that the new actor was closer to Ian Fleming's conception of Bond, and there was a general view that Dalton would make a more serious, hard-edged Bond than his predecessor. John Glen elaborated on the differences between Dalton and Moore thus:

> Roger had done three or four films before I directed him and he knew his role backwards, his style ... Timothy Dalton was very different, much more sinister in the sense he's very real – you can believe he's going to kill someone. He's very much nearer Fleming's Bond. He's the hardest Bond we've ever had ... He's very agile, extremely fit and keen, and very professional.[1]

Dalton's style of performance, in fact, is different both from the eyebrow-acting of Moore and from the brawny physicality of Connery. His Bond is more intense, saturnine, byronic; he moves purposefully, and smiles only rarely. Dalton brought a brooding, dangerous quality to the character which differentiates his Bond from all the others. The film-makers emphasised this in their advertising strategy for his two Bond films, which used the slogans 'The new James Bond ... living on the edge' (*The Living Daylights*) and 'His bad side is a dangerous place to be' (*Licence to Kill*).

In many respects Dalton *is* closer to Fleming's Bond. Dalton, for example, is clearly less comfortable than either Connery or Moore with the witty asides and one-liners, which are downplayed in his films so that he becomes something closer to the Bond of the books, who rarely displays a sense of humour. Dalton's Bond also exhibits some of the self-doubts with which Fleming occasionally endowed his hero. One critic observed that 'Timothy Dalton promises to become the first James Bond with angst, a moody spy for the *fin de siècle*'.[2] Dalton himself evidently saw Bond as something more than just an action hero, as a character riddled with all sorts of moral ambiguities:

> One is constantly reminded by Fleming, both from Bond himself and through the mouths of other characters, that Bond really is as bad as the bad guys. He is a killer, but he does have a moral sense of what good is. That throws him into conflict because of his self-knowledge of who he is and what he does. I find that interesting because it does go back to the Hero; to what it is that makes a hero, to what it is that real people respond to in a hero. We know that good and evil are combined in an individual, and that good must triumph. But unless you have both, you don't have the conflict either within the individual or within the world. It's one of the curious fascinations that made the character inter-esting, believable.[3]

While this may sound like the voice of a serious actor trying to convince himself that he is not slumming it by starring in popular action movies, Dalton certainly brought a dimension to the role that has not been present in any of Bond's other screen incarnations. Nor was it entirely fanciful for him to speak as he did about the combination of good and evil in the character of the hero. In this respect Dalton's Bond can be seen in the same context as the revisionist tendencies in the characterisation of other mythical hero figures at this time. The hugely successful *Batman* (1989), to take the most prominent example, explored, albeit in a neutered sort of way, the psychosis of its hero figure, a dark avenger far removed from the campy excess of the 1960s television series. The casting of comic actor Michael Keaton as Bruce Wayne/Batman was downright quirky, but no more so than the casting of a classically trained Shakespearean actor as James Bond.

The moral ambiguities of Bond's profession had been foregrounded in the short story from which Dalton's first Bond film took its title. In 'The Living Daylights', Bond had been sent to Berlin to cover the escape of a British agent across the no-man's land between the Russian and British sectors. His job is to kill a KGB sniper who has been detailed to shoot the agent. Bond watches for three nights, and takes a fancy to a girl who plays the cello in an orchestra which practises nearby. On the third night, as the agent makes his escape, Bond sights the enemy sniper, who turns out to be the girl cellist. At the last moment Bond alters his aim and wounds the girl rather than killing her outright, as he had been ordered to do.

The Living Daylights follows *For Your Eyes Only* and *Octopussy* in that it uses Fleming's story as a starting point and works out from there into a much more expansive narrative. After a pre-title sequence in which an unknown killer disrupts a Double-O training exercise in Gibraltar, Bond is assigned to cover the defection of General Koskov (Jeroen Krabbé) and, as in the original story, changes his aim when the apparent sniper turns out to be a beautiful girl. Koskov says he is defecting because his superior, General Pushkin (John Rhys-Davies), Gogol's successor as head of the KGB, has initiated an operation called *Smiert Spionam* ('Death to Spies') to kill off British agents. When Koskov is snatched back from a safe house, Bond reluctantly accepts his assignment to kill Pushkin. Bond discovers that the sniper was in fact Koskov's girl-friend Kara Milovy (Maryam d'Abo) and that her rifle was loaded with blanks. Realising that Koskov's defection had been an elaborate ruse, Bond poses as Koskov's friend in order to discover from Kara what he is up to. Koskov is in league with an American arms dealer, Brad Whitaker (Joe Don Baker), in a convoluted drugs-and-arms deal that will net them millions of dollars. The plot to kill British agents turns out to have been instigated by Koskov, and was intended to get the British to kill Pushkin, who had been about to have Koskov arrested before his 'defection'.

In its narrative structure and ideologies, *The Living Daylights* is a film split eloquently down the middle in several key respects. On one level, it straddles the boundary between the sensational and realist lineages of the spy thriller. While the narrative clearly belongs to the sensational thriller in that it revolves round the requisite action sequences, fights, chases and so on, the convoluted plot of a defection that is not really a defection at all is closer to the world of John le Carré, with its themes of treachery and deception, than to the more familiar world of the Bond films where the lines of opposition are usually clearly drawn. Moreover, *The Living Daylights* refers to one of the most celebrated

British thrillers, Carol Reed's *The Third Man* (1949), a reference which may have been intentional in so far as John Glen had worked on that film as an assistant editor. *The Third Man*, with its Graham Greene script and its expressionist photography by Robert Krasker, had created its own world of moral ambiguity and uncertainty in post-war Vienna during the Allied occupation. The Viennese section of *The Living Daylights* presents, in every respect, an image of the city that is precisely the opposite of *The Third Man*, and does it so thoroughly that it seems deliberate. Thus, whereas the Vienna of *The Third Man* was a bleak black-and-white landscape of crumbling buildings and bomb sites, the Vienna of *The Living Daylights* is a colourful fairy-tale land of plush hotels, opera houses and Strauss waltzes. It presents the usual romanticised tourist's-eye view: Bond and Kara arrive at the Schonbrunn Palace in a horse-drawn carriage while brightly costumed dancers twirl around in the open air. When Bond and Kara go on the ferris wheel at the Wiener Prater, it is impossible not to recall the famous meeting between Joseph Cotten and Orson Welles at the same location. James Bond meets Harry Lime, and the sensational and realist lineages of the British thriller converge.

While, on one level, it is caught between different traditions of the thriller, on another level *The Living Daylights* is also, like *A View to a Kill*, caught between the discourses of Cold War and détente, with the result that the film performs an uncomfortable sort of ideological splits. Uniquely, *The Living Daylights* manages simultaneously both to enforce and to transgress the geopolitical boundaries of the Cold War. The Cold War background is highly prominent, with much of the story taking place behind the Iron Curtain in Czechoslovakia (filmed in Vienna) and in Russian-occupied Afghanistan (filmed in Morocco). The film takes for granted the existence of the secret war between Soviet and Western intelligence services, a war in which Britain plays a prominent role. When Koskov is apparently snatched back by the KGB it comes as a severe blow to the British government, who are 'the laughing stock of the intelligence community' according to the minister of defence. When the action moves to Afghanistan, and Bond teams up with the Mujaheddin, who launch a full-scale attack on a Russian air base, the film is unequivocally taking the side of the Afghan resistance against the Red Army. In the sort of conceit which only the Bond films can pull off successfully, the Mujaheddin leader Kamran Shah (Art Malik) turns out to have been educated at Oxford. This is a not insignificant point: Kamran, alone among the Mujaheddin, does not burst into laughter when Bond reveals that he works for the British government. Only the foreigner who has lived in Britain understands what the British are really like; the old boy network is alive and well in the Khyber Pass.

Yet at the same time as taking a pronounced anti-Russian stance as far as the war in Afghanistan is concerned, *The Living Daylights* is also, paradoxically, concerned to distance itself from the political dimensions of the Cold War through its suggestion that Soviet Communism is not, as Raymond Durgnat puts it, 'enemy No. One'.[4] It borrows from *Octopussy* the idea of a renegade Russian general in league with a more conventional Bond villain and whose conspiracy does not have official sanction. However, there is no suggestion of any political or ideological rationale behind Koskov, who in this sense is more akin to Zorin of *A View to a Kill* in that he is motivated purely by greed. The complicated drugs-and-arms deal, in which Koskov deals not only with an American arms dealer but with the Afghan resistance fighters whom the weapons are destined to be used against, crosses both geographical and ideological boundaries. Durgnat, among others, identified certain topical references which suggested the films were moving in yet another direction:

> Although *The Living Daylights* involves heavier references to Second World oppression (not inappropriate in a Czechoslovakian setting), it eschews any further concessions to Cold War revival, *Rambo*-style, instead attributing trouble to collusion between deviationist ultras on both sides ... Here, Afghanistan, ambivalence and amorality call the tune. If the plot is rarely coherent, let alone plausible, its penultimate twists are quite fascinating. They happily mix, into a moral chiaroscuro worthy of Machiavelli himself, (a) a mercenary-capitalist dressed as a US general (virtually an incarnation of the 'contra' spirit), (b) a Russian equivalent of Irangate, and (c) freedom fighters who keep going by dealing dope.[5]

The 'Irangate' affair which Durgnat mentions – a complex scheme to free American hostages held by terrorists in Lebanon by selling arms illegally to Iran, and then secretly diverting the proceeds to provide financial support for the Contra guerrillas in Nicaragua – once again provided a Bond film with a degree of topicality which the film-makers may not have intended. Details of the Iran–Contra affair, which was to plague the last years of the Reagan administration, came to light in

November 1986, when *The Living Daylights* was already in an advanced stage of production. While it would therefore be misleading to suggest that the plot was based directly on 'Irangate', there are nevertheless some intriguing similarities. It is certainly tempting to see the character of Whitaker, a zealous right-wing extremist who has a 'personal pantheon of great commanders' (Hitler, Napoleon, Julius Caesar, Genghis Khan, Alexander the Great) modelled in his own image, as a thinly veiled representation of Colonel Oliver North, the officer most closely implicated in the Iran–Contra dealings.

If the conspiracy plot of *The Living Daylights* is somewhat confused, however, that is not to say that the film is unsuccessful in terms of its other ideological operations. Quite the contrary, in fact, for there are various aspects of the film which nuance, often in a very subtle way, some of the conventions of the Bond series. For a start, Bond's relationship to the secret service is problematised for the first time since he had threatened resignation in *On Her Majesty's Secret Service*. Whereas the Roger Moore films had asserted unequivocally Bond's sense of duty and loyalty ('I'm not for hire' he had told Octopussy), Dalton's Bond has an altogether more ambiguous relationship towards the service and towards his superiors. When a fellow agent admonishes him for not shooting to kill when he first sighted Kara and says he will report to M that Bond deliberately disobeyed orders, Bond's reply hints at an underlying sense of bitterness which hitherto had been the preserve only of the literary Bond: 'Stuff my orders! I only kill professionals. That girl didn't know one end of a rifle from the other. Go ahead – tell him what you want. If he fires me I'll thank him for it.' Scenes like this would seem to have been written especially for Dalton – it is hard to imagine either Roger Moore or Pierce Brosnan, who had been widely tipped to take over from him, carrying it off as convincingly – and foreshadow *Licence to Kill* in which Bond actually repudiates the service and embarks on a personal vendetta.

It is Dalton's performance which, in large measure, is responsible for the success of *The Living Daylights*. Memorably introduced in the pre-title sequence – sight of his face is withheld until the moment when another Double-O man falls to his death from a cliff face, and there is a close-up of Dalton as he turns and reacts – his Bond clearly means business. The hard edge which he brought to the role is best displayed in the key confrontation scene between Bond and Pushkin, in which Bond holds the KGB chief at gunpoint in his hotel room.

Dalton himself suggested that 'the movie had been written for Roger Moore, and originally they were just to sit across the table having a glass of champagne with each other'.[6] In the scene as played, however, Bond is tougher and more ruthless: he savagely clubs both Pushkin and his KGB minder with his gun, tears off the dress of Pushkin's mistress, and makes Pushkin kneel on the floor while holding his gun against Pushkin's forehead.

The greater seriousness of Dalton's Bond is also evident in his relationship with the heroine. *The Living Daylights* is unique among the Bond films in that there is only one love interest for the hero. Even in previous films where Bond's relationship with the girl had been conducted on a slightly more romantic basis, such as *On Her Majesty's Secret Service* and *For Your Eyes Only*, there had still been one or two incidental conquests along the way. The disavowal of casual liaisons in *The Living Daylights* was linked by some commentators to the new sexual climate which had supposedly emerged in the wake of the AIDS scares of the mid-1980s – Raymond Benson, for instance, believes that 'the AIDS epidemic was changing everyone's outlook on sex, and motion pictures and television were just beginning to reflect the new attitudes'[7] – but this seems an unlikely explanation given that the Bond character has never been a role model for notions of political correctness. A rather more likely reason for the existence of a sole Bond girl this time around is the decision by the film-makers to return to something more akin to Fleming's Bond, who was far from being the sort of Casanova that some critics alleged. 'Bond collects almost exactly one girl per excursion abroad, which total he exceeds only once, by one,' observes Kingsley Amis. 'This is surely not at all in advance of what any reasonably personable, reasonably well-off bachelor would reckon to acquire on a foreign holiday or a trip for his firm.'[8]

The release of *The Living Daylights* was something of a milestone in that it marked the twenty-fifth anniversary of the Bond series. The publicity and marketing strategy, like the film itself, was split down the middle. On the one hand there was an understandable urge to celebrate the silver anniversary of the series, which was illustrated in the congratulatory special editions of the trade papers *Variety* and the *Hollywood Reporter* which paid lavish tribute to the achievement of the Bond films in becoming far and away the most successful series of films in box-office history. But on the other hand there was the necessity of introducing the new James Bond, and of proving that while the series had been running for such a long time it was still fresh and vital. In the event *The Living Daylights* did well enough at the box-office, with worldwide grosses of $191 million (against a production cost of approximately $32 million). However, when broken down, these grosses represented a ratio of nearly three-to-one between overseas and North American revenues, thus once again highlighting the importance of non-US markets for the Bond films.[9]

Critical reaction to *The Living Daylights* followed the direction of the advertising in highlighting continuity and change – though there was some difference of opinion as to how much in the way of change there really was in the film. 'A new 007, Timothy Dalton, but generally the Bond mixture as before – relentless action, pretty girls, labyrinthine plot and comic-strip acting,' opined *Screen International*, complaining that 'the script seems feebler than usual and three baddies don't really compensate for one really colourful villain (as of yore)'.[10] *Films and Filming*, however, felt that 'within the limitations of that well-oiled formula, *The Living Daylights* could be termed a modest departure from the norm'. It approved, with some qualifications, of Dalton, who brought new vigour to the proceedings:

> Under the lightweight influence of jolly Roger Moore, the Bond series had deteriorated into something of an arthritic joke heavily reliant on the expertise of the backroom team and death-defying stuntmen. The introduction of Timothy Dalton has afforded the makers an opportunity to return to the drawing board and take Bond back to basics. The Dalton Bond is a more flavourful character than of late; a rugged, romantic hero, anti-authoritarian, tinged with a streak of self-disgust and brusque to the point of rudeness. His one fault is perhaps a certain lack of humour, once handled with impeccably sardonic aplomb by Sean Connery, still the original and best inhabitant of the role.[11]

American critics also differed in their assessment of the degree of change evident in the film. 'Carry On, James' was the title of Janet Maslin's review for the *New York Times*. 'At this late date, the James Bond formula doesn't require much modification,' she wrote. 'Keeping it afloat, as *The Living Daylights* succeeds in doing, is achievement enough.'[12] But *Variety* thought it was 'a healthy cut above the series norm of super hero fantasy' which provided 'a human dimension for Bond not hitherto plumbed'. Showing one of its occasional flashes of socio-political insight, *Variety* detected 'a more mature story of its kind ... Early apprehensions of yet more ho-hum Cold War shenanigans become tempered. By the conclusion, there's even a strong hint of the new *glasnost* spirit – in both directions, with more than one Soviet honcho sporting a decidedly human face.'[13] *Variety* was not alone in reading into the ending of the film overtones of the policy of *glasnost* ('openness') initiated by new Soviet leader Mikhail Gorbachev. General Gogol, who has now moved from the KGB to the Russian foreign service, is seen alongside M and, quite bizarrely, Kamran's guerrillas, in attending Kara's cello recital, where it is revealed that he has arranged a special visa so that she can travel freely between East and West.

With Dalton's performance having attracted critical plaudits, especially from the hard core of the Bond fan culture, the next film was tailored specially for his more serious interpretation of Bond. *Licence to Kill* was the first Bond film not to use an original Fleming title – those that remained, such as 'Quantum of Solace' and 'The Hildebrand Rarity' hardly offered exciting possibilities – though the phrase itself is part of the lexicography of the Bond mythology and thus had the sort of resonance which would identify it as a 'Bondian' title. Originally the film was to have been called *Licence Revoked*, but this was dropped after audience research in the United States revealed that too many cinema-goers did not understand what it meant.[14] Plans to set the film in China fell through when political and logistical difficulties became insurmountable. The story idea was that Bond would be pitted against an evil oriental drugs lord. In the event the drugs theme was maintained but the action was relocated to the Florida Keys and to a fictional Latin American country called Isthmus. The production base for the film was moved to Churubusco Studios in Mexico City, as the exchange rate made filming the $35 million production there more economical.

Licence to Kill represents a complete change of direction for the Bond series on several different levels. The Cold War background of the previous four films disappears entirely. Instead, the enemy is a drug cartel headed by Franz Sanchez (Robert Davi), who operates from a power base in Isthmus City where he has killed or bribed all the politicians and controls the military. Julian Petley was among the commentators who read this as a reflection of the late-1980s *Zeitgeist* which had seen a marked thawing in the Cold War following the new openness evident in the Soviet Union:

The fact that the villains on this occasion are tied up with extreme right-wing forces, however, does show that the Bond myth is fairly flexible in an ideological sense. On the whole, the films have served as a rather good barometer of East–West relations, and it would be difficult to imagine an anti-Soviet Bond in this era of *glasnost*. Instead, the universally reviled figure of the drug baron provides a much more effective target, and the film abounds with scenes in which dealers get their just deserts.[15]

If Whitaker of *The Living Daylights* had been a spiritual cousin of Colonel Oliver North, then Sanchez bears comparison to General Manuel Noriega of Nicaragua, whom the Americans were shortly later to 'snatch' and put on trial for conspiring to distribute drugs in the United States. The film begins with Sanchez being captured by the American DEA (Drug Enforcement Agency) when he makes a lightning visit to the Bahamas to reclaim his mistress who has run off with another man. Sanchez subsequently escapes and threatens to shoot down an American airliner with Stinger missiles unless the DEA leaves him alone. In taking on Sanchez, Bond is effectively relocated from the secret war against the Soviet Union to America's war against the para-military drug cartels in its own back yard.

However, a major difference between *Licence to Kill* and previous films in which Bond had adopted the role of a surrogate American hero (*Diamonds are Forever*, *Live and Let Die*) is that his pursuit of Sanchez amounts to a personal vendetta rather than an officially sanctioned mission. In an incident borrowed from Fleming's *Live and Let Die*, Felix Leiter (David Hedison, who had also played Leiter in the film of *Live and Let Die*) – now working for the DEA – is captured by Sanchez's men and thrown into a shark tank. He survives, though loses his leg; his newlywed bride, however, is murdered (and by implication raped) by Sanchez's men.[16] Upon discovering what has happened, Bond vows revenge and sets out to kill Sanchez and destroy his operation. This course of action puts him at odds with the DEA, who are restricted by legal procedures ('It just so happens we have laws in this country, commander,' says Leiter's colleague after Bond has killed several heavies; 'Do you have a law against what they did to Leiter?' Bond replies bitterly). Even more significantly, Bond disobeys the order given to him by M to leave the whole thing to the Americans ('This personal vendetta of yours could easily compromise Her Majesty's Government').

The key confrontation between Bond and M, in which Bond proffers his resignation and M informs him that his licence to kill is revoked, represents a fundamental shift in the underlying ideology of the Bond mythology. Fleming's Bond had always been fiercely loyal towards M, if occasionally resentful; the filmic Bond, particularly in the Connery films, had been rather more ironic and slightly rebellious towards his superior, though there had never been any question about his loyalty. Petley points out just how far *Licence to Kill* reconfigures, even violates, the relationship between Bond and M: 'The scene in which Bond is disciplined by M and ends up assaulting both his boss and his fellow agents will be as outrageous to Fleming purists as Marlowe's shooting of Terry Lennox in Robert Altman's *The Long Goodbye* was to Chandler disciples.'[17] If M represents Bond's symbolic father-figure, as has often been suggested (by Eco and Bennett among others), then this scene is acting out an oedipal scenario otherwise absent from the Bond films (though present in the novels). In fact, Bond does not physically assault M (that would be going too far), though he does punch and kick M's minders. For the rest of the film Bond is a rogue agent, operating outside the secret service and thus cut off from official resources, though the venerable Q does take leave to equip and assist him in the field. However, in assigning Bond to a personal vendetta rather than an official mission, the film repudiates the professional code of ethics that Bond himself had so often asserted in the past ('When I kill it's on the specific orders of my government,' as he had told Scaramanga in *The Man with the Golden Gun*).

It is not only in its narrative ideology that *Licence to Kill* breaks with the usual codes of the Bond series. It significantly remodels the generic conventions of the Bond narrative so that many of the expected incidents and situations are missing from the film. For example, there is no scene in which M briefs Bond with details of his mission, and no opportunity for the playful flirtation between Bond and Miss Moneypenny that had been one of the hallmarks of the series ever since *Dr No*. While this may be seen as an attempt to ring the changes on the Bond formula, it can be argued that the changes made are so drastic that *Licence to Kill* loses the distinctive generic identity of a Bond film and instead comes to resemble something more like *Dirty Harry* or *Lethal Weapon*. In his relentless pursuit of Sanchez, Bond crosses the boundary from secret agent with a 'licence to kill' to vengeance-driven cop or vigilante – a familiar figure from Hollywood action movies, but far removed from the cool, sophisticated hero audiences are accustomed to in the Bond films.

Licence to Kill also differs stylistically from other Bond movies. The visual style is less glossy than usual: the cinematography is more low-key, the colour definition less pronounced. The Florida locations and designer clothes are more *Miami Vice* than James Bond. The restrained elegance of Bond's usual tailored suits gives way to Dalton's more casual, dressed-down look. The music, too, is less distinctive than usual. Composed by Michael Kamen, the score for *Licence to Kill* – with the exception of the title song performed à la Bassey by Gladys Knight – is bland and undistinguished, too similar to his scores for *Lethal Weapon* (1987) and *Die Hard* (1988) and lacking the lush orchestrations that John Barry had brought to most previous Bond films. The result is that *Licence to Kill* lacks the distinctive 'feel' of a Bond film, again seeming more like a run-of-the-mill action movie.

In various ways, therefore, *Licence to Kill* does not 'fit' into the generic pattern of the Bond series; it is a break from what has gone before, not a natural evolution. However, this is not to say that it entirely lacks 'Bondian' characteristics. While not being the usual madman bent on world domination, Sanchez is one of the most charismatic and physically threatening villains in the series' recent history. Like Bond, he has his own code of ethics ('Loyalty is more important to me than money'), though he is also vicious and, it is suggested, a sexual sadist, whipping his treacherous girlfriend Lupe (Talisa Soto) with the hide of a stingray. This incident was taken from Fleming's story 'The Hildebrand Rarity', in which a boorish American called Milton Krest uses a similar instrument to beat his wife; in the film Krest (Anthony Zerbe) becomes one of Sanchez's associates. The Fleming villain whom Sanchez most closely resembles is Scaramanga of *The Man with the Golden Gun*: a Latin American gangster involved in narcotics who takes Bond on as one of his men for no obvious reason, though in both cases it might be inferred that the villain finds Bond sexually attractive. There is certainly a suggestion of homo-eroticism in the relationship between Sanchez and Dario (Benicio del Toro), a baby-faced young killer.

After the monogamous Bond of *The Living Daylights*, *Licence to Kill* again provides him with more sexual interest, though Latin temptress Lupe Lamora is little competition for main Bond girl Pam Bouvier (Carey Lowell). The character of Pam is an illustration of how far the Bond series has gone towards incorporating discourses of feminism into its representation of women while still maintaining the sexist code that is essential to the make-up of the Bond character. On their first meeting Pam is completely indifferent to Bond; on their second meeting she is shown to be capable of taking care of herself in a bar-room brawl and handles a pump-action shotgun with ease. But as well as being the possessor of a mighty phallic weapon (she tut-tuts when Bond reveals he is armed only with his trusty Walther PPK), Pam is also possessed of dainty feminine guile, keeping a small Beretta .25 (the pistol so contemptuously referred to as a 'lady's gun' by Major Boothroyd in *Dr No*) concealed in her garter. When Bond's speedboat runs out of fuel, Pam's ironic 'I haven't heard that one in a long time' recalls, whether intentionally or not, the ending of *Dr No* in which Bond and Honey had found themselves similarly stranded. A former army pilot, Pam flies Bond into Isthmus City and stays around to help him. She resents having to masquerade as Bond's 'executive secretary', but is firmly put in her place by Bond, who reasserts the sexist code ('We're south of the border – it's a man's world'). An assertive woman at the beginning, by the end of the film Pam adopts a more conventional nice-girl-next-door role when, seeing Lupe kissing Bond, she runs away and cries. Whereas earlier in the film Pam had taken the initiative, at the end she waits for Bond to kiss her first; their dialogue from the boat ('Why don't you wait until you're asked?' 'Then why don't you ask me?') is reversed.

Critical reaction to *Licence to Kill* was sharply divided. Indeed, of all the latter-day Bond films it was the one which most polarised critical opinion, with some responding favourably to its harder-edged style but others thinking that it had strayed too far away from traditional 'Bondian' territory. Even the American trade press, which generally tends to speak with much the same voice, was divided over its merits. *Variety* was enthusiastic. 'The James Bond production team has found its second wind with *Licence to Kill*, a cocktail of high-octane action, spectacle and drama,' it declared. 'It's a sure-fire click worldwide for the 16th in the United Artists 007 series and one that will rate among the best.'[18] But a rather more negative note was sounded by the *Hollywood Reporter*, which felt it lacked the usual panache of the Bond series and was rather more violent than usual:

It's neither shaken nor stirred, but rather blasted, this latest James Bond. If this movie were compared to the peripatetic secret agent's favored vodka martini, it would be of the airport bar variety –

formulaic, pre-measured and dispensed through a hose. A harsh refreshment that the discerning Mr Bond would send straight back to its maker. ... Although there are dollops of drollery throughout, *Licence* has little of the champagne-comic sparkle of vintage James Bond; instead, under John Glen's heavy-artillery direction, it has gory carnage and murder death scenes of such explicit gruesomeness that the series' armchair aficionados are likely to find their stomachs soured and their sensibilities nettled.[19]

This criticism was not without some justification. *Licence to Kill* is the most violent of the Bond movies. Several scenes – including Sanchez whipping Lupe, Leiter's descent into the shark tank, Krest's gory death in a depressurisation chamber, and Sanchez's final fiery demise – attracted the attention of censors in both the United States and Britain. In America it was given a 'PG-13' rating ('special parental guidance recommended for those younger than 13'), while in Britain it was given a more restrictive '15' certificate which denied it the usual family audience that the Bond films traditionally attracted. Some commentators wondered whether the more violent than usual content was a deliberate strategy to compete with Hollywood action movies. 'While this must clearly restrict the box office potential in the UK – where 11–14 year olds have been a huge and loyal audience for years – the reasoning may be that a "realistic" storyline about drugs allied to some graphic violence will more than help to compensate in other markets, notably the US where Bond has never [*sic*] been a giant drawing card,' *Screen International* suggested.[20] However, Broccoli was highly critical of the BBFC's category decision: 'What I also found hard to take was the harsh reaction of the British censor in restricting the age group for our picture while giving *Batman* a clean bill of health.'[21] In fact, *Batman* was only slightly less restricted than *Licence to Kill* in that it caused the BBFC to introduce a new '12' certificate.

Licence to Kill performed less well at the box-office than *The Living Daylights*. Its total worldwide grosses were $157 million, approximately the same as *A View to a Kill*, but only $36 million of that (roughly equal to the film's negative cost) came from North America – a disappointing return in an age when a big-budget film needs to earn back three times its production cost to be in the black. Its relatively disappointing showing at the box-office can be attributed partly to the fact that it was released during Hollywood's blockbuster summer of 1989 when

Indiana Jones and the Last Crusade, *Batman* and *Lethal Weapon 2* all provided stiff competition. *Batman* grossed more on its opening weekend ($40.5 million) than *Licence to Kill* did throughout its entire run in US cinemas. It is unlikely that the more restrictive certificates given to *Licence to Kill* made any significant difference, as *Lethal Weapon 2* was 'R-rated' in the USA and classified '18' in Britain. The *Lethal Weapon* series, which starred Mel Gibson as a maverick Los Angeles cop, was representative of a new style of violent action movie that had emerged in Hollywood, which also included the *Die Hard* films with Bruce Willis and the films of Arnold Schwarzenegger, such as *Commando* (1985), *Raw Deal* (1986) and *Red Heat* (1988). All these films copied from the Bond series the one-liners which the hero makes after dispatching the latest heavy, the difference being that the deaths were that much more violent and gory: the violence of *Licence to Kill* seems mild in comparison to the bloody, bullet-riddled bodies of *Lethal Weapon* and *Die Hard*.

Some commentators again expressed their doubts about the future of the Bond films. *Screen International* observed that 'a question mark seems to hang over the whole future of the series as the jury remains out on this new-look "adult" Bond'.[22] Broccoli conceded that *Licence to Kill* had deviated too far from the usual formula of the Bond series, that 'in making Bond an altogether tougher character, we had lost some of the original sophistication and wry humour', though he remained adamant that Dalton was the right man for the role.[23] However, there was to be a six-year hiatus between *Licence to Kill* and the next Bond film. The lukewarm reception of *Licence to Kill* caused the production team to rethink the Bond formula, and it was even reported (inaccurately as it turned out) that Broccoli was considering selling the Bond franchise.[24] The main reason for Bond's absence from the screen for the first half of the 1990s, however, was that Broccoli's company Danjaq, which holds copyright in the Bond films, entered into a protracted legal dispute with MGM/UA Communications – itself the subject of an abortive take-over by Giancarlo Parretti's Pathé Communications – which, it was alleged, had sold video and television rights for the Bond films at a cut-price rate. The dispute was resolved in 1993, at which time Dalton was still set to star in the forthcoming 'Bond 17'. However, the production was delayed further by script rewrites, and Dalton dropped out of the running. When Bond returned to the screen in *GoldenEye* in 1995, it was to be in the more lightweight persona of Pierce Brosnan.

8

Millennial Bond: *GoldenEye, Tomorrow Never Dies, The World is not Enough, Die Another Day*

The return of the Bond series in the mid-1990s following a six-year production hiatus once again demonstrates how the producers have negotiated structural changes in the film industry and in the popular tastes of cinema audiences. The four Bond films starring Pierce Brosnan – *GoldenEye* (dir. Martin Campbell, 1995), *Tomorrow Never Dies* (dir. Roger Spottiswoode, 1997), *The World is not Enough* (dir. Michael Apted, 1999) and *Die Another Day* (dir. Lee Tamahori, 2002) – successfully reinvigorated the franchise and turned Bond once again into a major box-office attraction. The worldwide grosses of the films increased progressively – $331 million (*GoldenEye*), $347 million (*Tomorrow Never Dies*), $353 million (*The World is not Enough*) and $425 million (*Die Another Day*) – and when adjusted for inflation the series had matched the level of the late 1970s and early 1980s.[1] Significantly, furthermore, each of these films passed $100 million in North America, regarded by the industry as the yardstick for a major box-office hit: *Die Another Day* was the fastest to this figure, taking just ten days. While these figures must be seen in the context of an upward trend in the industry at large, it is evident, nevertheless, that the Bond series had recovered from the doldrums of the late 1980s. *GoldenEye*, for example, took more at the box-office than *The Living Daylights* and *Licence to Kill* combined. 'Old wine in new bottles' would be an apt phrase to describe the four Brosnan films as the content remains essentially the same but the presentation is newer, slicker and more expensive than before. This is demonstrated, for example, in the new design of the iconic 'Bond' gun-barrel logo at the beginning of the films which now acquires a fluid three-dimensional effect. While each of the Brosnan films had a different director and the style varied accordingly, continuity at the level of production was maintained as the films were produced by Michael G. Wilson and Barbara Broccoli, stepson and daughter of 'Cubby' Broccoli, who died in 1996.

The popular success of the Brosnan Bonds is all the more remarkable given that the thirty-five-year-old series faced stiffer than ever competition in the action-movie market. The early 1990s had seen a wave of rival action thrillers which threatened to displace the Bond films from their position as the premier action-movie series. The *Lethal Weapon* and *Die Hard* series, which combined explosive and violent action with the sort of tongue-in-cheek humour pioneered by the Bond movies back in the 1960s, had both run to three films before the release of *GoldenEye*. The success of the Cold War thriller *The Hunt for Red October* (1990), starring Sean Connery as a Russian nuclear submarine commander playing cat-and-mouse with the Soviet and American navies as he attempts to defect, led to a further two film adaptations of Tom Clancy's high-tech novels, *Patriot Games* (1992) and *Clear and Present Danger* (1994), in which Harrison Ford took over the role of CIA agent Jack Ryan, a suited hero described in the promotional discourse as a 'James Bond for the 90s'. Another 'James Bond for the 90s' was threatened when Arnold Schwarzenegger recovered from the flop of *The Last Action Hero* (1993) with the Bond-derivative *True Lies* (1994), a massively-budgeted ($100 million-plus) action movie in which the Austrian *übermensch* played an American secret agent called Harry Tasker, the 'twist' being that his wife (Jamie Lee Curtis) believes him to be a boring computer salesman and is contemplating an affair with a used-car salesman who pretends he is a secret agent. 'I thought this could be made into a James Bond kind of movie,' Schwarzenegger remarked. 'But instead of having Bond with a playboy bunny waiting at every port, he would have a more realistic [*sic*] situation with a wife and child.'[2] That the Bond movies were a point of reference is evident from the outset, as Schwarzenegger emerges from the water and removes his wetsuit to reveal an immaculate dinner suit *à la* Connery in *Goldfinger*: imitation is the sincerest form of flattery. But for all its expensively staged pyrotechnics, *True Lies* lacks the unique generic identity of the Bond films, and Schwarzenegger himself can never be anything more than an *ersatz* Bond, despite his fetching deadpan way with heavily accented one-liners.

In relaunching the Bond series, the producers were at pains to differentiate Bond from the many competitors in the action market. Wilson described the Bonds as 'action-adventure' rather than simply 'action' films and emphasised the global scale of Bond's adventures. 'There are very few action-adventure films,' he states. 'Action films tend to be located in one particular city or one building, plane, boat or airport. So I never think of them as direct competition.'³ This is one of the key differences between the Bond series and the *Die Hard* and *Lethal Weapon* films. Another difference, as *GoldenEye* director Martin Campbell put it, is that Bond is a 'white collar hero' whereas the other action heroes are all 'blue collar'.⁴ Campbell, who had directed the acclaimed BBC thriller serial *Edge of Darkness* (1986) and the futuristic action film *No Escape* (1994), nevertheless admitted that he entertained some reservations about directing a Bond picture:

> I thought long and hard about it. I felt that Bond was getting very tired. I thought that the franchise had slightly passed its sell-by date and that the 17th film would need a shot in the arm. I questioned whether Bond was part of the '90s or an anachronism. It was a question of deciding whether he was relevant or not, whether he could still be as entertaining and successful as he had been in the past.⁵

The casting of Irish actor Pierce Brosnan as the new James Bond had a certain air of inevitability about it. Brosnan had been considered for the role in 1986, but was tied to a contract for the television series *Remington Steele*, even though it had been cancelled by the NBC network. In the absence of any other likely candidates for the role – though Mel Gibson had been touted in the media – the choice of Brosnan was virtually a *fait accompli*. Now in his early forties, Brosnan was the right age for Bond, and with his old-fashioned, darkly handsome matinée idol looks he certainly had the right image for the part. Some critics alleged that he had little to offer beyond his looks. 'The choice of Brosnan is less a piece of casting and more a masterstroke of art direction: those

Littlewood-catalogue looks; hair in all the right places ... the man looks as though he was born to model jumpers,' wrote Tom Shone in the *Sunday Times*.[6] 'Pierce Brosnan, a classless Celt, has a superficial resemblance to Sean Connery but ... the agency you'd associate him with is the one that supplies escorts, not spies,' observed Philip French.[7] Comparisons to his illustrious predecessors were inevitable. 'We know 007 is a tailor's dummy wired for wisecracks,' said Nigel Andrews. 'But Connery and Moore suggested wit and mischief in reserve. Brosnan seems to have signed on at the charm clinic and come away with a personality by-pass.'[8] Brigit Grant confessed that 'I was secretly pining for Sean Connery and felt that Brosnan was more of a Milk Tray man who failed to deliver'.[9]

Other critics, however, were more charitable to the new 007. Geoff Brown thought he was 'undoubtedly the best Bond since Sean Connery'.[10] Comparisons between Brosnan and his immediate predecessor tended to be in the new man's favour, as critics welcomed his lighter and more relaxed style of performance following the intensity and seriousness of Dalton's Bond. 'He [Brosnan] has the sexual mischief of the old James with a superman's derring-do and self-confidence in handling wit and weaponry,' said Alexander Walker. 'The last licence-holder, Timothy Dalton, pre-eminently a stage actor, seldom looked fully at ease in front of the camera.'[11] And Mariella Frostrup felt that the popular success of Brosnan's Bond 'is proof that the martini-swilling superhero has been successfully reinvented since the dire Dalton days'.[12] Such comments are indicative of a trend, particularly among the popular press, to disparage Dalton's Bond in hindsight, even though his performance had been well received by most critics at the time.

GoldenEye was the most expensive Bond film to date, though its $50 million budget was less than half that of *True Lies* and much of the cost was offset by product placement (BMW cars, Omega watches, IBM computers, Perrier water). Although the Bond series came back to Britain, Pinewood Studios was full to capacity at the time of production and so Eon converted a disused Rolls-Royce factory at Leavesden Aerodrome, near Watford, into a makeshift studio facility. This logistical improvisation certainly had no adverse effect on the quality of the film itself, which is a more polished and sophisticated Bond thriller than *Licence to Kill*, and one which adheres closer to the generic conventions of the series. Even so, *GoldenEye* is not without its contradictions.

The fact that Brosnan had so nearly been Bond instead of Dalton some eight years earlier adds a particular *frisson* to the pre-title sequence of *GoldenEye*, which, unusually for a Bond film, is set in the past, some nine years before the main story. Assuming that the main narrative is contemporaneous with the film's release (1995), then the pre-title sequence takes place in 1986, the year in which Brosnan had lost the Bond role to Dalton when he was unable to free himself from his television contract. It is almost as if the film is turning the clock back to suggest that Brosnan should really have been Bond all along, that Dalton had been an aberration. In this sense it can be compared to *Diamonds are Forever*, which had set out to erase the memory of George Lazenby by emphasising that Sean Connery was back as James Bond.

The main ideological imperative for *GoldenEye* was to find a place for Bond in the changing world of the 1990s. This was acknowledged in the publicity, exemplified by the following extract from a marketing document produced by international distributors UIP:

> It is six and a half years since the last Bond film (*Licence to Kill*) was released, and the 'classic' Bond films (as Nos. 1–16 are now referred) are a memory, a past associated with the pre-Glasnost era. The world has changed – the Berlin Wall has come down and those that were regarded as enemies are now our allies, and some who were friends cannot necessarily be regarded as so. 'Political correctness' is now taken for granted. Is there still a place in the modern world for a Secret Agent like 007?
>
> The answer is emphatically *yes*. *GoldenEye* presents a Bond for the 90s. This is a *contemporary* action film clearly reflecting the world in which we live. There are many elements that position the story in today's world – from bungee-jumping and computer hacking to a female M, and a sports car that hasn't even been launched yet![13]

This sort of publicity material illustrates the way in which a film is intended to be received, and as such it represents an attempt to pre-determine critical interpretation from an 'official' point of view. What is interesting about *GoldenEye*, however, is that the film itself does not entirely conform to the intended meaning that is here being overlaid on to it by the official publicity machine. While in some respects *GoldenEye* does present a 'Bond for the 90s', in other respects it offers the pos-sibility for alternative readings which are ignored or marginalised by the official publicity discourse. Indeed, close analysis reveals a considerable tension between official pronouncements on the one hand and the film itself on the other.

On one level, certainly, *GoldenEye* does perform the role assigned to it by the official publicity in locating Bond in the 1990s. Most obviously this involves taking account of the end of the Cold War. Since the release of *Licence to Kill* in the summer of 1989, the geopolitical map of Europe had been substantially redrawn: the Communist regimes in Eastern Europe had collapsed, the Berlin Wall had fallen, the two Germanys had been reunified, the Soviet Union had been dismantled and new democratic governments had been elected in most former Soviet bloc states. *GoldenEye* straddles the end of the Cold War by setting its pre-title sequence in the past. Thus, the film begins with Bond and his colleague 006, Alec Trevelyan (Sean Bean), penetrating a Soviet chemical weapon research centre near Archangel. Trevelyan is apparently shot by Colonel Ourumov (Göttfried John), but Bond blows up the centre and escapes. Nine years later, when a Russian satellite weapon known as 'Goldeneye', which uses an electro-magnetic pulse to knock out anything with an electronic circuit (shades of *A View to a Kill*), is hijacked by an unknown enemy, Bond is assigned to investigate. Travelling to St Petersburg, Bond discovers that Ourumov, now a general, is in league with the 'Janus' crime syndicate. The mysterious Janus is none other than Trevelyan, who it turns out was not killed, but who has been permanently scarred by the explosive charges which Bond set off. As the publicity material indicates, a degree of realignment between friend and foe has taken place: Bond's former friend is now his sworn enemy, while Bond turns for help to former KGB agent Valentin Zukovsky (Robbie Coltrane).

On closer inspection, however, the relocation of Bond to a post-Cold War context needs to be nuanced rather more subtly. For all that the old Communist regime has fallen, the threat still emanates from Russia. General Ourumov, a renegade military commander who plots his own personal conspiracy, recalls similar characters in *Octopussy* and *The Living Daylights*. And *glasnost* extends only so far: when the Russians claim the firing of Goldeneye was 'an accident during a routine training exercise', Bond detects a familiar cover-up ('Governments change, the lies stay the same'). In a sense, it could be argued that *GoldenEye* does not really modify the ideological content of the Bond narrative to any great degree. It still belongs squarely in the generic lineage of the British spy thriller in which Russia had always been represented as a mysterious and sinister enemy, even before the rise of Communism overlaid a more overt political dimension on to the genre. It could be argued, in fact, that for all its contemporary references to the powerful Russian Mafia which had emerged after the fall of Communism, *GoldenEye* simply represents a continuation of the tradition of Russian villains which had been a staple of the British imperialist spy thriller since the days of William Le Queux and E. Phillips Oppenheim.

There is another respect, too, in which *GoldenEye* looks to the past. The reason why Trevelyan turns against Britain is rooted in a historic betrayal. It is revealed that his parents were Lienz Cossacks, Russians who fought for the Germans during the Second World War and surrendered to the British in 1945, but were handed back to Stalin, who executed them ('Not exactly our finest hour,' Bond observes ruefully). Trevelyan plans to use the Goldeneye weapon on London, after hacking into the computer of the Bank of England to transfer money to his own accounts, which he sees as his own revenge on the country that betrayed his parents ('England is about to learn the cost of betrayal – inflation-adjusted for 1945').

In *GoldenEye*, therefore, the conspiracy is once again directed against England, relocating Bond within the generic lineage of the imperialist spy thriller following his excursion into *Lethal Weapon* territory in *Licence to Kill*. *GoldenEye* recalls *On Her Majesty's Secret Service* in its foregrounding of the codes of patriotism and duty. As Bond and Trevelyan set out on their mission together in the pre-title sequence, Trevelyan asserts the patriotic code which they both share ('For England, James'). When they come face to face nine years later, however, Trevelyan scorns and rejects that code. The dialogue exchange between the two men rehearses some familiar ideologies:

BOND: Why?

TREVELYAN: Hilarious question, particularly coming from you. Did you ever ask why? Why we toppled all those dictators, undermined all those regimes? Only to come home, 'Well done, good job, but sorry, old boy, everything you risked your life and limb for has changed.'

BOND: It was the job we were chosen for.

TREVELYAN: Of course you'd say that. James Bond, Her Majesty's loyal terrier, defender of the so-called faith.

This confrontation between former friends, one of whom no longer holds the values they once shared and who now scorns the other for clinging to outmoded boy-scout beliefs, recalls the similar exchange between Holly Martins and Harry Lime in *The Third Man*, thereby again reinforcing *GoldenEye*'s generic links within the thriller genre. Just as Martins kills Lime at the end of *The Third Man*, the climax of *GoldenEye* has Bond taking a personal relish at his former friend's demise. 'For England, James?' Trevelyan says, ironically recalling his earlier words; 'No, for me,' Bond replies, letting Trevelyan fall to his death from a great height.

Another way in which the publicity discourse tried to suggest that *GoldenEye* had updated the Bond series to reflect the world of the 1990s was in its representation of women. 'What is different about this film is that gone are the bimbos!' declared the publicity material. 'Izabella Scorupco and Famke Janssen play the two female leads. Both play highly intelligent and highly independent characters who have their own opinions and course of action, which are integral to the storyline of the film.'[14] But this was far from being a new discourse, as similar statements had been made about the women in every Bond film since *The Spy Who Loved Me* in 1977. And, moreover, as had been the case with previous films, the supposed intelligence and independence attributed to the female characters needs to be qualified. Heroine Natalya Simonova (Scorupco) is a computer programmer who possesses certain skills that Bond does not, though her independence is expressed mainly through bossiness rather than intelligence. And villainess Xenia Onatopp (Janssen), who gets her kicks from asphyxiating men between her legs during sex – as her name implies, she likes to go on top – is simply the latest in a long tradition of beautiful but deadly females such as Fiona Volpe and Fatima Blush who live fast (she drives a Ferrari) and die spectacularly.

This is not to say, however, that *GoldenEye* makes no concessions to feminism at all. Its strategy for incorporating feminist discourses is not to alter Bond's attitude towards women, but rather to alter the attitudes of the women around him to Bond himself. Indeed, the film presents Bond as being beleaguered by women in positions of power and authority. These women are no longer confined solely to the realms of villainy, such as Onatopp, but are also to be found on Bond's own side. Thus, the main narrative begins with Bond being evaluated by a female secret service psychologist, though she quickly melts when he turns on the charm ('I have no problem with female authority'). Miss Moneypenny suggests that his flirtation could be construed as sexual harassment, though she is still clearly flattered by the attention. The most obvious challenge to Bond's male chauvinism, however, comes from the new M, played by Judi Dench. In making M a middle-aged career woman, the film drew obvious comparisons to the real-life appointment of mother-of-two Stella Rimington as Director-General of MI5. However, the casting of a female M should be seen not merely as another example of the Bond series' topical contemporary references, but also as a deliberate strategy for renegotiating the sexist code which remains essential to the make-up of the Bond character. In the most-quoted line of the film, M makes it clear to Bond that she regards him as an anachronism, telling him to his face that he is 'a sexist, misogynist dinosaur, a relic of the Cold War whose boyish charms, though wasted on me, obviously appealed to that young woman I sent out to evaluate you'. Thus the film diffuses the obvious criticisms that could be made of the Bond character (that his attitude towards women is out of date in the 1990s) by voicing them itself through the agency of a female authority figure.

In its narrative ideologies, therefore, *GoldenEye* offers only a partial reworking of the Bond formula in a 1990s context. The tension between the film and the publicity discourses around it is evident at other levels too. For example, although the publicity material had claimed that the previous Bond films were now nothing more than a 'memory' – 'Pierce Brosnan *is* James Bond. Forget all who have preceded him'[15] – *GoldenEye* explicitly locates Brosnan in the Bond heritage by showing him, immediately following the title sequence, driving a silver-grey Aston Martin DB5, thus immediately invoking the memory of Connery who had driven the same vehicle in *Goldfinger* and *Thunderball*.[16]

The visual style of *GoldenEye* also represents a mixture between new and traditional elements. It restores the rich visual texture of earlier Bond films, following the more low-key look of *Licence to Kill*. The main title sequence, designed by pop video and commercial director Daniel Kleinman, is a stunning *tour de force* which pays homage to the late Maurice Binder while surpassing his most recent title designs in its level of visual imagination. Kleinman uses the title sequence as a metaphor for the plot itself, something which Binder did only occasion-ally, providing a surrealistic illustration of the fall of Communism: giant hammers and sickles float against a red background, women smash them with sledgehammers, statues of Lenin are toppled. There is a Daliesque quality to some of the imagery, especially the floating guns and the giant 'golden eye' which serves as a linking motif. The titles also anticipate the key confrontation scene between Bond and Trevelyan, which takes place symbolically among the relics of Russia's Communist past in a 'statue park' in St Petersburg. Elsewhere in the film, Peter Lamont's production design recalls the heyday of Ken Adam, particularly in the multi-layered Goldeneye control centre which resembles Dr No's gantried laboratory, and in the hidden satellite dish which rises from beneath the surface of a lake rather like the volcano base in *You Only Live Twice*. The new M's office eschews the traditional wood panels and leather-backed furniture in favour of a clinical modernist functionalism, while the secret service operations room features walls of giant monitor screens which emphasise the technological sophistication of modern spying. In the midst of all this technological modernity, however, Bond himself has a comfortingly 'retro' appearance through the elegant sophistication of Brosnan's tailored suits, complete with tucked-in pocket handkerchief. Phil Méheux's cinematography, furthermore, recalls the bright, glossy, high-contrast style of Ted Moore's work on the 1960s Bonds. This might be seen as a form of product differentiation, as the tendency in most other action thrillers of the 1990s, including the *Lethal Weapon* and *Die Hard* films, had been towards a grainier, grittier look in which much of the action is under-lit.

In locating *GoldenEye* in the lineage of the Bond series, the films which it most closely resembles are those directed by Guy Hamilton and John Glen. Martin Campbell's direction recalls Hamilton's in its visual extravagance and foregrounding of signs of conspicuous consumption (*Goldfinger* in particular springs to mind) and Glen's in its highly efficient staging of protracted action sequences. The film strikes a nice balance between action as spectacle, exemplified in the chase through the streets of St Petersburg with Bond at the controls of an unusually manoeuvrable T-64 tank which demolishes everything in its path, and more intimate set pieces such as the bruising close-quarters fight between Bond and Trevelyan at the film's end which recalls the train compartment fight of *From Russia with Love* and the lift fight in *Diamonds are Forever*. Where the film lacks the distinctive Bond style, however, is once again in its music: Eric Serra's synthesised score eschews John Barry's orchestral flourishes in favour of a more restrained electronic sound and makes only sparing use of the 'James Bond Theme'. 'The absence of the latter', said one critic, 'is sure to throw some audience members into a two-hour Pavlovian twitch.'[17]

The reception of *GoldenEye* was mixed, with some critics welcoming Bond's return to the screen after his extended leave of absence while others lamented that the film was so formulaic it felt as if he had never really been away at all. Geoff Brown belonged to the former camp, averring that *GoldenEye* marked a return to the high camp style of the classic Bond films and was stylish enough to put the over-muscled action men of Hollywood back in their place. 'Other action heroes may have sprung up in the 1980s while the Bond series nosedived with dull Timothy Dalton and then disappeared into legal wrangles; but, as Bond gets to work in his tailored clothing, you feel Schwarzenegger and Stallone shrivelling,' he wrote. 'Camp fun has returned to action movies.'[18] Todd McCarthy of *Variety* felt that the film 'breathes fresh creative and commercial life into the 33-year-old series' and that Bond 'has been shrewdly repositioned in the '90s in ways that will amuse longtime fans and prove engaging for viewers not born when Bond started saving the world'.[19] But there were other voices in the trade who doubted that a Bond film could hold its own in the age of the modern action cinema. Mike Goodridge, London critic of *Screen International*, thought *GoldenEye* was 'hampered by a feeble story, flabby pacing and too strict an adherence to the series' traditional formula. A 1995 Bond pic needs tighter plotting and more palpable suspense to seduce a generation groomed on the never-let-up tension of *Die Hard*, *Speed* and *True Lies*.' Goodridge felt that the film would appeal most to existing fans rather than the mainstream cinema audience: 'The marketing frenzy surrounding a new 007 picture – and a new 007 – will be enough to get ageing Bond fans into the cinema … but beyond that, this dated package might drop off dramatically at the box office, missing the target with the cinema's core 16-to-24-year-old audience.'[20] This was hardly the sort of verdict the producers wanted to hear, as much of their marketing strategy had been designed to attract new audiences to Bond.

For all the doubts of some critics, however, the popular success of *GoldenEye* proved that the Bond series could still prosper in the film culture of the 1990s. The eighteenth film, *Tomorrow Never Dies*, consolidated that success, though its production was anything but a trouble-free process. It was hampered by constant rewrites, by a hastily revised location when plans to film in Vietnam fell through at the last moment, and by friction on the set between director Roger Spottiswoode and writer Bruce Feirstein which was widely reported in the press. The start of principal photography was delayed until 1 April 1997 for a film due to be released at the end of the year, and the budget escalated to an estimated $80 million. Once again a makeshift studio was built to accommodate the production, this time in a former supermarket warehouse at Frogmore in Hertfordshire, though some work was done at Pinewood, while the underwater sequences were filmed at the massive tank built in Baja by Twentieth Century-Fox for James Cameron's *Titanic*. Considering the difficulties involved, the completion of the film to meet its December release date was an achievement in itself.[21]

Tomorrow Never Dies was originally to have revolved around the handover of Hong Kong from Britain to China, though that story was dropped because it was deemed too political. Instead the film features a megalomaniac multimedia baron, Elliot Carver (Jonathan Pryce), who plots to start a war between Britain and China. The film presents the figure of the media mogul as the modern equivalent of the traditional Bond villain, a man whose control of the channels of communication allows him to manipulate the course of governments. The publicity discourse hinted that Carver was a caricature of media tycoons such as Ted Turner and Rupert Murdoch, though a more useful comparison would be to William Randolph Hearst: Carver even quotes the famous dictum attributed to Hearst ('You provide the pictures, I'll provide the war'). Carver uses a secret satellite encoder to send a British frigate off course into Chinese territorial waters and a Stealth boat that is invisible to radar to sink it, making it look as if the Chinese are responsible.

Like *GoldenEye*, therefore, *Tomorrow Never Dies* locates Britain at the centre of the conspiracy and assigns to it the status of a world power. While the story itself bears no relation to Ian Fleming, one of the narrative ideologies of the original stories is still evident through the playing out of the *Pax Britannica*. If Fleming's novels had provided an imaginary reversal of Britain's decline on the world stage following the Suez Crisis, the main point of reference for *Tomorrow Never Dies* is the Falklands War. The sinking of the frigate HMS *Devonshire* is a blow to national pride which recalls the very real shock felt when ships were lost in the Falklands. In the imaginary world of the Bond film, however, Britain sets out to take on not a tin-pot South American dictatorship but the military might of Red China. 'We're sending the fleet to China,' Moneypenny tells Bond, in a gloriously anachronistic assertion of Britain's maritime power. Moreover, the film also recalls the jingoistic extremes of the British tabloid press during the Falklands War: 'The Empire Will Strike Back' screams one headline in a manner reminiscent of the *Sun*'s notorious 'Gotcha!' and 'Stick It Up Your Junta' banners of 1982. America's role, meanwhile, is sidelined: 'Uncle Sam is completely neutral in this turkey shoot,' CIA agent Jake Wade (Joe Don Baker) tells Bond. 'We have no interest in World War Three, unless we start it.'

The politics of *Tomorrow Never Dies* are intriguing. Red China, which at various times in the past had been a shadowy threat lurking in the background of the Bond movies, here assumes a position of much greater prominence, the collapse of the Soviet Union leaving China as the world's leading Communist power. At a time when there had been friction between China and Taiwan, as the Chinese navy carried out belligerent manoeuvres off the Taiwanese coast, the Bond films were once again reflecting the international political situation through references to Chinese military strength. However, *Tomorrow Never Dies* replays the narrative strategies of *From Russia with Love* and *The Spy Who Loved Me* in that the conspiracy revolves around a third party trying to provoke conflict, and Bond teams up with a Chinese agent, Wai Lin (Michelle Yeoh), to defeat the villain. Carver is in league with a renegade Chinese warlord, General Chang, but the possibilities of internal dissent within China are never fully explored. Indeed, although Chang is mentioned frequently he is glimpsed only fleetingly, and as a character serves no narrative function.

Tomorrow Never Dies is replete with topical references. There are some teasing in-jokes as to which media tycoon Carver might have been modelled on. 'The PM would have my head if he knew we were investigating *him*,' M remarks, a line which could be read as a veiled comment on new British Prime Minister Tony Blair's political friendship with Rupert Murdoch, whose News International Corporation owns *The Times* and *Sun* newspapers and whose support, after years of siding with the Conservative Party, was seen by some as a major factor in Labour's 1997 general election victory. When, at the end of the film, M covers up Carver's role in the crisis by issuing a press statement to the effect that he is missing after falling overboard from his yacht, the mysterious death of disgraced newspaper proprietor Robert Maxwell, owner of the Mirror Group, springs irresistibly to mind. One scene even suggests that Carver is blackmailing the (unnamed) US president with a 'video of him with the cheerleader in the Chicago motel room' – a not entirely fanciful scenario given President Bill Clinton's much-publicised sexual peccadilloes.

As well as providing a topical modern variation on the figure of the Bond villain, *Tomorrow Never Dies* also features the most progressive heroine of the series to date. The character of Wai Lin performs the same ideological role as Anya Amasova of *The Spy Who Loved Me* in that she represents the feminine face of Communism. However, as played by Michelle Yeoh, the foremost female star of Hong Kong action cinema, Wai Lin actually has less in common with previous Bond girls than she does with another tradition of popular cinema: the fighting woman. Yeoh is the latest in a lineage of martial-arts heroines in the cinema which includes Angela Mao Ying (the female Bruce Lee of the 1970s), Tamara Dobson, Pam Grier and Cynthia Rothrock. While these performers made their name in non-mainstream genres such as Hong Kong 'chop socky' and 'blaxploitation', the figure of the fighting woman crossed over into mainstream Hollywood movies during the 1980s and 1990s, the two foremost examples being Sigourney Weaver in the *Alien* films and Linda Hamilton in *Terminator 2*, women who adopt masculine characteristics through their assertiveness, physical courage and ability to handle big guns. *Tomorrow Never Dies* provides plenty of scope for Yeoh to display her martial-arts skills, even to the extent of borrowing one of the conventions of Hong Kong action cinema when she combats a whole gang of villains. Initially resistant to Bond both sexually and ideologically (she calls him 'the decadent agent of a corrupt western power'), it is only at the very end of the film, when the mission has been accomplished, that she succumbs to the inevitable.

Like so many of its predecessors, *Tomorrow Never Dies* foregrounds technology, particularly through its emphasis on systems of communication and military hardware. The pre-title sequence, in which Bond is transmitting camera pictures of a terrorist arms bazaar on the Russian-Afghan border back to the Ministry of Defence in London, establishes a motif of technological spying which is a key thematic concern of the film. Both the MOD and Carver's high-tech headquarters in Hamburg are dominated by a wall of giant video screens which transmit pictures from around the world, while Carver's associate Gupta (Ricky Jay) uses sophisticated eavesdropping equipment to listen in on a conversation between Bond and Carver's wife Paris (Teri Hatcher), who is one of Bond's old girlfriends. Modern military technology is represented in the form of the ship-launched Cruise missile which can unerringly find its target, with the film recalling the media coverage of the Gulf War in which 'smart' weapons had been portrayed as the most efficient and clinical means of hitting enemy targets. 'One strike and we take out half the world's terrorists,' remarks the belligerent Admiral Roebuck (Geoffrey Palmer), unwittingly anticipating the US Cruise missile strikes on terrorist training camps in Afghanistan in the summer of 1998. But, just as in reality 'smart' weapons are not as accurate as they are widely supposed to be, the film ends with the Royal Navy reverting to tried and trusted methods: when radar contact with the damaged Stealth boat is too weak for a missile lock, the British flagship destroys it 'the old-fashioned way' with its 4.5-inch gun.

While the narrative ideologies of *GoldenEye* and *Tomorrow Never Dies* have much in common through their reassertion of the patriotic code of the Bond series, the films are quite different in style. If *GoldenEye* is more polished and visually sumptuous, then *Tomorrow Never Dies* has a rawness and urgency that recalls the Bond films of Terence Young and Peter Hunt. The pace is extremely swift; Spottiswoode's direction creates a sense of constant movement, and his *mise-en-scène* is full of busy detail, especially in the first half of the film. For example, rather than the usual sit-down office scene, Bond's briefing with M takes place on the move, in the back of a limousine speeding to the airport surrounded by police motorcycle outriders. It is as if the speed at which the film was made is reflected in the urgency of the narration: it was the first Bond film for over two decades with a running time under two hours (though only just). If the film lacks the deep visual texture of other Bond films (the one it most closely resembles in this sense is *Licence to Kill*), it compensates by providing more action highlights than is common. The pre-title sequence contains enough explosions and spectacular destruction to provide the climax to most action movies, but here it serves as a prelude to a succession of action sequences and extended chases which punctuate the film at regular intervals. Richard Williams in the *Guardian* felt that the aim of the film had been 'to match the non-stop energy of movies by such action specialists as John Woo and Wolfgang Petersen'.[22] The highlight is a motorcycle chase through the backstreets of Saigon (actually filmed in Thailand and on the studio lot) which mirrors the tank chase in *GoldenEye*: it occurs about two-thirds of the way through the film as Bond and the heroine are making their escape from the villains, but this time on a vehicle which is completely exposed and which depends on speed and manoeuvrability rather than armour-plated bulk. In so far as Bond and Wai Lin are handcuffed together throughout this sequence, the film borrows a motif from Hitchcock's *The 39 Steps*, but whereas in Hitchcock's film the situation had been used to generate sexual tension (the handcuffed couple, who dislike each other, have to spend the night together), here it becomes simply a logistical exercise (how to drive a bike while cuffed together). It is only towards the end that the pace flags, with the climax on Carver's Stealth boat resembling the *Lethal Weapon* and *Die Hard* films as Brosnan struts around firing a submachine-gun with one hand in a manner too reminiscent of Gibson and Willis. Finally, after the disappointing scores of the two preceding films, *Tomorrow Never Dies* marks a return to the distinctive sound of the Bond series through the music of David Arnold, a worthy successor to John Barry, whose score mixes Barry-esque motifs with the pop and rock music of the 1990s. The 'James Bond Theme' is restored to prominence following its virtual absence in *GoldenEye*, with Arnold's heavier bass arrangement comparable to the way in which Lalo Schifrin's original music was rejigged for the Brian De Palma–Tom Cruise film of *Mission: Impossible* (1996).

However, critical reaction was generally less favourable than for *GoldenEye*. Alexander Walker, who had liked *GoldenEye*, declared that 'the new Bond is a shambles. Made in admitted haste and chaos, the 18th in the series looks that way, too.' He disliked the technological modernity of the film and longed for the style of the Bond of yesteryear: 'Give me the old words, the old weapons. For all its new-fangled, computerised, multiscreen razzmatazz, *Tomorrow Never Dies* can't match the bold hokum of the cartoon-styled classic 007 adventures.'[23] In contrast, José Arroyo in *Sight and Sound* felt that the film bore too much of a resemblance to its predecessors and echoed the same journal's review of *The Spy Who Loved Me* some two decades earlier: 'The film-makers' attempts at making this Bond film bigger and better seem to have taken the form of cannibalising the series' history.' Thus the crop-haired blonde German heavy Stamper (Götz Otto) recalls Robert Shaw's Grant in *From Russia with Love*, the Far Eastern archipelago where Bond and Wai Lin sail in search of the Stealth boat is the same location as *The Man with the Golden Gun*, and the main title sequence uses motifs from both *Goldfinger* and *Diamonds are Forever*. Arroyo concluded that '*Tomorrow* is like a photocopy of a collage of previous Bonds: there's more, but it looks second-generation.'[24]

For all its derivative content, however, *Tomorrow Never Dies* was another box-office success that consolidated Brosnan in the starring role. There is a sense in which the second film of each Bond actor is just as important as, if not more so than, his first. Curiosity will bring out audiences to see the new James Bond, but it is the second film that proves whether or not he has been accepted. The diminishing returns for Dalton's second film, for example, suggest that he had not been as widely accepted in the role by fans as he had by most critics. During the production of *The World is not Enough* the production discourse stressed what it called the 'Third Film Theory': the idea that the third film of both the longest-serving Bonds (*Goldfinger* for Connery and *The Spy Who Loved Me* for Moore) were those which most fully represented the ideal balance of 'Bondian' elements and in so doing perfected the formula. Brosnan, in particular, was keen that Bond should be 'more of a flesh and blood man' than in *Tomorrow Never Dies*, a view shared by new writers Neal Purvis and Robert Wade:

> We thought some of the core Fleming elements in the story had been lost. Rather than blasting at people with a machine gun as 007 did in *Tomorrow Never Dies*, it was felt he should make the difference by picking up his Walther PPK and firing one shot. We also decided to delve deeper into Bond's character and to make the new film a little bit Hitchcockian. After all, the screen Bond of the 1960s owed a lot to Hitchcock pictures like *Foreign Correspondent* and *North by Northwest*.[25]

Purvis and Wade had come to the Broccolis' attention through their screenplay for *Let Him Have It!* (1991), based on the case of Derek Bentley, an eighteen-year-old hanged for inciting the shooting of a policeman. They devised the original story of *The World is not Enough* and wrote the screenplay, which was then polished by Feirstein.

The World is not Enough is one of the better of the original screen stories for the Bond series in so far as it gives the impression of having been more carefully constructed (Bond screenplays are probably best described as 'constructed' rather than 'written') and, in marked contrast to *Tomorrow Never Dies*, the first half of the film at least seems more than a succession of set pieces laid end to end (though this criticism may be fairly levelled against the second half). Bond is assigned to protect Elektra King (Sophie Marceau), heiress to the business empire of Sir Robert King, an old school friend of M who is assassinated in the pre-title sequence. Elektra has continued her father's project to build an oil pipeline from the Caucasus to Istanbul, but its construction has been hampered by terrorist attacks. The villain responsible for the attacks on the pipeline is anarchist Renard (Robert Carlyle), whose 'only goal is chaos'. Renard had once kidnapped Elektra and held her for ransom – a ransom which her father, on M's advice, refused to pay – though she escaped by shooting one of her captors. However, it turns out that behind Renard is none other than Elektra herself, who has engineered her own father's death for revenge and to inherit his fortune. Renard – whose days are numbered because of a bullet lodged in his brain that is gradually destroying his nervous system – steals a nuclear warhead from the Russian Atomic Agency and intends to blow up Istanbul by inserting a plutonium rod into the reactor of a hijacked nuclear submarine.

The politics of *The World is not Enough* are intriguing in that the conspiracy posits an alliance between international terrorism and corporate capitalism. Renard represents the forces of chaos and anarchy that have emerged following the end of the Cold War: according to MI6 intelligence he has worked in Moscow, North Korea, Afghanistan, Bosnia, Iraq, Iran, Beirut and Cambodia ('All the romantic vacation spots'). Renard is associated with what President Clinton had described in 1998 as an 'unholy alliance of terrorists, drug traffickers and organised international criminals' who threatened to be the 'predators of the twenty-first century'.[26] While Renard is motivated by nothing more than a desire to create chaos, Elektra is driven by what she regards as her family's legacy. The contamination of the Bosphorous by a nuclear meltdown will leave her pipeline as the only route for oil to the West, meaning that 'the whole world will know my name, my grandfather's name, the glory of my people'. The film, once again, is rooted in contemporary geopolitics, reflecting international tensions over the control of energy supplies. It also refers to concerns over the nuclear stockpiles of the former Soviet Union and what might happen if weapons-grade plutonium were to fall into the wrong hands. To this extent the geopolitics that inform *The World is not Enough* are more plausible than those of either *GoldenEye* or *Tomorrow Never Dies*.

Sexual politics are also more prominent in *The World is not Enough* than in the two previous films. *The World is not Enough* is built around a complex set of narrative codes based on sexual power relationships. Elektra is initially characterised as the victim; Bond is attracted by her apparent vulnerability and is angered by the fact that Renard raped her in captivity. When he realises the link between Elektra and Renard he assumes that Elektra has become a victim of 'Stockholm Syndrome' and that Renard holds a power over her. Renard suggests as much when he blames M for Elektra's fate: 'When I took her she was promise itself, and you left her at the mercy of a man like me.' It transpires, however, that it is Elektra who controls Renard. She uses her sexuality to exercise power over men. The theme of sexual control is a recurring motif: 'I seduced the guards, used my body, gave me control'; 'I've always had a power over men'. Elektra has 'turned' Renard and, or so she thinks, Bond. Elektra, therefore, is another one of the women in the Bond films who is resistant to being repositioned ideologically. She refuses to be subject to male authority – Bond, Renard, her father – and her killing of her own father enacts a form of oedipal scenario that is rather more sophisticated than usual for a Bond narrative. Mapped on to this is a theme of sexual jealousy. Renard, who has lost all physical sensation, is unable to satisfy Elektra in bed and is jealous of Bond ('He was … he was a good lover?'). For the first time since *Live and Let Die*, therefore, the contest between Bond and the villain is represented symbolically as a contest for control of the woman's body.

The promotional discourse of *The World is not Enough* once again stressed the role of female agency and asserted the 'strong' roles for women in the film. On this occasion the claim was, perhaps, at least partially justified. Elektra is certainly one of the strongest-written parts in the series since the 1960s and the performance of Sophie Marceau, an accomplished French actress who had come to the attention of Anglo-American audiences following her role in Mel Gibson's *Braveheart* (1995), is undoubtedly the best by a 'Bond girl' since Diana Rigg in *OHMSS*. It might be suggested that *The World is not Enough* responds to one of the recurring narrative problems of recent Bond films – the increasing blandness of the villains in contrast to the (supposedly) more fully-developed female characterisations – by turning the principal woman into the villain. However, the secondary heroine, a nuclear scientist called Christmas Jones (Denise Richards), turns out to be nothing more than Holly Goodhead lite, and critics had their inevitable fun with Richards's acting (on a par with Tanya Roberts) and with the idea that her 'work clothes consist of halter top and hot pants'.[27]

That said, however, the gender politics of *The World is not Enough* are rather more complex than in *Tomorrow Never Dies*. As in *GoldenEye* Bond is beleaguered by female authority, including M ('I will not tolerate insubordination 007!') and even the comely MI6 doctor whom he needs to give him 'a clean bill of health' (Bond has damaged his shoulder at the beginning of the film and carries the injury throughout, part of the attempt to characterise him as 'more of a flesh and blood man'). The theme of female power and domination takes on a physical dimension in a highly-charged scene towards the end of the film in which Bond is captured and tortured by Elektra, who straddles and kisses him while he is strapped into an Ottoman torture chair. Elektra is clearly gaining satisfaction from the situation as she turns the screw that will break Bond's neck and taunts him with her knowledge that he is aroused by the sensation ('You know what happens when a man is strangled?') This was the first of three successive scripts by Purvis and Wade including a torture sequence – a motif that was frequent enough in the books but had tended to be downplayed in the films until now.

The presence of a torture sequence in *The World is not Enough* can be seen as part of the desire to maintain some of 'the core Fleming elements'. Indeed, the film employs more Fleming motifs than any since *The Living Daylights*. The title, for example, is a reference to the Bond family motto from the book and film of *On Her Majesty's Secret Service*. The film also borrows an idea from the short story 'For Your Eyes Only' in which Bond had been sent by M to avenge the murder of two of M's friends by gangsters. On this occasion M feels person-ally involved because she had advised King not to pay the ransom for Elektra. When King is murdered, she rationalises her personal desire for revenge thus: 'This will not stand ... We will find the people who committed this atrocity. We'll follow them to the farthest ends of the earth if needs be. And we will bring them to justice.' M is more closely involved in the narrative than in any previous film: and when she is lured to Istanbul and captured by Renard the film borrows an aspect from the plot of Kingley Amis's *Colonel Sun* in which Bond has to rescue M from the villain's clutches.

In its style *The World is not Enough* is closer to the more polished *GoldenEye* than to the restless kinetic energy of *Tomorrow Never Dies*. It is the most attractively photographed Bond since *The Spy Who Loved Me* and, for once, the locations (Azerbaijan, Baku, Istanbul) are integral to the plot rather than being an extended travelogue. The production design lays less emphasis on high-tech trappings than the previous two films: when MI6 headquarters in London is attacked (shortly after the film's release an IRA splinter group attempted to mortar the MI6 building near Vauxhall Bridge) the secret service decamps wholesale to a lochside Scottish castle replete with all the traditional trappings one would expect (pipers, kilts) from such a location. As in *GoldenEye*, again, there is a balance between narrative and spectacle, which may reasonably be attributed to director Michael Apted, whose reputation was based on more character-driven films (*Coal Miner's Daughter*, *Gorky Park*, *Gorillas in the Mist*) than on action cinema. Apted was keen, in particular, that the extended pre-title sequence (the longest to date in a Bond film at nearly a quarter of an hour) should be integrated into the main narrative rather than being an add-on: 'Lots of Bond films have opening sequences which are irrelevant to the story that follows. I wanted to lay in the beginnings of the plot into our opening.'[28] What is unique about the pre-title sequence of *The World is not Enough*, however, is that it is really two sequences in one. The first, in which Bond retrieves $5 million that King paid for a stolen intelligence report from a corrupt Swiss banker in Bilbao, recalls the pre-title sequences of early films such as *Goldfinger* and *Thunderball* in that it is relatively low-key: Bond escapes from the office by abseiling down the building. This is followed by a more spectacular action sequence of the sort that became the norm with *The Spy Who Loved Me* as, following the death of King and an attack on MI6 headquarters itself, Bond pursues the 'Cigar Girl' assassin in a powerboat chase down the River Thames concluding in an explosive climax on the Millennium Dome. This contrast between intimacy and spectacle recurs throughout the film, in which several well-written 'character' moments are punctuated by a succession of action set pieces. Like *Tomorrow Never Dies*, however, it runs out of steam towards the end: critics predictably described the climax on board a sinking submarine as 'waterlogged'. The fight between Bond and Renard is something of an anti-climax following the previous sequence in which Bond has shot and killed Elektra ('I never miss') when she refuses to call off her lover.

The World is not Enough, perhaps predictably, opened to excellent box-office and disparaging reviews. Several critics made reference to the fact that the title song was performed by a pop group called Garbage, perhaps the biggest hostage to fortune since Roger Moore posed as his own wax effigy in *The Man with the Golden Gun*. What was most interesting about the critical reception, however, was that the attempt to introduce a greater psychological depth to the narrative was thought to have been misguided. Anthony Quinn in the *Independent* felt that the attempt to offer more plausible characterisation 'has induced a kind of schizophrenia in the film-makers, nowhere more apparent than in Bond himself ... The film-makers are terrified of Bond seeming dated, but they allow him to do the usual gentleman-spy things like bed beautiful women, visit a casino, trash a lot of scenery and – a real hangover from the Sixties, this – save the planet from a nuclear catastrophe.'[29] Kim Fletcher in the *Spectator* also remarked upon the familiarity of the plot: 'There is also – for never accuse the Bond team of failing to give the audience what they expect – a Russian submarine, a nuclear bomb and an unexpected instrument of death.'[30] Arroyo's review for *Sight and Sound* demonstrated how far Bond criticism had changed since the 1960s:

> The makers of *The World is not Enough*, of whom director Michael Apted should be singled out for blame, have attempted to depict all-too fleshy characters who desire, lack and feel. It's what is valued in a Ken Loach film, but it acts as an explosive and un-settling expulsion from the fantasies Bond films invite us to. One can't name a patricidal character Elektra and then expect the audi-ence not to giggle at the film's attempts to psychoanalyse her; one can't have Denise Richards play a nuclear physicist and make any claim to conventional believability. Robert Carlyle striving to imbue a character with truth and depth is almost always a good thing, but when that character is a Bond villain who wants to conquer the world, one has to ask what the director was thinking of. Worst of all they've done the same to Bond, not understanding that deep feelings don't go easily with nonchalance, suavity, elegance or cool, much less with killing people as a profession.[31]

What is interesting here is that Arroyo criticises the film for attempt-ing to do what Bond films had so often been accused of not doing: taking itself seriously. In fairness, though, it should be said that the 'joke' ending – in which satellite surveillance captures Bond in bed with Dr Jones – represents a return to the juvenile humour of the Roger Moore films.

The charge of imbuing Bond with too much psychological depth was not a criticism that could be made of *Die Another Day*. Brosnan's fourth outing was a double landmark for the Bond series: it was both the twentieth official film and marked the fortieth anniversary of *Dr No*. It might have been expected that the production team would have responded to the expectations generated by these landmarks to produce a film that, like *Goldfinger* or *The Spy Who Loved Me*, adhered closely to the Bond formula. However, *Die Another Day* is one of those Bond films that attempts to vary the formula – 'pushing the envelope' as Brosnan says *ad nauseam* on his DVD commentary – but not, unfortunately, to its best advantage. It is a much less satisfying anniversary film than *The Living Daylights* and, like *The World is not Enough*, suggests a degree of uncertainty within the production team. *Die Another Day* turns out to be not so much another *Goldfinger* as another *A View to a Kill*: caught in two minds as to what sort of Bond movie it wants to be with the result that it is unbalanced, uneven and lacking the distinctive 'feel' of the classic Bonds. All that said, however, the film, like *A View to a Kill*, is not without some points of interest.

Die Another Day is yet again rooted in contemporary geopolitics as a renegade North Korean who dreams of 'the day all Korea is ruled by the North' plots to use the 'Icarus' satellite – capable of harnessing the sun's energy and directing it against targets on earth – to destroy the minefield that divides the Korean peninsula as a prelude to establishing Korean hegemony throughout Southeast Asia: 'Japan is a bug waiting to be squashed, and the West will shake with fear.' Purvis and Wade explained the reasoning thus:

> We saw the 38th Parallel as a fantastic image and the fact that it's full of mines. Bill Clinton, who was President at the time we started writing, said it was the scariest place on earth and we did think it was a flashpoint. And we were also trying to think, 'What's the worst situation that Bond can get into?' And it's to be held prisoner in North Korea. You couldn't get much worse than that.[32]

As so often happens the film's topicality was boosted when, shortly before its release, US President George W. Bush referred to North Korea as part of an 'axis of evil' that, along with Iraq, Iran and Syria, was responsible for promoting terrorism and destabilising international relations. To this extent *Die Another Day* can be located in the context of the US-led 'War on Terror' following the attacks on the World Trade Center and the Pentagon on 11 September 2001 in which it was not just terrorist networks like Al-Qaeda but also rogue states that were identified as a major threat to global security. The idea that North Korea had militaristic ambitions – even if *Die Another Day* makes it clear that Moon is a renegade – has been lent credence by the on-going international tension over its nuclear weapons programme. The 9/11 terrorist attacks are alluded to obliquely in the film, further, as M tells Bond: 'While you were away, the world changed.' The internal timeline of the film suggests that Bond's fourteen-month incarceration in North Korea spanned the pre-9/11 and post-9/11 periods.

Die Another Day once again relocates Bond in the context of Anglo-American power relations. The United States had been a marginal presence in both *GoldenEye* and *Tomorrow Never Dies* and had been absent entirely from *The World is not Enough*, a point noted by one critic who thought that 'the absence from it of any admitted transatlantic element' rendered it less plausible and felt that 'it's a bold solution to take out of the international-spy formula the only surviving superpower'.[33] This absence is redressed in *Die Another Day* where America has a more visible presence than in any film since *Moonraker*. Bond is teamed with an agent of the US National Security Administration, Jinx (Halle Berry), and for the first time in the series an American intelligence chief, Falco (an under-used Michael Madsen), also appears. If, on the one hand, this narrative strategy represents the continuing links between Britain and America in the War on Terror – shortly after the film's release Britain was part of the US-led 'coalition of the willing' in the invasion of Iraq in 2003 – on the other hand the film reflects something closer to the reality of the 'special relationship' than previous Bond movies. Falco is dismissive of Britain's contribution: he is brusque towards M ('Put your house in order or we're gonna do it for you') and is not prepared to countenance Bond's excursion into North Korea without America also being represented ('You think I'd leave this in the hands of the British?'). British technological ingenuity is no longer sufficient on its own: Bond requires American technology to enter North Korean airspace (he and Jinx use aiborne 'switchblades' to avoid radar). Colonel Moon is even more contemptuous of Britain's continued pretensions to world power status ('It's pathetic that you British still believe you have the right to police the world') and there are further references to the decline of British power when Bond meets Chinese agent Mr Chang ('Hong Kong's our turf now, Bond'). To this extent *Die Another Day* presents a more accurate representation than most other Bond films of Britain's role on the world stage at the beginning of the twenty-first century.

Yet despite rooting its conspiracy in a geopolitical context, *Die Another Day* is rather less successful than *The World is not Enough* in making the conspiracy plausible. This is due in large measure to a tension running throughout the film between a grounding in reality on the one hand and out-and-out fantasy on the other. When the narrative switches from North Korea to Cuba and Iceland, the content becomes more fantastic. In Cuba Bond discovers a clinic offering 'gene replacement therapy' and later discovers that Colonel Moon, believed dead in the pre-title sequence, has turned himself into an Anglophone entrepreneur called Gustav Graves (Toby Stephens). This is a somewhat implausible plot device even for a Bond movie and seems like a throwback to the movie serials of yesteryear: in *Manhunt of Mystery Island* (1945), for example, the villain had used a 'Transformation Machine' to turn himself into a likeness of the pirate Captain Mephisto! The 'Icarus' satellite is yet another super-laser, recalling *Diamonds are Forever* and *GoldenEye*, suggesting that the writers were struggling to find new variations on familiar science-fiction tropes. Consequently *Die Another Day* uneasily straddles the gap between plausible political threat and the madman-with-death-ray-bent-on-world-domination theme that the production discourse of the Brosnan films insisted was no longer part of Bond's world.

This tension between reality and fantasy is evident on other levels, too. The device of Bond's capture at the end of the pre-title sequence and his torture in a North Korean hell-hole is one of the grittiest episodes in a Bond movie, though most of his ordeal is represented in a stylised way as it takes place during the title sequence. Nevertheless the torture sequence is harrowing enough in what it depicts – repeated beatings, immersion in freezing water, hot pokers and, a suitably Flemingesque touch, being stung by scorpions and then injected with an anti-venom – to suggest that *Die Another Day* is going to be a darker-toned Bond than usual. Bond's chief tormentor is a silent female guard reminiscent of Fu Manchu's cruel daughter (a role played by Bond girl Tsai Chin in the Fu Manchu films of the 1960s): again, as in *The World is not Enough*, there is a suggestion of sado-masochism as the woman caresses Bond's face and pouts at him. However, if this seems to suggest that *Die Another Day* will be more realistic – *The Ipcress File* (1965), for example, had included a similar incarceration/torture sequence – this is not the direction the film subsequently takes. Thus Bond's escape from the hospital ship where he is taken for examination after his release is too easy by far: there is no explanation of how he is able to feign a cardiac arrest other than an oblique reference in the title song lyrics ('I'm gonna shut my body down'). It is when the film moves to Iceland, however, that it shifts to outright fantasy with an ice hotel and a succession of implausible action sequences that at one point has Bond paragliding on a tidal wave of melting ice caused by the Icarus laser. This represents the most cartoonish moment in the entire series: perhaps appropriately it is painfully obvious that the figure of Bond in this scene is an animation. (For a film with a budget reported to be around $140 million, indeed, some of the visual effects in *Die Another Day* are rather less than special.) Purvis and Wade themselves had doubts about the surfing scene at the beginning of the film, where Bond and two other agents land in North Korea, feeling that it 'was a great idea, but whether it was an implausible level of action, that is another question'.[34] The presence of this scene was taken by some critics to suggest that the producers were concerned about the competition of rival action films such as *xXx* (2002) which featured Vin Diesel as an extreme sports enthusiast recruited as a secret agent.

It is not only at the level of narrative that *Die Another Day* is unsatisfying. The visual style of the film is rather schizophrenic, as if, on this occasion, neither designer Peter Lamont nor director Lee Tamahori could quite decide how he wanted it to look. The subterranean MI6 headquarters in a disused London Underground station ('An abandoned station for abandoned agents') has a suitably dilapidated, retro-1950s look, while Graves's fencing club, with its wood panelling, cavalier busts and display cases, locates this part of the film within the clubland world to which Fleming's Bond was heir. The fencing club sequence, indeed, is the best part of the film, exhibiting a characteristically Bondian delight in the gratuitous destruction of property as Bond and Graves wreck the furnishings in a 'friendly' sabre duel that is substantially more exciting than their fight for real at the end of the film. Elsewhere, however, the sets foreground technological modernity, such as Graves's Icelandic lair and the US Command Bunker in South Korea with its banks of screens and monitors that recalls very similar sets in previous Brosnan films. A lack of visual imagination is suggested by the set for the 'dream machine' in the Cuban clinic where Bond enters a hall of mirrors resembling Scaramanga's in *The Man with the Golden Gun*. And in contrast to *The World is not Enough* the scenery is uninteresting: the film fails to make effective use of the stunning landscapes of Iceland as most of the Icelandic scenes are either indoors or are special effects sequences.

Die Another Day makes far more extensive use of CGI (computer-generated imaging) than previous Bonds. According to Tamahori this was part of a strategy to modernise the look of the film: 'It would be churlish for me to say I have reinvented the genre, but I think I have succeeded in some ways. I do think *Die Another Day* looks like a Bond movie and it does have some style and panache that was not evident in the last three. We are definitely modernising it in terms of the way it is cut and some of the way it is shot.'[35]

The editing, in particular, has been enhanced by computer effects, giving the effect of fast camera dollies – seemingly influenced by the likes of *The Matrix* and *Spiderman* – while there are selective slow-motion shots in some of the fight sequences. The 'look' of the film is slick but, contrary to Tamahori's assertion, is not in the tradition of the Bond films. The action and chase sequences seem artificial: at times it feels more like watching a computer game than a film. Indeed, the 'duel' between Bond's Aston Martin and Zao's equally gadget-laden Jaguar seems more like a trailer for spin-off games such as *007: Nightfire* than an action sequence in its own right. The presence of the Aston Martin (a new Vanquish V12 model) is one of the film's many references to the Bond heritage (Brosnan had driven a BMW as his 'official' car in each of his three previous outings), though on this occasion the imagination of the writers was allowed perhaps too much free rein. Among the many gadgets of his car is an 'adaptive camouflage system' that renders it invisible to the naked eye – a device that is motivated by special effects rather than by narrative logic and oversteps the rule of plausibility.

For all its stylistic makeover, however, *Die Another Day* does not lose sight of the fact that it was an anniversary Bond film. It includes several visual references to the series' past. Halle Berry's iconic entrance, for example, emerging from the waves on a Cuban beach, is clearly intended as a homage to Ursula Andress in *Dr No*. Classic Bond moments are here reworked for other characters: thus it is Jinx who is spread-eagled beneath the industrial laser (*Goldfinger*) and Graves who deploys the Union Jack parachute (*The Spy Who Loved Me*). On this occasion Bond is alert to the camera concealed behind the mirror of his hotel suite (*From Russia with Love*), though he might have recalled when bedding MI6 agent Miranda Frost (Rosamund Pike) that a bed designed like a giant swan had been thought too *outré* even for *Diamonds are Forever*. Memories of Bond films past are evoked by the visit to

Q's underground workshop, which is full of old props: the briefcase and Rosa Klebb's spiked shoe (*From Russia with Love*), the Acrostar jet and crocodile submarine (*Octopussy*), Kara's cello (*The Living Daylights*) and the Bell jet pack (*Thunderball*). Bond's casual remark on seeing the latter ('Does this still work?') was taken by several critics as a comment on the Bond formula itself. One of the aims of this sequence is to establish John Cleese as the new Quartermaster, though it also has the unfortunate effect of reminding fans of better Bond films than this one. There is a moment for the Fleming buffs when Bond picks up a copy of *Field Guide to the Birds of the West Indies*, the name of whose author Fleming adopted for his hero, and assumes the guise of an ornithologist. Other Fleming references can be identified in the illicit trade in African conflict diamonds (*The Diamond Smugglers*) and in Frost's line 'Remember I know all about you, 007 – sex for dinner, death for breakfast – well it's not going to work with me.'[36] As this is about the most memorable line in the film, however, *Die Another Day* can hardly be regarded as one of the better Bond scripts.

The sexual politics of the film are less complex than in *The World is not Enough*, though the script again imbues the villain with an oedipal complex: Moon/Graves rejects the authority of his moderate father ('I hoped a western education would help him become a bridge between our worlds') and eventually kills him. The two Bond girls are straightforward archetypes: Jinx represents another in the line of 'female James Bonds' (Anya Amasova, Wai Lin) given her own action sequences, while Miranda is another bad girl (she is a double agent working for Graves) who refuses to be ideologically repositioned when she sleeps with Bond ('I enjoyed last night James, but this time it really is death for breakfast'). The suggestion of internal treachery within MI6 is a new departure for the Bond films, however, and would be more fully explored in the next (post-Brosnan) instalment. The contrast between Jinx (warm, friendly, sexually available) and Miranda (cool, reserved, initially resistant) can also be seen as part of an under-developed 'fire and ice' motif within the film, though one critic preferred a different metaphor when he described the film as 'a whole pick'n'mix of eye candy, from the meltingly sweet Halle Berry to the tart citrus sorbet of Rosamund Pike and the old Black Magic box charm of Pierce Brosnan's Bond'.[37]

The critical reception of *Die Another Day* was even cooler than Miranda Frost, with a majority reckoning it to have overdosed on technology and special effects. 'In their efforts to outpace technology, the producers seem to have gone a little mad,' wrote Catherine Shoard in the *Sunday Telegraph*, adding that 'Tamahori struggles to pitch the tone right, and usually loses'.[38] Sukhdev Sandhu in the *Daily Telegraph* felt that the special effects 'conceal their manipulation with the subtlety of a schoolchild performing magic tricks for the first time' and that the script 'veers between plodding liberalism and double entendres of floor-groaning awfulness'.[39] Nicholas Barber in the *Independent on Sunday* thought it 'too disjointed, too self-referential, too loud and too long – arguably the worst of the Brosnan Bonds'.[40] Anthony Quinn in the *Independent* damned it with faint praise as 'a highly competent, thoroughly impersonal "action spectacular"', but was underwhelmed by the experience on the grounds that 'when you've seen one masterplan for global domination, you've seen the lot'.[41] A dissenter from the generally dismissive response, however, was Alexander Walker, in what would be his last review of a Bond movie, who felt that it was 'hugely enjoyable' and reprimanded his fellow critics who had expressed their boredom with the formula with a sentiment that would ring true with the fans: 'He who is tired of Bond is tired of life.'[42]

The popular reception of *Die Another Day* would indeed suggest that audiences were very far from being tired of Bond as it set new box-office records for the series. It also received what amounted to an official seal of approval when it became the first Bond movie selected for the Royal Film Performance (previous films had had royal premières, but none had been chosen for the prestigious annual showcase for the British film industry). The Bond series had never seemed in a better state of economic health and there was soon speculation about another film in 2004 teaming Brosnan with leading Bollywood star Aishwarya Rai. In the event, however, it would be four years until the next instalment in the franchise and Brosnan had worn Bond's dinner jacket for the last time (though he did make one more appearance as 007 in the computer game *Nightfire*). The critical mauling of *Die Another Day* within the fan culture, where it soon became a leading contender for worst Bond movie (largely on account of the invisible car), did not go unnoticed by the producers who were evidently keen to keep faith with their die-hard fans as well as the general audience. Their next step, indeed, was to be one of the boldest and most radical in the series' history: to go 'back to basics' by filming the very first Bond novel *Casino Royale*.

9

Revisionist Bond: *Casino Royale*

C *asino Royale* (dir. Martin Campbell, 2006) was the first new Bond film for four years and represented an entirely new departure for the franchise. The acquisition by Eon Productions of the rights to Fleming's first novel and their declared intention to adapt it for the screen (as there would be little point in using just the title and nothing else) determined the decision to make *Casino Royale* a 'reboot' of the series. On the face of it, perhaps, this was an unusual decision as *Die Another Day* had been the biggest-grossing Bond to date and a radical change to the formula might risk alienating fans who preferred their Bonds full of spectacle and CGI. The strategy of the 'reboot' – a term used to describe the process whereby a genre or series is entirely reinvented – is usually applied to ailing franchises (as had been the case with *Batman Begins* in 2005) or when a character is revived following a long hiatus (*Superman Returns* in 2006 was the first Superman film since 1987). For the Bond series the gap between films had not been as long as the hiatus between *Licence to Kill* and *GoldenEye*, while a \$432 million worldwide gross for the previous instalment suggested that the franchise was hardly ailing. That said, however, there was a view within the production team that *Die Another Day* had been too excessive. 'Even though the last film was the most commercially successful,' said Wilson, 'I think we felt we were getting away from our roots, which is what made Bond so special. And that's what we were trying to find here – our basic Bond.'[1] The 'back to basics' approach adopted for *Casino Royale* needs to be seen as one of the series' periodic attempts to reinvent itself by returning to more plausible, if not strictly realistic, narratives – *For Your Eyes Only* and *The Living Daylights* are the comparative examples here – though this time the reinvention would be significantly more far-reaching than on previous occasions.

The decision to return to Bond's roots – from an early stage in the scripting process it was agreed that the film would dramatise his first mission after achieving Double-o status – made a change of star almost inevitable. That said, it was not until 2004 that Pierce Brosnan was finally ruled out and not until 2005 that a new James Bond was announced. The casting of Daniel Craig, controversially preferred to other candidates including Hugh Jackman, Clive Owen and Ewan McGregor, was the clearest indicator of the producers' intent. Other than a supporting role in *Lara Croft: Tomb Raider* (2001), Craig's reputation was very much that of a serious actor, with roles in the acclaimed television drama *Our Friends in the North* (1996) and as Ted Hughes in *Sylvia* (2003) to his credit. However, Craig had also demonstrated a rugged leading man persona in the British gangster film *Layer Cake* (2004) that had evidently impressed the Broccolis. The replacement of Brosnan by Craig is comparable, perhaps, to the replacement of Moore by Dalton: the Bond with the implausibly handsome male model looks succeeded by the more rugged specimen with serious acting credentials. Indeed, the publicity that attended Craig's casting recalled that surrounding Dalton's interpretation of Bond. Craig himself spoke of finding a 'dark side' to the character: 'One of the things I was criticised for was that I looked like a bad guy, but I was happy with that because I think true good guys have to step into the dark side to do their job. I wanted people to question Bond's morals and his judgement.'[2] The promotional discourse for *Casino Royale*, in which 'gritty', 'realistic' and 'tough' were the most prominent adjectives, recalled *Licence to Kill*.

The 'back to basics' production discourse of *Casino Royale* can again be seen as part of the continuing strategy of the Bond series to respond to changes in film culture. Just as *Die Another Day* had been seen as being in competition with the kinetic *xXx*, the reference point during production of *Casino Royale* were the two Jason Bourne films, *The Bourne Identity* (2002) and *The Bourne Supremacy* (2004), adapted from the novels by Robert Ludlum. The Bourne films – a third, *The Bourne Ultimatum*, followed in 2007 – were notable for a greater level of psychological complexity than usual in the action thriller in so far as the protagonist (played by Matt Damon) is a former government agent who has lost his memory. *The Bourne Supremacy*, moreover, also shared a motif with *Mission: Impossible 3* (2006) in that it begins with the hero living in happy domesticity with his girlfriend and trying to leave his secret past behind. It would be misleading, however, to regard the Bourne films as direct competition for Bond, not least because they were 'not in the same box-office league' as recent instalments of the Bond franchise.[3] The greater psychological depth implied for Bond in *Casino Royale*, rather than being seen as a response to other films – or, indeed, to television series such as *24* and *Spooks* which had made spies and secret agents the subjects of primetime drama for the first time since the 1960s – should, instead, be understood as a natural consequence of the decision to adapt the Fleming novel. Eco suggests that Fleming's *Casino Royale* is informed by a degree of psychological realism – 'the treacherous life of moral meditation and of psychological anger' – that was largely absent from the later stories.[4]

The production arrangements of *Casino Royale* demonstrate the complexities of the international film industry in the early twenty-first century. In 2005 MGM had been bought by an international consortium whose partners included the Sony Corporation of America, who also owned Columbia Pictures, co-producer of *Casino Royale*. It is tempting to speculate that Sony's acquisition of MGM was motivated, at least in part, by its desire to gain control of the Bond franchise since the late 1990s. The escalating costs of film production – *Casino Royale* was budgeted at an estimated $132 million – meant that, as had been the case with *Moonraker* and *Licence to Kill*, the production moved overseas, this time to the Czech Republic where the Barrandov Studios in Prague offered state-of-the-art technical facilities at a more economical cost. To this extent the production exemplifies the re-emergence of the 'runaway' trend in the era of the global blockbuster. As Campbell put it: 'Like everybody, we're heading off to where we can get a good exchange rate.'[5]

Casino Royale is the first film in the Bond series since *Dr No* in which the credits actually state: 'Based on the novel by Ian Fleming'. It is not, however, the closest to Fleming, bearing less similarity to its source than the early films and *On Her Majesty's Secret Service*. The screenplay was by Purvis and Wade, with revisions by Paul Haggis, the Academy Award-winning writer of *Crash* and *Million Dollar Baby*, who was brought in as a 'script doctor' shortly before production began. It is difficult to disentangle the contributions of the different writers, though it would seem that the content and structure of the story were Purvis and Wade's and that Haggis's main input was in the 'character' dialogue. Wade described the screenplay as 'a very faithful adaptation updated'. He elaborated thus: '[The book] doesn't have the global vista and it doesn't have the level of action which the cinematic Bonds have become synonymous with. We've opened it up but tried to keep the action fairly contained, and of realistic proportions.'[6]

The critical response to the new Bond was largely positive and, on balance, probably more favourable than it had been for *GoldenEye*. There were, of course, dissenters, such as Cosmo Landesman of the *Sunday Times* who averred that 'no new face can hide the fact that *Casino Royale* is the same old tosh the producers of the Bond franchise have been serving up since the glory days of the 1960s'.[7] And Catherine Shoard of the *Sunday Telegraph* thought that it 'is an overstuffed turkey – uncertain, unwieldy and only patchily revamped to match its modernised hero'.[8] The most frequent criticism was the film's length (at 144 minutes it was the longest Bond to date) and there was a feeling that it would have benefited from some judicious editing. Otherwise, however, the reception was positive, both for the film itself and, especially, for Craig's performance. Todd McCarthy, senior *Variety* critic, felt that 'Craig comes closer to the author's original conception of this exceptionally long-lived male fantasy figure than anyone since early Sean Connery' and that '*Casino Royale* sees Bond recharged with fresh toughness and arrogance, along with balancing hints of sadism and humanity, just as the fabled series is reinvigorated by going back to basics'.[9] The popular press rhapsodised about Craig's performance ('The best Bond since Connery' was a recurring review headline) and this enthusiasm rubbed off on the *Daily Telegraph* ('The best Bond for decades').[10] *The Times* thought it an 'immensely enjoyable' film and suggested that 'Craig brings a brutally efficient physicality to the role and a thrilling undercurrent of sadistic cruelty – his is a Bond you feel gains real job satisfaction from his licence to kill'.[11] Charlie Higson – the writer commissioned by the Fleming estate to write a series of 'Young Bond' novels for juvenile readers – identified 'a greater depth to the movie and to the central character'.[12] Kim Newman told readers of *Empire* that 'this has almost everything you could want from a Bond film, plus qualities you didn't expect they'd even try for' and concluded that '*Casino Royale* is the most exciting Bond film, in conventional action terms but also in dramatic meat, since *On Her Majesty's Secret Service*'.[13] While this was the sort of sentiment designed to appeal to the Bond aficionados, what was perhaps most remarkable about the reception of *Casino Royale* was that it also won over long-serving film critics. Derek Malcolm, only occasionally a Bond fan in the past, felt that 'Craig's Bond helps propel Martin Campbell's film into the realm of a serious thriller' and that the 'well-produced film steers Bond into the 21st century with what looks like certain box-office success'.[14] Perhaps the ultimate accolade came from the *Guardian* critic: 'For the first time in ages, I am actually looking forward to the next James Bond movie.'[15]

Casino Royale is a revisionist Bond narrative in the sense that it places Bond at the start of his career as if events in previous films had not taken place. While this strategy was not entirely as new as some commentators suggest – other Bonds, notably *Diamonds are Forever* and *GoldenEye*, had written out their immediate predecessors from the series' continuity – it had never been done to such a complete degree. In fact the revisionist strategy of *Casino Royale* is not without its contradictions, not least in the continued presence of Judi Dench's M, whose relationship with Bond is prickly to say the least ('I knew it was too early to promote you'). Dench is the one cast member maintained from the Brosnan films: there is no place for either Q or Miss Moneypenny, while the MI6 staff are all entirely new. There is a certain tension, moreover, in the fact that while *Casino Royale* strips the Bond mythology down to its bare essentials it still expects the audience to be familiar with aspects of that mythology. It is still, largely, the mythology of the films rather than the books, though Craig does order a vodka martini according to Fleming's recipe. The presence of the Aston Martin – both a 1964 vintage that Bond wins in a poker game and a brand-new DBS model – is perhaps intended to reassure fans that this is still the same Bond. Wade attempted to explain it thus: 'The book is the story of what actually forges James Bond as a secret agent. There is a James Bond that everyone knows, but it would be nice just once to show how he got there.'[16]

The revisionist strategy of *Casino Royale* was necessitated by the film's relationship to its source material. Herein is the source of both the film's strength and its main structural weakness. Fleming purists welcomed the fidelity to the novel, including the notorious torture sequence as well as the preservation of some of Fleming's best lines – notably Bond's bitter 'The bitch is dead'. There were some who objected to the change of card game from baccarat to a variation of poker known as 'Texas Hold 'Em', though this can be seen as necessary for comprehension as the game occupies a significant amount of screen time and more spectators would be likely to understand poker than baccarat: there is no easy way for a film to explain the rules as Bond does to Vesper over several pages in the book. However, the two principal flaws of the novel are repeated in the film. The first is that we (and Bond) are denied the satisfaction of Bond killing the villain who has tortured him: Le Chiffre is shot by a member of his own organisation. The second flaw is a structural one: that the climax comes two-thirds of the way into the book. This is resolved in the film by the addition of another act, though Newman felt that 'a collapsing building in Venice is a gimmick too many in an emotional finale which would play better without all the noise'. Structurally, *Casino Royale* is like two films bolted together: a Fleming-based narrative in the middle with the spectacular action set pieces expected of a Bond movie grafted on to the beginning and end.

That said, however, there is a structural symmetry to *Casino Royale* that is not at all unsatisfying. The narrative may be seen as an 'arc' in which we see the transformation of Bond from a rough-edged assassin (M calls him as 'a blunt instrument' and remarks acidly that 'any thug can kill') to someone approaching 'the gentleman agent with a licence to kill' described in trailers for the early films. The closing scene of the film, for example, refers back to the beginning. The pre-title sequence shows Bond's first two 'kills' necessary for the award of his Double-o status: the clinical assassination of a corrupt section chief in Prague ('M really doesn't mind you earning a little money on the side, Dryden, she would just prefer if it wasn't selling secrets') and a vicious fight in a toilet ('Made you feel it, did he?').[17] These incidents, intercut with one another and shot in grainy low-contrast monochrome, give the opening of *Casino Royale* a certain *film noir* mood and style that recalls, though probably unintentionally, the under-rated television production of the story from 1954. The sequence ends with Bond in the toilet, with his back to the camera, turning and firing at the other man: this is the cue for the iconic gun-barrel point-of-view shot and the trickle of blood down the screen. The contrast between the monochrome and the red recalls, though again perhaps not intentionally, a similar effect in Hitchcock's *Spellbound* (1945) where there is a sudden flash of red as the killer turns a gun on himself. The sordidness of Bond's first 'kill' (Dryden is the second, though we see it first) is contrasted with the clinical precision of his shooting of 'Mr White' with a high-powered rifle at the end of the film: Bond shoots him in the back of the knee and, walking up to his victim, introduces himself as 'Bond. James Bond'. This time Bond is suited rather than wearing casuals and it is only now that we hear in full for the first time David Arnold's bass-heavy arrangement of 'The James Bond Theme'. In this sense Craig's traditional 'Bondian' introduction comes at the end rather than at the beginning: the film has shown us how he acquires the trappings and accoutrements of 'Bond. James Bond'.

The modernisation of Fleming's story, for its part, is done effectively, stripping away the Cold War trappings and updating it to an era of global terrorism and financial intrigue. In the novel Le Chiffre is the Soviet-backed paymaster for a Communist-controlled trade union ('an important fifth column in the event of war with Redland') who has been defrauding his masters by diverting funds for his own use and who sets up a high-stakes card game in a desperate attempt to make good his losses. In the film he has become 'private banker to the world's terrorists', investing their money in the stock market: he has lost $100 million of his clients' money betting the wrong way. Behind Le Chiffre is the shadowy 'Organisation', an international cabal providing financial services for terrorists and African 'freedom fighters'. The film therefore refers to the economy of terrorism: shortly before its release, indeed, a US State Department report had suggested that the main terrorist threat to the United States was not another 9/11-style attack but came from the existence of wealthy sponsors of terrorism with connections to the world of high finance. M makes this very point when she reprimands Bond for his execution-style killing of a bomber in Madasgascar: 'We're trying to find out how an entire network of terrorist groups is financed and you give us one bomb-maker. Hardly the big picture, wouldn't you say?'

This strategy of updating the source material is standard practice for the Bond series, of course, though there are some more subtle changes that demonstrate an admirable fidelity to the original. The characterisation of Vesper Lynd, for example, is more rounded than in the book: here she becomes a Treasury agent ('I'm the money') and is assigned a more significant role in terms of narrative agency than Fleming's rather two-dimensional character. In line with the strategy of the Brosnan films to address Bond's sexism through the agency of female authority figures, a Fleming line ('Women were for recreation') here becomes a point made by Vesper herself to Bond ('Having just met you I wouldn't go as far as calling you a cold-hearted bastard … but it wouldn't be a stretch to imagine that you think of women as disposable pleasures rather than meaningful pursuits'). Bond's preference for married women ('It keeps things simple') is also a characteristic inherited from the books.

Elsewhere, however, the film introduces a level of introspection and psychoanalytical apparatus that was less evident in Fleming. There are several references to Bond's ego which suggest that the writers (probably Haggis) were introducing a Freudian subtext. Thus M tells Bond that 'I want you to take your ego out of the equation' and Vesper issues a scathing put-down: 'There isn't room for me and your ego.' Bond is characterised as impetuous, impulsive and even reckless: he shoots an unarmed bomber in full view of a CCTV camera and casually dispenses with his cover when he checks into the Hotel Splendide under his own name. Bond is controlled by female authority: not only M but also Vesper, who controls the purse strings and whose decision it is whether or not to stake him in Le Chiffre's poker game. It has been argued, especially by Tony Bennett, that it is M who endows Bond with phallic authority: the difference here is that the pistol with its huge silencer ('I love you too M') is a gift from a woman. Bond's arrogance may be seen as his reaction to the emasculation of his authority, especially when Vesper refuses to release further funds when Bond is apparently wiped out by Le Chiffre due to his own impatience which prompts his only angry outburst in the film. Bond is further threatened with emasculation by Le Chiffre, who, as in the novel, makes both a literal and a symbolic assault on Bond's manhood: 'I never understood all those elaborate tortures. It is the simplest thing to cause more pain than a man can possibly endure. And of course it is not only the immediate agony, but the knowledge that if you do not yield soon enough there will be little left to identify you as a man.' It is tempting here to interpret Le Chiffre as the Id to Bond's Ego – the monster unleashed from his unconscious – though this would perhaps be stretching the point. The way in which the torture scene is played, however, is suggestive of homoeroticism: Le Chiffre admires Bond's nakedness ('You've taken good care of your body') and Bond goads him into beating him again so that 'the whole world's going to know that you died scratching my balls'.

Casino Royale, indeed, seems to offer up Bond's (or rather Craig's) body as an object of spectacle. The film contains numerous scenes of Craig in swimming trunks (he even sends emails topless) while the camera lingers on his torso, smooth-skinned and revealing a bulkier musculature than previous Bonds (even including former 'Mr Scotland' contestant Connery). Whether this was a conscious attempt to counter the old charge that Bond films have tended to objectify women by turning Bond himself into an object of the female gaze is a moot point, though it certainly had this effect on female critics. One called the film 'an homage to the six-pack, a celebration of musculature', while another rhapsodised about 'Bond emerging from the ocean, his toned and rippling musculature glistening in the tropical sunshine'.[18] To this extent the film can be seen as representative of changing discourses of masculinity in the twenty-first century towards 'heteroeroticism' rather than homoeroticism, as represented by men's health magazines and in the pop videos of performers such as Justin Timberlake and Robbie Williams. One article suggested that 'Craig in his swimming trunks has cemented the emergence of a new type of adoration of the male form'.[19]

The style of *Casino Royale* falls somewhere between the visual excess of *Die Another Day* and the more realistic look of, say, *From Russia with Love*. The cinematography of Phil Méheux (returning to the series for the first time since *GoldenEye*) again recalls Ted Moore's work, especially in its effective use of locations (Prague, the Bahamas, Lake Como, Venice), while Peter Lamont's production design abandons the high-tech trappings and control rooms of the Brosnan films in favour of the 'elegant scene' of gambling rooms and luxury hotels so memorably evoked in Fleming's books. The outstanding set is one of the simplest: the barge where Le Chiffre tortures Bond is lit in low-key expressionist style that contrasts sharply with the glossy elegance of the preceding casino sequence. *Casino Royale* exhibits a certain 'retro' style, which was welcomed by commentators following the overdose of CGI effects in *Die Another Day*. Daniel Kleinman's best title sequence to date, for example, recalls the pulp covers of paperback editions of the novel with its playing-card motif, while the fighting silhouette figures hark back to the titles of the sixties television series *The Saint*. One scene in particular locates the film in the heritage of the spy thriller as Bond and Vesper engage in dining-car psychology on the train to Montenegro. Several critics compared the scene to the celebrated sequence between Cary Grant and Eva Marie Saint in *North by Northwest*, though one complained that, unlike Hitchcock, the scene here was 'stilted, utterly unsexy and largely incomprehensible owing to [Eva] Green's mangled accent'.[20]

Where *Casino Royale* certainly does distinguish itself, however, is in its return to the tradition of real stunts and action sequences that 'emphasize the physicality of the stunt work rather than special effects'.[21] This is best exemplified in the first major action set piece, an extended foot-chase in which Bond pursues a terrorist suspect across an African construction site – contrasting the extraordinary agility of the 'free running' specialist Sébastien Foucan with Bond's bull-in-a-chinashop physicality – and into the fictional Nambutu Embassy which Bond proceeds to shoot up before killing the bomber and making his escape. The sequence is done for 'real', unlike, for example, the paragliding in *Die Another Day*, with CGI effects used only for enhancement. A later set piece, admittedly, as Bond chases another bomber at Miami airport, seems repetitive and somewhat redundant. Nevertheless, in locating the action sequences in recognisable physical environments rather than ice palaces or underground lairs Campbell achieves some of the most plausible action highlights in the series since *OHMSS*. Roger Clarke, reviewing the film for *Sight and Sound*, felt that the action scenes were more fully integrated into the thematic structure of the film than usual:

> The best set pieces all revolve around architecture, the most incredible romp being set on a building site in Madagascar, where Bond pursues a lead and leaps from steel girder to steel girder and from crane to crane. There is also a spectacular demolition of a Venetian palazzo, the very fabric of the building unable to sustain the pummelling it receives from Bond and the villains trying to kill him. With the film-makers resisting the temptation to compare the palazzo's collapse to that of a famous structure in New York, Bond's feverish fight to save the woman he loves disappearing into the murky waters of the Grand Canal while trapped in an elevator cage is Bond's journey into the subconscious; and the heroine's chaotic and watery demise evokes both Leonardo Di Caprio's amniotic sinking into the Atlantic in *Titanic* and Olivia de Havilland's wide-eyed and raging Cornelia Hilyard in Walter Grauman's *Lady in a Cage*.[22]

Here, perhaps, speaks the voice of the critic reading too much into the film, though *Casino Royale* certainly maintains one tradition of the Bond series: it positively delights in the gratuitous destruction of property. The moment when Bond writes off his brand-new Aston Martin, crashing spectacularly to avoid running over a bound-and-gagged Vesper in the road, is more painful to some male viewers than the torture scene that follows.

The promotional discourse of *Casino Royale* stressed its realistic action sequences as well as the greater psychological depth of the narrative. These factors also combined to make it one of the most violent Bond movies: certainly the most violent since *Licence to Kill* and arguably the most 'sadistic' since *Dr No*. Bond kills in cold blood (the execution of Dryden, whom Bond knows is unarmed, recalls the shooting of Professor Dent in *Dr No*) and shows a callous disregard for diplomatic protocol when he shoots the bomber Mollaka ('You violated the only absolutely inviolable rule of international relationships!' declares a shocked M). Bond also, for the first time, is seriously seen to bleed. He emerges plausibly cut and bruised from the Madagascar and Miami sequences, though the most sordid sequence is the fight with Obanna and his henchman – the African terrorists who have threatened Le Chiffre – in a hotel stairwell that leaves Bond covered in blood (his own as well as the Africans') and Vesper in a psychologically plausible state of shock. (Compare her reaction to, say, Tiffany's 'Oh my God, you've just killed James Bond!' after the lift-fight in *Diamonds are Forever* and we see the extent to which *Casino Royale* attempts to make Vesper a real person.) For all this, however, *Casino Royale* received nothing more restrictive than a 12A certificate in Britain – actually less prohibitive than the censors' ratings for the first three Brosnan films – and a PG13 in the United States. This would suggest that tolerance of screen violence has changed significantly since *Licence to Kill*, where the violence is no more brutal than in *Casino Royale*. The evidence concerning the effects of screen violence, as ever, is mixed. One eleven-year-old girl, for example, felt that 'it was more serious than the other Bonds. Some bits were quite violent – I didn't like the strangling bit at all, and the black-and-white opening was quite scary.' An eight-year-old boy in the same survey, however, found it 'fantastic': he 'loved all the action and shooting', though complained there was 'too much snogging'.[23]

Too much snogging or not, *Casino Royale* surpassed *Die Another Day* at the box-office: after three months it had grossed $454 million worldwide.[24] While this may be due to the effect of ticket-price inflation in the four years between the films, it proved, nevertheless, that the much-vaunted reboot of the series had paid off handsomely. The fact that both films performed exceptionally well at the box-office, moreover, would seem to suggest that there was an audience for both visually-enhanced fantasy Bond and back-to-basics stripped-down Bond. Like its predecessor *Casino Royale* was chosen for the Royal Film Performance, marking the sixtieth anniversary of that institution. Moreover, it was nominated for nine British Film and Television Academy Awards, including 'Outstanding British Film of the Year' and 'Actor in a Leading Role', suggesting that the achievement of the Bond series was at last being recognised by its native film industry, though in the event the only award it won was for visual effects. Its popular and critical success demonstrates, yet again, the durability of the Bond formula and its ability to respond to changes in popular taste. There remains every indication that, for the foreseeable future at least, the James Bond films are likely to go on being what they have always been: a unique and very special kind of popular cinema.

Notes

For the endnotes, books are cited by the place of publication and the date of the edition used. Full details of all books referred to are given in the Bibliography. Where film reviews or newspaper articles are cited without a page reference, the source is the British Film Institute's microfiche collection, which does not usually include page numbers. Reviews from *Variety* are taken from *Variety's Film Reviews* and *Variety's Television Reviews*; reviews and articles from the *New York Times* are taken from *The New York Times Film Reviews* and *The New York Times Encyclopedia of Film*.

Introduction: Taking James Bond Seriously

1. Ian Fleming, 'How to Write a Thriller', *Books and Bookmen*, May 1963, p. 14.

2. Quoted in John Pearson, *The Life of Ian Fleming* (London, 1966), p. 206.

3. Many extravagant claims have been made about Fleming's war. A made-for-television film, *Spymaker: The Secret Life of Ian Fleming* (1992), had Fleming undertaking a secret mission in Lisbon, where he kills a German agent, and included an entirely fictional sequence in which Fleming takes part in a commando raid on German secret service headquarters in Norway which owes more to *Where Eagles Dare* than the reality of Fleming's wartime service. In an intriguingly inter-textual piece of casting, Fleming was played by Jason Connery. An even more bizarre fiction is offered by ex-actor John Ainsworth-Davis, writing as Christopher Creighton, in his book *Op. JB: The Last Great Secret of the Second World War* (London, 1996), in which he claims that during the dying days of the war in 1945 Fleming masterminded and led a secret mission into Germany to kidnap Hitler's deputy, Martin Bormann. The reality, according to intelligence experts Norman Polmar and Thomas B. Allen in their definitive *Spy Book: The Encyclopedia of Espionage* (London, 1997) was rather less dramatic: 'Most of Fleming's espionage work was cerebral and deskhound, though he occasionally carried a commando knife and a fountain pen that he said contained tear gas' (p. 212).

4. Jack Fishman, '007 and Me, by Ian Fleming', in Sheldon Lane (ed.), *For Bond Lovers Only* (London, 1965), pp. 10, 15.

5. Quoted in Andrew Lycett, *Ian Fleming* (London, 1995), pp. 289–90.

6. Paul Johnson, 'Sex, Snobbery and Sadism', *New Statesman*, 5 April 1958, p. 431.

7. Quoted in Laura Lilli, 'James Bond and Criticism', in Oreste Del Buono and Umberto Eco (eds), *The Bond Affair*, trans. R. A. Downie (London, 1966), p. 172.

8. Kingsley Amis, *The James Bond Dossier* (London, 1966), p. 9.

9. Ibid., p. 144.

10. Terry Eagleton, *Literary Theory: An Introduction* (Oxford, 1983), p. 96.

11. Umberto Eco, 'The Narrative Structure in Fleming', in Del Buono and Eco (eds), *The Bond Affair*, p. 58.

12. Anthony Burgess, 'The James Bond Novels: An Introduction', for the Hodder and Stoughton 1987 edition of the novels (unpaginated in the Coronet paperback editions of the same).

13. *Daily Worker*, 6 October 1962.

14. Quoted in the *Evening Standard*, 18 May 1965. The quotation is from an article entitled 'The James Bond Case' in the Vatican newspaper *Osservatore Romano*.

15. *Observer*, 7 October 1962.

16. *Saturday Review*, 1 June 1963 (Arthur Knight).

17. *Variety*, 17 October 1962 ('Rich').

18. *Monthly Film Bulletin*, 34/403, August 1967, p. 122.

19. Ronald Bergan, *The United Artists Story* (London, 1986), p. 305.

20. John Brosnan, *James Bond in the Cinema* (London, 1981), p. ix.

21. Albert R. Broccoli, with Donald Zec, *When the Snow Melts: The Autobiography of Cubby Broccoli* (London, 1998), p. 308.

22. Robin Wood, *Hitchcock's Films* (London, 1977), p. 96. Noting that *Goldfinger* was awarded 'three stars' (out of a possible four) in *Sight and Sound*'s 'Guide to Current Films', which lists 'films of special interest to *Sight and Sound* readers', Wood was prompted to ask 'do *Sight and Sound* readers accept such blackening of their characters?'

23. Ibid., p. 38.

24. Roy Armes, *A Critical History of British Cinema* (London, 1978), pp. 254–7.

25. Sarah Street, *British National Cinema* (London, 1997), p. 87.

26. Burgess, 'The James Bond Novels', n.p.

27. Alan Barnes and Marcus Hearn, *Kiss Kiss Bang! Bang!: The Unofficial James Bond Film Companion* (London, 1997), p. 5.

28. Tony Bennett, 'Text and Social Process: The Case of James Bond', *Screen Education*, 41 (Winter/Spring 1982), p. 11.

29. Julian Petley, 'The Lost Continent', in Charles Barr (ed.), *All Our Yesterdays: 90 Years of British Cinema* (London, 1986), p. 98.

30. Julian Petley and Alan Burton, 'Introduction', *Journal of Popular British Cinema*, 1, 'Genre and British Cinema' (1998), pp. 2, 4.

31. Film critic David Robinson (*Financial Times*, 11 October 1963) was so impressed with the stylistic similarities between *From Russia with Love* and the Hammer horror films that he confused Bond director Terence Young with Hammer director Terence Fisher: 'Terence Fisher brings to the assignment a technical proficiency gained over a 30-year career in pictures ... and which was probably sharpened up on the run of horror films that he directed in the late 50s, *The Curse of Frankenstein*, *Dracula*, *The Hound of the Baskervilles*, and so on ...'

32. '007 Sights \$2-Bil in Ducats Overall', declared *Variety* on 13 May 1987, p. 57. For those unfamiliar with *Variety*'s particular style of journalese, this meant that the Bond films, in their twenty-fifth year, were approaching total box-office earnings of \$2 billion (i.e. \$2,000,000,000). 'No other celluloid concept has come close to a similar giga-take: i.e. hitting 10-digit sales twice over,' said trade journalist Roger Watkins. In 2002 the

total gross of the Bond series until *Die Another Day*, excluding television, video and DVD sales, was $3.6 billion. When adjusted for inflation this figure was an estimated $8.4 billion. See Jeff Chu, 'The Man with the Golden Run', *Time*, 11 November 2002, pp. 64–71.

33. Raymond Williams, *Keywords: A Vocabulary of Culture and Society* (London, 1983), p. 237.

34. Nick Roddick, '"If the United States spoke Spanish, we would have a film industry ..."', in Nick Roddick and Martyn Auty (eds), *British Cinema Now* (London, 1985), p. 4.

35. Lee Drummond, *American Dreamtime: A Cultural Analysis of Popular Movies and Their Implications for a Science of Humanity* (Lanham, 1996), pp. 128–9.

36. Tony Bennett and Janet Woollacott, *Bond and Beyond: The Political Career of a Popular Hero* (London, 1987), p. 1.

37. Ibid., pp. 5–6.

38. Ibid., p. 7.

39. Ibid., p. 24.

40. Ibid., p. 29.

41. Ibid., p. 38. The practice of showing a Bond film on Christmas Day – and, where possible, the television première of a particular Bond film – lasted for some fifteen years until it petered out in the 1990s, by which time the advent of home video, satellite broadcasting and cable television meant that all the films became more easily and frequently available to domestic audiences, and the television broadcast of a Bond film was no longer the 'event' that it had been in the 1970s and 1980s. Even so, television schedulers still tend to save Bond films for holiday periods. Along with *The Great Escape*, Bond has become a staple of Christmas, Easter and bank holiday television schedules.

42. 'Four Just Men Rolled into One', *The Times*, 10 October 1963.

43. Raymond Durgnat, *A Mirror for England: British Movies from Austerity to Affluence* (London, 1970), p. 151.

44. Andrew Rissik, 'Indiana Jones and the 007 Myth', *Films and Filming*, 362 (November 1984), p. 13.

45. Jim Harmon and Donald F. Glut, *The Great Movie Serials: Their Sound and Fury* (London, 1973), p. 368.

46. Larry Gross, 'Big and Loud', *Sight and Sound*, New Series 5/8 (August 1995), p. 8.

47. Quoted in 'Bond of Gold', *Screen International*, 17 November 1995, p. 22.

48. Janet Woollacott, 'The James Bond Films: Conditions of Production', in James Curran and Vincent Porter (eds), *British Cinema History* (London, 1983), p. 210.

1. The Contexts of Bond

1. Interviewed for the television programme *30 Years of James Bond*, broadcast on the ITV network on 30 September 1992.

2. Quoted in John Pearson, *The Life of Ian Fleming* (London, 1966), p. 284.

3. Ian Fleming, 'How to Write a Thriller', *Books and Bookmen*, May 1963, p. 14.

4. Tony Bennett and Janet Woollacott, *Bond and Beyond: The Political Career of a Popular Hero* (London, 1987), pp. 26–7.

5. John A. Sutherland, *Fiction and the Fiction Industry* (London, 1978), p. 176.

6. 'An Extremely Engaging Affair', *The Times Literary Supplement*, 17 April 1953, p. 249.

7. *The Listener*, 23 April 1953, p. 695.

8. Richard Usborne, 'Introduction', to 'Sapper', *Bulldog Drummond* (London, 1983 edn), p. vi. The novel itself was first published by Hodder & Stoughton in 1920.

9. Jack Fishman, '007 and Me, by Ian Fleming', in Sheldon Lane (ed.), *For Bond Lovers Only* (London, 1965), pp. 12–13.

10. Bernard Bergonzi, 'The Case of Mr Fleming', *Twentieth Century*, March 1958, pp. 220–8.

11. 'The Exclusive Bond', *Manchester Guardian*, 31 March 1958, p. 6.

12. James Price, 'Our Man in the Torture Chamber', *London Magazine*, July 1962, pp. 67–70.

13. Umberto Eco, 'The Narrative Structure in Fleming', in Oreste Del Buono and Umberto Eco (eds), *The Bond Affair* , trans. R. A. Downie (London, 1966), p. 37.

14. Ibid., p. 52.

15. Ibid., p. 51.

16. Ibid., p. 39.

17. Ibid., p. 60.

18. The mythical imagery of the Bond novels is the subject of an interesting, if rather fanciful monograph by Ann Boyd, *The Devil with James Bond!* (Westport, 1975 edn). Approaching the novels from a Christian/moralist perspective, Boyd argues that Bond is 'one of the seven legendary champions of Christendom' and reads his adventures in terms of man's struggle against the seven deadly sins, particularly that of sloth, as represented by the villain. However, her reading is overdetermined by Fleming's own statements – including his series of essays on 'The Seven Deadly Sins' – and does not account sufficiently for contradictory evidence within the novels themselves. Given that the books would hardly seem to regard lust as a sin – indeed there is much evidence to the contrary – then Boyd's attempt to overlay a Christian dimension on to them is problematic.

19. Tony Bennett, 'James Bond as Popular Hero', *Politics, Ideology and Popular Culture* 2 (Milton Keynes, 1982), p. 13.

20. Kingsley Amis, *The James Bond Dossier* (London, 1966 edn), p. 23.

21. David Cannadine, 'James Bond and the Decline of England', *Encounter*, 53/3, November 1979, p. 46.

22. Amis, *The James Bond Dossier*, p. 96.

23. Harold Perkin, *The Rise of Professional Society: England Since 1880* (London, 1990), p. 359.

24. Price, 'Our Man in the Torture Chamber', p. 69.

25. Cannadine, 'James Bond and the Decline of England', p. 55.

26. Arthur Marwick, *British Society Since 1945* (Harmondsworth, 1996 edn), p. 110.

27. Quoted in Pearson, *The Life of Ian Fleming*, p. 304.

28. Andrew Bear, 'Intellectuals and 007: High Comedy and Total Stimulation', *Dissent*, Winter 1966, p. 24.

29. Christopher Booker, *The Neophiliacs: A Study in the Revolution in English Life in the Fifties and Sixties* (London, 1969), pp. 42–3.

30. Fleming, 'How to Write a Thriller', p. 14.

31. Michael Denning, *Cover Stories: Narrative and Ideology in the British Spy Thriller* (London, 1987), pp. 109–10.

32. Eco, 'The Narrative Structure in Fleming', p. 59.

33. Andrew Lycett, *Ian Fleming* (London, 1995), p. 221.

34. In his book *James Bond: The Authorised Biography of 007* (London, 1975), Fleming biographer John Pearson puts forward the imaginative notion that Bond was a real

person and that the books were grossly exaggerated accounts of his adventures designed to create a 'myth' of Bond as part of a Cold War plot to confuse the Russians. In the SMERSH conference in *From Russia, with Love*, the conspirators talk about 'the myth of Scotland Yard, of Sherlock Holmes, of the Secret Service'. The idea of the Fleming books themselves existing in the fictional world of Bond – a device inherited from the Sherlock Holmes stories in which Holmes makes disparaging reference to Dr Watson's literary efforts – is suggested in M's 'obituary' of Bond in *You Only Live Twice*: 'The inevitable publicity, particularly in the foreign Press, accorded some of these adventures, made him, much against his will, something of a public figure, with the inevitable result that a series of popular books came to be written about him by a personal friend and former colleague of James Bond. If the quality of these books, or their degree of veracity, had been any higher, the author would certainly have been prosecuted under the Official Secrets Act. It is a measure of the disdain in which these fictions are held at the Ministry, that action has not yet – I emphasise the qualification – been taken against the author and publisher of these high-flown and romanticised caricatures of episodes in the career of an outstanding public servant.'

35. Bennett and Woollacott, *Bond and Beyond*, p. 99.

36. Amis, *The James Bond Dossier*, p. 70.

37. Lycett, *Ian Fleming*, p. 264.

38. Several versions of the television *Casino Royale* have been released on VHS. In the United Kingdom it was issued by Retro Video in 1995 and by Visual Corporation Ltd in 1996. Both feature the same telerecording of the broadcast, in which the last minute (approximately) is missing. The most complete version of *Casino Royale* currently available is the 'Collector's Edition' released in the United States by Spy Guise and Cara Entertainment. This restores the ending, missing from other versions, in which the apparently dead Le Chiffre suddenly springs up again and threatens Vesper with a razor blade held against her breasts, before Bond shoots him dead; it also contains the original end credits. Although a story persists that during the live broadcast of *Casino Royale* Peter Lorre was seen getting to his feet and walking off to his dressing room after his 'death', this is not to be seen on any of the versions currently available.

39. Steven Jay Rubin, *The James Bond Films: A Behind the Scenes History* (London, 1981), p. 2; Alan Barnes and Marcus Hearn, *Kiss Kiss Bang! Bang!: The Unofficial James Bond Film Companion* (London, 1997), p. 3.

40. Peter Haining, *James Bond: A Celebration* (London, 1987), p. 88.

41. *Daily Variety*, 26 October 1954 ('Helm').

42. Quoted in Lycett, *Ian Fleming*, p. 337. In his autobiography Cubby Broccoli quotes the same 'Editorial Notes', which Fleming gave him while preparing the first Bond film. Albert R. Broccoli, with Donald Zec, *When the Snow Melts: The Autobiography of Cubby Broccoli* (London, 1998), pp. 159–60.

43. Richard Maltby, with Ian Craven, *Hollywood Cinema: An Introduction* (Oxford, 1995), p. 70.

44. Sue Harper and Vincent Porter, *British Cinema of the 1950s: The Decline of Deference* (Oxford, 2003), p. 114.

45. 'Britain "Turning Prople Out" Says Bond Producer', *Screen International*, 9 September 1978, p. 4.

46. Pat McGilligan (ed.), *Backstory: Interviews with Screenwriters of Hollywood's Golden Age* (Berkeley, 1986), p. 284.

47. Quoted in Lycett, p. 250.

48. Harper and Porter, *British Cinema of the 1950s*, p. 44.

49. Roy Moseley, *Evergreen: Victor Saville in His Own Words* (Carbondale, 2000), p. 197.

The manuscript copy of Saville's memoir held by the British Film Institute has a slightly different version: 'I made four [*sic*] films and said "I've got the successor now to the Spillanes. There's a man named Fleming who's written a book called 'Dr No'. I'm sure it's the best there is and I have an option [*sic*] on the rest of his work. " I went to United Artists who turned me down. I was foolish. I'd become too rich to care … I don't regret not making them. They are rather poor really and I don't know that I would necessarily have been good at them. They're all so unreal. I always have to cling on to some piece of sanity.' BFI Victor Saville Collection Item 1, typescript entitled 'Shadows in a Screen', dated November 1974.

50. *Kinematograph Weekly*, 1 October 1959, p. 21.

51. See, for example, John Brosnan, *James Bond in the Cinema* (London, 1981 edn), pp. 1–9, and Alexander Walker, *Hollywood, England: The British Film Industry in the Sixties* (London, 1986 edn), pp. 178–85. Broccoli's own account is given in *When the Snow Melts*, pp. 146–53.

52. Quoted in Walker, *Hollywood, England*, p. 185.

53. *Kinematograph Weekly*, 20 July 1961, p. 17. A UA press release announced that the first film would be either *Thunderball* or *Diamonds are Forever*. (I am grateful to Gary J. Firuta for this item of Bondiana.)

54. *Motion Picture Herald*, 3 April 1963, p. 785.

55. Eight Drummond films were made by Paramount: *Bulldog Drummond Escapes* (1937), starring Ray Milland, and *Bulldog Drummond Comes Back* (1937), *Bulldog Drummond's Revenge* (1937), *Bulldog Drummond's Peril* (1938), *Bulldog Drummond in Africa* (1938), *Arrest Bulldog Drummond* (1939), *Bulldog Drummond's Bride* (1939) and *Bulldog Drummond's Secret Police* (1939), all with John Howard. There was also a brace of British films: *The Return of Bulldog Drummond* (1934) with Ralph Richardson and *Bulldog Drummond at Bay* (1937) with John Lodge. Walter Pidgeon played an ageing Drummond in the British-made *Calling Bulldog Drummond* (1951).

56. The eight Saint films by RKO were: *The Saint in New York* (1938), starring Louis Hayward; *The Saint Strikes Back* (1939), *The Saint in London* (1939), *The Saint's Double Trouble* (1940), *The Saint Takes Over* (1940) and *The Saint in Palm Springs* (1941), all starring George Sanders; *The Saint's Vacation* (1941) and *The Saint Meets the Tiger* (1941), both with Hugh Sinclair. Hayward also starred in *The Saint's Girl Friday* (1954), made in Britain by Hammer.

57. In production order the films were *Dick Barton – Special Agent*, *Dick Barton at Bay* and *Dick Barton Strikes Back*. The release of *Dick Barton at Bay* was held back, however, until 1950 so that *Dick Barton Strikes Back*, generally reckoned to be the best of the series with some exciting location action sequences on Blackpool Tower, was the second to be released. There were plans for a fourth film, *Dick Barton in Africa*, though the series was aborted following star Don Stannard's death in a car accident in July 1949.

58. Richard Schenkman, 'The Terence Young Interview', *Bondage*, 10 (1981), p. 3.

59. Kristin Thompson and David Bordwell, *Film History: An Introduction* (New York, 1994), p. 394.

60. In *Thunderball* Giuseppe Petachi muses: 'Rather a bind missing *North by Northwest* at the Odeon. But one would catch up with it at Southampton.' Film critic Philip French avers that 'Fleming often spoke of [*North by Northwest*] as his favourite movie' (*Observer*, 19 November 2006).

61. James Naremore (ed.), *North by Northwest; Alfred Hitchcock, director* (New Brunswick, 1993), p. 6.

62. Broccoli, *When the Snow Melts*, p. 164.

63. Robin Wood, *Hitchcock's Films* (London, 1977 edn), p. 96.

64. Richard Maibaum, 'James Bond's 39 Bumps', *New York Times*, 13 December 1964.

65. Schenkman, 'The Terence Young Interview', p. 3.

2. Snobbery with Violence: *Dr No, From Russia with Love, Goldfinger*

1. Quoted in Roy Armes, *A Critical History of British Cinema* (London, 1978), p. 231.

2. Linda Wood (ed.), *British Film Industry: BFI Information Guide No. 1* (London, 1980), p. A-1.

3. Robert Murphy, *Sixties British Cinema* (London, 1992), p. 164.

4. Quoted in ibid., p. 28.

5. 'The Gilt-Edged Bond', *Business Observer*, 16 January 1972.

6. John Francis Lane, 'Young Romantic', *Films and Filming*, 13/5, February 1967, p. 58.

7. Arthur Marwick, '*Room at the Top, Saturday Night and Sunday Morning*, and the "Cultural Revolution" in Britain', *Journal of Contemporary History*, 19/1, January 1984, p. 138; Jeffrey Richards, *Films and British National Identity: From Dickens to Dad's Army* (Manchester, 1997), p. 163.

8. Sarah Street, *British National Cinema* (London, 1997), p. 87.

9. Lane, 'Young Romantic', p. 58.

10. The annual assessments of box-office winners offered by *Kinematograph Weekly*, the British fan magazine *Picturegoer* and the American trade paper *Motion Picture Herald* are correlated and analysed in Janet Thumim, 'The "Popular", Cash and Culture in the Postwar British Cinema Industry', *Screen*, 32/3, Autumn 1991, pp. 245–71.

11. 'Three British Films Head the General Releases', *Kinematograph Weekly*, 13 December 1962, p. 5.

12. Dalton was speaking on the television programme *30 Years of James Bond*, broadcast on the ITV network on 30 September 1992.

13. 'British Films Again Ahead on General Release', *Kinematograph Weekly*, 19 December 1963, p. 5.

14. Lane, 'Young Romantic', p. 58.

15. Andrew Lycett, *Ian Fleming* (London, 1995), p. 297.

16. Richard Schenkman, 'The Terence Young Interview', *Bondage*, 10, 1981, p. 7.

17. *Kinematograph Weekly*, 27 July 1961, pp. 13f.

18. Pat McGilligan (ed.), *Backstory: Interviews with Screenwriters of Hollywood's Golden Age* (Berkeley, 1986), p. 284. Aubrey Mather was in fact a British character actor.

19. Schenkman, 'The Terence Young Interview', p. 7.

20. BFI S6500: *Dr No. From the Novel by Ian Fleming*. Fourth Draft Screenplay, by Richard Maibaum and Wolf Mankowitz, 12 December 1961. This script contains some features which did not, fortunately, find their way into the finished film. For example, after assigning Bond to his mission, the script has M wishing him luck and shaking hands – a fundamental misunderstanding of the relationship between Bond and his boss. Honey has the tedious habit of referring to animals by their full Latin names. The script contains none of the famous Bond one-liners. Lines such as Connery's droll 'I think they were on their way to a funeral' after the hearse pursuing him has plunged over a cliff and exploded into flames were apparently devised on the set by Young and Connery himself.

21. Tony Bennett and Janet Woollacott, *Bond and Beyond: The Political Career of a Popular Hero* (London, 1987), p. 33.

22. Raymond Durgnat, *A Mirror for England: British Movies from Austerity to Affluence* (London, 1970), p. 151.

23. Andrew Rissik, *The James Bond Man: The Films of Sean Connery* (London, 1983), p. 50.

24. Schenkman, 'The Terence Young Interview', p. 4.

25. Ibid., p. 9.

26. Laura Mulvey, 'Visual Pleasure and Narrative Cinema', *Screen*, 16/3, Autumn 1975, pp. 6–18.

27. All the female voices in *Dr No*, except Miss Moneypenny (Lois Maxwell) and Miss Taro (Zena Marshall), were dubbed by actress Nikki Van Der Zyl, who also dubbed Shirley Eaton in *Goldfinger* and Claudine Auger in *Thunderball*. Daniela Bianchi in *From Russia with Love* was dubbed by British actress Barbara Jefford.

28. *Sunday Times*, 7 October 1962.

29. *Monthly Film Bulletin*, 29/345, October 1962, p. 136.

30. *Spectator*, 12 October 1962.

31. Derek Hill, 'The Infallible *Dr No*', *Scene*, 4, October 1962, p. 19.

32. *The Times*, 5 October 1962.

33. Thomas Wiseman, 'Is Mr Bond Your Idea of a Hero?', *Sunday Express*, 7 October 1962.

34. *Daily Worker*, 6 October 1962.

35. *Films and Filming*, 9/2, November 1962, p. 36.

36. John Trevelyan, *What the Censor Saw* (London, 1973), p. 90.

37. There is some anecdotal evidence of censorship of *Dr No*. Broccoli told authors Lee Pfeiffer and Philip Lisa that in the scene where Bond shoots Professor Dent, originally he 'gives Dent six shots. They made us cut out three shots.' Quoted in Lee Pfeiffer and Philip Lisa, *The Incredible World of 007* (London, 1992), p. 192. Bond actually shoots Dent twice in the film.

There was some comment at the time over another scene which was excised from the finished film, which some attributed to censorial intervention. According to Isabel Quigley (*Spectator*, 12 October): 'In the book we are told that Honey ... is staked out to be eaten by land-crabs, and this episode was mentioned in one or two notices of the film. Only in the version I saw it was never stated at all. True, she was chained in a dungeon with the water rising through a sluice, but we were not told she was going to be eaten. This was either deleted by the censor or furnished by the critics. I should like to know which.' The scene was evidently filmed, as production stills showing the crabs crawling over Ursula Andress do exist, and it was mentioned in reviews by Alexander Walker (*Evening Standard*, 4 October 1962) and Leonard Mosley (*Daily Express*, 5 October 1962). According to Mosley: 'The beautiful blonde has been shackled to the ground and a couple of Oriental villains are grinning lasciviously as poison spiders [*sic*] crawl over her limbs.' Editor Peter Hunt later said that, rather than having anything to do with the censors, the scene was removed because it looked too silly.

38. 'No, No, a Thousand Times No', *Time*, 19 October 1962.

39. Michael Davie (ed.), *The Diaries of Evelyn Waugh* (London, 1976), p. 789.

40. According to Josh Billings (*Kinematograph Weekly*, 25 October 1962, p. 4): 'Every night of the week there are long queues waiting to get into the London Pavilion to see *Dr No*, although it's on show in the suburbs at nearly half the price. The Ian Fleming thriller is marvellous escapist fare and obviously just the medicine the cash customers need. What a box-office tonic!'

41. J. Hoberman, 'When Dr No Met Dr Strangelove', *Sight and Sound*, New Series, 3/12, December 1993, p. 18.

42. *New York Times*, 30 May 1963, p. 20.

43. 'Hairy Marshmallow', *Time*, 31 May 1963.

44. *Motion Picture Herald*, 3 April 1963, p. 785.

45. 'James Bond's 25th Anniversary', *Hollywood Reporter*, 14 July 1987, p. S-26.

46. Albert R. Broccoli, with Donald Zec, *When the Snow Melts: The Autobiography of Cubby Broccoli* (London, 1998), p. 177. According to the *Hollywood Reporter* (25 March 1963, p. 3), *Dr No* 'will première in the US with a massive 450-theater engagement in the midwest and southwest starting May 8'. It was not so much the number of cinemas where the film was shown that Broccoli objected to as it was their location in the sticks.

47. McGilligan (ed.), *Backstory*, p. 284.

48. BFI S6501: *Ian Fleming's From Russia with Love*. Final Draft Screenplay by Richard Maibaum, 18 March 1963.

49. Albert R. Broccoli, 'Introducing James Bond', in Jay McInnerney et al., *Dressed To Kill: James Bond, the Suited Hero* (Paris, 1996), p. 9.

50. Richard Roud (*Guardian*, 11 October 1963) wondered whether there was political pressure behind the plot changes: 'Those who have read the book will wonder at my calling the divine Klebb *former* head of the Russian secret service; I was surprised, too. For some reason (Foreign Office? post-test-ban-euphoria? distribution in the uncommitted countries?) the straight fight between us and the Russians has been changed in the film to a battle between us and "Spectre", the international crime syndicate which preys on Communists and capitalists alike.'

51. Penelope Gilliat, 'Laughing It Off with Bond', *Observer*, 13 October 1963.

52. *Kinematograph Weekly*, 24 October 1963, p. 11.

53. *New Statesman*, 11 October 1963.

54. Thomas Wiseman, 'Such Jolly Fun – This Latest Bond 007 Epic', *Sunday Express*, 13 October 1963.

55. Nina Hibbin, 'No, James Bond is not "Fun" – He's Just Sick', *Daily Worker*, 12 October 1963.

56. *Esquire*, September 1964.

57. *Saturday Review*, 18 April 1964.

58. McGilligan (ed.), *Backstory*, p. 285.

59. Brian McFarlane (ed.), *An Autobiography of British Cinema* (London, 1997), p. 275.

60. John Brosnan, *James Bond in the Cinema* (London, 1981), p. 75.

61. In the screenplay, Bond's hands are also painted gold, as if to suggest his responsibility for Jill's death. BFI S6508: *Ian Fleming's Goldfinger*. Final Draft Screenplay by Richard Maibaum and Paul Dehn, 26 February 1964.

62. BFI microfiche for *Goldfinger*: undated press release.

63. Richard Maibaum, 'James Bond's 39 Bumps', *New York Times*, 13 December 1964.

64. G. B. Zorzoli, 'Technology in the World of James Bond', in Oreste Del Buono and Umberto Eco (eds), *The Bond Affair*, trans. R. A. Downie (London, 1966), p. 127.

65. Quoted in Laura Lilli, 'James Bond and Criticism', in Del Buono and Eco (eds), *The Bond Affair*, pp. 161 2.

66. Janet Thumim, *Celluloid Sisters: Women and Popular Cinema* (London, 1992), p. 204.

67. Graham Rye, *The James Bond Girls* (London, 1989), p. 11.

68. *The Daily Cinema*, 21 September 1964, p. 2.

69. Nina Hibbin, 'Bond's Latest Film Repeats the Dose', *Daily Worker*, 16 September 1964.

70. Penelope Houston, '007', *Sight and Sound*, 34/1, Winter 1964–65, p. 16.

3. Bondmania: *Thunderball, Casino Royale, You Only Live Twice, On Her Majesty's Secret Service*

1. John Brosnan, *James Bond in the Cinema* (London, 1981), p. 99.

2. 'James Bond's 25th Anniversary', *Hollywood Reporter*, 14 July 1987, p. S-26.

3. Nicholas Anez, 'James Bond', *Films in Review*, 18/9–10, September/October 1992, p. 316.

4. Lietta Tornabuoni, 'A Popular Phenomenon', in Oreste Del Buono and Umberto Eco (eds), *The Bond Affair*, trans. R. A. Downie (London, 1966), p. 19.

5. *Daily Telegraph*, 1 March 1965.

6. 'Bondomania', *Time*, 11 June 1965, p. 59.

7. Alexander Walker, *Hollywood, England: The British Film Industry in the Sixties* (London, 1986), p. 198.

8. *New York Times*, 26 January 1966.

9. 'Bondomania', p. 59.

10. Quoted in Arthur Marwick, *The Sixties: Cultural Revolution in Britain, France, Italy, and the United States, c. 1958–1974* (Oxford, 1998), p. 476.

11. Tony Bennett and Janet Woollacott, *Bond and Beyond: The Political Career of a Popular Hero* (London, 1987), p. 32.

12. Tornabuoni, 'A Popular Phenomenon', p. 19.

13. Marwick, *The Sixties*, p. 456.

14. Bennett and Woollacott, *Bond and Beyond*, pp. 34–5.

15. In my discussion of various aspects of the 'cultural revolution', I am drawing on the work of my Open University colleague Professor Arthur Marwick, to whose exhaustive researches this particular section of the book is heavily indebted.

16. *Punch*, 30 September 1964.

17. Marwick, *The Sixties*, p. 18.

18. *Sunday People*, 26 June 1977.

19. Quoted in Bennett and Woollacott, *Bond and Beyond*, p. 231.

20. 'Whatever Happened to the Bond Girls?', *Telegraph Sunday Magazine*, 17 September 1978.

21. Marwick, *The Sixties*, p. 680.

22. Drew Moniot, 'James Bond and America in the Sixties: An Investigation of the Formula Film in Popular Culture', *Journal of the University Film Association*, 28/3, Summer 1976, p. 32.

23. Ibid., p. 30.

24. The cinema trailer for *Our Man Flint* had this voice-over: 'I know – you're tired of those British super secret agents. Now, here's your chance to buy American. Our Man Flint is here. ... He's the clean shaven, red-blooded, super-American secret agent everybody turns to when the world is really in trouble.' The film itself is replete with sideswipes at the Bond movies, such as an Agent 0008 and the assertion that the criminal syndicate GALAXY is 'bigger than SPECTRE'.

25. *The Man from U.N.C.L.E.* (an acronym of United Network Command for Law and Enforcement) ran on the American NBC television network from 1964 to 1968. Executive producer Norman Felton was a friend of Ian Fleming, who had been involved

at the inception of the show and suggested the name of the hero Napoleon Solo (played in the series by Robert Vaughn). Eight movies, stitched together from double episodes of the TV series, were released theatrically outside America by MGM: *To Trap a Spy* (1965), *The Spy with My Face* (1965), *One of Our Spies is Missing* (1966), *One Spy Too Many* (1966), *The Spy in the Green Hat* (1966), *The Helicopter Spies* (1967), *The Karate Killers* (1967) and *How to Steal the World* (1968).

26. Some indication of the glut of 'spaghetti' spy movies is provided by the number of them listed in the *Monthly Film Bulletin* between 1965 and 1968 (referred to here by their English titles). Agent 077, the 'Italian James Bond', had his own series with *Mission Bloody Mary*, *From the Orient With Fury* and *Killers Are Challenged*, though *DA 077: Espionage in Lisbon* seems to have been about a different character entirely; Agent oSS 17, the 'French James Bond', featured in *Mission for a Killer* and *Terror in Tokyo*; two other secret agents, *Coplan – Agent 005* and *Secret Agent FX 18*, would somehow seem to have merged into one with *Coplan FX 18: The Exterminators*; the Italian heroes of *Agent OS 14: Operation Poker* and *Agent 3. S. 3: Passport to Hell* seem only to have had one outing each, as did the West German *Agent 505*. However, these titles represent only those films that were released in Britain, and would therefore be the tip of an iceberg of films which never travelled beyond their own shores. Several Italian films used a variation on the 'Mr Kiss Kiss Bang Bang' tag attached to Bond, including *Kiss Kiss, Kill Kill* and *Kiss the Girls and Make Them Die*. Not all European spy films were necessarily derivative of Bond: *That Man in Rio* (1964), starring Jean-Paul Belmondo, and Claude Chabrol's *An Orchid for the Tiger* (1965) were quite favourably reviewed. Tornabuoni mentions a film called *002 Secret Agents and the Goldfinger Mission*, though I have been unable to verify the existence of this particular title.

27. Quoted in Tornabuoni, 'A Popular Phenomenon', p. 23.

28. I am using the word 'epic' in its proper sense, from the Greek *epos*, as referring to a type of narrative (such as epic poetry) which celebrates and eulogises the endeavours of a heroic character. The film version of *You Only Live Twice* is an epic in the sense in which the term is now more usually understood, particularly in respect of films, as a 'big' picture, with high production values, an expensive budget and a large canvas on which the story unfolds.

29. *Kinematograph Weekly*, 5 December 1963, p. 5.

30. Steven Jay Rubin, *The James Bond Films: A Behind the Scenes History* (London, 1981), p. 55.

31. BFI microfiche on *Thunderball*: 'Advance Production Story'.

32. Richard Schenkman, 'The Terence Young Interview', *Bondage*, 10, 1981, p. 6.

33. Lee Pfeiffer and Philip Lisa, *The Incredible World of 007* (London, 1992), p. 44; Alan Barnes and Marcus Hearn, *Kiss Kiss Bang! Bang!: The Unofficial James Bond Film Companion* (London, 1997), p. 47.

34. *The Times*, 29 December 1965.

35. *Daily Worker*, 1 January 1966.

36. *New York Times*, 26 December 1965, S2, p. 1; 22 December 1965, p. 23.

37. *Kinematograph Weekly*, 5 August 1965, p. 14.

38. Robert Murphy, *Sixties British Cinema* (London, 1992), p. 246.

39. Clive Hirschhorn, *The Columbia Story* (London, 1989), p. 266.

40. *Variety*, 19 April 1967 ('Rich').

41. '007's Oriental Eyefuls', *Playboy*, June 1967, p. 87.

42. This particular line features in the trailer for *Thunderball* – Connery says, 'The things I do for England!' as Fiona Volpe removes his shirt – but the scene was dropped from the finished film.

43. *New York Times*, 14 June 1967, p. 40.

44. Quoted in Herb A. Lightman, 'The "Cinemagic" of 007', *American Cinematographer*, 51/3, March 1970, pp. 204–5.

45. Lazenby did, however, make a cameo appearance in the 1983 television movie *The Return of the Man from U.N.C.L.E.,* as a character known as 'JB' whose rocket-firing Aston Martin helps Napoleon Solo out of a tight spot.

46. Pat McGilligan (ed.), *Backstory: Interviews with Screenwriters of Hollywood's Golden Age* (Berkeley, 1986), pp. 286–7.

47. *Village Voice*, 24 December 1969.

48. 'Richard Maibaum: 007's Puppetmaster', *Starlog*, 68, March 1983, p. 27.

49. Alexander Walker, *National Heroes: British Cinema in the Seventies and Eighties* (London, 1985), p. 56.

50. Ibid., p. 57.

51. Derek Malcolm, 'Off-the-peg Bond', *Guardian*, 16 December 1969.

52. *Films and Filming*, 16/4, February 1970, p. 38.

53. *Today's Cinema*, 19 December 1969, p. 5.

54. *New Yorker*, 27 December 1969.

55. *Variety*, 16 December 1969 ('Rick').

56. *Hollywood Reporter*, 17 December 1969.

57. *New York Times*, 1 February 1970, S2, p. 19 (A. Marks).

58. In programme notes for a screening of *OHMSS* at the National Film Theatre on 22 February 1992, Andrew Pilkington of the James Bond 007 International Film Club wrote: 'To most informed Bond fans it is considered possibly the best film in the entire series. The film features consistently in the top three of the Bond Fan Club's "running" poll, often in the Number One slot.' This is an example of how the Bond fan culture distinguishes itself from the general audience, identifying qualities in the film that others have missed. But it is not only the die-hard Bond fans who now rate the film so highly. American critic Danny Peary, for example, while preferring Connery's Bond and finding that 'it's impossible to ever fully adjust to Lazenby', nevertheless adds, 'I think that it might still be the best Bond film, as many Bond cultists claim. At the very least, it ranks with *Goldfinger*, Connery's best film … and *The Spy Who Loved Me*, Roger Moore's one top-flight Bond film.' See his *Cult Movies 3* (New York, 1988), pp. 172–6. Nicholas Anez is even more certain, describing *OHMSS* as 'a perfect movie and the crowning achievement of the series'. See his 'James Bond (Part 2)', *Films in Review*, 18/11–12, November/December 1992, pp. 383–8. However, this view is still by no means widespread. Even Robert Murphy, so often the champion of under-valued movies, finds *OHMSS* 'a very dull film despite its ascension to cult status' (*Sixties British Cinema*, p. 317).

4. Bond in Transition: *Diamonds are Forever, Live and Let Die, The Man with the Golden Gun*

1. *Sunday People*, 8 July 1973 (Kenneth Bailey).

2. Alexander Walker, *National Heroes: British Cinema in the Seventies and Eighties* (London, 1985), p. 58.

3. 'Richard Maibaum: 007's Puppetmaster', *Starlog*, 68, March 1983, p. 63.

4. Quoted in Steven Jay Rubin, *The James Bond Films: A Behind the Scenes History* (London, 1981), p. 112.

5. *Observer*, 8 July 1973.

6. *Spectator*, 14 July 1973.

7. Tony Bennett and Janet Woollacott, *Bond and Beyond: The Political Career of a Popular Hero* (London, 1987), p. 37.

8. Christopher Booker, *The Seventies: Portrait of a Decade* (London, 1980), p. 32.

9. Walker, *National Heroes*, p. 15.

10. *The Times*, 6 July 1973.

11. *New York Times*, 18 December 1971.

12. That is not to say that debates about the violence of the Bond films did not still exist; rather, the participants in the debate were no longer the film critics. A correspondence in *The Times* in March 1972 was concerned with the subject of children at Bond films. One correspondent complained that, in taking children to see *Diamonds are Forever*, parents were 'irresponsibly encouraging infants to enjoy unsuitable entertainment. ... Mrs Whitehouse does have the courage to speak out with conviction and consistently'. Another correspondent, however, believed that the film 'was pure slapstick which made it impossible to identify with either the hero or the victims, and contained less sadism and reality than a Tom and Jerry cartoon'.

13. *Observer*, 8 July 1973.

14. Bennett and Woollacott, *Bond and Beyond*, p. 40.

15. Felix Barker, 'Is James Bond Running Out of Steam?', *Evening News*, 19 December 1974.

16. 'Richard Maibaum: 007's Puppetmaster', p. 27.

17. BFI S6502 *Diamonds are Forever*, Final Draft Screenplay, by Tom Mankiewicz. The script is undated, but several yellow revision pages are marked 14 April 1971.

18. Walker, *National Heroes*, p. 57.

19. *Esquire*, June 1972.

20. Quoted in Andy Medhurst, 'Batman, Deviance and Camp', in Roberta E. Pearson and William Uricchio (eds), *The Many Lives of the Batman: Critical Approaches to a Superhero and His Media* (London, 1991), p. 155.

21. *Monthly Film Bulletin,* 39/457, February 1972, p. 30.

22. 'James Bond's 25th Anniversary', *Hollywood Reporter*, 14 July 1987, p. S-26.

23. Peter Schjeldahl, 'Bond is Back – and "Diamonds" Got Him', *New York Times*, 28 December 1971.

24. *Village Voice*, 16 December 1971.

25. John Belton, *American Cinema/American Culture* (New York, 1994), p. 291.

26. 'Richard Maibaum: 007's Puppetmaster', p. 63.

27. *New Statesman*, 6 July 1973.

28. *Monthly Film Bulletin*, 40/475, August 1973, p. 172.

29. *Spectator*, 14 July 1973.

30. *The Times*, 6 July 1973.

31. Richard Schickel, 'Dirty Trick', *Time*, 9 July 1973.

32. *Sunday Times*, 8 July 1974.

33. Kenneth O. Morgan, *The People's Peace: British History 1945–1990* (Oxford, 1990), p. 363.

34. *Guardian*, 19 December 1974.

35. *Observer*, 22 December 1974.

36. Jay Cocks, 'Water Pistols', *Time*, 13 January 1975.

5. Keeping the British End Up: *The Spy Who Loved Me*, *Moonraker*

1. 'James Bond's 25th Anniversary', *Hollywood Reporter*, 14 July 1987, p. S-26.

2. *Screen International*, 5 December 1997, p. 21.

3. Alexander Walker, *National Heroes: British Cinema in the Seventies and Eighties* (London, 1985), pp. 135–6.

4. Linda Wood (ed.), *British Film Industry: BFI Information Guide No. 1* (London, 1980), p. A-2.

5. Walker, *National Heroes*, p. 276.

6. 'Cubby Counts the Cost of Keeping 007 in the Manner …', *Screen International*, 26 August 1976, p. 11.

7. Ibid.

8. 'No More Bond Films to be Made in Britain?', *Screen International*, 26 March 1977, p. 6.

9. 'Britain "Turning People Out" Says Bond Producer', *Screen International*, 9 September 1978, p. 4.

10. Anthony Burgess, 'The James Bond Novels: An Introduction', n.p.

11. 'Midas Touch', *Screen International*, 17 November 1995, p. 28.

12. 'Richard Maibaum: 007's Puppetmaster', *Starlog*, 68, March 1983, p. 63.

13. BFI S4498: *The Spy Who Loved Me*. Revised Final Shooting Script, 23 August 1976. Although there are no references to SPECTRE in this script, some traces of the SPECTRE formula remain, such as Sandor referring to Stromberg as 'Number One', the designation used for Blofeld in the SPECTRE films.

14. John Brosnan, *James Bond in the Cinema* (London, 1981), p. 256.

15. One Bond fan listed no fewer than forty-six specific plot similarities between *You Only Live Twice* and *The Spy Who Loved Me*: Saul Fischer, 'The Spy Who Lived Twice', *Bondage*, 7 (no date).

16. Tony Bennett et al., *The Making of 'The Spy Who Loved Me'* (Milton Keynes, 1977), pp. 29–30.

17. Quoted in Janet Woollacott, 'The James Bond Films: Conditions of Production', in James Curran and Vincent Porter (eds), *British Cinema History* (London, 1983), p. 221.

18. *Screen International*, 16 July 1977, p. 16.

19. *Monthly Film Bulletin*, 44/523, August 1977, p. 176.

20. Frank Rich, 'Why James Bond is Still a Crowd Pleaser', *New York Times*, 21 August 1977, S2, p. 11.

21. For an informed discussion of the significance of *Jaws* and *Star Wars* for the film industry, see Thomas Schatz, 'The New Hollywood', in Jim Collins et al., *Film Theory Goes to the Movies* (London, 1993), pp. 8–36.

22. 'No More Bond Films to be Made in Britain?', *Screen International*, 26 March 1977, p. 6.

23. Albert R. Broccoli, with Donald Zec, *When the Snow Melts: The Autobiography of Cubby Broccoli* (London, 1998), p. 254.

24. BFI microfiche on *Moonraker*: typed notes entitled 'The Book', undated.

25. Eric Burgess, 'The Making of *Moonraker*', *New Scientist*, 21 June 1979, p. 984.

26. *Screen International*, 7 July 1979, p. 17.

27. *Monthly Film Bulletin*, 46/547, August 1979, p. 180.

28. Dilys Powell, 'Inhuman Bondage', *Punch*, 4 July 1979.

6. Cold Warrior Reborn: *For Your Eyes Only, Octopussy, Never Say Never Again, A View to a Kill*

1. Albert R. Broccoli, with Donald Zec, *When the Snow Melts: The Autobiography of Cubby Broccoli* (London, 1998), p. 254.
2. *Screen International*, 5 December 1997, p. 21.
3. In Fleming's novels, secret service headquarters is in a 'gloomy building overlooking Regent's Park' (*Casino Royale*, p. 23).
4. Sarah Street, *British National Cinema* (London, 1997), p. 87.
5. Margaret Thatcher, *The Downing Street Years* (London, 1993), p. 90.
6. 'Bond is back with a new spy master', *Screen International*, 3 January 1981, p. 13.
7. BFI S17894: *For Your Eyes Only*. Screen Story and Screenplay by Richard Maibaum and Michael G. Wilson, 12 August 1980.
8. 'Richard Maibaum: 007's Puppetmaster', *Starlog*, 68, March 1983, p. 63.
9. *Screen International*, 11 June 1981, p. 15.
10. *Variety*, 19 June 1981 ('Cart').
11. BFI S18120: *Octopussy*. Screenplay by Richard Maibaum and Michael G. Wilson, based on a Draft Screenplay by George MacDonald Fraser, 10 June 1982.
12. *Monthly Film Bulletin*, 50/594, July 1983, p. 192.
13. 'Independent Way for Mr Fixit', *Screen International*, 20 November 1982, p. 13.
14. Ibid.
15. *Monthly Film Bulletin*, 50/599, December 1983, pp. 334–5.
16. *Variety*, 1 October 1983 ('Cart').
17. Nicholas Anez, 'James Bond (Part 3)', *Films in Review*, 19/1–2, January/February 1993, p. 34.
18. Tony Bennett and Janet Woollacott, *Bond and Beyond: The Political Career of a Popular Hero* (London, 1987), p. 287.
19. Ibid., p. 288.
20. Ibid., pp. 289–90.
21. *Films and Filming*, 370, July 1985, p. 46.
22. *Variety*, 21 May 1985 ('Jagr').
23. *Films and Filming*, 351, December 1983, p. 41 (Brian Baxter).

7. Continuity and Change: *The Living Daylights, Licence to Kill*

1. 'James Bond Returns', *Starburst*, 107, July 1987, p. 12.
2. *New York Times*, 14 July 1989, p. C-8 (Caryn James).
3. Quoted in Richard Schenkman, 'Timothy Dalton Revisited', *Bondage*, 16, Winter 1989, pp. 22–3.
4. *Monthly Film Bulletin*, 54/643, August 1987, p. 244.
5. Ibid.
6. Schenkman, 'Timothy Dalton Revisited', p. 22.
7. Raymond Benson, *The James Bond Bedside Companion* (London, 1988), p. 258.
8. Kingsley Amis, *The James Bond Dossier* (London, 1966), p. 46.
9. *Screen International*, 5 December 1997, p. 21.
10. *Screen International*, 4 July 1987, p. 38.
11. *Films and Filming*, 395, August 1987, p. 35 (Allan Hunter).
12. *New York Times*, 31 July 1987, p. C-3.
13. *Variety*, 1 July 1987 ('Pit').

14. There were mischievous reports in the British press that the title was changed because most Americans did not understand the meaning of the word 'revoked', though this rather distorted the truth which was that American audiences associated the title *Licence Revoked* with having their driving licence recalled. There were further problems over the title in so far as 'licence' is spelled 'license' in American English. The shooting script for the film held by the British Film Institute (S18050) is entitled *License to Kill*, but for the finished film the Queen's English was restored.

15. *Monthly Film Bulletin*, 56/666, July 1989, p. 208.

16. Bizarrely, in John Gardner's novelisation of the screenplay, which maintains a semblance of continuity with the literary Bond, this is the *second* occasion on which Bond has found Leiter in this state. This time around the shark had managed to chew off Leiter's false arm and leg, which Sanchez and his men had not noticed!

17. *Monthly Film Bulletin*, 56/666, July 1989, p. 208.

18. *Variety*, 14 June 1989 ('Coop').

19. *Hollywood Reporter*, 30 June 1989, pp. 4f.

20. *Screen International*, 17 June 1989, p. 22.

21. Albert R. Broccoli, with Donald Zec, *When the Snow Melts: The Autobiography of Cubby Broccoli* (London, 1998), p. 294.

22. *Screen International*, 17 June 1989, p. 22.

23. Broccoli, *When the Snow Melts*, p. 295.

24. This story was broken in *Variety* on 8 August 1990: 'Bond Bombshell: 007 Goes on the Block', p. 1. It was repeated, and slightly modified, in the British press, for example the *Sunday Times* on 12 August: 'Hollywood Mogul Puts $200m Price on James Bond's Head', S1, p. 3.

8. Millennial Bond: *GoldenEye, Tomorrow Never Dies, The World is not Enough, Die Another Day*

1. Jeff Chu, 'The Man with the Golden Run', *Time*, 11 November 2002, pp. 70–1.

2. 'Big Bang Theory', *Time Out*, 3 August 1994, p. 16.

3. 'The Avatar of Espionage', *Screen International*, 5 December 1997, p. 21.

4. *In Search of James Bond ... with Jonathan Ross*, ITV network, 9 December 1995.

5. 'Bond of Gold', *Screen International*, 17 November 1995, p. 22.

6. Tom Shone, 'The Gilt-edged Bond', *Sunday Times*, S10, 19 November 1995, p. 67.

7. Philip French. 'Oh, Put It Away, James', *Observer: Review*, 14 December 1997, p. 12.

8. *Financial Times*, 23 November 1995, p. 21.

9. Brigit Grant, 'Deadly but Dull', *Sunday Express Classic Magazine*, 26 November 1995, p. 49.

10. Geoff Brown, 'Bond Comes in from the Cold', *The Times*, 23 November 1995.

11. Alexander Walker, 'Bond Rescues Action Man', *Evening Standard*, 23 November 1995, p. 13.

12. *News of the World*, 14 December 1997.

13. Quoted in *GoldenEye: Film Education Study Guide 3* (London, 1997), p. 3.

14. Ibid.

15. Ibid.

16. Eagle-eyed Bond fans may have spotted that the number plates of the cars are different, however. The Aston Martin DB5 in *Goldfinger* and *Thunderball* had been BMT 216A, whereas the car Brosnan drives in *GoldenEye* is BMT 214A. The fascinating story

of the various different cars which have featured in the Bond films is told in Dave Worrall's book *The Most Famous Car in the World: The Complete History of the James Bond Aston Martin DB5* (Christchurch, 1991, and subsequent editions).

17. *New York Times*, 17 November 1995, p. C-17 (Janet Maslin).

18. Geoff Brown, 'Bond Comes in from the Cold', *The Times*, 23 November 1995.

19. *Variety*, 20 November 1995.

20. *Screen International*, 17 November 1995.

21. Some indication of the trials and tribulations is provided by Garth Pearce, *The Making of Tomorrow Never Dies* (London, 1997), though even so the book was endorsed by Eon Productions and was clearly intended, in some measure, to downplay the on-set frictions. This was also strongly evident in the television interviews given by Pierce Brosnan to promote *Tomorrow Never Dies*.

22. Richard Williams, 'Premium Bond', *Guardian*, 12 December 1997, p. 10.

23. Alexander Walker, 'Unshaken and Totally Unstirred', *Evening News*, 11 December 1997, p. 27.

24. *Sight and Sound*, New Series 8/2 (February 1998), p. 53.

25. Quoted in York Membery, 'No, Mr Bond, I Want You to Live', *Sunday Times*, S2, 21 February 1999, p. 4.

26. Quoted in Jeremy Black, *The Politics of James Bond: From Fleming's Novels to the Big Screen* (Westport, 2001), p. 207.

27. Alexander Walker, 'This World is More than Enough for Non-stop 007', *Evening Standard*, 8 November 1999, p. 3.

28. Quoted in David Gritten, 'The Man Who Made 007 What He is Today', *Daily Telegraph*, 25 November 1999, p. 30.

29. Anthony Quinn, 'Hanging by a Thread', *Independent: Review*, 26 November 1999, p. 11.

30. Kim Fletcher, 'Millennial Bond', *Spectator*, 27 November 1999, p. 74.

31. *Sight and Sound*, New Series 10/1 (January 2000), p. 63.

32. Kevin Conroy Scott (ed.), *Screenwriters' Masterclass: Screenwriters Talk About Their Greatest Movies* (London, 2005), p. 367.

33. Adam Mars-Jones, 'On Her Majesty's Civil Service', *The Times*, 25 November 1999, p. 51.

34. Conroy Scott, *Screenwriters' Masterclass*, p. 367.

35. 'A View to a Thrill . . . Lee Tamahori', *Screen International*, 15 November 2002, p. 11.

36. Chapter 11 of *On Her Majesty's Secret Service* is entitled 'Death for Breakfast', while 'Love for Breakfast' is Chapter 19.

37. Michael Gove, 'Gung-ho 007 Returns to Torture the Anti-capitalist Pigs', *The Times*, 19 May 2002, p. 7.

38. Catherine Shoard, 'More Sex, Bigger Gadgets', *Sunday Telegraph: Review*, 24 November 2002, p. 7.

39. Sukhdev Sandhu, 'Bond Loses the Plot', *Daily Telegraph*, 20 November 2002, p. 25.

40. Nicholas Barber, 'Nobody Does It Better? Not on the Strength of This, James Old Boy', *Independent on Sunday: Arts*, 24 November 2002, p. 10.

41. Anthony Quinn, 'Beyond Salvation', *Independent: Review*, 22 November 2002, p. 8.

42. Alexander Walker, 'Licence to Chill', *Evening Standard*, 20 November 2002, p. 51.

9. Revisionist Bond: *Casino Royale*

1. *The Times*, S2, 6 November 2006, p. 13.
2. 'I Want to Find Bond's Dark Side', *Daily Telegraph*, 7 November 2006, p. 27.
3. 'The Bond Supremacy', *Screen International*, 11 March 2005, p. 8.
4. Umberto Eco, 'The Narrative Structure in Fleming', in Oreste Del Buono and Umberto Eco (eds), *The Bond Affair*, trans. R. A. Downie (London, 1966), p. 37.
5. 'The Bond Supremacy', p. 8.
6. 'Campbell Trades Masks for Martinis', *Screen International*, 28 October 2005, p. 18.
7. Cosmo Landesman, *Sunday Times: Culture*, 12 November 2006, p. 11.
8. Catherine Shoard, 'A Bit Shaken, but Hardly Stirred', *Sunday Telegraph: Seven*, 19 November 2006, p. 22.
9. *Variety*, 9 November 2006: http://www.variety.com/VE1117932077.html (accessed 19.02.07).
10. Sukhdev Sandhu, 'The Best Bond for Decades', *Daily Telegraph*, 17 November 2006, p. 29.
11. Wendy Ide, 'Craig Gambles with the Winning Hand', *The Times*, S2, 16 November 2006, p. 16.
12. Charlie Higson, 'It's Got Everything You Want from a Bond Film', *Daily Telegraph*, 17 November 2006, p. 29.
13. *Empire*, November 2006: http://www.empireonline.com/reviews/CasinoRoyale.html (19.02.07).
14. Derek Malcolm, 'This 007 Leaves You Shaken', *Evening Standard*, 16 November 2006, p. 34.
15. *Guardian G2*, 10 November 2006, p. 9.
16. 'The Bond Supremacy', p. 8.
17. Philip French suggests that the toilet killing takes place in London (*Observer: Review*, 19 November 2006, p. 18). In the Final Production Script of 20 December 2005 (copy in the possession of the author) the location is identified as the Lahore cricket ground in Pakistan during a match between a Pakistani and a 'British' team (England played a Test match against Pakistan at Lahore between 29 November and 3 December 2005). In the film the only suggestion of this location is prints of Asian cricketers on the wall of the toilet where the fight takes place.
18. Sarah Sands, 'Double Oh Heaven', *Independent on Sunday*, 12 November 2006, p. 42; Sandhu, 'The Best Bond for Decades', p. 29.
19. Zoe Williams and Paul Flynn, 'The Spy Who Buffed Up', *Guardian G2*, 16 November 2006, p. 7.
20. Kirk Honeycutt, *Hollywood Reporter*, 10 November 2006: http://www.hollywood reporter.com/hr/film/reviews/CasinoRoyale.jsp (19.02.07).
21. Shoard, 'A Bit Shaken, but Hardly Stirred', p. 23.
22. *Sight and Sound*, New Series, 17/1 (January 2007), p. 54.
23. Francesca Steele, 'Is the New Bond Movie Too Violent for Children?', *The Times*, S2, 24 November 2006, p. 10.
24. 'Casino Tops Bond at Box Office': http://news.bbc.co.uk/1/hi/entertainment/6211929.stm (19.02.07).

Filmography

The filmography lists all the James Bond 'films' (including the television *Casino Royale*) in chronological order. Note that the 1967 *Casino Royale* and *Never Say Never Again* were produced outside the 'official' James Bond series. The filmography is compiled from the credits of the films themselves and the information provided by the *Monthly Film Bulletin*; credits vary according to different terminology and industry conventions.

Casino Royale

Columbia Broadcasting System. 1954.

Climax! television series. *Hosted by:* William Lundigan. *Director:* William H. Brown. *Producer:* Bretaigne Windust. *Written for television by:* Antony Ellis and Charles Bennett. *Associate producer:* Elliott Lewis. *Art direction:* Robert Tyler Lee and James De Val. *Running time:* 50 minutes.

Cast: Barry Nelson (James Bond), Linda Christian (Valerie Mathis), Peter Lorre (Le Chiffre), Michael Pate (Clarence Leiter), Eugene Borden (Chef de Partie), Jean Del Val (Croupier), Gene Roth (Basil), Kurt Katch (Zoltan).

Dr No

United Artists/Eon Productions. 1962.

Director: Terence Young. *Producers:* Harry Saltzman and Albert R. Broccoli. *Screenplay:* Richard Maibaum, Johanna Harwood and Berkeley Mather. *Production manager:* L. C. Rudkin. *Editor:* Peter Hunt. *Director of photography:* Ted Moore. Technicolor. *Production designer:* Ken Adam. *Art director:* Syd Cain. *Costume de-*

signer: Tessa Welborn. *Stunt arranger:* Bob Simmons. *Special effects:* Frank George. *Main titles:* Maurice Binder. *Music:* Monty Norman. *Orchestrated by:* Burt Rhodes. *Conducted by:* Eric Rodgers. 'The James Bond Theme' *played by:* The John Barry Orchestra. *Certificate:* A. *Running time:* 111 mins.

Cast: Sean Connery (James Bond), Ursula Andress (Honey Ryder), Joseph Wiseman (Dr No), Jack Lord (Felix Leiter), Bernard Lee (M), Anthony Dawson (Professor Dent), Zena Marshall (Miss Taro), John Kitzmiller (Quarrel), Eunice Gayson (Sylvia Trench), Lois Maxwell (Miss Moneypenny), Peter Burton (Major Boothroyd), Yvonne Shima (Sister Lily), Michele Mok (Sister Rose), Marguerite Lewars (Girl photographer), Lester Prendergast (Puss-Feller), William Foster-Davis (Superintendent), Louis Blaazer (Pleydell-Smith), Tim Moxon (Strangways), Dolores Keator (Mary), Reggie Carter (Jones), Colonel Burton (General Potter).

From Russia with Love

United Artists/Eon Productions. 1963.

Director: Terence Young. *Producers:* Harry Saltzman and Albert R. Broccoli. *Screenplay:* Richard Maibaum. *Adaptation:* Johanna Harwood. *Production manager:* Bill Hill. *Editor:* Peter Hunt. *Director of photography:* Ted Moore. Technicolor. *Art director:* Syd Cain. *Costume designer:* Jocelyn Rickards. *Stunt arranger:* Peter Perkins. *Special effects:* John Stears. *Assisted by:* Frank George. *Main titles:* Robert Brownjohn. *Assisted by:* Trevor Bond. *Music:* John Barry. *Title song performed by:* Matt Monro. *Lyrics:* Lionel Bart. *Certificate:* A. *Running time:* 116 mins.

Cast: Sean Connery (James Bond), Daniela Bianchi (Tatiana Romanova), Pedro Armendariz (Kerim Bey), Lotte Lenya (Rosa Klebb), Robert Shaw (Grant), Bernard Lee (M), Eunice Gayson (Sylvia), Walter Gotell (Morzeny), Vladek Sheybal (Kronsteen), Lois Maxwell (Miss Moneypenny), Francis de Wolff (Vavra), George Pastell (Orient Express conductor), Nadja Regin (Kerim's girl), Alizia Gur (Vida), Martine Beswick (Zora), Leila (Belly dancer), Fred Haggerty (Krilencu), Peter Bayliss (Benz), Desmond Llewelyn (Boothroyd – Q),* Neville Jason (Kerim's chauffer), Nushet Ataer (Mehmet), Peter Brayham (Rhodes), Jan Williams (Masseuse), Peter Madden (McAdams).**

---

* Llewelyn took over the role of the Armourer, Major Boothroyd, when Peter Burton who had played him in *Dr No* was unavailable for *From Russia with Love*. Llewelyn appeared in every subsequent Bond film except *Live and Let Die*, until *The World is not Enough*, and holds the record for most appearances in the series. He was first billed as 'Q' in *Goldfinger* and generally has been known by that designation ever since, though in *The Spy Who Loved Me* Anya Amasova does say to him 'Good morning, Major Boothroyd'.

Goldfinger

United Artists/Eon Productions. 1964.

Director: Guy Hamilton. *Producers:* Harry Saltzman and Albert R. Broccoli. *Screenplay:* Richard Maibaum and Paul Dehn. *Production manager:* L. C. Rudkin. *Editor:* Peter Hunt. *Director of photography:* Ted Moore. Technicolor. *Production designer:* Ken Adam. *Art director:* Peter Murton. *Wardrobe supervisor:* Elsa Fennell. *Action sequences:* Bob Simmons. *Special effects:* John Stears. *Assisted by:* Frank George. *Main titles:* Robert Brownjohn. *Music:* John Barry. *Title song performed by:* Shirley Bassey. *Lyrics:* Leslie Bricusse, Anthony Newley. *Certificate:* A. *Running time:* 109 mins.

Cast: Sean Connery (James Bond), Honor Blackman (Pussy Galore), Gert Frobe (Goldfinger), Shirley Eaton (Jill Masterson), Tania Mallet (Tilly Masterson), Harold Sakata (Oddjob), Bernard Lee (M), Cec Linder (Felix Leiter), Martin Benson (Solo), Richard Vernon (Colonel Smithers), Lois Maxwell (Miss Moneypenny), Bill Nagy (Midnight), Hal Galili (Strap), Lenny Rabin (Henchman), Austin Willis (Simmons) Michael Mellinger (Kisch), Peter Cranwell (Johnny), Burt Kwouk (Mr Ling), Desmond Llewelyn (Q), Mai Ling (Mai Lei), Alf Joint (Capungo), Nadja Regin (Bonita), Margaret Nolan (Dink), Raymond Young (Sierra), Varley Thomas (Swiss gatekeeper).

Thunderball

United Artists/Eon Productions. 1965.

Director: Terence Young. *Producer:* Kevin McClory. *Executive producers:* Harry Saltzman and Albert R. Broccoli. *Screenplay:* Richard Maibaum and John Hopkins. From an original screenplay by Jack Whittingham. Based on an original story by Kevin McClory, Jack Whittingham and Ian Fleming. *Production supervisor:* David Middlemas. *Supervising editor:* Peter Hunt. *Director of photography:* Ted Moore. Panavision. Technicolor. *Underwater photography:* Ricou Browning. *Production designer:* Ken Adam. *Art director:* Peter Murton. *Costume designer:* Anthony Mendleson. *Action sequences:* Bob Simmons. *Special effects:* John Stears. *Main titles:* Maurice Binder. *Music:* John Barry. *Title song performed by:* Tom Jones. *Lyrics:* Don Black. *Certificate:* A. *Running time:* 132 mins.

Cast: Sean Connery (James Bond), Claudine Auger (Domino), Adolfo Celi (Largo), Luciana Paluzzi (Fiona Volpe), Rik Van Nutter (Felix Leiter), Guy

---

** Ernst Stavro Blofeld, who made his first screen appearance in *From Russia with Love*, was billed on the end credits as a mysterious '?'; it seems that he was in fact played by Anthony Dawson, while Eric Pohlmann provided his voice.

Doleman (Lippe), Molly Peters (Patricia Fearing), Martine Beswick (Paula), Bernard Lee (M), Desmond Llewelyn (Q), Lois Maxwell (Miss Moneypenny), Roland Culver (Home Secretary),* Earl Cameron (Pinder), Paul Stassino (Palazzi), Rose Alba ('Widow'), Mitsuoko (French liaison agent), Philip Locke (Vargas), George Pravda (Kutze), Michael Brennan (Janni), Leonard Sachs (Group Captain Prichard), Edward Underdown (Air Vice Marshal), Reginald Beckwith (Kenniston), Harold Sanderson (Hydrofoil captain).**

Casino Royale

Columbia Pictures/Charles K. Feldman. 1967.

Directors: John Huston, Kenneth Hughes, Val Guest, Robert Parrish, Joseph McGrath. *Additional sequences:* Val Guest. *Producers:* Charles K. Feldman and Jerry Bresler. *Screenplay:* Wolf Mankowitz, John Law, Michael Sayers. *Associate producer:* John Dark. *Editor:* Bill Lenny. *Director of photography:* Jack Hildyard. Panavision. Technicolor. *Additional photography:* John Wilcox, Nicolas Roeg. *Second unit directors:* Richard Talmadge, Anthony Squire. *Production designer:* Michael Stringer. *Art directors:* John Howell, Ivor Beddoes, Lionel Couch. *Costume designer:* Julie Harris. *Special effects:* Cliff Richardson, Roy Whybrow. *Titles and montage effects:* Richard Williams. *Music:* Burt Bacharach. *Lyrics:* Hal David. *Main title theme played by:* Herb Alpert and the Tijuana Brass. 'The Look of Love' *performed by:* Dusty Springfield. *Certificate:* A. *Running time:* 130 mins.

Cast: Peter Sellers (Evelyn Tremble – 'James Bond 007'), Ursula Andress (Vesper Lynd – 'James Bond 007'), David Niven (Sir James Bond), Orson Welles (Le Chiffre), Joanna Pettet (Mata Bond), Daliah Lavi (The Detainer – 'James Bond 007'), Woody Allen (Jimmy Bond/Dr Noah), Deborah Kerr (Agent Mimi, *aka* Lady Fiona), William Holden (Ransome), Charles Boyer (Le Grand), John Huston (McTarry – M), Kurt Kasznar (Smernov), George Raft (Himself), Jean-Paul Belmondo (French Legionnaire), Terence Cooper (Agent Cooper – 'James Bond 007'), Barbara Bouchet (Moneypenny), Jacqueline Bisset (Miss Goodthighs), Angela Scoular (Buttercup), Gabriella Licudi (Eliza), Tracey Crisp (Heather), Elaine Taylor (Peg), Alexandra Bastedo (Meg), Anna Quayle (Frau Hoffer), Ronnie Corbett (Polo), Bernard Cribbins (Taxi driver), Derek Nimmo (Hadley), Geoffrey Bayldon (Q), John Wells (Q's assistant), John Bluthal (Casino doorman & MI5 man), Tracy Reed (FANG Leader), Duncan MaCrea (Inspector Mathis), Richard Wattis (British Army officer),

---

* Roland Culver is actually listed on the credits as 'Foreign Secretary' but is referred to as 'Home Secretary' in the film itself.

** Blofeld is again uncredited, though his voice is clearly that of Joseph Wiseman (not, on this occasion, Eric Pohlmann as suggested by some sources).

Vladek Sheybal (Le Chiffre's representative), Graham Stark (Cashier), Chic
Murray (Chic), Jonathan Rowth (John), Percy Herbert (1st Piper), Penny Riley
(Control girl), Jeanne Roland (Captain of the Guard).*

You Only Live Twice

United Artists/Eon Productions. 1967.

Director: Lewis Gilbert. *Producers:* Harry Saltzman and Albert R. Broccoli.
Screenplay: Roald Dahl. *Additional story material:* Harold Jack Bloom. *Produc-
tion supervisor:* David Middlemas. *Second unit director and supervising editor:* Peter
Hunt. *Director of photography:* Freddie Young. Panavision. Technicolor. *Aerial
photography:* John Jordan. *Underwater photography:* Lamar Boren. *Production designer:*
Ken Adam. *Art director:* Harry Pottle. *Wardrobe supervisor:* Elsa Fennell. *Action
sequences:* Bob Simmons. *Special effects:* John Stears. *Main titles:* Maurice Binder.
Music: John Barry. *Title song performed by:* Nancy Sinatra. *Lyrics:* Leslie Bricusse.
Certificate: A. *Running time:* 116 mins.

Cast: Sean Connery (James Bond), Donald Pleasence (Ernst Stavro Blofeld),
Akiko Wakabayashi (Aki), Mie Hama (Kissy Suzuki), Tetsuro Tamba (Tiger
Tanaka), Teru Shimada (Osato), Karin Dor (Helga Brandt), Bernard Lee (M),
Lois Maxwell (Miss Moneypenny), Desmond Llewelyn (Q), Charles Gray (Hend-
erson), Tsai Chin (Chinese girl – Hong Kong), Burt Kwouk (SPECTRE #3),
Michael Chow (SPECTRE #4), Ronald Rich (Hans), Jeanne Roland (Bond's
masscuse), David Tiguri (Bedroom assassin), Alexander Knox (American presid-
ent), Robert Hutton (President's aide), John Stone (Submarine captain), Richard
Marner (Russian officer), Anthony Ainley, Patrick Jordan (Military policemen),
Norman Jones, Paul Carson (Astronauts: 1st American spacecraft), Laurence
Herder, Richard Graydon (Astronauts: Russian spacecraft), Bill Mitchell, George
Roubeck (Astronauts: 2nd American spacecraft).

On Her Majesty's Secret Service

United Artists/Eon Productions. 1969.

Director: Peter Hunt. *Producers:* Albert R. Broccoli and Harry Saltzman. *Screenplay:*
Richard Maibaum. *Additional dialogue:* Simon Raven. *Associate producer:* Stanley
Sopel. *Production supervisor:* David Middlemas. *Editor and second unit director:* John
Glen. *Director of photography:* Michael Reed. Panavision. Technicolor. *Aerial
photography:* John Jordan. *Ski photography:* Willy Bogner, Alex Barbey. *Stock car
sequence director:* Anthony Squire. *Production designer:* Syd Cain. *Art director:* Peter

---

* Peter O'Toole made an uncredited appearance as a Scottish piper.

Lamont. *Costume designer:* Marjory Cornelius. *Stunt arranger:* George Leech. *Special effects:* John Stears. *Main titles:* Maurice Binder. *Music:* John Barry. *Lyrics:* Hal David. 'We Have All the Time in the World' *performed by:* Louis Armstrong. 'Do You Know How Christmas Trees are Grown?' *performed by:* Nina. *Certificate:* A. *Running time:* 140 mins.

Cast: George Lazenby (James Bond),* Diana Rigg (Tracy), Telly Savalas (Ernst Stavro Blofeld), Gabriele Ferzetti (Draco), Ilse Steppat (Irma Bunt), George Baker (Sir Hilary Bray), Lois Maxwell (Miss Moneypenny), Bernard Lee (M), Bernard Horsfall (Campbell), Desmond Llewelyn (Q), Yuri Borienko (Grunther), Virginia North (Olympe), Geoffrey Cheshire (Toussaint), Irvin Allen (Che Che), Terry Mountain (Raphael), James Bree (Gumbold), John Gay (Hammond), Brian Worth (Manuel), Norman McGlen (Janitor), Dudley Jones (Hall porter), John Crewdson (Draco's helicopter pilot), Josef Vasa (Piz Gloria reception-ist), Les Crawford (Felsen), George Cooper (Braun), Reg Harding (Blofeld's driver), Richard Graydon (Draco's driver), Bill Morgan (Klett), Bessie Love (American guest), Steve Plytas (Greek tycoon), Robert Rietty (Chef de Jeu), Elliott Sullivan (American guest). *The Girls:* Angela Scoular (Ruby), Catherina von Schell (Nancy), Julie Ege (Scandinavian), Mona Chong (Chinese), Sylvana Henriques (Jamaican), Dani Sheridan (American), Joanna Lumley (English), Zara (Indian), Anoushka Hempel (Australian), Ingrit Back (German), Helena Ronee (Israeli), Jenny Hanley (Irish).

Diamonds are Forever

United Artists/Eon Productions. 1971.

Director: Guy Hamilton. *Producers:* Albert R. Broccoli and Harry Saltzman. *Screenplay:* Richard Maibaum and Tom Mankiewicz. *Associate producer:* Stanley Sopel. *Production managers:* Milton Feldman, Claude Hudson. *Editors:* John W. Holmes, Bert Bates. *Director of photography:* Ted Moore. Panavision. Technicolor. *Production designer:* Ken Adam. *Art directors:* Bill Kenney, Jack Maxsted. *Wardrobe supervisors:* Elsa Fennell, Ted Tetrick. *Stunt arrangers:* Bob Simmons, Paul Baxley. *Special effects:* Whitey McMahon, Leslie Hillman. *Main titles:* Maurice Binder. *Music:* John Barry. *Title song performed by:* Shirley Bassey. *Lyrics:* Don Black. *Certificate:* A. *Running time:* 120 mins.

Cast: Sean Connery (James Bond), Jill St John (Tiffany Case), Charles Gray (Ernst Stavro Blofeld), Lana Wood (Plenty O'Toole), Jimmy Dean (Willard Whyte), Bruce Cabot (Bert Saxby), Bruce Glover (Mr Wint), Putter Smith

---

* Lazenby was dubbed by George Baker during his impersonation of Sir Hilary Bray.

(Mr Kidd), Norman Burton (Felix Leiter), Joseph Furst (Dr Metz), Bernard Lee (M), Desmond Llewelyn (Q), Lois Maxwell (Miss Moneypenny), Laurence Naismith (Sir Donald Munger), Leonard Barr (Shady Tree), Margaret Lacey (Mrs Whistler), Joe Robinson (Peter Franks), David de Keyser (Doctor), David Bauer (Morton Slumber), Donna Garratt (Bambi), Trina Parks (Thumper), Burt Metcalf (Maxwell), Ed Bishop (Klaus Hergersheimer), Henry Rowland (Dentist), Marc Lawrence, Michael Valente (Gangsters), Shane Rimmer (Tom), Constantin de Goguel (Aide to Metz), Clifford Earle (US Immigration officer), Max Latimer (Blofeld's double), Frank Olegario (Man in fez), Denise Perrier (Marie).

Live and Let Die

United Artists/Eon Productions. 1973.

Director: Guy Hamilton. *Producers:* Harry Saltzman and Albert R. Broccoli. *Screenplay:* Tom Mankiewicz. *Production supervisor:* Claude Hudson. *Editors:* Bert Bates, Raymond Poulton, John Shirley. *Director of photography:* Ted Moore. Eastman Colour. *Supervising art director:* Syd Cain. *Costume designer:* Julie Harris. *Choreography:* Geoffrey Holder. *Stunt co-ordinators:* Bob Simmons, Ross Kananga, Jerry Comeaux, Bill Bennet, Eddie Smith, Joie Chitwood. *Special effects:* Derek Meddings. *Main titles:* Maurice Binder. *Music:* George Martin. *Title song by:* Paul and Linda McCartney. *Performed by:* Paul McCartney and Wings. *Certificate:* A. *Running time:* 121 mins.

Cast: Roger Moore (James Bond), Yaphet Kotto (Kananga/Mr Big), Jane Seymour (Solitaire), Clifton James (Sheriff Pepper), Julius W. Harris (Tee Hee), Geoffrey Holder (Baron Samedi), Gloria Hendry (Rosie), Bernard Lee (M), Lois Maxwell (Miss Moneypenny), Tommy Lane (Adam), Earl Jolly Brown (Whisper), Roy Stewart (Quarrel Jr), Lon Satton (Strutter), Arnold Williams (Cab driver), Ruth Kempf (Mrs Bell), Joie Chitwood (Charlie), Madeline Smith (Italian girl), Michael Ebbin (Dambala), Kubi Chaza (Sales girl), B. J. Arnau (Singer).

The Man with the Golden Gun

United Artists/Eon Productions. 1974.

Director: Guy Hamilton. *Producers:* Albert R. Broccoli and Harry Saltzman. *Screenplay:* Richard Maibaum and Tom Mankiewicz. *Associate producer:* Charles Orme. *Production supervisor:* Claude Hudson. *Editors:* John Shirley, Raymond Poulton. *Directors of photography:* Ted Moore, Oswald Morris. Eastman Colour. *Production designer:* Peter Murton. *Art directors:* John Graysmark, Peter Lamont.

Wardrobe supervisor: Elsa Fennell. *Special effects:* John Stears. *Miniatures:* Derek Meddings. *Stunt co-ordinator:* W. J. Milligan Jr. *Main titles:* Maurice Binder. *Music:* John Barry. *Title song performed by:* Lulu. *Lyrics:* Don Black. *Certificate:* A. *Running time:* 125 mins.

Cast: Roger Moore (James Bond), Christopher Lee (Scaramanga), Britt Ekland (Mary Goodnight), Maud Adams (Andrea Anders), Hervé Villechaize (Nick Nack), Clifton James (J. W. Pepper), Richard Loo (Hai Fat), Soon Taik Oh (Hip), Bernard Lee (M), Lois Maxwell (Miss Moneypenny), Desmond Llewelyn (Q), James Cossins (Colthorpe), Marne Maitland (Lazar), Carmen Sautoy (Saida), Marc Lawrence (Hitman), Chan Yiu Lim (Chula), Gerald James (Frazier), Michael Osborne (Naval lieutenant), Michael Fleming (Communications officer).

The Spy Who Loved Me

United Artists/Eon Productions. 1977.

Director: Lewis Gilbert. *Producer:* Albert R. Broccoli. *Screenplay:* Christopher Wood and Richard Maibaum. *Associate producer:* William P. Cartlidge. *Production manager:* David Middlemas. *Special assistant to the producer:* Michael G. Wilson. *Second unit directors:* Ernest Day, John Glen. *Editor:* John Glen. *Director of photography:* Claude Renoir. Panavision. Eastman Colour. *Ski photography:* Willy Bogner. *Underwater photography:* Lamar Boren. *Production designer:* Ken Adam. *Art director:* Peter Lamont. *Wardrobe supervisor:* Rosemary Burrows. *Action sequences:* Bob Simmons. *Ski jump performed by:* Rick Sylvester. *Special visual effects:* Derek Meddings. *Main titles:* Maurice Binder. *Music:* Marvin Hamlisch. 'Nobody Does It Better' *performed by*: Carly Simon. *Lyrics:* Carole Bayer Saiger. *Certificate:* A. *Running time:* 125 mins.

Cast: Roger Moore (James Bond), Barbara Bach (Anya Amasova), Curt Jurgens (Stromberg), Richard Kiel (Jaws), Caroline Munro (Naomi), Walter Gotell (General Gogol), Geoffrey Keen (Sir Frederick Gray),* Bernard Lee (M), George Baker (Captain Benson), Robert Brown (Admiral Hargreaves), Shane Rimmer (Commander Carter), Desmond Llewelyn (Q), Lois Maxwell (Miss Moneypenny), Edward de Souza (Sheik Hossein), Nadim Sawalha (Fekkesh), Vernon Dobtcheff (Max Kalba), Michael Billington (Sergei), Sue Vanner (Log cabin girl),

---

* The character of the Minister of Defence, played by Keen from *The Spy Who Loved Me* until *The Living Daylights*, is referred to by name, as Sir Frederick Gray, in both *The Spy Who Loved Me* and *Moonraker*. Bond calls him 'Freddie' in *The Spy*, but reverts to a more formal 'Minister' thereafter. Sir Frederick is unique as the only Cabinet minister to have served in successive Labour *and* Conservative governments!

Eva Rueber-Staier (Rublevich),* Milton Reid (Sandor), Sidney Tafler (*Liparus* Captain), Valerie Leon (Hotel receptionist), Marilyn Galsworthy (Stromberg's assistant), Cyril Shaps (Dr Bechmann), Milo Sperber (Professor Markovitz), Rafiq Anwar (Mujaba Club waiter), Albert Moses (Barman), Bryan Marshall (Captain Talbot), Felicity York, Dawn Rodriques, Anika Pavel, Jill Goodall and The Egyptian Folklore Group (Arab beauties).

Moonraker

United Artists/Eon Productions and Les Productions Artistes Associes. 1979.

Director: Lewis Gilbert. *Producer:* Albert R. Broccoli. *Screenplay:* Christopher Wood. *Executive producer:* Michael G. Wilson. *Associate producer:* William P. Cartlidge. *Production managers:* Jean-Pierre Spiri-Mercanton (France), Terence Churcher (GB). *Second unit directors:* Ernest Day, John Glen. *Editor:* John Glen. *Director of photography:* Jean Tournier. Panavision. Technicolor. *Production designer:* Ken Adam. *Art directors:* Max Douy, Charles Bishop. *Costume designer:* Jacques Fonteray. *Action sequences:* Bob Simmons. *Space consultant:* Eric Burgess. *Visual effects supervisor:* Derek Meddings. *Visual effects art director:* Peter Lamont. *Main titles:* Maurice Binder. *Music:* John Barry. *Title song performed by:* Shirley Bassey. *Lyrics:* Hal David. *Certificate:* A. *Running time:* 126 mins.

Cast: Roger Moore (James Bond), Lois Chiles (Holly Goodhead), Michael Lonsdale (Drax), Richard Kiel (Jaws), Corinne Clery (Corinne Dufour), Emily Bolton (Manuela), Toshiro Suga (Chang),** Geoffrey Keen (Sir Frederick Gray), Bernard Lee (M), Desmond Llewelyn (Q), Lois Maxwell (Miss Moneypenny), Michael Marshall (Colonel Scott), Walter Gotell (General Gogol), Irka Bochenko (Blonde beauty), Anne Lonnberg (Museum guide), Nicholas Arbez (Drax's boy), Blanche Ravelac (Dolly), Arthur Howard (Cavendish), Alfie Bass (Consumptive Italian), Lizzie Warville (Gogol's girl), Jean-Pierre Castaldi (Pilot, private jet), Leila Shenna (Hostess, private jet), Douglas Lambert (Mission Control director), Brian Keith (US Shuttle captain), George Birt (Boeing 747 captain), Kim Fortune (RAF officer), Claude Carliez (Gondolier), Chichinou Kaeppler, Christina Hui, Françoise Gayat, Nicaise Jean-Louis, Catherine Serre and Beatrice Libert (Drax's Girls).

---

* Former Miss World Eva Rueber-Staier had cameo roles in three Bond films as General Gogol's secretary, and on each occasion her character's name was spelled differently on the credits: as 'Rubelvitch' in *The Spy Who Loved Me*, 'Rublevich' in *For Your Eyes Only* and 'Rublevitch' in *Octopussy*. I have opted for 'Rublevich'.

** The character is credited as 'Chang', but is referred to as 'Char' in the film itself.

For Your Eyes Only

United Artists/Eon Productions. 1981.

Director: John Glen. *Producer:* Albert R. Broccoli. *Screenplay:* Richard Maibaum and Michael G. Wilson. *Executive producer:* Michael G. Wilson. *Associate producer:* Tom Pevsner. *Production supervisor:* Bob Simmonds. *Second unit director and photographer:* Arthur Wooster. *Editor:* John Grover. *Director of photography:* Alan Hume. Panavision. Technicolor. *Ski photography:* Willy Bogner. *Aerial photography:* James Devis. *Underwater photography:* Al Giddings. *Production designer:* Peter Lamont. *Art director:* John Fenner. *Costume designer:* Elizabeth Waller. *Action sequences:* Bob Simmons. *Driving stunts:* Remy Julienne. *Visual effects supervisor:* Derek Meddings. *Visual effects photography:* Paul Wilson. *Main titles:* Maurice Binder. *Music:* Bill Conti. *Title song performed by:* Sheena Easton. *Lyrics:* Michael Leeson. *Certificate:* A. *Running time:* 127 mins.

Cast: Roger Moore (James Bond), Carole Bouquet (Melina Havelock), Topol (Columbo), Lynn-Holly Johnson (Bibi), Julian Glover (Kristatos), Cassandra Harris (Lisl), Jill Bennett (Jacoba Brink), Michael Gothard (Locque), John Wyman (Kriegler), Jack Hedley (Sir Timothy Havelock), Lois Maxwell (Miss Moneypenny), Desmond Llewelyn (Q), Geoffrey Keen (Minister of Defence), Walter Gotell (General Gogol), James Villiers (Tanner),* John Moreno (Ferrara), Toby Robins (Iona Havelock), Graham Crowden (First Sea Lord), Noel Johnson (Vice-Admiral), Charles Dance (Claus), Paul Angelis (Karageorge), Jack Klaf (Apostis), Stag Theodore (Nikos), Stefan Kalipha (Gonzales), William Hoyland (McGregor), Eva Rueber-Staier (Rublevich), Fred Bryant (Vicar), Robbin Young (Girl in flower shop), Graham Hawks (Mantis Man), John Wells (Denis), Janet Brown (Prime Minister), Lalla Dean, Evelyn Drogue, Laoura Hadzivageli, Koko, Chai Lee, Kim Mills, Tula, Vanya, Viva, Lizze Warville and Alison Worth (Girls at poolside).

Octopussy

MGM-United Artists/Eon Productions. 1983.

Director: John Glen. *Producer:* Albert R. Broccoli. *Screenplay:* Richard Maibaum and Michael G. Wilson. *Story:* George MacDonald Fraser. *Executive producer:*

---

* Bill Tanner is the British Secret Service Chief of Staff in Fleming's novels. When Bernard Lee died shortly before filming his scenes for *For Your Eyes Only*, it was decided not to replace him in this film. Moneypenny tells Bond that M is 'on leave'. The script reveals that the lines written for M were simply assigned to Tanner. It also reveals that the scene later in the film where Bond meets Q in disguise as a Greek Orthodox priest was originally to have been for M.

Michael G. Wilson. *Associate producer:* Tom Pevsner. *Production supervisor:* Hugh Harlow. *Second unit director and photographer:* Arthur Wooster. *Supervising editor:* John Grover. *Director of photography:* Alan Hume. Panavision. Technicolor. *Production designer:* Peter Lamont. *Art director:* John Fenner. *Costume designer:* Emma Porteous. *Action sequences:* Bob Simmons. *Driving stunts:* Remy Julienne. *Special effects supervisor:* John Richardson. *Main titles:* Maurice Binder. *Music:* John Barry. 'All Time High' *performed by:* Rita Coolidge. *Lyrics:* Tim Rice. *Certificate:* PG. *Running time:* 131 mins.

Cast: Roger Moore (James Bond), Maud Adams (Octopussy),* Louis Jourdan (Kamal Khan), Kristina Wayborn (Magda), Steven Berkoff (General Orlov), Kabir Bedi (Gobinda), David Meyer (Twin One), Anthony Meyer (Twin Two), Vijay Amritraj (Vijay), Desmond Llewelyn (Q), Robert Brown (M),** Lois Maxwell (Miss Moneypenny), Michaela Clavell (Penelope Smallbone), Walter Gotell (General Gogol), Geoffrey Keen (Minister of Defence), Douglas Wilmer (Fanning), Albert Moses (Sadruddin), Andy Bradford (009), Bruce Boa (US General), Paul Hardwick (Soviet Chairman), Suzanne Jerome (Gwendoline), Cherry Gillespie (Midge), Peter Porteous (Lankin), Dermot Crowley (Kamp), Eva Rueber-Staier (Rublevich), Jeremy Bullock (Smithers), Tina Hudson (Bianca), William Derrick (Yo-yo thug), Stuart Saunders (Major Clive), Patrick Barr (British Ambassador), Ken Norris (Colonel Toro), Tony Arjuna (Mufti), Gertan Klauber (Bubi), Hugo Bower (Karl), Brian Coburn (South American VIP), Mary Stavin, Carolyn Seaward, Carole Ashby, Cheryl-Anne, Jani-Z, Julie Martin, Joni Flynn, Julie Barth, Kathy Davies, Helene Hunt, Gillian De Terville, Safira Afzal, Louise King, Tina Robinson, Alison Worth, Janine Andrews and Lynda Knight (The Octopussy Girls), Suzanne Dando (Gymnasts supervisor), Teresa Craddock, Kirsten Harrison, Christine Cullers, Lisa Jackman, Jane Aldridge, Christine Gibson, Tracy Llewellyn and Ruth Flynn (Gymnasts), Robert Germains (Ringmaster), Richard Graydon (Francisco the Fearless), The Hassani Troupe, The Flying Cherokees, Carol Richter, Josef Richter, Vera Fossett, Shirley Fossett and Barrie Winship (Circus Performers).

---

* Maud Adams, who had previously played Scaramanga's mistress in *The Man with the Golden Gun*, is the only actress to have had two major parts as a 'Bond girl'.

** Robert Brown, the new M, had previously played Admiral Hargreaves in *The Spy Who Loved Me*, though it seems likely that his M is meant to be the same character previously played by the late Bernard Lee. He played M for four films, until *Licence to Kill*. Brown had previously played Gurth to Roger Moore's Ivanhoe in the Anglo-American television series *Ivanhoe* (1957–58).

Never Say Never Again

Warner Bros./Taliafilm/Woodcote Productions. 1983.

Director: Irvin Kershner. *Producer:* Jack Schwartzman. *Screenplay:* Lorenzo Semple Jr. Based on an original story by Kevin McClory, Jack Whittingham and Ian Fleming. *Executive producer:* Kevin McClory. *Associate producer:* Michael Dryhurst. *Production supervisor:* Alex de Grunwald. *Second unit director:* Michael Moore. *Underwater sequences director:* Ricou Browning. *Supervising editor:* Robert Lawrence. *Director of photography:* Douglas Slocombe. Panavision. Technicolor. *Production designers:* Philip Harrison, Stephen Grimes. *Supervising art director:* Leslie Dilley. *Costume designer:* Charles Knode. *Stunt co-ordinator:* Vic Armstrong. *Supervisor of special visual effects:* David Dryer. *Music:* Michael Legrand. *Title song performed by:* Lani Hall. *Trumpet solo:* Herb Alpert. *Lyrics:* Alan and Marilyn Bergman. *Certificate:* PG. *Running time:* 134 mins.

Cast: Sean Connery (James Bond), Klaus Maria Brandauer (Largo), Max Von Sydow (Blofeld), Barbara Carrera (Fatima Blush), Kim Basinger (Domino), Bernie Casey (Felix Leiter), Alec McCowen (Q – Algernon), Edward Fox (M), Pamela Salem (Miss Moneypenny), Rowan Atkinson (Nigel Small-Fawcett), Valerie Leon (Lady in Bahamas), Milow Kirek (Kovacs), Pat Roach (Lippe), Anthony Sharp (Lord Ambrose), Prunella Gee (Patricia Fearing), Gavan O'Herlihy (Captain Jack Petachi), Ronald Pickup (Elliott), Robert Rietty and Guido Adorni (Italian ministers), Vincent Marzello (Culpepper), Christopher Reich (No. 5), Billy J. Mitchell (Captain Pedersen), Manning Redwood (General Miller), Saskia Cohen Tanugi (Nicole), Anthony Van Laast (Kurt), Sylvia Marriott (French Minister), Dan Meaden (Bouncer), Michael Medwin (Dr Wain), Lucy Hornak (Nurse), Derek Deadman (Porter), Joanna Dickens (Cook), Tony Alleff (Auctioneer), Paul Tucker (Steward), Brenda Kempner (Masseuse), Jill Meager (Receptionist at health spa), Roy Bowe (Ship's captain), John Stephen Hill (Communications officer), Wendy Leech (Girl hostage).

A View to a Kill

MGM-United Artists/Eon Productions. 1985.

Director: John Glen. *Producers:* Albert R. Broccoli and Michael G. Wilson. *Screenplay:* Richard Maibaum and Michael G. Wilson. *Associate producer:* Tom Pevsner. *Production supervisor:* Anthony Waye. *Second unit director and photographer:* Arthur Wooster. *Ski director:* Willy Bogner. *Editor:* Peter Davies. *Director of photography:* Alan Hume. Panavision. Technicolor. *Production designer:* Peter Lamont. *Art director:* John Fenner. *Costume designer:* Emma Porteous. *Action sequences:* Martin Grace. *Driving stunts:* Remy Julienne. *Special effects supervisor:*

John Richardson. *Main titles:* Maurice Binder. *Music:* John Barry. *Title song performed by:* Duran Duran. *Written by:* Duran Duran and John Barry. *Certificate:* PG. *Running time:* 131 mins.

Cast: Roger Moore (James Bond), Christopher Walken (Max Zorin), Tanya Roberts (Stacey Sutton), Grace Jones (May Day), Patrick Macnee (Sir Godfrey Tibbett), Patrick Bachau (Scarpine), David Yip (Chuck Lee), Fiona Fullerton (Pola Ivanova), Manning Redwood (Bob Conley), Alison Doody (Jenny Flex), Willoughby Gray (Dr Carl Mortner), Desmond Llewelyn (Q), Robert Brown (M), Lois Maxwell (Miss Moneypenny),* Walter Gotell (General Gogol), Geoffrey Keen (Minister of Defence), Jean Rougerie (Aubergine), Mary Stavin (Kimberley Jones), Daniel Benzali (Howe), Bogdan Kominowski (Klotkoff), Papillon Soo Soo (Pan Ho), Dominique Risbourg (Butterfly act compere), Carole Ashby (Whistling girl), Anthony Chin (Taiwanese tycoon), Lucien Jerome (Taxi driver), Joe Flood (US police captain), Gerard Buhr (Auctioneer), Dolph Lundgren (KGB man), Tony Sibbald (Mine foreman), Bill Ackridge (O'Rourke), Sian Adey-Jones, Samina Afzal, Celine Cawley, Nike Clark, Helen Clitherow, Maggie Defreitas, Gloria Douse, Caroline Hallett, Deborah Hanna, Josanne Haydon-Pearce, Ann Jackson, Terri Johns, Karen Loughlin, Angela Lyn, Patricia Martinez, Kim Ashfield Norton, Elke Ritschel, Lou-Anne Ronchi, Helen Smith, Jane Spencer, Paula Thomas, Mayako Torigai and Toni White (The Girls).

The Living Daylights

MGM-United Artists/Eon Productions. 1987.

Director: John Glen. *Producers:* Albert R. Broccoli and Michael G. Wilson. *Screenplay:* Richard Maibaum and Michael G. Wilson. *Associate producers:* Tom Pevsner and Barbara Broccoli. *Production supervisor:* Anthony Waye. *Second unit director and photographer:* Arthur Wooster. *Editors:* John Grover, Peter Davies. *Director of photography:* Alec Mills. Panavision. Technicolor. *Production designer:* Peter Lamont. *Art director:* Terry Ackland Snow. *Costume designer:* Emma Porteous. *Stunt supervisor:* Paul Weston. *Driving stunts:* Remy Julienne. *Aerial stunt arranger:* B. J. Worth. *Special visual effects:* John Richardson. *Main titles:* Maurice Binder. *Music:* John Barry. *Title song performed by:* a-ha. *Written by:* Pal Waaktaar

---

* *A View to a Kill* marked Lois Maxwell's farewell apprearence as Miss Moneypenny, having played the role of M's secretary in fourteen consecutive films from *Dr No*. Hereafter a new actress has been cast as Moneypenny opposite each new James Bond. Maxwell claims she suggested to the producers that after stepping down as Moneypenny, she should herself play M, though the idea was turned down. A female M was of course introduced with Dame Judi Dench in *GoldenEye*.

284 Licence to Thrill

and John Barry. 'Where Has Everybody Gone' and 'If There Was a Man' *performed by:* The Pretenders. *Lyrics:* Chrissie Hynde. *Certificate:* PG. *Running time:* 131 mins.

Cast: Timothy Dalton (James Bond), Maryam d'Abo (Kara Milovy), Jeroen Krabbé (General Georgi Koskov), Joe Don Baker (Brad Whitaker), John Rhys-Davies (General Leonid Pushkin), Art Malik (Kamran Shah), Andreas Wisniewski (Necros), Thomas Wheatley (Saunders), Desmond Llewelyn (Q), Robert Brown (M), Geoffrey Keen (Minister of Defence), Caroline Bliss (Miss Moneypenny), Walter Gotell (General Anatol Gogol),* John Terry (Felix Leiter), Virginia Hey (Rubavitch),** John Bowe (Colonel Feyador), Julie T. Wallace (Rosika Miklos), Kell Tyler (Linda), Catherine Rabett (Liz), Dulice Liecier (Ava), Nadim Sawalha (Chief of Police, Tangier), Alan Talbot (KGB man), Carl Rigg (Imposter), Frederick Warder (004), Glyn Baker (002), Tony Cyrus (Chief of the Snow Leopard Brotherhood), Ken Sharrock (Russian jailer), Peter Porteous (Gas works supervisor), Derek Hoxby (Sergeant Stagg), Anthony Carrick (Male secretary, Blaydon), Bill Weston (Butler, Blaydon), Leslie French (Lavatory attendant), Michael Moor, Sumar Khan (Mujaheddin), Odette Benatar, Dianna Casale, Sharon Devlin, Femi Gardiner, Patricia Keefer, Ruddy Rodriguez, Mayte Sanchez, Cela Savannah, Karen Seeberg, Waris Walsh and Karen Williams (The Girls).

Licence to Kill

MGM-United Artists/Eon Productions. 1989.

Director: John Glen. *Producers:* Albert R. Broccoli and Michael G. Wilson. *Screenplay:* Michael G. Wilson and Richard Maibaum. *Associate producers:* Tom Pevsner and Barbara Broccoli. *Production supervisor:* Anthony Waye. *Second unit director and photographer:* Arthur Wooster. *Editor:* John Grover. *Director of photography:* Alec Mills. Panavision. Technicolor. *Production designer:* Peter Lamont. *Art director:* Michael Lamont. *Costume designer:* Jodie Tillen. *Stunt co-ordinator:* Paul Weston. *Driving stunts:* Remy Julienne. *Aerial stunt supervisor:* 'Corkey' Fornof. *Special visual effects:* John Richardson. *Main titles:* Maurice Binder. *Music:* Michael Kamen. *Title song performed by:* Gladys Knight. 'If You Asked Me to' *performed by:* Patti LaBelle. *Written by:* Diana Warren. *Certificate:* 15. *Running time:* 133 mins.

---

* This was the only occasion on which Gogol's first name was included in the credits: although billed here as 'Anatol', M had called him 'Alexis' in *The Spy Who Loved Me.*

** This character, Pushkin's mistress, is presumably not the same as Gogol's secretary Rublevich, despite the similarity in their names – unless successive heads of the KGB keep the same female companion.

Cast: Timothy Dalton (James Bond), Carey Lowell (Pam Bouvier), Robert Davi (Franz Sanchez), Talisa Soto (Lupe Lamora), Anthony Zerbe (Milton Krest), Frank McRae (Sharkey), Everett McGill (Killifer), Desmond Llewelyn (Q), Wayne Newton (Professor Joe Butcher), Pedro Armendariz Jr (President Hector Lopez), Don Stroud (Heller), David Hedison (Felix Leiter),* Pamela Barnes (Della Churchill), Robert Brown (M), Caroline Bliss (Miss Moneypenny), Benicio del Toro (Dario), Anthony Starke (Truman-Lodge), Grand L. Bush (Hawkins), Cary-Hiroyuki Tagawa (Kwang), Alejandro Bracho (Perez), Guy de Saint Cyr (Braun), Rafer Johnson (Mullens), Diana Lee-Hsu (Loti), Christopher Neame (Fallon), Claude Brook (Montelongo), Jeannine Bisignano (Stripper), Edna Bolkan (Waitress), Eddie Enderfield (Clive), Cynthia Fallo (Consuello), Teresa Blake (Ticket agent), Samuel Benjamin Lancaster (Della's uncle).

GoldenEye

MGM-United Artists/Eon Productions. 1995.

Director: Martin Campbell. *Producers:* Michael G. Wilson and Barbara Broccoli. *Screenplay:* Bruce Feirstein. *Story:* Jeffrey Caine and Michael France. *Executive producer:* Tom Pevsner. *Associate producer:* Anthony Waye. *Editor:* Terry Rawlings. *Director of photography:* Phil Méheux. Panavision. Technicolor. *Additional photography:* Arthur Wooster. *Production designer:* Peter Lamont. *Supervising art director:* Neil Lamont. *Costume designer:* Lindy Hemming. *Stunt co-ordinator:* Simon Crane. *Driving stunts:* Remy Julienne. *Parachute stunt co-ordinator:* B. J. Worth. *Special effects supervisor:* Chris Corbould. *Miniatures:* Derek Meddings. *Main titles:* Daniel Kleinman. *Music:* Eric Serra. *Title song performed by:* Tina Turner. *Written by:* Bono and The Edge. 'The Experience of Love' *written and performed by:* Eric Serra. *Certificate:* 12. *Running time:* 130 mins.

Cast: Pierce Brosnan (James Bond), Sean Bean (Alec Trevelyan), Izabella Scorupco (Natalya Simonova), Famke Janssen (Xenia Onatopp), Joe Don Baker (Jack Wade), Judi Dench (M), Robbie Coltrane (Valentin Zukovsky), Gottfried John (General Ourumov), Tcheky Karyo (Defence Minister Dimitri Mishkin), Alan Cumming (Boris Grishenko), Desmond Llewelyn (Q), Samantha Bond (Miss Moneypenny), Michael Kitchen (Tanner), Serena Gordon (Caroline), Billy J. Mitchell (Admiral Chuck Farrel), Minnie Driver (Irina), Michelle Arthur (Anna), Simon Kunz (Severnaya duty officer).

---

* Hedison is the only actor to have played Felix Leiter twice, having previously appeared in *Live and Let Die*.

Tomorrow Never Dies

MGM-United Artists/Eon Productions. 1997.

Director: Roger Spottiswoode. *Producers:* Michael G. Wilson and Barbara Broccoli. *Screenplay:* Bruce Feirstein. *Line producer:* Anthony Waye. *Second unit director:* Vic Armstrong. *Aerial director:* Marc Wolff. *Underwater director:* Pete Romano. *Editors:* Dominique Fortin, Michel Arcand. *Director of photography:* Robert Elswit. Panavision. Technicolor. *Production designer:* Allan Cameron. *Art directors:* Stephen Scott, Giles Masters, Tony Reading, Jonathan Lee, Ken Court. *Costume designer:* Lindy Hemming. *Stunt supervisor:* Dicky Beer. *HALO Jump co-ordinator:* B. J. Worth. *Special effects supervisor:* Chris Corbould. *Miniatures:* John Richardson. *Main titles:* Daniel Kleinman. *Music:* David Arnold. *Title song performed by:* Sheryl Crow. *Written by:* Sheryl Crow and Mitchell Froom. *End title song performed by:* k. d. lang. *Certificate:* 12. *Running time:* 119 mins.

Cast: Pierce Brosnan (James Bond), Jonathan Pryce (Elliot Carver), Michelle Yeoh (Wai Lin), Teri Hatcher (Paris Carver), Joe Don Baker (Jack Wade), Ricky Jay (Henry Gupta), Götz Otto (Stamper), Vincent Schiavelli (Dr Kaufman), Judi Dench (M), Desmond Llewelyn (Q), Samantha Bond (Miss Moneypenny), Colin Salmon (Robinson), Geoffrey Palmer (Admiral Roebuck), Julian Fellowes (Minister of Defence), Terence Rigby (General Bukharin), Cecilie Thomsen (Professor Inga Bergstrom), Nina Young (Tamara Steele), Daphne Deckers (Carver's PR girl), Colin Stinton (Dave Greenwalt), Michael Byrne (Admiral Kelly), Mark Spalding (Stealth Boat captain), Bruce Alexander (Captain of HMS *Chester*), Christopher Bowen (Captain of HMS *Devonshire*), Philip Kwok (General Chang).

The World is not Enough

MGM-United Artists/Eon Productions. 1999.

Director: Michael Apted. *Producers:* Michael G. Wilson and Barbara Broccoli. *Screenplay:* Neil Purvis & Robert Wade and Bruce Feirstein. *Story:* Neil Purvis & Robert Wade. *Line producer:* Anthony Waye. *Second unit director:* Vic Armstrong. *Additional unit director:* Arthur Wooster. *Editor:* Jim Clark. *Director of photography:* Adrian Biddle. Panavision. De Luxe. *Production designer:* Peter Lamont. *Supervising art director:* Neil Lamont. *Costume designer:* Lindy Hemming. *Stunt co-ordinator:* Simon Crane. *Special effects supervisor:* Chris Corbould. *Main titles:* Daniel Kleinman. *Music:* David Arnold. *Title song performed by:* Garbage. *Lyrics:* Don Black. *Certificate:* 12. *Running time:* 128 mins.

Cast: Pierce Brosnan (James Bond), Sophie Marceau (Elektra King), Robert

Carlyle (Renard), Denise Richards (Christmas Jones), Robbie Coltrane (Valentin Zukovsky), Judi Dench (M), Desmond Llewelyn (Q),* John Cleese (R), Samantha Bond (Miss Moneypenny), Michael Kitchen (Tanner), Colin Salmon (Robinson), Maria Grazia Cucinotta (Cigar Girl), Serena Scott Thomas (Dr Molly Warmflash), Goldie (Mr Bullion), David Calder (Sir Robert King), Ulrich Thomsen (Davidov), Claude-Oliver Rudolph (Colonel Akakievich), Patrick Malahide (Lachaise), Omid Djalili (Foreman), Jeff Nuttall (Dr Arkov), Diran Meghreblian (Coptic priest), Justus von Dohnányi (Captain Nikolai), Martyn Lewis (Newsreader), Daisy Beaumont (Nina), Nina Muschallik (Verushka), Lawrence Makoare (Elektra's bodyguard), Daz Crawford (Casino thug).

Die Another Day

MGM/Twentieth Century-Fox/Eon Productions. 2002.

Director: Lee Tamahori. *Producers:* Michael G. Wilson and Barbara Broccoli. *Screenplay:* Neil Purvis & Robert Wade. *Executive producer:* Anthony Waye. *Co-producer:* Callum McDougall. *Production supervisor:* Janine Modder. *Second unit director:* Vic Armstrong. *Editor:* Christian Wagner. *Director of photography:* David Tattersall. Panavision. De Luxe. *Additional unit direction and photography:* Shaun O'Dell, Arthur Wooster, Don King. *Production designer:* Peter Lamont. *Supervising art director:* Simon Lamont. *Costume designer:* Lindy Hemming. *Co-stunt co-ordinator:* George Aguilar. *Special effects supervisor:* Chris Corbould. *Main titles:* Daniel Kleinman. *Music:* David Arnold. *Title song performed by:* Madonna. *Certificate:* 12A. *Running time:* 132 mins.

Cast: Pierce Brosnan (James Bond), Halle Berry (Jinx), Toby Stephens (Gustav Graves), Rosamund Pike (Miranda Frost), Rick Yune (Zao), Judi Dench (M), John Cleese (Q), Michael Madsen (Falco), Colin Salmon (Robinson), Samantha Bond (Miss Moneypenny), Kenneth Tsang (General Moon), Will Yun Lee (Colonel Moon), Emilio Echevarria (Raoul), Michael Gorevoy (Vlad), Lawrence Makoare (Mr Kil), Ben Wee (Snooty desk clerk), Ho Yi (Hotel manager), Rachel Grant (Masseuse), Ian Pirie (Creep), Simón Andreu (Dr Alvarez), Mark Dymond (Van Bierk), Deborah Moore (Air hostess), Oliver Skeete (Concierge), Joaquin Martinez (Old man in cigar factory), Paul Darrow (Doctor), Michael G. Wilson (General Chandler), Daryl Kwan (General Han),

---

* *The World is not Enough* marked the last appearance in the series of Llewelyn, who tragically died in a car accident shortly after the film's release. That the producers were already preparing for a future without the 84-year-old stalwart of seventeen Bonds is evidenced in the introduction of John Cleese as 'the young man I'm grooming to replace me' and in the 'exit' scene written for Q in this film.

Vincent Wong (General Li), Stuart Ong (General Dong), Tymarah (Korean scorpion guard).*

Casino Royale

MGM/Columbia Pictures/Eon Productions and Casino Royale Productions. 2006.

Director: Martin Campbell. *Producers:* Michael G. Wilson and Barbara Broccoli. *Screenplay:* Neil Purvis & Robert Wade and Paul Haggis. *Executive producers:* Anthony Waye, Callum McDougall. *Associate producer:* Andrew Noakes. *Second unit director:* Alexander Witt. *Editor:* Stuart Baird. *Director of photography:* Phil Méheux. Panavision. De Luxe. *Production designer:* Peter Lamont. *Supervising art director:* Andrew Lamont. *Costume designer:* Lindy Hemming. *Stunt co-ordinator:* Gary Powell. *Free running stunts:* Sébastien Foucan. *Special effects and miniature effects supervisor:* Chris Corbould. *Main titles:* Daniel Kleinman. *Music:* David Arnold. 'You Know My Name' *performed by:* Chris Cornell. *Written and produced by:* David Arnold and Chris Cornell. *Certificate:* 12A. *Running time:* 144 mins.

Cast: Daniel Craig (James Bond), Eva Green (Vesper Lynd), Mads Mikkelsen (Le Chiffre), Judi Dench (M), Jeffrey Wright (Felix Leiter), Giancarlo Giannini (Mathis), Caterina Murino (Solange), Simon Abkarian (Dimitrios), Ivana Milicevic (Valenka), Isaach De Bankole (Obanno), Jesper Christensen (Mr White), Tobias Menzies (Villiers), Claudio Santamaria (Carlos), Sébastien Foucan (Mollaka), Malcolm Sinclair (Dryden), Richard Sammel (Gettier), Ludger Plator (Mendel), Joseph Millson (Carter), Daud Shah (Fisher), Clamens Schick (Kratt), Emmanuel Avena (Leo), Tom Chadbon (Stockbroker), Peter Notley (MI6 Technician), Paul Bhattacharjee, Crispin Bonham Carter (Hot Room Doctors), Simon Cox, Rebecca Gethings (Hot Room Technicians), Valentine Nonyela (Nambutu Embassy official), Michael Offel (Obanno's lieutenant). *Casino Royale players:* Ade (Infante), Urbano Barberini (Tomelli), Tsai Chin (Madame Wu), Charlie Levi Leroy (Gallardo), Lazar Ristovski (Kaminofsky), Tom So (Fukutu), Veruschka (Gräfin von Wallenstein), Daniel Andreas (Dealer), Carlos Leal (Tournament director).

---

* Madonna has a cameo appearance in the film as fencing instructor 'Verity'. It was reported in the press that Sir Sean Connery was paid $1 million for a cameo appearance in the Reform Club as Bond's father, though the scene does not appear in the film or on the DVD special features. Bond is, of course, an orphan. In *GoldenEye* Alec Trelyan refers to Bond's parents having been killed in a climbing accident – an aspect of Bond's personal history revealed in his 'obituary' in the novel *You Only Live Twice*.

Bibliography

The James Bond novels

This bibliography lists all the James Bond novels, by various authors, in chronological order. The publication details refer to the original editions; the Ian Fleming titles have subsequently been published in paperback editions by Pan, Triad and Coronet (the paperback division of Hodder and Stoughton). The editions currently available in the United Kingdom are published by Penguin. Novelisations of film screenplays are indicated by an asterisk (*).

By Ian Fleming:

Casino Royale (London: Jonathan Cape, 1953).
Live and Let Die (London: Jonathan Cape, 1954).
Moonraker (London: Jonathan Cape, 1955).
Diamonds are Forever (London: Jonathan Cape, 1956).
From Russia, with Love (London: Jonathan Cape, 1957).
Dr No (London: Jonathan Cape, 1958).
Goldfinger (London: Jonathan Cape, 1959).
For Your Eyes Only (London: Jonathan Cape, 1960).
Thunderball (London: Jonathan Cape, 1961).
The Spy Who Loved Me (London: Jonathan Cape, 1962).
On Her Majesty's Secret Service (London: Jonathan Cape, 1963).
You Only Live Twice (London: Jonathan Cape, 1964).
The Man with the Golden Gun (London: Jonathan Cape, 1965).
Octopussy and the Living Daylights (London: Jonathan Cape, 1966).

(When first published, the last volume comprised just two short stories, 'Octopussy' and 'The Living Daylights'. A third story, 'The Property of a Lady', originally written for Sotheby's yearbook, was included in later editions and the volume entitled just *Octopussy*. The Coronet paperback title reverted to *Octopussy and the Living Daylights*. The current Penguin edition also includes a fourth story, '007 in New York', originally published in the *New York Herald Tribune*.)

By *Kingsley Amis (writing as Robert Markham):*

Colonel Sun (London: Jonathan Cape, 1968).

By *Christopher Wood:*

James Bond, the Spy Who Loved Me (London: Triad/Panther, 1977).*
James Bond and Moonraker (London: Triad/Panther, 1979).*

By *John Gardner:*

Licence Renewed (London: Jonathan Cape/Hodder and Stoughton, 1981).
For Special Services (London: Jonathan Cape/Hodder and Stoughton, 1982).
Icebreaker (London: Jonathan Cape/Hodder and Stoughton, 1983).
Role of Honour (London: Jonathan Cape/Hodder and Stoughton, 1984).
Nobody Lives for Ever (London: Jonathan Cape/Hodder and Stoughton, 1986).
No Deals, Mr Bond (London: Jonathan Cape/Hodder and Stoughton, 1987).
Scorpius (London: Hodder and Stoughton, 1988).
Win, Lose or Die (London: Hodder and Stoughton, 1989).
Licence to Kill (London: Hodder and Stoughton/Coronet, 1989).*
Brokenclaw (London: Hodder and Stoughton, 1990).
The Man from Barbarossa (London: Hodder and Stoughton, 1991).
Death is Forever (London: Hodder and Stoughton, 1992).
Never Send Flowers (London: Hodder and Stoughton, 1993).
Sea Fire (London: Hodder and Stoughton, 1994).
GoldenEye (London: Hodder and Stoughton/Coronet, 1995).*
Cold (London: Hodder and Stoughton, 1996).

By *Raymond Benson:*

Zero Minus Ten (London: Hodder and Stoughton, 1997).
Tomorrow Never Dies (London: Hodder and Stoughton/Coronet, 1997).*
The Facts of Death (London: Hodder and Stoughton, 1998).
High Time to Kill (London: Hodder & Stoughton, 1999).
The World is not Enough (London: Hodder & Stoughton, 1999).*
Doubleshot (London: Hodder & Stoughton, 2000).
Never Dream of Dying (London: Hodder & Stoughton, 2001).
The Man with the Red Tattoo (London: Hodder & Stoughton, 2002).
Die Another Day (London: Hodder & Stoughton, 2002).*

British Film Institute unpublished scripts

S6500: *Dr No. From the Novel by Ian Fleming.* Fourth Draft Screenplay, by Richard Maibaum and Wolf Mankowitz, 12 December 1961.

S6501: *Ian Fleming's From Russia with Love.* Final Draft Screenplay, by Richard Maibaum, 18 March 1963.

S6508: *Ian Fleming's Goldfinger.* Final Draft Screenplay, by Richard Maibaum and Paul Dehn, 26 February 1964.

S6502: *Diamonds are Forever.* Final Draft Screenplay, by Tom Mankiewicz, no date.

S4498: *The Spy Who Loved Me.* Revised Final Shooting Script [by Christopher Wood], 23 August 1976.

S17894: *For Your Eyes Only*. Screen Story and Screenplay, by Richard Maibaum and Michael G. Wilson, 12 August 1980.

S18120: *Octopussy*. Screenplay by Richard Maibaum and Michael G. Wilson, based on a draft screenplay by George MacDonald Fraser, 10 June 1982.

S18050: *License to Kill* [*sic*]. Final Draft Screenplay, by Michael G. Wilson and Richard Maibaum, no date.

Newspapers and periodicals

My chapter notes indicate which newspapers and periodicals I have used for film reviews. Many of these are taken from the press clippings provided on the British Film Institute's microfiche collection, an invaluable source for researchers, though occasionally prone to inaccuracy. I have quoted from reviews and articles appearing in the following British newspapers and periodicals: *Daily Express*, *Daily Telegraph*, *Daily Worker*, *Evening News*, *Evening Standard*, *Financial Times*, *Guardian*, *Independent*, *New Statesman*, *News of the World*, *Observer*, *Punch*, *Scene*, *Spectator*, *Sunday Express*, *Sunday People*, *Sunday Times* and *The Times*. These represent a range of opinion from both the quality and the popular press and from across the political spectrum. For the United States I have quoted from the following newspapers and periodicals: *Esquire*, *New York Times*, *New Yorker*, *Playboy*, *Saturday Review*, *Time* and *Village Voice*. Reviews of the Bond films can be found in the following volumes of *The New York Times Film Reviews*: *1959–1968*, *1969–1970*, *1971–1972*, *1973–1974*, *1977–1978*, *1979–1980* (all published in New York by Times Books and Arno Press, 1970, 1971, 1973, 1975, 1979 and 1981 respectively), and *1981–1982*, *1983–1984*, *1985–1986*, *1987–1988*, *1989–1990*, *1995–1996* (all published in New York by Times Books and Garland Publishing, 1984, 1986, 1988, 1990, 1992 and 1998 respectively). Some film-related articles are extracted from Gene Brown (ed.), *The New York Times Film Encyclopedia* (New York: Times Books, 1984).

Film journals and trade papers

Again sources can be traced through the chapter notes. For reviews I have drawn on *Films and Filming* as representative of the middle-brow film journalism in Britain for much of the period during which the Bond films have been made, and on the *Monthly Film Bulletin* and *Sight and Sound* as (until their merger and subsequent dumbing-down) the nearest thing to an intellectual film culture in Britain. Separate articles on the Bond films, as distinct from reviews, are listed under 'articles and chapters' below. For background on the British film industry I have used the trade papers *Kinematograph Weekly* and *Today's Cinema* until the end of the 1960s, and *Screen International* thereafter. *American Cinematographer* provided much useful technical information on the Bond films, while US trade papers *Hollywood Reporter*, *Motion Picture Herald* and *Variety* have been used for reviews and information about the reception of the films in the United States. Reviews of the Bond films from *Variety* can be found in the following volumes of *Variety's Film Reviews* (all published by R. R. Bowker, New York until *Vol. 18*, thereafter R. R. Bowker, New Providence, NJ): *Vol. 10: 1959–1963* (1983), *Vol. 11: 1964–1967* (1983), *Vol. 12: 1968–1970* (1983), *Vol. 13: 1971–1974* (1983), *Vol. 14: 1975–1977* (1983), *Vol. 15: 1978–1980* (1983), *Vol. 17: 1981–1982* (1983), *Vol. 18: 1983–1984* (1986), *Vol. 19: 1985–1986* (1988), *Vol. 20: 1987–1988* (1991), *Vol. 21: 1989–1990* (1991) and *Vol. 24: 1995–1996* (1997). (*Vol. 16* [1983] is the *Index of Titles, 1907–1980*.)

The review of the television *Casino Royale* from *Daily Variety* on p. 38 is taken from *Variety's Television Reviews, Vol. 1: 1946–1956* (New York: Garland Publishing, 1988). Statistics regarding the negative costs and box-office performance of the Bond films can be found in the following trade paper special issues: 'James Bond: 25 Years', *Variety*, 13 May 1987; 'James Bond's 25th Anniversary', *Hollywood Reporter*, 14 July 1987; and '35 Years of Unrivaled Success', *Screen International*, 5 December 1997; and 'The Man With the Midas Touch', *Screen International*, 15 November 2002.

Fan magazines and websites

'Fanzines' represent a different type of source to film journals and trade papers, being celebratory, anecdotal and uncritical, but magazines such as *Cinefantastique*, *Starburst* and *Starlog* provide background information on the production of the films and sometimes feature interviews with actors and production personnel. In addition, the following James Bond fanzines are worthy of particular mention: *Bondage* (published by the now defunct James Bond 007 Fan Club of America), *007 Magazine* (published by the British-based James Bond 007 International Fan Club) and *Goldeneye* (published by the US-based Ian Fleming Foundation). The articles and correspondence in these publications provide a useful insight into the ways in which the James Bond fan culture engages with the films. *007 Magazine* became an online publication in 2005 (http://www.007magazine.co.uk) following a change in organisation of the James Bond International Fan Club (http://www.007.info/). Since the first edition of this book was published the number of James Bond-related websites has expanded faster than Mr Big after swallowing a gas pellet: among the most informative are Universal Exports (http://www.universalexports.net) and Commander Bond (http://commanderbond.net). The official Bond website is http://www.jamesbond.com.

Biographies, autobiographies and diaries

Broccoli, Albert R., with Donald Zec, *When the Snow Melts: The Autobiography of Cubby Broccoli* (London: Boxtree, 1998).

Creighton, Christopher, *Op. JB: The Last Great Secret of the Second World War* (London: Simon and Schuster, 1996). (An example of the 'secret history' genre of fiction, the author's account of a secret mission entitled 'Operation James Bond' supposedly undertaken with Ian Fleming in April and May 1945.)

Davie, Michael (ed.), *The Diaries of Evelyn Waugh* (London: Weidenfeld and Nicolson, 1976).

Eaton, Shirley, *Golden Girl* (London: B.T. Batsford, 1999).

Fiegel, Eddi, *John Barry, a Sixties Theme: From James Bond to Midnight Cowboy* (London: Constable, 1998).

Freedland, Michael, *Sean Connery: The Untouchable Hero* (London: Virgin, 1993).

Glen, John, with Marcus Hearn, *For My Eyes Only* (London: B.T. Batsford, 2001).

Hernu, Sandy, *Q: The Biography of Desmond Llewelyn* (Seaford: S.B. Publications, 1999).

Lycett, Andrew, *Ian Fleming* (London: Weidenfeld and Nicolson, 1995).

Moore, Roger, *Roger Moore as James Bond: Roger Moore's Own Account of Filming Live and Let Die* (London: Pan, 1973).

Moseley, Roy, *Evergreen: Victor Saville in His Own Words* (Carbondale: Southern Illinois University Press, 2000).

Moseley, Roy, with Philip and Martin Masheter, *Roger Moore: A Biography* (London: New English Library, 1985).

Pearson, John, *The Life of Ian Fleming* (London: Jonathan Cape, 1966).

— *James Bond: The Authorised Biography of 007* (London: Sidgwick and Jackson, 1973). (An ingenious 'fictional biography' based on the premise that James Bond was a real person, and Fleming his biographer.)

Simmons, Bob, with Kenneth Passingham, *Nobody Does It Better: My 25 Years of Stunts with James Bond and Other Stars* (Poole, Dorset: Javelin Books, 1987).

Thatcher, Margaret, *The Downing Street Years* (London: HarperCollins, 1993).

Trevelyan, John, *What the Censor Saw* (London: Michael Joseph, 1973).

Wood, Christopher, *James Bond, the Spy I Loved* (London: Twenty First Century, 2006)

Young, Freddie, *Seventy Light Years: A Life in the Movies* (London: Faber and Faber, 1999).

Books and monographs

Aldgate, Anthony, *Censorship and the Permissive Society: British Cinema and Theatre 1955–1965* (Oxford: Clarendon Press, 1995).

Amis, Kingsley, *The James Bond Dossier* (London: Jonathan Cape, 1965; Pan Books, 1966).

Armes, Roy, *A Critical History of British Cinema* (London: Secker and Warburg, 1978).

Barnes, Alan, and Marcus Hearn, *Kiss Kiss Bang! Bang!: The Unofficial James Bond Film Companion* (London: B.T. Batsford, 1997).

Barr, Charles, *Ealing Studios*, rev. edn (London: Studio Vista, 1993).

Belton, John, *American Cinema/American Culture* (New York: McGraw-Hill, 1994).

Bennett, Tony, et al., *The Making of 'The Spy Who Loved Me': DE 353 Broadcasting Handbook 3* (Milton Keynes: Open University Press, 1977).

Bennett, Tony, and Janet Woollacott, *Bond and Beyond: The Political Career of a Popular Hero* (London: Macmillan, 1987).

Benson, Raymond, *The James Bond Bedside Companion* (London: Boxtree, 1988).

Bergan, Ronald, *The United Artists Story* (London: Octopus, 1986).

Black, Jeremy, *The Politics of James Bond: From Fleming's Novels to the Big Screen* (Westport: Praeger, 2001).

Booker, Christopher, *The Neophiliacs: A Study of the Revolution in English Life in the Fifties and Sixties* (London: Collins, 1969).

— *The Seventies: Portrait of a Decade* (London: Allen Lane, 1980).

Bouzerau, Laurent, *The Art of Bond* (London: Boxtree, 2006).

Boyd, Ann S., *The Devil with James Bond!* (Richmond: John Knox Press, 1967; Westport: Greenwood Press, 1975).

Brosnan, John, *James Bond in the Cinema*, 2nd edn (London: Tantivy Press, 1981).

Cawelti, John G., *Adventure, Mystery, and Romance: Formula Stories as Art and Popular Culture* (Chicago: University of Chicago Press, 1976).

Commentale, Edward P., Stephen Watt and Skip Willman, *Ian Fleming & James Bond: The Cultural Politics of 007* (Bloomington: Indiana University Press, 2005).

Cork, John, and Bruce Scivally, *The James Bond Phenomenon* (London: Boxtree, 2002).

D'Abo, Maryam, and John Cork, *Bond Girls are Forever: The Women of James Bond* (London: Boxtree, 2003).

Del Buono, Oreste, and Umberto Eco (eds), *The Bond Affair*, trans. R. A. Downie (London: Macdonald, 1966).

Denning, Michael, *Cover Stories: Narrative and Ideology in the British Spy Thriller* (London: Routledge and Kegan Paul, 1987).

Dickinson, Margaret, and Sarah Street, *Cinema and State: The Film Industry and the British Government, 1927–84* (London: British Film Institute, 1985).

Drummond, Lee, *American Dreamtime: A Cultural Analysis of Popular Movies and Their Implications for a Science of Humanity* (Lanham, Maryland: Littlefield Adams, 1996).

Durgnat, Raymond, *A Mirror for England: British Movies from Austerity to Affluence* (London: Faber and Faber, 1970).

Eagleton, Terry, *Literary Theory: An Introduction* (Oxford: Basil Blackwell, 1983).

Haining, Peter, *James Bond: A Celebration* (London: Planet Books, 1987).

Harmon, Jim, and Donald F. Glut, *The Great Movie Serials: Their Sound and Fury* (London: Woburn Press, 1973).

Harper, Sue, *Women in British Cinema: Mad, Bad and Dangerous to Know* (London: Continuum, 2000).

Harper, Sue, and Vincent Porter, B*ritish Cinema of the 1950s: The Decline of Deference* (Oxford: Oxford University Press, 2003).

Hibbin, Sally, *The Official James Bond 007 Movie Book* (London: Hamlyn, 1987).

Hirschhorn, Clive, *The Columbia Story* (London: Pyramid, 1989).

Johnstone, Iain, *The World is not Enough: A Companion* (London: Boxtree, 1999).

Landy, Marcia, *British Genres: Cinema and Society, 1930–1960* (Princeton: Princeton University Press, 1991).

Lane, Andy, and Paul Simpson, *The Bond Files: The Unofficial Guide to the World's Greatest Secret Agent* (London: Virgin, 1998).

Lane, Sheldon (ed.), *For Bond Lovers Only* (London: Panther, 1965).

Lindner, Christoph (ed.), *The James Bond Phenomenon: A Critical Reader* (Manchester: Manchester University Press, 2003).

McFarlane, Brian (ed.), *An Autobiography of British Cinema* (London: Methuen, 1997).

McGilligan, Pat (ed.), *Backstory: Interviews with Screenwriters of Hollywood's Golden Age* (Berkeley: University of California Press, 1986).

McInnerney, Jay, Nick Foulkes, Neil Norman, Nick Sullivan, with Colin Woodhead, *Dressed to Kill: James Bond, the Suited Hero* (Paris: Flammarion, 1996).

Marwick, Arthur, *British Society Since 1945*, 3rd edn (London: Penguin, 1996).

—— *The Sixties: Cultural Revolution in Britain, France, Italy, and the United States c.1958–1974* (Oxford: Oxford University Press, 1998).

Merry, Bruce, *Anatomy of the Spy Thriller* (Dublin: Gill and Macmillan, 1977).

Morgan, Kenneth O., *The People's Peace: British History 1945–1990* (Oxford: Oxford University Press, 1990).

Murphy, Robert, *Sixties British Cinema* (London: British Film Institute, 1992).

Naremore, James (ed.), *North by Northwest; Alfred Hitchcock, director* (New Brunswick: Rutgers University Press, 1993).

Palmer, Jerry, *Thrillers: Genesis and Structure of a Popular Genre* (London: Edward Arnold, 1978).

Pearce, Garth, *The Making of GoldenEye* (London: Boxtree, 1995).

—— *The Making of Tomorrow Never Dies* (London: Boxtree, 1997).

Pearson, Roberta E., and William Uricchio (eds), *The Many Lives of the Batman: Critical Approaches to a Superhero and His Media* (London: British Film Institute, 1991).

Peary, Danny, *Cult Movies 3* (New York: Simon and Schuster, 1988).

Perkin, Harold, *The Rise of Professional Society: England Since 1880* (London: Routledge, 1989).

Perry, George, *The Great British Picture Show* (London: Michael Joseph, 1974).

— *Movies from the Mansion: A History of Pinewood Studios* (London: Pavilion, 1986).

Petrie, Duncan, *The British Cinematographer* (London: British Film Institute, 1996).

Pfeiffer, Lee, and Philip Lisa, *The Incredible World of 007* (London: Boxtree, 1992).

Pfeiffer, Lee, and Dave Worrall, *The Essential Bond: The Authorized Guide to the World of 007* (London: Boxtree, 1998).

Polmar, Norman, and Thomas B. Allen, *The Spy Book: The Encyclopedia of Espionage* (London: Greenhill, 1997).

Ray, Robert B., *A Certain Tendency of the Hollywood Cinema, 1930–1980* (Princeton: Princeton University Press, 1985).

Richards, Jeffrey, *Films and British National Identity: From Dickens to Dad's Army* (Manchester: Manchester University Press, 1997).

Rissik, Andrew, *The James Bond Man: The Films of Sean Connery* (London: Elm Tree Books, 1983).

Roddick, Nick, and Martin Auty (eds), *British Cinema Now* (London: British Film Institute, 1985).

Rubin, Steven Jay, *The James Bond Films: A Behind the Scenes History* (London: Talisman Books, 1981).

Rufo, Patrick, *The James Bond Story* (Paris: WIN Productions, 1987).

Ryall, Tom, *Alfred Hitchcock and the British Cinema* (London: Croom Helm, 1986).

Rye, Graham, *The James Bond Girls* (London: Boxtree, 1989).

Scott, Kevin Conroy (ed.), *Screenwriters' Masterclass: Screenwriters Talk About Their Greatest Movies* (London: Faber and Faber, 2005).

Snelling, O. F., *James Bond: A Report* (London: Panther, 1965).

Street, Sarah, *British National Cinema* (London: Routledge, 1997).

Sutherland, John A., *Fiction and the Fiction Industry* (London: Athlone Press, 1978).

Thompson, Kristin, and David Bordwell, *Film History: An Introduction* (New York: McGraw-Hill, 1994).

Thumim, Janet, *Celluloid Sisters: Women and Popular Cinema* (London: Macmillan, 1992).

Truffaut, François, with Helen G. Scott, *Hitchcock*, rev. edn (London: Paladin, 1986).

Turner, Adrian, *Goldfinger: Bloomsbury Movie Guide No. 2* (London: Bloomsbury, 1998).

Usborne, Richard, *Clubland Heroes: A Nostalgic Study of Some Recurrent Characters in the Romantic Fiction of Dornford Yates, John Buchan and Sapper*, rev. edn (London: Barrie and Jenkins, 1974).

Walker, Alexander, *Hollywood, England: The British Film Industry in the Sixties* (London: Michael Joseph, 1974; rev. edn London: Harrap, 1986).

— *National Heroes: British Cinema in the Seventies and Eighties* (London: Harrap, 1985).

Watson, Colin, *Snobbery with Violence: English Crime Stories and Their Audience*, rev. edn (London: Methuen, 1987).

Williams, Greg, *Bond on Set: Filming Die Another Day* (London: Boxtree, 2002).

— *Bond on Set: Filming Casino Royale* (London: DK Publishing, 2006).

Williams, Raymond, *Keywords: A Vocabulary of Culture and Society*, rev. edn (London: Fontana, 1983).

Winder, Simon, *The Man Who Saved Britain: A Personal Journey into the Disturbing World of James Bond* (New York: Farra, Straus and Giroux, 2006).

Wood, Linda (ed.), *British Film Industry: BFI Information Guide No. 1* (London: British Film Institute, 1980).

Wood, Robin, *Hitchcock's Films*, rev. edn (London: Tantivy Press, 1977).

Worrall, Dave, *The Most Famous Car in the World: The Complete History of the James Bond Aston Martin DB5* (Christchurch: Solo Publishing, 1991).

Articles and chapters

Anez, Nicholas, 'James Bond', *Films in Review*, 18/9–10, September/October 1992, pp. 311–19; 'James Bond (Part 2)', 18/11–12, November/December 1992, pp. 383–8; 'James Bond (Part 3)', 19/1–2, January/February 1993, pp. 30–6.

Baron, Cynthia, '*Doctor No*: Bonding Britishness to Racial Sovereignty', *Spectator: The University of Southern California Journal of Film and Television Criticism*, 14/2, Spring 1994, pp. 68–81.

Bear, Andrew, 'Intellectuals and 007: High Comedy and Total Stimulation', *Dissent*, Winter 1966, pp. 23–7.

Bennett, Tony, 'Text and Social Process: the Case of James Bond', *Screen Education*, 41, Winter/Spring 1982, pp. 3–14.

— 'James Bond as Popular Hero', Unit 21 of Open University course U203 *Popular Culture*, in *Politics, Ideology and Popular Culture 2* (Milton Keynes: Open University Press, 1982).

— 'James Bond in the 1980s', *Marxism Today*, 27/6, June 1983, pp. 37–9.

Bergonzi, Bernard, 'The Case of Mr Fleming', *Twentieth Century*, March 1958, pp. 220–8.

Black, Jeremy, 'The Geopolitics of James Bond', *Intelligence and National Security*, 19/2 (Summer 2004), pp. 290–303.

Burgess, Eric, 'The Making of *Moonraker*', *New Scientist*, 21 June 1979, pp. 984–7.

Cannadine, David, 'James Bond and the Decline of England', *Encounter*, 53/3, November 1979, pp. 46–55.

Dodds, Klaus, 'Licensed to Stereotype: Popular Geopolitics, James Bond and the Spectre of Balkanism', *Geopolitics*, 8/2 (Summer 2003), pp. 125–56.

— 'Screening Geopolitics: James Bond and the Early Cold War Films', *Geopolitics*, 10/3 (Autumn 2005), pp. 266–89.

Douglas, Andy, 'Bond Never Dies', *British Film and Television Facilities Journal*, 9, Winter 1998, pp. 17–27.

Fleming, Ian, 'How to Write a Thriller', *Books and Bookmen*, May 1963, pp. 14–19.

Gow, Gordon, 'Thrill a Minute: Adventure Movies of the '60s', *Films and Filming*, 13/4, January 1967, pp. 5–11.

Grant, Barry Keith, 'Introduction', Grant B. K. (ed.), *Film Genre Reader II* (Austin: University of Texas Press, 1995), pp. xv–xx.

Gross, Larry, 'Big and Loud', *Sight and Sound*, New Series, 5/8, August 1995, pp. 6–10.

Hoberman, J., 'When Dr No Met Dr Strangelove', *Sight and Sound*, New Series, 3/12, December 1993, pp. 16–21.

Hochscherf, Tobias, and Christoph Laucht, 'Reel Spies Die Another Day: Continuity and Change in the 007 Film Series', *Literatur in Wissenschaft und Unterricht*, 36/4 (2003), pp. 347–67.

Houston, Penelope, '007', *Sight and Sound*, 34/1, Winter 1964–65, pp. 14–16.

'James Bond Special', *Film Review*, Special 21, 1997, pp. 18–59.

Johnson, Ian, '007 + 4', *Films and Filming*, 12/1, October 1965, pp. 5–8.

Kirkham, Pat, 'Dots and Sickles', *Sight and Sound*, New Series, 5/12, December 1995, pp. 10–12.

Lane, John Francis, 'Young Romantic', *Films and Filming*, 13/5, February 1967, pp. 58–60.

Marwick, Arthur, '*Room at the Top*, *Saturday Night and Sunday Morning*, and the "Cultural Revolution" in Britain', *Journal of Contemporary History*, 19/1, January 1984, pp. 127–52.

Moniot, Drew, 'James Bond and America in the Sixties: An Investigation of the Formula Film in Popular Culture', *Journal of the University Film Association*, 28/3, Summer 1976, pp. 25–33.

Mulvey, Laura, 'Visual Pleasure and Narrative Cinema', *Screen*, 16/3, August 1975, pp. 6–18.

Petley, Julian, 'The Lost Continent', in Charles Barr (ed.), *All Our Yesterdays: 90 Years of British Cinema* (London: British Film Institute, 1986), pp. 98–119.

Petley, Julian, and Alan Burton, 'Introduction', *Journal of Popular British Cinema*, 1, 'Genre and British Cinema', 1998, pp. 2–5.

Price, James, 'Our Man in the Torture Chamber', *London Magazine*, July 1962, pp. 67–70.

Richler, Mordecai, 'Ian Fleming: A Voice for Little England', *Nova*, January 1970, pp. 2–12.

Rissik, Andrew, 'Indiana Jones and the 007 Myth', *Films and Filming*, 362, November 1984, p. 13.

Schatz, Thomas, 'The New Hollywood', in Jim Collins, Hilary Radner and Ava Preacher Collins, *Film Theory Goes to the Movies* (London: Routledge, 1993), pp. 8–36.

Thumim, Janet, 'The "Popular", Cash and Culture in the Postwar British Cinema Industry', *Screen*, 32/3, Autumn 1991, pp. 245–71.

Wills, Ron, 'Sadism for the Family', *Cinema* (Berkeley), 1/5, August/September 1963, pp. 32–3.

Woollacott, Janet, 'The James Bond Films: Conditions of Production', in James Curran and Vincent Porter (eds), *British Cinema History* (London: Weidenfeld and Nicolson, 1983), pp. 208–25.

Index

ABC (American Broadcasting Company), 38

Adam, Ken, 19, 47, 63–4, 75, 84, 134, 140, 153, 186

Adams, Maud, 146, 180

Al-Qaeda, 234

Alfie, 128

Alien, 163, 225

Allen, Irving, 40, 43, 97

Allen, Woody, 106

Alpert, Hollis, 79

Altman, Robert, 207

Altria, Bill, 55

Ambushers, The, 97

American Dreamtime (book), 14

Amis, Kinglsey, 3–4, 27, 28, 34, 203, 231

Amorous Adventures of Moll Flanders, The, 80

Amritraj, Vijay, 183

Anderson, Lindsay, 50, 51, 77

Anderson Tapes, The, 132

Andress, Ursula, 66, 95, 106, 238

Andrews, Nigel, 134, 215

Anez, Nicholas, 188

Apted, Michael, 212, 232, 233

Armendariz, Pedro, 76

Armes, Roy, 8

Armstrong, Louis, 118

Arnold, David, 227, 247

Around the World in 80 *Days*, 42

Arroyo, José, 227, 233

Assignment K, 98

Atkinson, Rowan, 186

Attenborough, Richard, 180

Auger, Claudine, 66, 95–6

Austen, David, 119

auteur theory, 7,

Avengers, The, 38, 86, 117, 155, 193

Babuscio, Jack, 132–3

Bach, Barbara, 159

Baker, Joe Don, 199, 224

Barber, Nicholas, 240

Barnes, Alan, 9, 36, 104

Barrandov Studios, 243

Barry, John, 19, 63, 111, 117–8, 140, 208, 221, 227

Basinger, Kim, 187

Bassey, Shirley, 83, 92, 208

Bates, Alan, 51

Batman, 198, 210, 211

Batman Begins, 241

Battle Beneath the Earth, 110

Battle of Britain, 127

Battlestar Galactica, 165

Bean, Sean, 217

Bear, Andrew, 30

Beatles, The, 44, 93, 127

Belger, Thomas, 131

Belmondo, Jean-Paul, 106

Bennett, Charles, 35

Bennett, Tony, 9–10, 14–16, 26–7, 33, 60, 92, 93–4, 102, 127, 128, 129, 156, 189, 190–1, 248

Benson, Raymond, 203

Bergan, Ronald, 6

Bergonzi, Bernard, 24–5

Berkoff, Steven, 180, 182

Bernstein, Elmer, 168

Berry, Halle, 235, 238, 239

Bianchi, Daniela, 66, 76, 98

Big Boss, The, 147

Bilbow, Marjorie, 119–20, 161, 167, 178

Billancourt (film studio), 151

Billings, Josh, 54

Billion Dollar Brain, 98

Billy Liar, 51

Binder, Maurice, 19, 63, 188, 220

Black Gunn, 137

Black Hole, The, 163

Blackmail, 35

Blackman, Honor, 82, 86, 95, 117

Blair, Tony, 224

'blaxploitation', 129, 136–7, 225

Blazing Saddles, 108

Bogart, Humphrey, 35
Bonicelli, Vittorio, 84
Bond and Beyond (book), 14–16
'Bondian' (production ideology), 18–19, 228
'Bondmania', 15, 86–8, 90–8, 120, 127
Bonnie and Clyde, 121
Booker, Christopher, 30–1, 127
Bordwell, David, 44, 46
Borehamwood Studios, 106
Borienko, Yuri, 112, 117
Boulogne (film studio), 151
Boulting brothers (John and Roy), 80
Bouquet, Carole, 174, 178
Bourne Identity, The, 242
Bourne Supremacy, The, 242–3
Box, Betty, 98
Boy and the Bridge, The, 42
Boyer, Charles, 106
Braine, John, 2, 51
Brandauer, Klaus Maria, 185, 188
Braveheart, 230
Brezhnev, Leonid, 181
British Board of Film Censors (BBFC), 69–70, 210
British Film Production Fund, 40
British Interplanetary Society, 165
British National Cinema (book), 8
'Britishness', and the Bond films, 13–14
Broccoli, Albert R. ('Cubby'), 5, 6, 22, 40, 42–3, 47, 72, 74, 76, 78, 95, 109, 149, 151, 153, 164, 170, 197, 210, 211, 213
Broccoli, Barbara, 213
Bronson, Charles, 129
Brooks, Mel, 108
Brosnan, John, 6, 80–1, 89, 154
Brosnan, Pierce, 182, 202, 211, 212, 213, 214–6, 221, 227, 228, 233, 234, 240, 242

Brown, Geoff, 215, 222
Brown, Janet, 177
Brown, Jim, 137, 147
Brownjohn, Robert, 77, 82
Bryce, Ivar, 41
Buchan, John, 16, 24
Bulldog Drummond, 45
Bulldog Drummond Strikes Back, 45
Bullitt, 133
Burgess, Anthony, 4–5, 9, 152
Burgess, Eric, 165–6
Burgess, Guy, 33
Buskin, Richard, 194
Butch Cassidy and the Sudance Kid, 118

Cahiers du Cinéma, 7
Cain, Syd, 75, 140
Caine, Michael, 93, 98
Call Me Bwana, 76
Callaghan, James, 151
Cameron, Ian, 68
Cameron, James, 223
camp, 132–3
Campaign for Nuclear Disarmament (CND), 181
Campbell, Martin, 19, 212, 214, 221, 241, 243, 245, 250
Canby, Vincent, 91–2, 128
Cannadine, David, 27–8, 29
Carlyle, Robert, 229, 233
Carrera, Barbara, 187
Carroll, Madeleine, 46
'Carry On' films, 8, 11, 54, 128, 148, 194
Carry On Nurse, 54
Carry On Sergeant, 54
Carry On Spying, 97, 108
Casablanca, 35
Casey, Bernie, 186
Casino Royale (novel), 2, 23–4, 25, 27, 33, 37, 42, 240, 243, 245–7
Casino Royale (television), 22, 34–9, 246
Casino Royale (film: 1967), 5, 90, 106–8
Casino Royale (film: 2006), 18, 241–52
Catch 22, 106

CBS (Columbia Broadcasting System), 34, 38
Celi, Adolfo, 98, 102
Central Intelligence Agency (CIA), 34, 129
Chandler, Raymond, 2, 24, 35, 207
Chaplin, Charles, 97
Chariots of Fire, 171
Charteris, Leslie, 45
Cheyney, Peter, 24
Chiles, Lois, 165
Chin, Tsai, 236
Chitty Chitty Bang Bang, 109
Christian, Linda, 35
Christie, Agatha, 75
Christie, Julie, 93, 95
Chrysler Corporation, 35
Churchill, (Sir) Winston, 28, 158
Churubusco Studios, 205
CIA (Central Intelligence Agency), 34, 129
Ciao Amici, 92
Citizen Kane, 130
Clancy, Tom, 213
Clarke, Roger, 250
Clear and Present Danger, 213
Cleese, John, 239
Cleopatra Jones, 137
Cleopatra Jones and the Casino of Gold, 137
Climax!, 34, 35
Clinton, Bill, 224, 229, 234
Clockwork Orange, A, 128
Close Encounters of the Third Kind, 165, 168
Clubland Heroes (book), 16
CND (Campaign for Nuclear Disarmament), 181
Coburn, James, 97
Cockleshell Heroes, 40
Cocks, Jay, 148
'cod war', 158
Cold War, 26, 32, 36, 60–1, 71, 75, 110, 156–7, 159, 170, 172–3, 175, 181–2, 186, 189–90, 200–1, 217–8, 247
Coleman, John, 78, 140
Colman, Ronald, 45, 64
Colonel Sun, 231
Coltrane, Robbie, 217

Columbia Pictures, 40, 43, 243
Comin' thro' the Rye, 172
Commander Jamaica (proposed tv series), 56
Commando, 211
Common Market (Europe), 28
'Confessions' series, 153
Confessions of a Window Cleaner, 150
Connery, Neil, 98
Connery, Sean, 4, 18, 20, 52, 64, 68, 75–6, 80, 93, 98, 106, 108, 112, 114, 122, 124, 131, 171, 184, 186, 187–8, 194, 204, 213, 214, 216, 220, 228, 249
Conservative Party, 224
Cooper, Gary, 64
Cotten, Joseph, 200
Cotton Comes to Harlem, 136–7
Courtenay, Tom, 51
Cover Stories (book), 16
Coward, Noël, 133
Craig, Daniel, 242, 244, 245, 247, 248, 249
Crash, 243
Critical History of the British Cinema, A (book), 8
Cromwell, 127
Crowther, Bosley, 71, 105, 111
Cruise, Tom, 227
Cuban Missile Crisis, 70–1
cultural studies, 14–16
Curse of Frankenstein, The, 50
Curtis, Jamie Lee, 213
Cushing, Peter, 50

d'Abo, Maryam, 199
Dahl, Roald, 108–9, 110
Daily Express, 15, 23, 48
Daily Telegraph, 240, 244
Daily Variety, 38
Daily Worker, 5, 68–9
Dalton, Timothy, 54, 55, 125, 196, 197–8, 202–3, 204, 211, 215, 216, 228, 242
Damon, Matt, 242
Danjaq, 43, 211
Darling, 93, 128

Darling Lili, 127
Davi, Robert, 205
David, Hal, 118
Davis, (Sir) John, 41, 51–2
Dawson, Anthony, 62, 98
Day the Earth Caught Fire, The, 57
De Gaulle, Charles, 28
De Palma, Brian, 227
Deadlier than the Male, 98
Deadly Affair, The, 84
Dean, Jimmy, 134
Death Wish, 129
Dehn, Paul, 80
Deighton, Len, 24, 33, 73, 98, 184
del Toro, Benicio, 208
Delaney, Shelagh, 51
Dench, Judi, 220, 245
Denning, Michael, 16, 31
Destination Moon, 166
Diamonds are Forever (novel), 129–30
Diamonds are Forever (film), 124, 128, 129, 130–6, 140, 143, 147, 153, 176, 186, 216, 221, 227, 236, 239, 245, 251
Diamond Smugglers, The, 239
Dick Barton – Special Agent (radio serial), 17
Dick Barton – Special Agent (film), 45
Dick Barton at Bay, 45
Dick Barton Strikes Back, 45
Die Another Day, 212, 233–40, 241, 242, 249, 250
Die Frau im Mond (*By Rocket to the Moon*), 166
Die Hard, 208, 211, 213, 218, 227
Diesel, Vin, 237
Dirty Dozen, The, 121
Dirty Harry, 129, 207
Dobson, Tamara, 137, 225
Doctor Dolittle, 127
Doctor in the House, 54
Doctor Zhivago, 111, 160
Dr No (novel), 3, 24–5, 27, 56–7, 79, 92, 172
Dr No (film), 4, 5, 21, 44, 49, 49, 52, 53, 54, 56, 57–72, 74, 75, 77, 80, 81, 83, 86,

89, 90, 97, 102, 118, 207, 209, 233, 238, 251
Donat, Robert, 46, 64
Dor, Karin, 111
Doyle, (Sir) Arthur Conan, 3
Dreigroschenoper, Die (*The Threepenny Opera*), 76
Drummond, Lee, 14
Durgnat, Raymond, 17, 61–2, 201

E.T.: The Extra-Terrestrial, 171
Eady Levy, 40, 42, 43, 150
Eagle Has Landed, The, 150
Eagleton, Terry, 4
Ealing comedies, 8
Eastwood, Clint, 128–9
Eaton, Shirley, 66, 83, 92
Eco, Umberto, 4, 25–6, 32, 243
Edge of Darkness, 214
Ekberg, Anita, 76
Ekland, Britt, 146
Elizabeth II, Queen, 28, 115, 158
Ellis, Antony, 35
Elstree Studios, 150
Empire, 244
Empire Strikes Back, The, 171
Enforcer, The (1950), 35
Enforcer, The (1976), 129
Enter the Dragon, 147
Entertainer, The, 51
Eon Productions, 43, 127, 153, 184, 185, 241
Epinay (film studio), 151
Esquire, 79, 131
Essential Bond: The Authorized Guide to the World of 007, The (book), 9

Falklands War, 174, 223
Far Pavilions, The, 180
Farewell, My Lovely, 35
Feirstein, Bruce, 222, 228
Feldman, Charles K., 106
Ferzetti, Gabriele, 114
Field Guide to the Birds of the West Indies, 239
Fielding, Henry, 44
Films and Filming, 52, 69, 119, 194, 204
Finney, Albert, 51

Fist of Fury, 147
Flash Gordon, 185
Fleming, Anne (*née* Charteris, *then* O'Neill, *then* Rothermere), 2, 30
Fleming, Ian Lancaster, 1–5, 15, 16, 20, 22, 23, 31, 34, 38, 40–2, 56, 59, 70, 93, 101, 109, 113, 125, 126, 152, 172, 174, 197, 208, 223, 231, 239, 243, 245, 247
Fletcher, Kim, 233
For Your Eyes Only (book), 38
'For Your Eyes Only' (short story), 174–5, 231
For Your Eyes Only (film), 163, 170, 171, 172, 174–9, 183, 189, 199, 203, 242
Ford, Harrison, 18, 213
Foreign Correspondent, 35, 228
Forster, E.M., 172
Forsyth, Frederick, 182
Foucan, Sébastien, 250
Four Just Men, The, 17, 155
Four Weddings and a Funeral, 13
Fourth Protocol, The, 182
Fox, Edward, 186
Foxy Brown, 137
France-Soir, 92
Frankenheimer, John, 71
French Connection, The, 133
French, Philip, 215
Frobe, Gert, 81, 130
Frogmore Studios, 223
'From a View to A Kill' (short story), 189
From Russia, with Love (novel), 23, 27, 33, 44, 57, 72–3
From Russia with Love (film), 7, 17, 18, 49, 52, 56, 72–9, 81, 82, 89, 90, 110, 113, 133, 140, 173, 174, 176, 221, 224, 227, 249
Frostrup, Mariella, 215
Full Monty, The, 13
Fullerton, Fiona, 190
Funeral in Berlin, 98
Furst, Joseph, 134

Gable, Clark, 64
Gainsborough melodramas, 8, 10–11

Gaitskell, Hugh, 30
Galeries Lafayette, 92
Game of Death, 147
Gandhi, 180
Garbage, 232
Gavin, John, 130
Gayson, Eunice, 66
genre, and the Bond films, 16–19, 44–5, 54, 89, 155–6
Gibson, Mel, 18, 193, 211, 214, 227, 230
Gilbert, Lewis, 19, 89, 111, 149, 152, 154, 174
Gilliat, Penelope, 5, 75
Glen, John, 19, 170, 174, 178, 194, 196, 197, 200, 210, 221
Glover, Bruce, 133
Glover, Julian, 175
Glut, Donald F., 17
Godard, Jean-Luc, 87
Goldcrest Films, 13, 180
GoldenEye, 19, 149, 211, 212–3, 215–22, 223, 226, 227, 229, 230, 231, 232, 235, 236, 241, 244, 245, 249
Goldfinger (novel), 26, 79–80
Goldfinger (film), 6–7, 8, 18, 49, 56, 79–87, 89, 90–1, 92, 94, 97, 98, 102, 105, 110, 113, 130, 132, 134, 140, 154, 191, 192, 214, 220, 221, 227, 228, 232, 234
Goldwyn, Sam, 45
Goodbye Mr Chips, 127
Goodridge, Mike, 222
Gorbachev, Mikhail, 157, 205
Gotell, Walter, 157, 175
Grade, Lew, 150
Grant, Brigit, 215
Grant, Cary, 7, 46, 47, 125, 249
Grauman's Chinese Theatre, 90
Gray, Charles, 132, 133
Great Escape, The, 77
Great Expectations, 172
Great Train Robbery, The, 63
Green, Eva, 250
Greene, Graham, 75, 200
Greenham Common, 181

Greening of America, The (book), 96
Grier, Pam, 137, 225
Gross, Larry, 18
Guardian, 226, 245
Guess Who's Coming to Dinner, 136
Guest, Val, 106
Gulf War, 225

Haggard, (Sir) Henry Rider, 3
Haggis, Paul, 243–4, 248
Haining, Peter, 37
Haley, Bill, 55
Half a Sixpence, 127
Hamilton, Donald, 97
Hamilton, Guy, 19, 49, 80, 82, 124, 130, 148, 152, 221
Hamilton, Linda, 225
Hammer Films, 45
Hammer horror films, 8, 10–11, 50–1, 55
Hammerhead, 98
Hammett, Dashiell, 24
Hard Day's Night, A, 13, 44
Harmon, Jim, 17
Harris, Richard, 51
Harvey, Laurence, 52
Harwood, Joanna, 58, 73
Haskell, Molly, 113
Hatcher, Teri, 225
Hayden, Sterling, 182
Hayward, Louis, 45
Hearn, Marcus, 9, 36, 104
Hearst, William Randolph, 223
Heat and Dust, 171–2
Hecht, Ben, 106
Hedison, David, 206
hegemony theory, 15
Hell Below Zero, 40
Heller, Joseph, 106
Hello Dolly, 127
Help!, 44
Hendry, Gloria, 140
Hepworth, Cecil, 172
'heritage' cinema, 10, 171–2, 180
Heroes of Telemark, The, 117
Hibbin, Nina, 5, 68–9, 79, 86–7, 105
'Hildebrand Rarity, The' (short story), 205, 208

Hildyard, Jack, 108
Hill, Derek, 68
Himes, Chester, 137
Hirschhorn, Clive, 108
Hitchcock, Alfred, 6–8, 16,
    35, 44, 46–8, 61, 65, 75,
    76, 130, 228, 246, 250
Hitchcock's Films (book), 6–7
Hoggart, Richard, 52
Holden, William, 106
Holder, Geoffrey, 141
Hollywood Reporter, 71, 120,
    203, 209–10
Hope, Bob, 76
Hopkins, John, 101
Houston, Penelope, 87–8
Howard, Leslie, 64
Howards End, 172
Hudson, Christopher, 141
Hughes, Howard, 130
Hughes, Kenneth, 106
Hunt for Red October, The, 213
Hunt, Peter, 19, 48, 89, 104,
    112, 226
Huston, John, 106

I, the Jury, 41, 69
In Like Flint, 97
In the Heat of the Night, 136
Incredible World of 007, The
    (book), 9
Independent, 232, 240
Independent on Sunday, 240
Indiana Jones and the Last
    Crusade, 18, 211
Indiana Jones and the Temple
    of Doom, 171
Ipcress File, The, 98, 236
'Irangate', 201–2
Iranian Embassy siege, 174
Ivory, James, 10, 171–2

Jackman, Hugh, 242
'James Bond' (newspaper
    strip), 15, 48
James Bond Bedside Companion,
    The (book) 9
James Bond Dossier, The
    (book), 3, 27
James Bond of the Secret Service
    (proposed film), 42, 184
'James Bond Theme, The',
    63, 221, 227, 247

James Gunn, Secret Agent
    (proposed tv series), 56
James, Clifton, 140
Janssen, Famke, 219
Jaws, 160, 163
Jay, Ricky, 225
Jewel in the Crown, The, 180
John, Göttfried, 217
Johnson, Paul, 3, 126
Johnson, Richard, 98
Jonathan Cape (publisher), 2
Jones, Grace, 171, 192, 194
Journal of Popular British
    Cinema, 11
Jourdan, Louis, 180
Juarez, 64
Jurassic Park, 12
Jurgens, Curt, 154

Kael, Pauline, 120
Kamen, Michael, 208
Kaye, M.M., 180
Keaton, Michael, 198
Keen, Geoffrey, 160
Kennedy, John Fitzgerald,
    44, 72, 94
Kennedy, Robert, 120
Kerr, Deborah, 106
Kershner, Irving, 171
Kid for Two Farthings, A, 57
Kiel, Richard, 160
Killers of Kilimanjaro, 40
Kind of Loving, A, 51
Kinematograph Weekly, 42, 43,
    54, 55, 57, 77
King, Martin Luther, 120
King Kong, 185
Kiss Me Deadly, 41, 69
Kiss Kiss Bang! Bang!: The
    Unofficial James Bond Film
    Companion (book), 9
Kitzmiller, John, 62
Kleinman, Daniel, 220, 249
Knight, Gladys, 208
Korda, (Sir) Alexander, 13,
    40–1
Korean War, 33, 182
Kotto, Yaphet, 138
Krabbé, Jeroen, 199
Krasker, Robert, 200
Krim, Arthur, 43
Kubrick, Stanley, 128, 130,
    182

kung fu cinema, 129, 147–8
Kwouk, Burt, 81

L'Anné derniere à Marienbad
    (Last Year at Marienbad),
    76
Labour Party, 93, 181, 224
Ladd, Alan, 144
Lady from Shanghai, The, 147
Lady Vanishes, The, 16, 75
Lamont, Peter, 19, 221, 237,
    249
Landesman, Cosmo, 244
Landis, John, 152
Lang, Fritz, 35, 64, 166
Lara Croft: Tomb Raider, 242
Last Action Hero, The, 213
Last Year at Marienbad
    (L'Anné derniere à
    Marienbad), 76
Law, John, 106
Lawrence of Arabia, 111, 160
Layer Cake, 242
Lazenby, George, 112, 114,
    115, 118–9, 125, 130, 216
le Carré, John, 24, 80, 98, 199
Le Queux, William, 218
Lean, David, 10, 111, 160,
    172, 180
Leaveseden Studios, 215
Lee, Bernard, 61, 98, 179
Lee, Bruce, 147, 225
Lee, Christopher, 50, 144
Lee, Spike, 143
Leigh, Janet, 130
Lejeune, C.A., 67
Lenya, Lotte, 76
Let Him Have It!, 228
Lethal Weapon, 207, 208, 211,
    213, 218, 221, 227
Lethal Weapon 2, 211
Life, 44, 72, 92
Licence to Kill, 196–7, 202,
    205–11, 213, 215, 216,
    217, 220, 241, 242, 243,
    251
Liquidator, The, 98
Lisa, Philip, 104
Live and Let Die (novel), 27,
    40, 56, 137, 206
Live and Let Die (film), 123,
    125, 128, 129, 136–43,
    144, 146

'Living Daylights, The' (short story), 198–9

Living Daylights, The (film), 18, 196, 199–205, 206, 213, 217, 231, 234, 242

Loach, Ken, 233

London Pavilion cinema, 77

Loneliness of the Long Distance Runner, The, 51

Long Goodbye, The (television), 35

Long Goodbye, The (film), 207

Longitude 78 West (proposed film), 42

Lonsdale, Michael, 164

Look Back in Anger, 42, 51

Lord, Jack, 62

Lorimar, 184

Lorre, Peter, 35, 37

Lowell, Carey, 208

Lucas, George, 163, 171

Ludlum, Robert, 242

Lumet, Sidney, 131

Lundigan, William, 35

Lycett, Andrew, 33

M, 35

McCarthy, Todd, 222, 244

McCartney, Paul, 141

McClory, Kevin, 41–2, 58, 101, 153, 184–5

McClusky, John, 48

McCowen, Alec, 186

McGrath, Joseph, 106

McGregor, Ewan, 242

McNeile, H.C., 16, 24

Maclean, Donald, 33

Macnee, Patrick, 155, 193

Madsen, Michael, 235

Magnificent Seven, The, 168

Magnum Force, 129

Maibaum, Richard, 19, 40, 44, 47–8, 57–8, 73, 80, 83, 101, 113, 125, 130, 138, 144, 152–3, 177–8, 196

Malcolm, Derek, 118, 148, 245

Malik, Art, 200

Mallet, Richard, 94

Mallet, Tania, 66

Maltese Falcon, The, 35

Man from U.N.C.L.E., The, 98

Man Who Knew Too Much, The, 16, 35

Man with the Golden Gun, The (novel), 23, 28, 144, 208

Man with the Golden Gun, The (film), 23, 123, 129, 140, 144–8, 149, 158, 183, 227, 232, 237

Manchester Guardian, 25

Manchurian Candidate, The, 71

Manhunt of Mystery Island, 236

Mankiewicz, Herman, 130

Mankiewicz, Joseph L., 130

Mankiewicz, Tom, 130, 138, 144

Mankowitz, Wolf, 57–8, 106

Mann, Anthony, 117

Mao Tse-tung, 110

Marceau, Sophie, 228, 230

Marks, A., 120

Martin, Dean, 97

Martin, George, 141

Marwick, Arthur, 30, 52, 93, 94, 96

Mask of Dimitrios, The, 35

Maslin, Janet, 204

Mason, James, 46

Mather, Berkeley, 58

Matrix, The, 238

Maugham, W. Somerset, 2

Maurice, 171

Maxwell, Lois, 98

Maxwell, Robert, 224

Méheux, Phil, 221, 249

Melly, George, 126

Merchant, Ismail, 10, 171–2

MGM/UA Communications, 211, 243

Miami Vice, 208

Million Dollar Baby, 243

Millionairess, The, 57

Milne, Tom, 148

Mirror Group, 224

Mission: Impossible, 227

Mission: Impossible 3, 243

Modern Times, 97

Modesty Blaise, 98

Molly Maguires, The, 132

Moniot, Drew, 96–7

Monogram Pictures, 45

Monthly Film Bulletin, 5–6, 67–8, 134, 161, 184, 188

Moonraker (novel), 26, 33, 40, 164

Moonraker (film), 20, 149, 151, 163–9, 170, 178, 180, 182, 183, 190, 192, 235, 243

Moore, Roger, 6, 20, 122, 123, 124–6, 131, 141, 143, 146, 148, 151, 170–1, 172, 176, 193–4, 197, 202, 204, 228, 232, 233, 242

Moore, Ted, 19, 221, 249

Morgan, Kenneth O., 145

Morgenthau, Henry, 56

Most Dangerous Man in the World, The, 110

Motion Picture Export Association, 39

Motion Picture Herald, 44, 71

Mulvey, Laura, 66

Muni, Paul, 64

Murder on the Orient Express (novel), 75

Murder on the Orient Express (film), 150

Murderer's Row, 97

Murdoch, Rupert, 223, 224

Murphy, Robert, 50–1, 108

Murton, Peter, 147

Naismith, Laurence, 132

Naremore, James, 46–7

NASA (National Aeronautics and Space Administration), 165

NATO (North Atlantic Treaty Organisation), 33, 102, 181, 186

Nelson, Barry, 35, 37

Neophiliacs, The (book), 30–1

Never Say Never Again, 171, 184–8, 193, 195

New Statesman, 3, 78

'new wave' cinema, Britain, 42, 51–3

New York Herald Tribune, 3

New York Times, 71, 91, 120, 135, 162, 204

Newman, Kim, 244, 246

News Chronicle, 80

News International Corporation, 224

Nightfire, 238, 240

'9/11' (terrorist attacks

on United States, 11
September 2001), 234–5,
247
Niven, David, 64, 106–7
Nixon, Richard, 129
No Escape, 214
'Nobody Does It Better', 154
Noriega, Manuel, 206
Norman, Monty, 63
North Atlantic Treaty
Organisation (NATO),
33, 102, 181, 186
North by Northwest, 6–7, 46–7,
61, 76, 228, 249–50
North, Oliver, 202, 206
Nouvelle Vague cinema,
France, 87

Observer, 5
'Octopussy' (short story),
179–80, 182
Octopussy (film), 163, 170, 171,
172, 179–84, 189, 217
*Octopussy and the Living
Daylights* (book), 23
Odeon cinema, Leicester
Square, 77, 86
Offence, The, 131
*Official James Bond 007 Movie
Companion, The* (book), 9
Oliver Twist, 172
Olivier, Laurence, 155, 197
On Her Majesty's Secret Service
(novel), 99–100, 231
On Her Majesty's Secret Service
(film), 18, 89, 90, 95, 99,
104, 105, 112–22, 123,
126, 130, 131, 132, 134,
158, 172, 174, 176, 178,
202, 203, 218, 230, 231,
243, 244, 250
OPEC (Organisation
of Petroleum Exporting
Companies), 145
Open University, 19
Operation Kid Brother, 98
Oppenheim, E. Phillips, 218
Organisation of Petroleum
Exporting Countries
(OPEC), 145
Ornstein, George H., 43
Osborne, John, 42, 44, 51
Otto, Götz, 227

Pabst, G.W., 76
Pal, George, 166
Palance, Jack, 144
Palmer, Geoffrey, 226
Paluzzi, Luciana, 103
Pan (publisher), 23, 92
Panavision, 101, 140, 153
Parretti, Giancarlo, 211
Parrish, Robert, 106
Passage to India, A, 180
Pasternak, Boris, 160
Pate, Michael, 36
Pathé Communications, 211
Patriot Games, 213
Payne. John, 41
Peck, Gregory, 110
Peckinpah, Sam, 128
Peeping Tom, 69
Perkin, Harold, 29
Persuaders!, The, 124
Petersen, Wolfgang, 226
Petley, Julian, 10, 205–6, 207
Pettet, Joanna, 106
Pfeiffer, Lee, 104
Picker, David, 131
Pike, Rosamund, 238, 239
Pinewood Studios, 43, 106,
150
Playboy, 31, 92, 96, 109
Pleasence, Donald, 110
Plon (publisher), 92
pornography, 31
Powell, Dick, 35
Powell, Dilys, 67, 142–3, 168
Powell, Michael, 69
Presley, Elvis, 55
Price, James, 25, 29
*Private Life of Henry VIII,
The*, 13
'Property of a Lady, The'
(short story), 180
Psycho, 130
Pulleine, Tim, 161–2, 167
Punch, 94
Purvis, Neal, 228, 231, 234,
237, 243–4

Q-Planes, 17, 155–6
Quant, Mary, 93

'Quantum of Solace' (short
story), 205
Quiller Memorandum, The, 98
Quinn, Anthony, 232–3, 240

Raft, George, 106
Rai, Aishwarya, 240
Raiders of the Lost Ark, 171,
186
Raise the Titanic!, 150
Rambo: First Blood, Part II,
173, 182
Rank Organisation, 13, 41, 77
Ratoff, Gregory, 106
Raven, Simon, 24
Raw Deal, 211
Reagan, Ronald, 173, 190
Red Tent, The, 132
Red Beret, The, 40, 43
Red Dawn, 173
Red Heat, 211
Reed, Carol, 200
Reed, Michael, 117
Reich, Charles, 96
Remains of the Day, The, 172
Remington Steele, 214
Renoir, Claude, 153
Renoir, Jean, 153
Republic Pictures, 45
Resnais, Alain, 76
*Return of Bulldog Drummond,
The*, 16
Return of the Jedi, 171
Reynolds, Burt, 140
Rhys-Davies, John, 199
Rich Man, Poor Man, 122
Rich, Frank, 162
Richard, Cliff, 54, 55
Richards, Denise, 230, 233
Richards, Jeffrey, 52
Richardson, Ralph, 155
Richardson, Tony, 42, 44,
Rigg, Diana, 95, 113, 117, 230
Rimington, Stella, 220
'Risico' (short story), 174–5
Rissick, Andrew, 17, 64
RKO Radio Pictures, 45
Roberts, Tanya, 190, 193,
194, 230
Roddick, Nick, 13, 184
Roeg, Nicolas, 108
Rohmer, Sax, 26, 57
Room at the Top, 51, 52

Room with a View, A, 172
Rothrock, Cynthia, 225
Roundtree, Richard, 137, 139
Rubin, Steven Jay, 36, 101
'runaway' productions, 39
Rye, Graham, 86

Sabotage, 35
Safari, 40
Saint, Eva Marie, 46, 47, 249
St John, Jill, 131
Saint, The, 124, 249
Sakata, Harold, 82
Saltzman, Harry, 5, 42–3, 52,
     70, 76, 78, 80, 98, 149,
     154
Sanders, George, 45
Sandhu, Sukhdev, 240
'Sapper' (H.C. McNeile),
     16, 24
Sarris, Andrew, 135–6
SAS (Special Air Service),
     174
Satton, Lon, 138
*Saturday Night and Sunday
     Morning*, 42, 51, 74
Saturday Review, 79
Savalas, Telly, 114
Saville, Victor, 41, 43
Saxon, John, 147
Sayers, Michael, 106
Schickel, Richard, 142
Schifrin, Lalo, 227
Schwartzman, Jack, 184–5
Schwarzenegger, Arnold, 18,
     19, 193, 211, 213–4
Scorupco, Izabella, 219
Scott, Paul, 180
Screen, 12
Screen International, 150, 204,
     210, 211, 222
Secret Agent, 16, 35, 65
Sellers, Peter, 57, 106
Semple, Lorenzo Jr, 185
serials, 17, 168
Serra, Eric, 221
Seven Days to Noon, 80, 81
Seven Year Itch, The, 106
sexploitation, 11, 128
*Sexton Blake and the Hooded
     Terror*, 16
Seymour, Jane, 139
Shaft, 137

Shaft in Africa, 137
Shaft's Big Score, 137
Shalako, 132
Shane, 144
Shaw, Robert, 76, 227
Shepperton Studios, 106
Shoard, Catherine, 240, 244
Shone, Tom, 215
Shout at the Devil, 150
Sight and Sound, 87, 227, 233,
     250
Silencers, The, 97
Silliphant, Stirling, 152
Sillitoe, Alan, 2, 51
Simmons, Bob, 19
Simon, Carly, 154
Sinclair, Hugh, 45
Slaughter, 137
Smith, Putter, 133
Smokey and the Bandit, 140
Some Girls Do, 98
Sony Corporation, 243
Soto, Talisa, 208
Spartacus, 130
Special Air Service (SAS), 174
Spectator, 68, 126, 233
Speed, 222
Spellbound, 246
Spielberg, Steven, 160, 163,
     171
Spillane, Mickey, 27, 41
Spiderman, 238
Spooks, 243
Spottiswoode, Roger, 212,
     222, 226
*Spy Who Came in from the Cold,
     The*, 80, 98
Spy Who Loved Me, The (novel), 151–2
Spy Who Loved Me, The (film),
     8, 18, 19, 20, 90, 130, 148,
     149, 150, 151–63, 165,
     166, 167, 170, 176, 182,
     189, 190, 219, 224, 225,
     227, 228, 231, 232, 234
Stallone, Sylvester, 18, 19,
     173, 193
Stamboul Train, 75
Stamp, Terence, 93
Star!, 127
Star Trek: The Motion Picture,
     163
Star Wars, 12, 162–3, 165

Stephens, Toby, 236
Stern, R.M., 3
Storey, David, 51
Straw Dogs, 128
Street, Sarah, 8, 53, 172
Strick, Philip, 141, 188
structuralism, 4, 25–6
Suez Crisis, 28, 223
Sun, 224
Sunday Express, 68
Sunday Telegraph, 240, 244
Sunday Times, 215, 244
Superfly, 137
Superman, 163
Superman Returns, 241
Sutherland, John, 23
'Swinging London' films, 8,
     10, 53
Sydow, Max Von, 185
Sylvia, 242

Tamahori, Lee, 212, 237,
     238, 240
Tamba, Tetsuro, 111
Taste of Honey, A, 51
Taylor, John Russell, 28, 142
Tearle, Godfrey, 46
Technicolor, 63
Terminator 2, 225
Thatcher, Denis, 177
Thatcher, Margaret, 157, 173,
     174, 176–7, 190
Third Man, The, 200, 219
39 Steps, The, 16, 35, 46, 227
This Sporting Life, 51, 77
Thomas, Ralph, 98
Thompson, Kristin, 44, 46
*Threepenny Opera, The (Die
     Dreigroschenoper)*, 76
Thumim, Janet, 85
Thunderball (novel), 42, 46, 56,
     61, 99, 152
Thunderball (film), 8, 18, 89,
     90, 91, 94, 95, 97, 98,
     101–5, 124, 149, 156, 184,
     185, 186, 187, 220
Time, 71, 91, 92, 93, 142, 148
Times, The, 17, 68, 105, 244
Times Literary Supplement, The,
     23–4
Titanic, 12, 223
Today's Cinema, 119
Todd, Mike, 42

Tom Jones, 13, 43–4, 77, 128
Tomorrow Never Dies, 212,
    222–7, 228, 229, 231,
    232, 235
Topol, 175
Townsend, Robert, 143
Trades Union Congress
    (TUC), 181
Trevelyan, John, 69–70
True Lies, 213–4, 215, 222
Turner, Ted, 223
24, 243
Two Faces of Dr Jekyll, The, 57

United Artists, 43–3, 72, 98,
    126, 127, 131,
United International
    Pictures, 216
Untouchables, The, 38
Usborne, Richard, 16, 24
Uses of Literacy, The, 52

Variety, 5, 108, 120, 178–9,
    188, 194, 203, 204–5, 209,
    222, 244
Verne, Jules, 3
Vietnam War, 120–1, 136
View to a Kill, A, 6, 170, 171,
    172, 188–95, 200, 201,
    210, 234
Village Voice, 113, 135
Villechaize, Hervé, 147

Wade, Robert, 228, 231, 234,
    237, 243–4
Walken, Christopher, 189
Walker, Alexander, 115, 118,
    124, 127–8, 149, 215, 240

Wallace, Edgar, 26, 57
'War on Terror', 234–5,
Warhead (proposed film), 184
Warsaw Pact, 181
Warwick Pictures, 40, 43, 44
Waterhouse, Keith, 51
Waugh, Evelyn, 2, 70
'We Have All the Time in the
    World', 118
Weaver, Sigourney, 225
Weill, Kurt, 76
Welland, Colin, 171
Welles, Orson, 106, 130, 147,
    200
Wells, John, 177
What's New Pussycat?, 106
Whelan, Tim, 155
Where Eagles Dare, 121
Where the Bullets Fly, 98
Where the Spies are, 98
Whitehall, Richard, 69
Whittingham, Jack, 42, 101
Who Dares Wins, 174
Wild Bunch, The, 121
Wild Geese, The, 150
Wilder, Billy, 106
Williams, Raymond, 12
Williams, Richard, 226
Willis, Bruce, 18, 19, 211
Wilson, Harold, 93, 94, 150
Wilson, Michael G., 196, 213,
    214, 241
Windust, Bretaigne, 35
Wings (rock group), 141
Wiseman, Joseph, 66
Wiseman, Thomas, 68, 78–9
Woo, John, 226
Wood, Christopher, 153

Wood, Robin, 6–8, 47
Woodfall Films, 42, 52
Woodhouse, Barbara, 183
Woollacott, Janet, 14–16, 19,
    33, 60, 92, 93–4, 102, 127,
    128, 129, 189, 190–1
World is not Enough, The, 212,
    228–33, 234, 235, 237,
    239
World Trade Centre ('9/11'),
    234
Wrecking Crew, The, 97

Xanadu Productions, 42
xXx, 237, 242

Yeoh, Michelle, 224, 225
Ying, Angela May, 225
Yom Kippur War, 145
You Asked for It, 37
You Only Live Twice (novel),
    26, 28–9, 100–1, 144
You Only Live Twice (film),
    5–6, 8, 89, 90, 94, 99, 106,
    108–12, 113, 121, 150,
    154, 156, 221
Young, Freddie, 111
Young, Terence, 19, 44, 45,
    48, 49, 52, 53, 56, 57, 64,
    66, 73, 76, 80, 89, 96, 101,
    102, 226
Young and Innocent, 35
Young Ones, The, 54
Youngstein, Max, 41

Zarak, 40
Zerbe, Anthony, 208
Zorzoli, G.B., 83